LINCOLN AND CONTINENTAL
CLASSIC MOTORCARS
THE EARLY YEARS

CLASSIC MOTORCARS

The Early Years

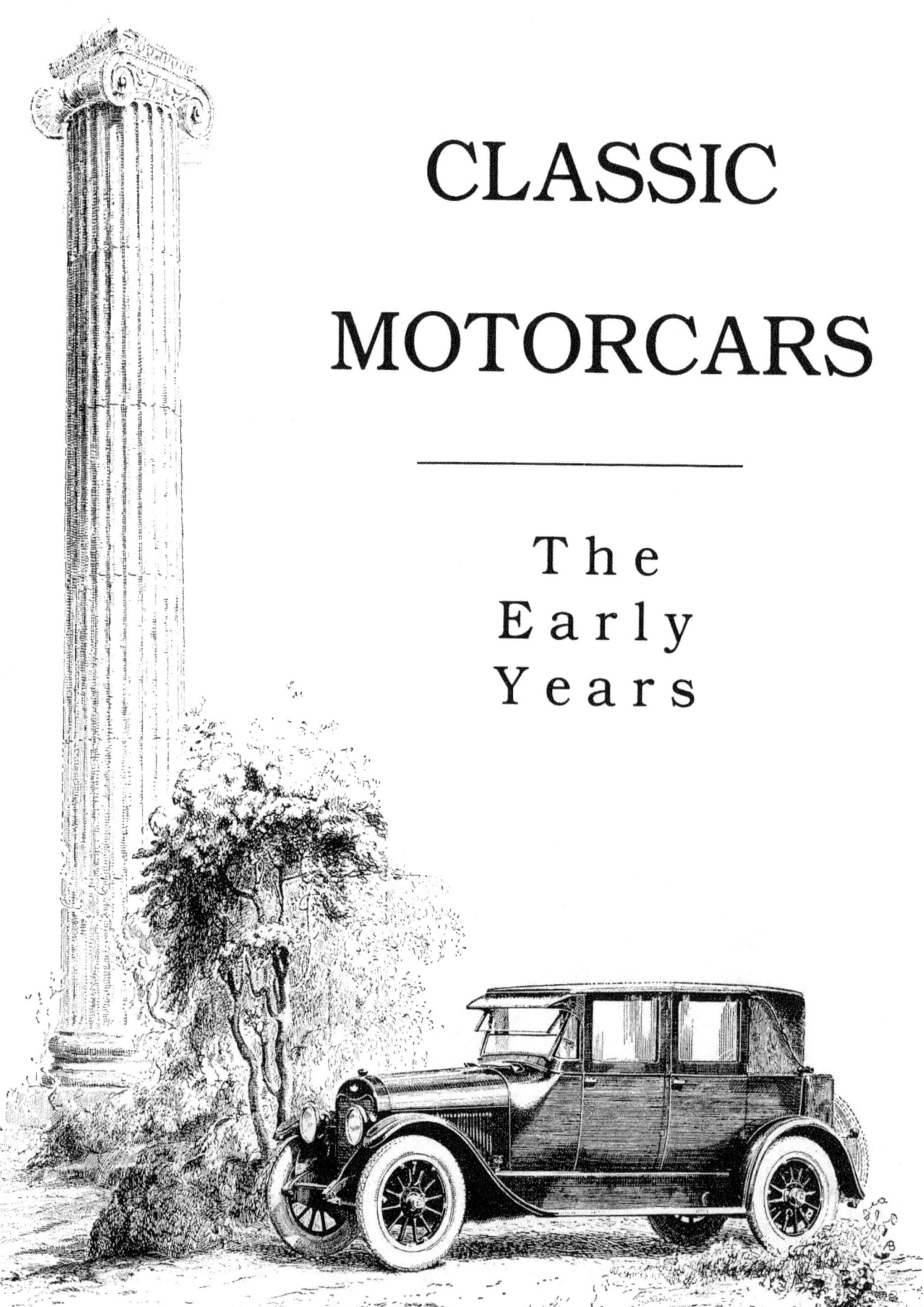

LINCOLN and CONTINENTAL

By

MARVIN ARNOLD

Lincoln and Continental
Classic Motorcars
The Early Years

Samco Publishing
Www.storydomain.com

© 1989, 2012 Marvin Arnold, All rights reserved
Published in the United States of America

Automobile – United States – History

Dewey Decimal Number 629.22

No part of this book may be reproduced, stored in retrieval system or transmitted by any means without the written permission of the author.

First published by Hallmark Edition Publication 1989
Fine Books Division, Taylor Publishing Company
ISBN: 0-87833-691-5 (hc)

Second publication by Samco Publishing 2012
ISBN-13: 978-0-615-59751-5 (sc)
ISBN-10: 0615597513 (sc)
ISBN: 978-1-4524-5441-2 (eBook)
ASIN: B0072PLJGO (Kindle)

| Samco Publishing | CreateSpace | Amazon |

This book is not dedicated to my children or your children, although I hope that they might read and enjoy it for years to come. This one is for my generation and the generation past, those who will fill in the blanks as they visit here.

To:

SUZANNE RAE BURROWS ARNOLD, my wife.

LOLA EVELYN SWANSON ARNOLD, my mother.

EARL MASON ARNOLD, my father, an appreciator of fine machinery and a heck of an engineer.

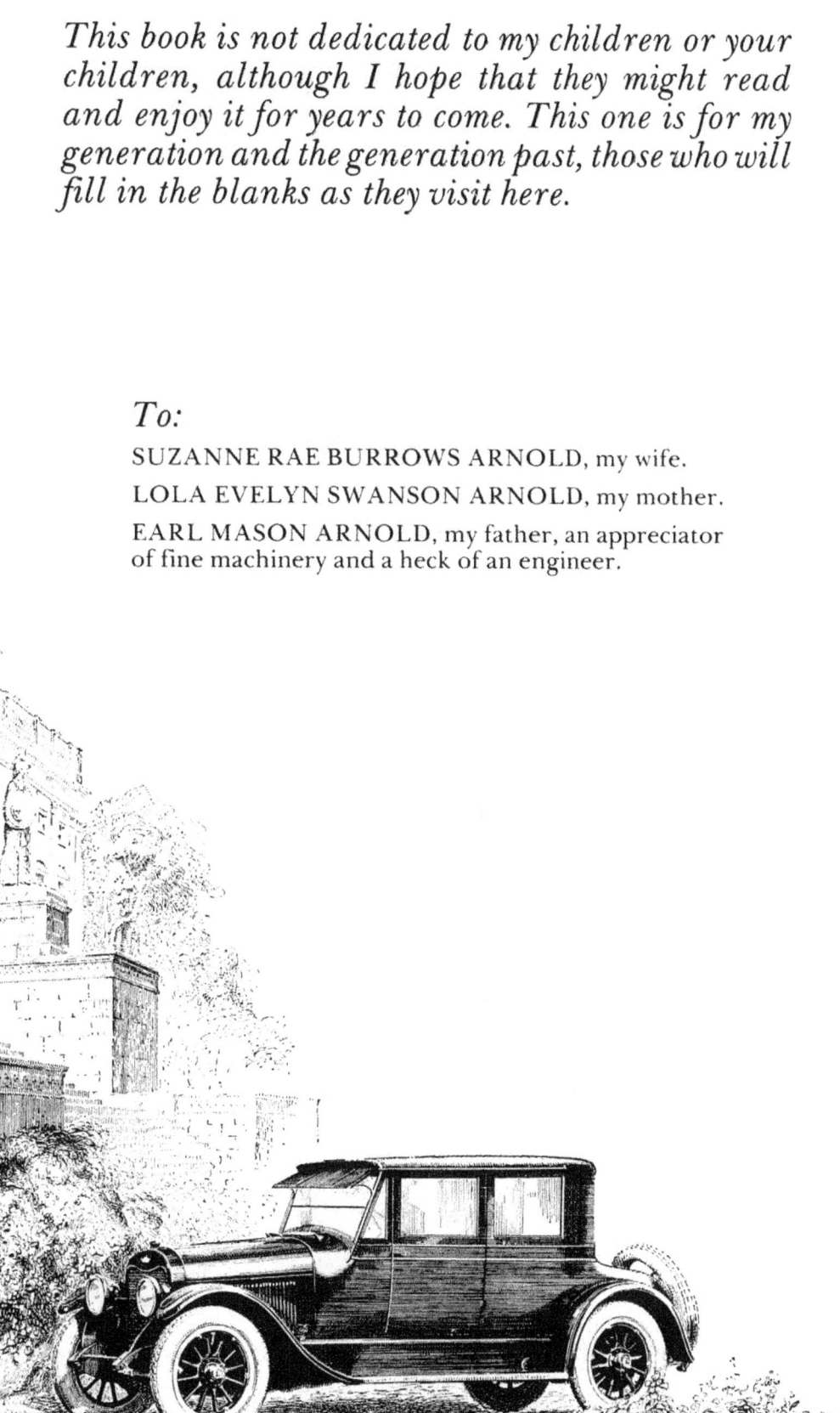

EARLY —
Henry Martyn Leland founds Cadillac and Lincoln. Henry Ford builds an automotive empire and his son Edsel Ford, takes over Lincoln. The Model L Lincolns (1919-1930) are recognized as the finest coachbuilt motorcars in the world, and become the aristocrats automobile in a time of opulence.

CLASSIC —
An era of Automobile Salons and custom coachbuilts. These are the chauffeur-driven Landaulets and Broughams, the Roadsters and Sedans of the rich and famous. The period of the Model K Lincoln (1931-1940) ushers in the V-12 engine and classic craftsmanship. The world is changing and soon these massive motorcars would give way to that progress and become the last of the big iron.

STREAMLINE —
These are the designs influenced by the age of Art Deco and aerodynamic appearances. The Zephyr automobile arrives (1935-1948), in an era of reconstruction and colossal World's Fairs. New manufacturing techniques, like unit body construction, create an all new model of automobile. From these designs evolve the famous Lincoln Continental, perceived today as the only modern classic.

MODERN —
America survives a world war and gets on with the business of building a better nation. These new designs are influenced by the tanks and bombers that preceded them. They are modern designs manufactured with an outdated technology. The bulbous era Lincolns and Cosmopolitans (1948-1951) are not the modern cars of today, but a major link in the evolution to that end result.

TABLE OF CONTENTS

CHAPTER ONE - THOSE EARLY YEARS
　　The Cadillac was a Ford reviews the establishment of automobile making in America and the early manufacturing endeavors of Henry Ford and H.M. Leland.

CHAPTER TWO - THE LELAND LINCOLNS
　　Where in the "L" do we go from here explains how the first Lincoln motorcars came into existence and Henry Leland

CHAPTER THREE - LINCOLN SURVIVES
　　A chrome greyhound leads the way is devoted to the Model-L Lincolns of the 1920s and a time of opulence.

CHAPTER FOUR - THE LINCOLN COACHBUILDERS
　　An American carrossiers who's who discusses the golden era of coachbuilding as it related to the Lincoln and the early Automobile Salons.

CHAPTER FIVE - THE CLASSIC SERIES
　　"K" is for king of the road follows the development and production of the Model-K Lincolns during the changing times of the 1930s.

CHAPTER SIX - ENTER THE ZEPHYR
　　Ride like the wind begins the development of a completely new Lincoln, the Zephyr. a design influenced by the age of Art Deco, streamlined passenger trains and colossal World's Fairs.

CHAPTER SEVEN - THE ORIGINAL CONTINENTAL
　　A Ford that was an Edsel relates what is believed to be the most nearly correct story of the original Lincoln Continental. Much research went into the separation of myth and legend from fact in this chapter. Included is an interview with designer Bob Gregorie.

CHAPTER EIGHT - THE LINCOLN LIBERATORS
　　Into the breach with Henry II covers the World War II years at Ford and Lincoln, the changing of the guard and the beginnings of a new Ford Motor Company.

CHAPTER NINE - THOSE COSMOPOLITAN TIMES
　　Of bulbous beauties concludes the early years at Lincoln. It is devoted to that rare and often forgotten era of bulbous Lincolns. They were not the old Lincolns, but they were not yet the modern Lincolns.

APPENDIX

GLOSSARY

The original custom-crafted Continental was the only American luxury car ever honored for design excellence at New York's Museum of Modern Art.

FOREWORD

I have had a keen interest in the Lincoln and Lincoln-Continental all my life and I must confess that the rich detail in Marvin Arnold's book includes many interesting facts that I did not know. This is a valuable reference work for the serious student of these cars.

Beyond that, this book contains a wealth of information about the beginnings of automotive design as a formalized discipline. My father, Edsel Ford, was a leader in this movement and surrounded himself with many of the most gifted industrial designers in the nation during the years between the wars. Mr. Arnold caught the spirit of the enormously creative team my father assembled and I thoroughly enjoyed reading about it.

William Clay Ford

PREFACE

In 1986, the year in which I sat down to write this book, the Lincoln motorcar had been around for sixty-six. The automobile industry celebrated its hundredth anniversary and I was half its age. I grew up in Oklahoma, along U.S. Highway 66, or as the song says, "Got my kicks on Route 66." Route 66 was the twentieth century's answer to the Santa Fe Trail. It carried many a Midwesterner to the golden shores of California and points in between. I remember "The War" (WWII). Although I was only a youngster at the time, I can still remember synthetic rubber, Plexiglas and gasoline "A" ration windshield stickers,

My first encounter with a Lincoln was in 1946, a Lincoln Continental coupe with push-button doors. It belonged to an Air Force captain, a neighbor whom I befriended the year my little brother was born. On reflection, I believe that the young officer or his wife must have been from a wealthy family in order to afford such a car on a captain's pay, or for that matter, get delivery on any new automobile in 1946.

The Ford industry was to play a major role in my informal education. Like many kids, I learned to drive on my grandfather's Fordson (Ford and Son) tractor. My cousins and I would argue over whose turn it was to drive. Being the smallest, I was usually last. One summer in the early fifties my family took a vacation to Sandusky, Ohio. I had always been fascinated by airplanes and my first ride aloft was out over Lake Erie in a Ford Tri-Motor. It was on that same visit, I got to drive a Model-T Ford, which belonged to my friend's grandfather. For the first time, I began to understand how much the automobile industry had progressed in just a few short decades.

My first Lincoln was a 1939 Zephyr three-window coupe. It was black with a dark maroon dash and gray velour interior. I always called it mohair or maybe it's the other way round. For winter it had a Southwind gasoline heater and a pair of large driving lamps mounted on the front bumper brackets. It had some minor damage to the left running board cover, which I never could afford to have repaired. I purchased the Zephyr in 1953. That summer, I accidentally rolled my father's brand new Ford Fordor. It was not a 1953 Cosmo and I was not Chuck Stevenson, as I quickly discovered.

After school and on Saturdays, I worked at Jaffe's Auto Supply to support the Zephyr, a 1940 Ford Tudor, a 1937 Ford Club Coupe and a 1939 Packard sedan. None of which I had paid over $125 for, except the Zephyr for which I paid a whopping $200. Like most mid-America suburban kids of the fifties, my life centered around the car culture.

Why I bought the Zephyr, I don't exactly know. I remember thinking that it was about the neatest car I had ever seen. I particularly liked the smooth center-console gearshift lever control and the Columbia two-speed vacuum shift rear axle that was controlled by a push-pull knob. You could drive along beside someone at 50 MPH in high-second, then amaze them by shifting again to low-third and then to high-third.

I installed hinges at the top of the small auxiliary rear seat's back that allowed at least three friends to crawl into the long, wood-decked trunk. It was a great way to sneak into the drive-in theater. Sam, a mechanic on the night shift at Delco Products, helped me grind the valves on that old flathead V-12. I experimented with a single-throat Studebaker carburetor to improve the V-12s fuel economy, but the engine lost too much acceleration power.

The motor mounts for a V-8 power plant had been welded in place a few inches rearward of the HV-12 mounts by the previous owner, who had an eight in it prior to reinstalling the twelve. A friend gave us a 5-9AB Mercury block engine, but my Dad and I never got around to installing it. The old Zephyr V-12 engine ran fine at a constant 12 miles to the gallon, so long as you did not operate the gasoline heater.

My folks owned a large turn-of-the-century house with a three-car garage, which had been converted from a stable. At times, my dad complained about not being able to find a parking place in the driveway. He had taught me mechanics, beginning with a Wizzer motorbike kit that we assembled when I was in my early teens.

My mother was always fond of telling this story about me, "He always looked like a grease monkey until a young girl in tight shorts walked past one day as he peered out from under one of his old cars. You know, he came in the house, cleaned up and I don't think I ever saw him under one of those machines again." My dad came home one day and announced that since he could still no longer get into his own garage, some of the cars had to go.

The Zephyr remained until we moved back to Oklahoma in 1955, when it was sold for about what I had paid for it. The last Ford product I owned before going off to college was a 1929 Model-A coupe, which I drove every day of my senior year.

While in the Navy, I owned a not-so-new, flamingo-pink, 1956 Lincoln Premier. One of those cars you didn't park, you docked. In the mid-sixties, after my wife and I made some money on a real estate transaction, we purchased a one-year-old Lincoln sedan. That Thanksgiving we drove it from Texas, where we now live, to Florida on vacation. That did it. Once again I was hooked on Lincolns, now called Continentals.

I will never again feel so affluent as I felt cruising down the Sunshine Parkway with the power seat rocked back, puffing on a good twenty-cent cigar. Thus began my affair with Lincolns and Continentals. I quit smoking years ago, but never lost my appreciation for the Lincoln.

Since my first ride in that Ford Tri-Motor, I have logged over 6,000 hours as pilot-in-command of a hundred different aircraft and work now as a design engineer. We have owned a succession of Lincolns, Marks and Continentals, including several presently. My wife has accused me of going out for a haircut and coming home with a different old car.

Once I picked up a friend from back East at the airport in our, then new, 1967 white Continental Coupe with brown leather seats. He said something that has always stayed with me, "This (the Lincoln) is what I call an automobile. The rest are just cars."

As a young man, Lincolns were engineering and design marvels to be disassembled, studied and reassembled. In later years, they were fine machines to be driven and enjoyed. Now my Lincolns are time machines that allow me to travel back, not only to my youth, but into the lives and pasts of millions of Americans. I have a hobby, an avocation called Lincoln motorcars and I would like to tell you about them.

Marvin Earl Arnold

INTRODUCTION

The year 1986, celebrated the 100th anniversary of the internal-combustion engine automobile. This centennial was based on the 1886 European patents of Gottlieb Daimler and Karl Benz. There were, however, many significant automotive contributions both before and after this date. The original Lincoln motorcar, designed in 1919, was one product of these evolutionary developments. Thus our book on Lincolns begins in the latter part of the nineteenth century. The appropriate format for a marque automobile book is difficult to determine. Should it trace the people and the company or be a chronology of the car itself? Should it be a narrative or a string of technical information? Complicating a by-the-model-year approach is the fact that designs sometimes overlap time periods. For example, Model-K Lincolns were still being produced near the end of the 1930s while the Model-H Zephyr Lincolns were introduced in late 1935. We have, therefore, divided this book into nine chapters based on significant model periods or eras. The stories, anecdotes, and technical aspects are related chronologically within those eras. Ten Appendices and a Glossary have been included to help the reader understand the specifications and terms applicable to this particular segment of the automotive industry.

Chapter One reviews the establishment of automobile making in America, and the early manufacturing endeavors of Henry Ford and H.M. Leland. Chapter Two explains how the Lincoln motorcar came into existence. Chapter Three is devoted to the Model-L Lincolns of the 1920s, a time of opulence. Chapter Four discusses the golden era of coachbuilding as it related to the Lincoln, and the early Automobile Salons. Chapter Five follows the development and production of the Model-K Lincolns during the changing times of the 1930s. Chapter Six begins the development of a completely new Lincoln, the Zephyr. It was a design influenced by the age of Art Deco, streamlined passenger trains, and colossal World's Fairs. Chapter Seven relates what is believed to be the most nearly correct story to date of the original Lincoln Continental. Much research went into the separation of myth and legend from fact in this chapter. Included is an interview with designer Bob Gregorie. Chapter Eight covers the World War II years at Ford and Lincoln, the changing of the guard, and the beginnings of a new Ford Motor Company. Chapter Nine concludes the early years at Lincoln. It is devoted to that rare and often forgotten era of bulbous Lincolns. They were not the "old" Lincolns, but they were not yet the "moderns".

The book's hardback cover color was chosen because gray was Edsel Ford's favorite color. The embossed silver represents nickel chrome accessories. The book's size is similar to that of the older magazines in which period Lincoln ads appeared. The typeset style was selected for its similarity to those used in many older automotive publications. Hundreds of books and periodicals were researched in order to supplement the author's experience with the various Lincoln models. This book is richly illustrated with advertising art from the respective periods. In addition to being beautiful art work, these graphics help the reader have a feeling for the motif of the era being discussed.

Only a few comprehensive books have been published on the Lincoln motorcar. Fifty Years of Lincoln - Mercury by G.H. Dammann was a pictorial history. It was assembled years ago when photos from the Henry Ford Museum archives were readily available for publication and are no longer accessible to the public.

The author would like to thank the following: Suzie Arnold for her many hours of typing, proofing, and letting the author win a few of the arguments; Dr. June Welch, historian for his encouragement; Dave Cole, early Continental expert, for his advice. Bob Gregorie, designer, and Bob Thomas, designer and author, for the interviews; David Freeman, Lincoln history for his input; Taylor Publishing Company's Neal Kimmel; Sarabeth Allen and Jewel Parr, librarians; Professor David Lewis, Ford historian and author; David Crippen of the Henry Ford Museum archives; Howard Pickard, retired Eagle L-M and quintessential Lincoln salesman; George Blesse, antique car dealer and auctioneer; the many Lincoln, Continental, and Zephyr hobbyists who have graciously shared their wealth of knowledge; and a special thanks to William Clay Ford, Vice-Chairman of the Ford Motor Company, for his written remarks.

Charles Rolls, partner of Henry Royce, believed that motorcars were for aristocrats alone. Rolls was killed in a flying accident in 1910 so he never knew how badly Henry Ford trod upon this idea. Many view automotive history as merely a specialized branch of industrial history, but to the automobile buff it is much more. The Lincoln motorcar, by virtue of limited production, lacks the popularity of some marques, but Lincoln is exemplary as an American marque.

Lincoln's history closely parallels that of the American automotive industry and the nation itself. It is the story of why a Cadillac was really a Ford, and the Lincoln a Cadillac. It is about a 1934 Lincoln that looked like a Volkswagen Beetle, and was named for a General Motors passenger train. It is about a lead-filled, custom-bodied cabriolet which is the only recognized modern classic automobile. It is about aluminum bodies, V-12 engines, and the iron-willed men who created them. The rich and colorful history of the Lincoln motorcar is the story of one of the finest series of automobiles ever conceived and produced. These automobiles were Town Sedans, Zephyrs and Continentals, the Lincolns

CHAPTER ONE

THOSE EARLY YEARS

The Cadillac Was A Ford

In 1886, the first patent was issued for a working internal-combustion engine automobile and children yet unborn were destined to shape the future of the motorcars, which became known as the Lincoln and the Lincoln Continental.

The automobile itself was not really an invention, but was the application of various engine designs to a land transport vehicle. The internal-combustion engine was an evolutionary result of the cylinder pump, the atomizer and Volta's spark pistol. As early as Leonardo da Vinci and even before his time the concept of a self-powered vehicle had been proposed.

The French word Automobile had not yet come to America when the news from Germany of Karl Benz' and Gottlieb Daimler's gasoline-powered carriages arrived. Benz was assisted by Emile Levassor and the third vehicle they built was exhibited at the 1887 Paris Exposition. A Belgian, J. Etienne Lenoir, had constructed a lamp gas-powered carriage in the late 1850s and reportedly sold it to the Czar of Russia in 1862.

In lawsuits that arose many years later, his design was singled out as the first example of a vehicle to be successfully powered by an internal-combustion engine.

John Lambert of Ohio City, Indiana, with his three-wheeler, may have been the first American to build a gasoline-powered automobile. He had used stationary engines extensively prior to experimenting with a powered vehicle.

Elwood Haynes of Kokomo, however, claimed to have been first. Haynes, with the assistance of the Apperson Brothers, used a Sintz boat engine to power a four-wheeled buggy. Charles and Frank Duryea of Springfield, Massachusetts, had been working on various designs and may have actually beaten Haynes by as much as a year. They were both bicycle mechanics like the Wright Brothers of powered flight fame.

Hiram Percy Maxim, a practicing projectile engineer and Massachusetts Institute of Technology graduate, lived in Lynn, Massachusetts. He had observed Nicolas Otto's lamp oil engine at work in the farm fields nearby. Maxim experimented with gasoline to power the three-cylinder, four-cycle engine for a tricycle, which he began constructing in early 1894. He was told at the local hardware store to leave gasoline alone because, "most of them who fooled with it blew 'em self up."

Then there was George Baldwin Selden of Rochester, New York, the inventor of Neophyte had also seen Otto's engine. Selden was granted U.S. patent number 549,160 on November 5, 1895, for an improved compression type road engine powered by liquid hydrocarbon. Using the guise of periodically revising his applications, Selden had been able to extend the effective life of his patent.

In the 1890s, Colonel Albert Pope was building electric motor carriages, which were more commonly called horseless carriages. Pope purchased an interest in the Selden patent and, with his associates, eventually tried to enforce this patent against all American auto manufacturers.

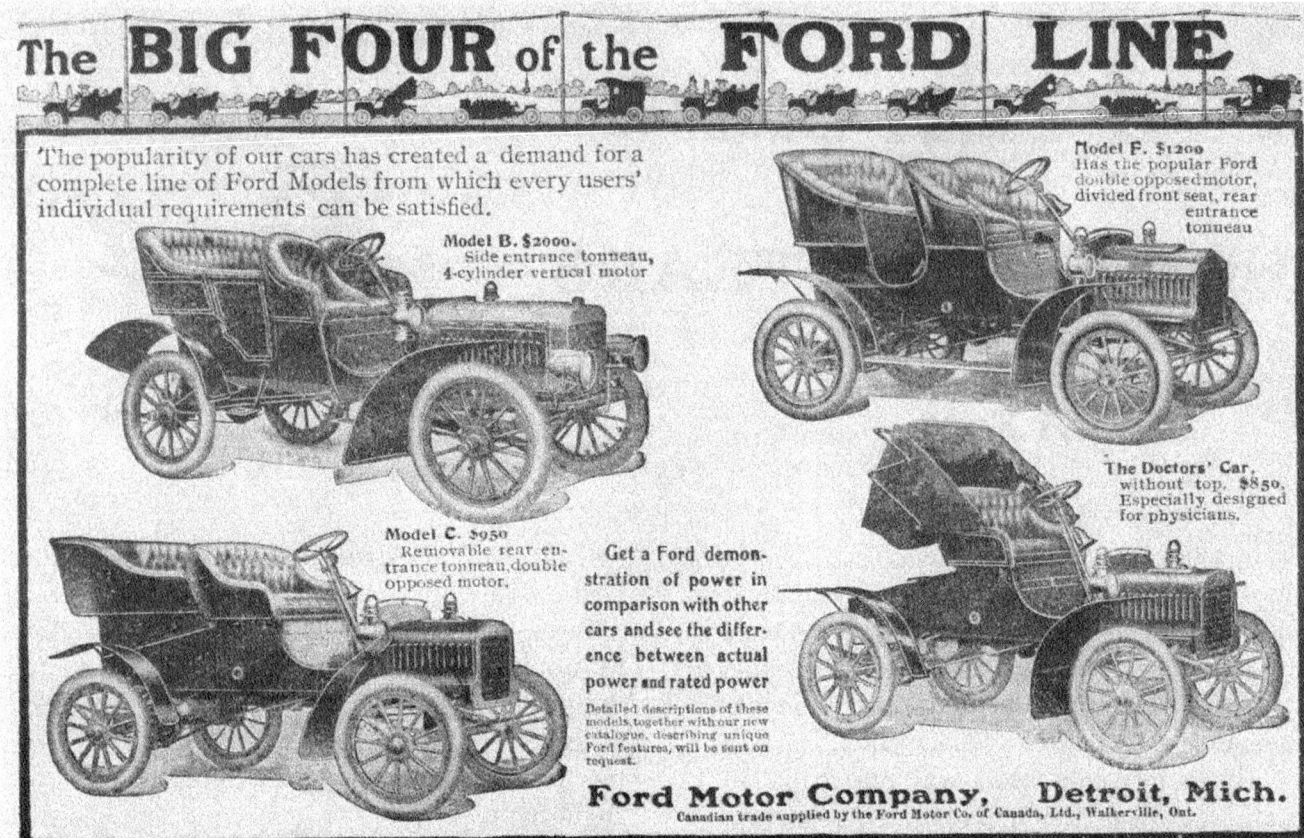

Charles Duryea in 1893, Haynes-Apperson in 1894 and Henry Ford and Charles King in 1896 had all constructed successful gasoline powered carriages. Charles King was what we might consider today a sports car enthusiast. In addition to being an early auto designer, he actually drove the Benz that finished second to Duryea in the Chicago Times Herald road race of November, 1895.

However, the second decade of the twentieth century, the court ruled that Selden's concept applied only to the two-cycle engine.

At the Chicago World's Fair of 1893, Ransom Olds displayed his steam-powered car. The word Car denotes a kinship to the railroad rolling stock and is slang or an abbreviated form of car'riage.

George Whitney, who inspired Francis E. and Freelan O. Stanley, had built a successful steamer in Boston prior to 1896. The Whites and Stanleys built reliable steam cars through the early twentieth century. Vehicles powered by gasoline engines, however, proved easier to start and to operate.

As for the Electrics, in 1899 Thomas A. Edison summed it up best when he said, "The need for constantly renewing is too great a handicap to overcome."

Olds soon abandoned steam power for gasoline engines. The buggy with its front floorboard curved up like a bobsled was called the Curved Dash Oldsmobile and was immortalized by the song "In My Merry Oldsmobile." So grand was the reputation of the Oldsmobile that the Reo Truck honored Ransom Eli Olds by using his initials. Alexander Winton, a bicycle builder, founded the Winton Motor Carriage Company of Cleveland, Ohio, in 1897.

The Winton became a major competitor of the Oldsmobile. Automobile manufacturing in the old days was a classic example of free enterprise and no-holds-barred competition. Alex Winton, it is said, even helped James Packard get started in the business. James Packard purchased Winton Number 12, but complained about it. He was told to go build a better one himself, if he could

Packard did just that and continued building premier motorcars for years to come.

Ol' Jim was working under a car one day when a prospective buyer inquired about its quality. Packard is said to have replied, "Ask a man who owns one." This became the Packard Company's motto.

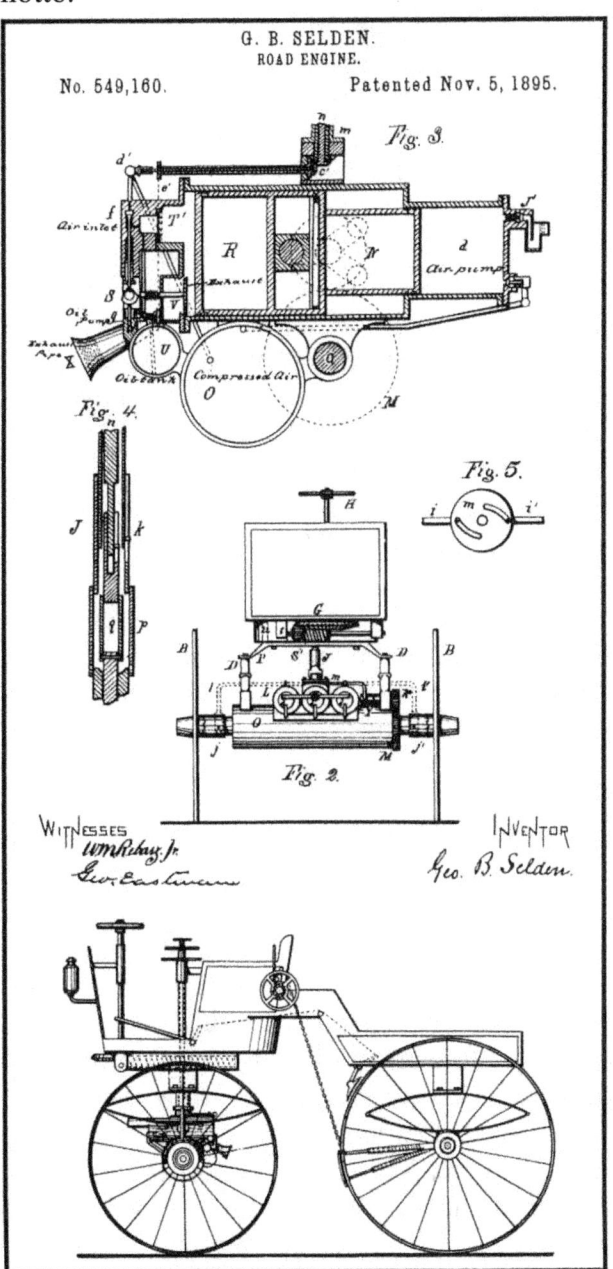

Opposite page: Siegfried Markus' gasoline car capable of 8 MPH. Karl Benz's 1-cylinder, 3-wheeler. Daimler's converted horse-carriage with 2-speed belt transmission. The Panhard-Levassor. Charles Duryea's 3-wheeler. Cross section of 1897 Daimler engine. J.H. Knight's experimental car. Left: 1877 George Baldwin Selden's road engine patent of 1895. The actual 4-wheel, 2-cycle vehicle was built in 1905 during the Selden-Ford Patent Trial.

Cars were not built to a standard configuration in those days. The average motorist of today would find it difficult to start and drive many of these older cars. By 1910 this began to change and today's drivers would feel quite at home behind the wheel of a 1920s car

One of the standardization adapted was Packard's H-pattern gearshift. Even Ford changed to this gear pattern at the end of the Model-T line.

The first president of the United States to ride in an automobile was William McKinley. On November 22, 1899, Horse Age magazine of New York reported that earlier in the week President McKinley had ridden in F.O. Stanley's Locomobile.

Theodore Roosevelt rode in many different makes of automobiles. One such occasion was in promoting A.P. Warner's new invention, the speedometer. Teddy's love for horses probably prevented him from considering the transition to the motorcar completely.

William Howard Taft's administration was the first to purchase and use automobiles. Taft had toured in a White Steamer during his campaign for office and after he became President, the executive branch purchased a Baker Electric, a White Steamer, two Pierce-Arrows and two motorcycles. Although Taft was issued Connecticut driver's license number 17,474, he was generally chauffeured by Quartermaster Corpsman George H. Robinson.

At the New York Automobile Show of 1900, some forty automakers displayed over three hundred models ranging in price from $280 to $4,000. By 1910, there were 458,500 motor vehicles registered in the United States. Automobile manufacturing was largely centered in New England and in the northeastern Midwest. They were referred to as the Eastern and Western companies. The Eastern companies adapted to the Vanderbilt, Astor and Winthrop type of clientele, making higher priced cars for upper class buyers. The Western companies engine. Oliver Barthel, George Gato, James W. Bishop and Edward S. "Spider" Huff

all helped or produced lower priced cars at higher production rates and catered to farmers and industrial workers.

After the turn of the century automobile companies sprang up all over and promoters sold motorcar company stocks as get-rich-quick schemes. Studebaker had been in the wagon and carriage building business for many years when the motorcar revolution exploded. Pierce-Arrow, a wire manufacturer building bird cages, entered the auto parts business by making spoke wheels.

White was a sewing machine company. In San Antonio, Texas, Sam Pandolfo manufactured about seven hundred automobiles before going to jail for pocketing too much of the stock revenue. The automobile spawned hundreds of other successful industries, two of which being the gasoline stations and tire companies.

Roads were poor prior to the First World War, especially in the West and South and automobile travel required the same planning as going on a safari. The Lincoln Highway Association was founded in 1913 to promote quality roads across the United States. There is no connection between the Lincoln Highway and the Lincoln Motor Company. Carl Graham Fisher of Indianapolis helped to raise four million dollars for construction of a public highway between Jersey City on the East Coast and San Francisco on the West Coast.

Named the Lincoln Memorial Highway by Fisher, it was not completed until the 1920s when it was designated as U.S. Route 30. In 1916, Congress passed the Federal Road Act based on powers granted for postal access roads, providing federal aid for state construction of highways. The Defense Highway Act of 1944 eventually gave this nation its superhighway system.

In 1933, a presidential commission concluded that no other invention so quickly influenced the national culture, transforming habits, thoughts and language as did the automobile. At a 1971 meeting in New York City, the American Historical Association formally recognized the growing interest in automotive history and the impact of the automobile on our society.

Many of us who enjoy automobilia look upon it as a form of modern art. The sculpturing of steel, wood and synthetics into the automobile is as much an art form as stone carving and pottery-making was to the ancients.

Thus, the stage was set for our story. America by the late 1900s was on a collision course for a love affair with the automobile. This story is about one such automobile called a Lincoln.

A century ago, two automobile geniuses met and set in motion one of the most interesting series of events in American motorcar history.

Henry Ford and the Quadricycle.

A TALE OF TWO HENRYS - Henry Ford was the eldest child of a rather humble Michigan farm family. He moved to Detroit in about 1885 and took a job as an electrician for the Edison Company. As early as 1889, he became interested in the internal-combustion engine. He had his own idea for a lightweight, self-propelled vehicle. Ford began work on his Quadricycle on New Year's Day, 1894 and test-drove it two years later on Bagley Avenue in Detroit.

Charles Brady King, also of Detroit, beat Henry by a couple of months. King and Ford were acquainted and both had read an article in the American Machinist on how to construct a simple gasoline worked on the first Ford automobile. The Quadricycle was sold to Charles Ashley of Detroit because Ford was dissatisfied with its lack of a reverse gear and other shortcomings.

Even if Henry Ford was not the inventor of the first automobile, he may have been the first used car dealer. The car Henry originally sold for $200 was later repurchased and now resides in a place of honor at the Henry Ford Museum in Dearborn, Michigan. Henry built hissecond car in 1897, but always claimed to have built an automobile prior to 1892. It was, however, a rather unsuccessful steam tractor. His experience with this vehicle probably motivated him to begin experiments with gasoline engines. It is interesting to note that early Ford company brochures mistakenly used the 1892 date for the Quadricycle.

Henry Martyn Leland was the son of a Vermont teamster. He was raised in a devoutly Christian home and named for a famous British missionary. At age seventeen, he went to work for a tool company that supplied machined parts to the Springfield Armory. It was here and later at Colt Arms, that young Henry Leland became a master machinist. He was strongly patriotic, a Unionist in political philosophy. It was during these early years that Leland adopted Abe Lincoln as his personal hero. He would later name his automobile company for the sixteenth President of the United States.

Leland worked for Brown & Sharpe as a precision tool representative and developed manufacturing techniques for Westinghouse. A little known fact about Henry Leland is that he invented mechanical barber clippers. Henry and Wilford Leland, Robert C. Faulconer and Charles H. Norton started a milling and casting business in Detroit.

By 1899, it became a major parts producer for Olds Motor Works. Alfred Sloan of Hyatt Roller Bearing Company finally convinced Leland to use roller bearings in his engines and transmissions, but only after the Hyatt company met Leland's accuracy standards. Sloan later became president of General Motors.

Leland's continued insistence on precision and accuracy made Leland-Built an industry byword for quality. The Leland & Faulconer Mfg. Co. had originally intended to build boat engines, but quickly became competitors with the Dodge Brothers and other contract automotive parts suppliers.

Both Henrys had sons. Leland's son, Wilford Chester, was born in 1869. Ford's son, Edsel Bryant, was born in 1893. Bryant was Mrs. Clara Ford's family name. Less flamboyant and less famous than their fathers, both sons nevertheless left their individual marks on the annals of automotive history.

Henry Ford is generally credited with having failed in three or four car companies, if you do not count experimental car companies,

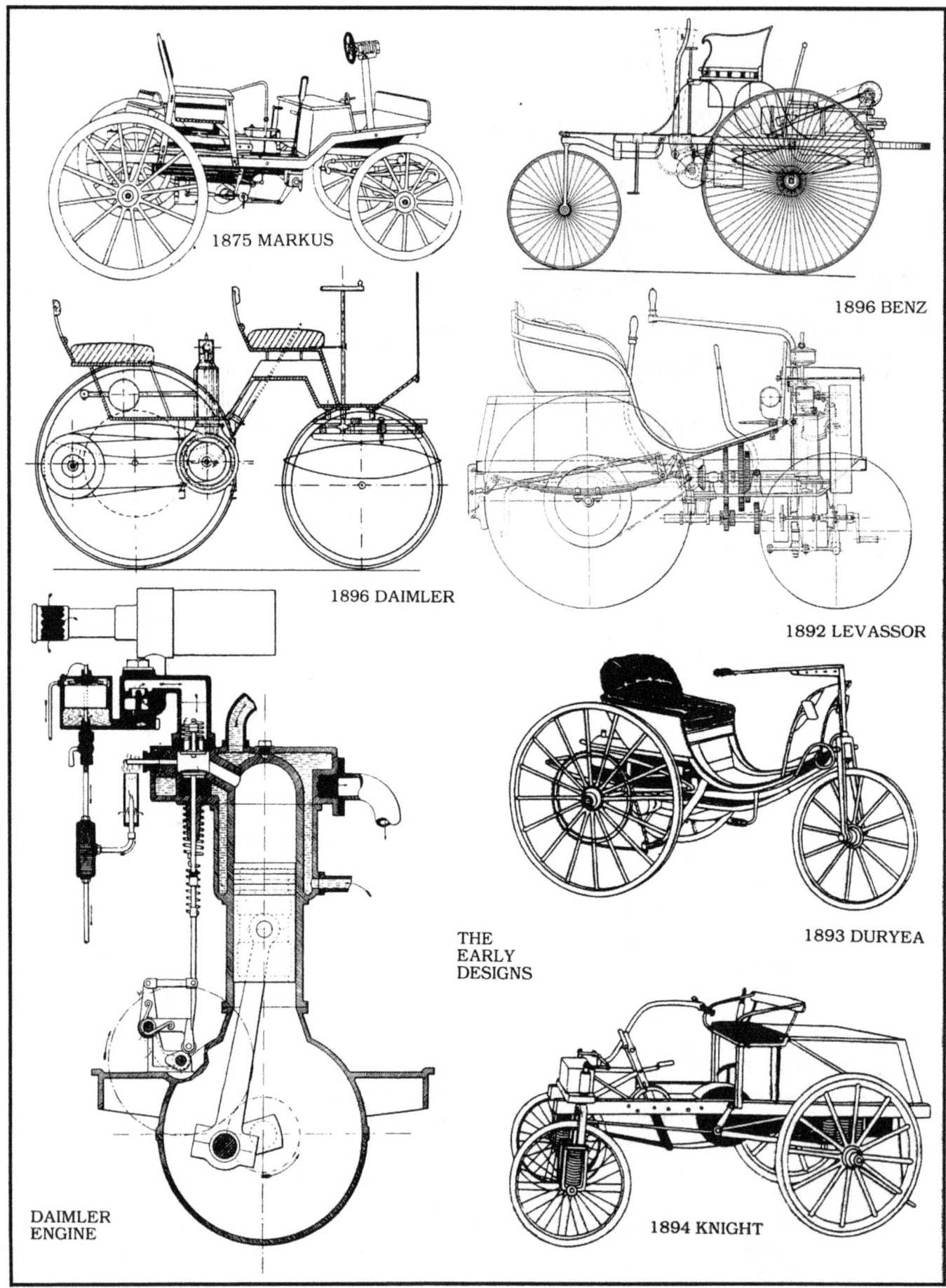

Elwood P. Haynes, 1894.

Frank Duryea, 1895.

Charles B. King, 1896.

And the race car ventures and corporate reorganizations, there was really only the first failure. His second of two ventures in association with William H. Murphy later became part of General Motors. Henry Ford's auto firm, in association with Alex Y. Malcomson, evolved into the Ford Motor Company.

In 1899, the Detroit Automobile Company was organized. The incorporators were Frank Hacke, Pat Ducy, Wil Maybury, Saf Delano, Frank Eddy, Bill Murphy, W.C. McMillian, Frank Alderman, Fred Osborn, Clarence Band and Henry Ford who was also chief engineer. Only about ten or twelve cars were ever produced by this company. Henry Ford was less than thrilled with his small interest in the company's profits. He was more interested in developing a new type of car than in producing substandard machines. The design he had in mind would eventually become the 1903 Ford Model-A.

Frank Alderman had been promoting sales of a new model Detroit automobile. In November 1901, he persuaded Murphy to endorse renaming and reorganizing the Detroit Automobile Company into the Henry Ford Company. Ford was given one-sixth interest and a cash advance to develop his new prototype. For the next eight months Henry fiddled while Murphy and the rest of the stockholders burned. Bill Murphy and Henry Leland attended the same local Presbyterian Church. One Sunday in the spring of 1902, the two were discussing production problems at the Henry Ford Company. At the request of Murphy, Leland agreed to have a look and make some suggestions. He did and Ford departed. This seemingly insignificant incident touched off a chain of events that affects the automobile industry to this day.

Henry M. Leland was a tall elderly, white-whiskered gentleman with a reputation for mechanical perfection. His analytical reasoning and quest for precision made Leland a role model for the modern automotive engineer. Henry Ford, on the other hand, was a wiry, shoot-from-the-hip, experimentation inventor. The two originally met at the Detroit Auto Show in 1901. It was not said that the two Henrys disliked one another. In fact, they seemed to have the highest regard for each other's professional achievements.

Leland just could not abide non-precision workmanship and thus was overly critical of Ford's designs. Leland knew that the Oldsmobile engine his company was currently building was already superior to Ford's engine. Ford probably did not give a damn. What he really wanted to do was build a race car that could challenge the Winton Bullet. To say that Ford and Leland locked automobile horns is a pun one can hardly pass up, but it was probably just time for a change of drivers.

Leland formally took over management of the Henry Ford Company at the shareholders' behest. In August, 1902, the corporation's name was changed to Cadillac Automobile Company. Thus the first Cadillac was really a Ford. The Faulconer & Leland shop provided the engines for the new Ford/Cadillac; it was good business for both companies. Other parts were obtained from contract vendors like the Dodge Brothers. The Dodge's machine shop had built transmissions and parts for the Oldsmobile.

The Dodges later became major suppliers to the Ford Motor Company and for a short time were stockholders. Ultimately, the Dodge Brothers would build their own automobiles.

Some General Motors historians try to overlook the Ford/Cadillac lineage. To disprove the similarity between the automobiles, they point to the improvements Leland made in the Ford design, most notably the two-cylinder versus the original one-cylinder engine. Ford had told the Detroit auto people that he himself thought it was an inferior product and needed more development. Murphy, however, continued to push for production. The L-section frame versus the original channel-type frame was another improvement implemented during early Cadillac production models.

The Leland spring design was semi-elliptical and attached with gooseneck hangers that resulted in a very smooth ride, but these too were modified and although minor, were some of the changes made to the early production Model-A Cadillac. Ford Motor Company went to some length to avoid mentioning Leland's role in the origination of the Lincoln design.

The ridiculous enters when one argues that the Model-A Cadillac came out before the Model-A Ford. Of course it did. Henry Ford had started the Detroit (Ford/Cadillac) automobile two years earlier. The absurd comes in when one argues that the Cadillac was left-hand steering and the Ford was European right-hand. A photo entitled, "First Cadillac" and dated 1902, shows Wilford Leland in the left seat with Alanson Bush behind the wheel on the right side.

Ford and Cadillac both went to left-hand steering shortly thereafter. In horse-drawn carriages, the driver often sat on the right to allow free use of a whip in the right hand. Automobiles switched the driver to the left side to allow passengers, often ladies, to exit to the generally less-muddy curb side. Note that the Ford Model-A, mentioned before, should not be confused with the famous Model-A built by Ford between 1929 and 1931. The original Model-A was the predecessor of the Ford Model-N and Model-T.

In 1905, Leland & Faulconer merged with the Cadillac Automotive Company and the new Cadillac motorcar became the industry standard. Henry and Wilford Leland retained about 19 percent ownership in Cadillac. The Cadillac won engineering awards like the Dewar Trophy from Great Britain for the precision manufacturing of standardized parts in 1908 and for its electrical system in 1912. Henry M. Leland was president of the SAE (Society of Automotive Engineers) for several terms. The title, "Master of Precision," given him by the British, became a synonym for Leland and will remain his personal badge of courage throughout automotive history.

A friend of Henry Leland, Byron Carter, once stopped to assist a lady driver crank start her automobile. The engine backfired and Carter was struck by the handle. He later died of the injury. This incident moved Leland to work closely with Charles Kettering of Dayton, Ohio to develop a self-starter. Kettering was a noted inventor and founder of the Dayton Electric Company. He adapted a high torque electric motor to the mechanical task of cranking the engine. His company, Delco, later became part of General Motors and Charles Kettering was influential in GM management for many years. Another starter, the Rushmore, was developed in 1911.

It was available on the Simplex and other automobiles at extra cost. The Rushmore design became known as the Bendix drive and its design was closer to starters today than was Kettering's design.

David Dunbar Buick had made considerable money by inventing a process for enameling bathroom fixtures. He turned his profits and efforts towards the development of an overhead valve engine in 1903. The Buick Motor Company, a partnership with David Buick and the Briscoe brothers, was sold to Billy Durant in 1904. And Benjamin Briscoe and Jonathan Maxwell founded the United States Motor Company, a consortium of 130 firms; all of which folded in 1912.

William Carpo Durant borrowed from Wall Street's J.P. Morgan to form International Motors Company. After a split with Morgan, Durant scratched out the word International on the company stationery and wrote General above it. Leland and Murphy sold Cadillac to Durant in July of 1909 and became General Motors stockholders. Wilford C. Leland was instrumental in saving the entire General Motors conglomerate from bankruptcy in 1910 through tactful negotiations with GM's New York bankers. The elder Leland was in Europe at the time, Wilford succeeded where Durant had failed.

The Touring model was the natural extension of the automobile from the carriage. Most early models began as Tourings and remained popular well into the 1920s. Page 18: Popular Touring models of the early 1900s, 1905 Peerless, 1905 Toledo, 1903 Pope, 1911 Duryea Landaulet, 1911 Lion, and 1907 Deere. Page 21: Ford Model N of 1898; Ford race car the "999." Below: Early Ford Model T ad. Opposite page: Ford's public declaration of the invalidity of the Selden claim. This open defiance eventually led to legal action between the Selden group and Ford.

Henry Ford had left the old Detroit Automobile Company in March of 1902 with the designs for his race car, a few hundred dollars in cash and the company's name, which was his birthright anyway. Ford took up racing with a passion. Automobile racing had come of age with the turn of the century. Most early races came down to who could finish at all, let alone who could finish first.

The first reported race in America was won by J. Frank Duryea in 1895. Only the Duryea and the Benz automobiles completed the race. The fifty mile run between Chicago and Evanston, Illinois, took nine hours. In 1901, the Cleveland built Winton came to Detroit to race. The hometown entry was Henry Ford's two-cylinder, seat-over engine racer. The Winton took the first turn in a cloud of dust, but developed engine problems. Ford won the race with an average speed of 44.8 miles per hour.

Henry was overheard saying, "I'll never do that again. I was scared to death."

Tom Cooper and Henry Ford built a new racer, naming it the ol' 999 for a famous locomotive of the era. It was a four-cylinder, seven-square engine that developed approximately eighty horsepower, so large that the driver was now placed behind the engine. This also resulted in a lower and improved center of gravity. This car was used by Barney Oldfield to set the first mile-a-minute record for an oval track. A bicycle racer, Berna Eli Oldfield had been hired as the Ford competition race driver.

In 1903, Carl Fisher organized a race at Indianapolis. Barney won it in the Red Devil a sister car to the Number 999 speedster and three new phrases were added to the American language. They were the Indy race, Barney O'field and Daredevil driver. Today, the 999 locomotive is on display at the Chicago Museum of Science beside the Burlington Zephyr. The 999 speedster is housed at the Henry Ford Museum in Dearborn, Michigan.

The last speed run Henry Ford ever drove was the Arrow Speedster when he set a new straight course world's record with a speed of 91.37 miles per hour on icy Lake St. Clair. Earlier records were set by Alex Winton in the Bullet Number 2 and by Ransom Olds in his eight hundred pound Pirate with a speed of 53.5 miles per hour at Daytona in 1903. Ford's record set in 1904 was broken in 1905 by Louis Ross in a Steamer traveling 94.73 miles per hour. In 1906, a Stanley Steamer set an astonishing record of 127.57 miles per hour. Either through luck or calculation, the publicity from racing created widespread public interest in Henry Ford's cars.

With the backing of Alex Malcomson, plus assistance by financial wizard James Couzens and metallurgist Harold Childe Wills, Henry incorporated the Ford Motor Company in June of 1903. Wills drafted the famous Ford script logo that is second only to the Coca-Cola logo in worldwide recognition. Henry Ford finally overcame his hang-ups about production and manufactured thousands of cars during the next five years. Dodge Brothers produced chassis and parts for the lightweight low-cost Model-N.

In 1908, the Model-T and a rather unsuccessful large car, the Model-K, were introduced. This Model-K was probably the namesake of the 1931 successor to the Model-L Lincoln. The Ford Model-K had a six-cylinder engine that Henry Ford disliked and upon which Chevrolet capitalized. Colorful, quotable Henry always claimed that an engine should have no more cylinders than a cow has teats. One assumes Henry had two cows in mind when he went to the V-8.

1898 experimental Ford car produced by Henry Ford prior to the organization of the Ford Motor Company, preceded the Model T by ten years. Even this early Ford had a radius rod front axle with the body mounted at the center of the transverse front spring. Manual throttle was a sidemounted lever. Drawing by John M. Perckham, courtesy Behr-Manning.

Swiss race driver Louis Chevrolet had designed a six-cylinder engine for the Buick in 1911. Durant was impressed with the name Chevrolet, which means Little Mountain Goat. He reintroduced the GM Republic calling it Chevrolet, but fired Louis for smoking cigars in his office. The Chevrolet Model-L known as the Light-six and Model-C both used six-cylinder engines. In 1914, the four-cylinder Model-H, Royal Mail Chevrolet was introduced to compete with Ford, thus beginning a long-standing rivalry. Louis Chevrolet's Frontenac Motor Company would later build racing equipment for modifying Model-T Fords.

In 1909, after acquiring Cadillac, Durant offered to purchase the Ford Motor Company. Selden and Pope had formed a group known as ALAM (Association of Licensed Automobile Manufacturers) to enforce Selden's patent, going first after Winton and then after Ford. Ford had just lost the first round of court battles when the Durant offer was made. Henry and Malcomson agreed to sell to GM for eight million dollars, but Henry wanted cold, hard, train-ridin' dollars. Durant had put most of his deals together through stock trades and was unable to borrow that kind of money, which was a fortunate turn of events for the fledgling American automobile industry.

Durant's general manager, Charles Nash, left GM to produce the Jeffery Rambler. He and James Storrow, also formerly of GM, formed the Nash Motor Company in 1917. Walter Percy Chrysler replaced Charles Nash and by 1920 was being paid a half-million dollars a year to manage General Motors. This arrangement ended abruptly during a dispute over building a new Buick plant in Flint, Michigan. The cause of the dispute was for the same reason as the Ford and Leland split. The one company was not large enough to support two large egos. Jonathan D. Maxwell had worked on some of the original Haynes cars in Indiana, but his automobile company was now floundering.

Walter Chrysler took over the Maxwell-Chalmers company and built it into the Chrysler Corporation. Chrysler bought out Dodge Brothers in 1928. Another dynamic automotive entrepreneur of this period was Erret Lobban Cord. He founded Cord, Auburn and Duesenberg. Cord was born in 1894. By the time he was thirty-five years old, he owned Lycoming Engine, American Airlines, Stenson Aircraft and New York Shipbuilders.

"999" RACER

World War I was now occupying much of America's industrial output. Billy Durant, like Henry Ford, was a devout pacifist. The Lelands were not. So H.M. and Wilford left General Motors to produce airplane engines for the war effort. They founded the Liberty Engine Company, that produced over six thousand, 400 horsepower, V-12 aircraft engines between August, 1917 and January, 1919. Most of these engines never saw action in Europe, but they became the mainstay of the Army Air Corps and the U.S. Air Mail Service for a decade to come.

The Liberty engine was used by Donald Douglas, creator of the famed DC-3, on an early aircraft that he built for D.P. Davis. The Liberty engine also powered the aircraft of Army Lieutenants Kelly and Macready, a Fokker T-2, on its record-setting nonstop transcontinental flight in May, 1923. The Allison Engine Company later became part of General Motors. The company began in Indianapolis as a shop where it converted Liberty engines into an inverted configuration.

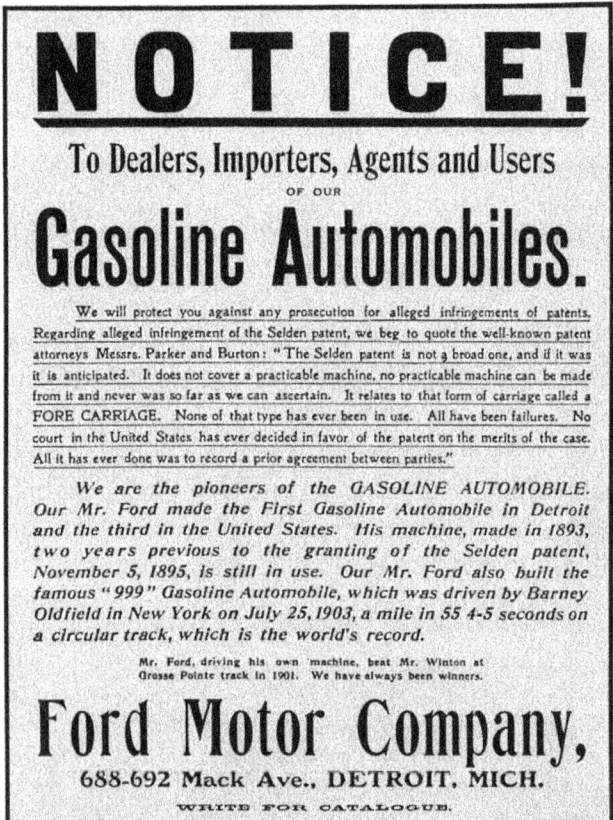

Of all those who disliked the Selden patent claim, Henry Ford opposed it the most. The Wright brothers tried to patent the airplane, but Glen Curtiss added an aileron to his wing and thus circumvented their claim. Ingenuity is the American way. In 1911, after the introduction of the famous Ford Model-T, the courts ordered the ALAM group and Ford to construct actual prototypes.

The Selden design was a paper only patent, no working Model-Had even been constructed. At last, Henry had the advantage. He based his working model on the 1860 Lenoir design and won the case. Henry Ford wanted control of the Ford Motor Company and by 1919, he had acquired controlling interest. The Ford Motor Company perfected mass production techniques, the assembly line and introduced the five-dollar workday. The rest, as they say, is history.

THE LINCOLN IS CONCEIVED - There were a few earlier Lincoln automobile companies, but none were very successful. The Lincoln Auto Company of Jersey City, organized in 1908 and the Lincoln Carriage and Automobile Company of New York in 1905, probably never built any motor cars. The Lincoln Square Garden Company of Long Island was organized to build and sell motor cars and motorcycles in about 1910, but there is no evidence that any were produced.

The Lincoln Automobile Company of Lincoln, Illinois, began in 1907 at the Kate's machine shop. Until 1909, they produced a Buggy, a Runabout and a Surrey model. All were seat-over-engine, two-cylinder, air cooled and chain driven. The earliest Lincoln was the Electric of Cleveland, Ohio. Built in 1900, it developed 2 1/2 horsepower and was powered by 420 pounds of Willard batteries. The vehicle received a lengthy write-up in the November 6th, 1900 issue of Motor Age. The company abandoned the Electric Runabout and returned to electrical component manufacturing the following year.

Sears, Roebuck and Company sold several versions of a seat-over-engine, two-cylinder Runabout between 1908 and 1912. Most of the parts for the 14 horsepower, tiller steering buggy were actually produced by the Lincoln Motor Car Works of Illinois. When Sears dropped the car from its catalog, Lincoln continued to market the Model-24 Runabout for $585. In 1913, they introduced a front-engine, three-passenger Light Touring for $650. The Lincoln motor works on Harrison Street in Chicago discontinued motor car production in 1914.

The Lincoln Highway Roadster was built by Lincoln Motor Car Company of Detroit in 1914. The company was the successor to American Motorette. Its design greatly resembled the Lincoln Works Light Touring, both had Renault-style front ends and odd seating arrangements. The Lincoln Highway had four-cylinders and sold for $500. Only a few were ever produced.

Henry Leland was a wealthy and successful industrialist, but found himself and the company he had built out of work at the end of World War I. Many dedicated and patriotic employees had followed him from Cadillac in 1917. Forming a new automobile company seemed the logical course of action and it would put his six thousand skilled employees back to work. More specifically, it would fulfill Leland's dream of building the Permanent Motorcar, an automobile built with such precision and care that it would run for decades with only routine maintenance. The Lincoln motorcar was born. The Boys, as Leland called them, began designing the first Lincoln in early 1919.

Most of the giant automobile makers crossed paths several times in the next decade and automotive historians refer to that era as, "The levee upon which great men stood."

By March of 1920 a Model-T Ford was selling for $570, production was approaching a million cars and trucks per year and unfilled orders were backed up for six months. There were, however, some signs that the auto market was softening. It was into this environment that the new Lincoln motorcar was introduced.

LINCOLN
MOTOR CARS

The ENCLOSED TYPES

THE first thing that impresses you about LINCOLN Enclosed Cars is their rich and dignified bearing, which naturally appeals to the more discerning types of citizens, and which in turn bespeaks the substantial type of owner.

LINCOLN Eight-Cylinder Enclosed Cars comprise eight styles, in standard and custom-built bodies, owner and chauffeur driven, and having accommodations for from four to seven persons.

Each is a model of its type, fashioned not merely to emulate fine creations with which you may be familiar, but rather to anticipate your ideals of a truly sumptuous car, and to enable you to realize those ideals in so far as it is humanly possible.

The ideals pictured were ideals of atmosphere and environment, emphasized and made more appealing by a mode of travel possessing even greater charm than motordom has been accustomed to experience.

LELAND-BUILT

LINCOLN MOTOR COMPANY
DETROIT, MICH.

CHAPTER TWO

THE LELAND LINCOLNS

Where In "L" Do We Go From Here

In 1920, within weeks of one another, two new luxury automobiles were introduced. They were Henry Leland's Lincoln and Fred Duesenberg's Model-A. Although the Lincoln motorcar was new to the industry, its people were not. The Boys at Lincoln had built the first precision Oldsmobile engines in 1902. Under Cadillac, they had introduced the Kettering electrical system in 1912 and developed a V-8 engine in 1914.

Automobile publications of the time gave the new Lincoln more publicity than it deserved or needed. The initial stock offering was over-subscribed and sold out the first day it was offered. On January 26, 1920, Lincoln Motor Company was officially organized as a Delaware corporation and assumed the liabilities and assets of the Lincoln Motor Company of Michigan. These included the business address, buildings, property and manufacturing equipment of the old Liberty engine company. Much of the early Model-L development had been accomplished under this company.

At the stock offering, plans were announced to manufacture three hundred cars per month with the first production models to be delivered in January. The new corporation was capitalized at $6.5 million. This was problem number one, a violation of the basic economic precept that everything costs more than you think it will. The Lincoln Motor Company turned out to be undercapitalized. The Lelands put up $1 million in cash and personally endorsed another $3 million in loans during the next two years.

The press continued to hype the Lincoln as the car of tomorrow, designed by the Master of Precision and founder of Cadillac, Henry M. Leland. They predicted that it would outperform everything on the road and run forever. Wilford Leland assumed more and more of the actual management, as Henry was now in his late seventies. The Lincoln turned out to be as finely-built and precision-engineered a machine as could be produced at that times.

In late 1918, Henry Leland called the boys together for one of his conferences. He was strong on conferences, always saying, "Nothing important should be left to the judgment of one man."

When H.M. called them into a meeting, they listened and he announced, "You have been telling me for years about this idea you all have for a quality-built, rugged and stable automobile. Well, we are ready to go ahead. You have an opportunity now such as you have never had before to make a thoroughly roadable car, a car that will not only go anywhere, but that will go there with ease to the driver and with comfort to the passengers, a car in which it will not be necessary to pick out only the good roads, a car that will enable people to travel less frequented highways and to go places they have not been able comfortably to go heretofore. Do the jobs as you have always been accustomed to doing, only do it better! After the experimental cars are finished, we want to figure on at least a year to prove them out so as to leave no shortcoming for the car owner to discover."

EARLY MODEL L CHASSIS

In about six months, they had designed several different prototypes and actually constructed two of them for testing.

According to Leland, "They were both truly wonderful cars, but we adopted the better of the two. Four engines were built, three of them were installed in chassis and the fourth was assigned for testing on the dynamometer followed by a refining process and ferreting out of deficiencies. The cars had been subjected to the most severe and the most practical punishment we could prescribe and have successfully withstood endurance tests equal to about five years of service in the hands of the average user. I believe motorists will agree that the ideal car should possess primarily six important virtues: good appearance, trustworthiness, long life, power, economy and comfort. The order of their importance is largely a matter of individual opinion. In appearance, the cars are substantial, well-proportioned and graceful."

Leland continued, "There is nothing extreme or overdone in any of the eight body types, just thoroughly dignified. They are cars such as the best citizens, persons of good judgment and refined taste will be proud to own. Their beauty is a type dictated not by passing fancy but by a desire for permanent attractiveness. The cars are replete with those many little conveniences, which contribute so much to real pleasure and enjoyment."

The chief engineer for Lincoln was Ernest Sweet. He and his people questioned the concept of geometry on the 90 degree V-engine with a single plane crank. Even during Lincoln's aircraft engine days, their engineers had considered going to a tighter degree engine. The new Lincoln's engine cylinders were opposed at approximately 60 degrees instead of the 90 degrees used on the V-8 introduced by Cadillac.

An engineer by the name of Heldt had published a paper in 1916, which suggested that such an engine would run smoother and it did. On a 60 degree engine, the firing stroke was alternated between 60 and 120 degrees of angle and the power stroke then added a push, which occurred alternately.

These engines were referred to as an Out-Of-Step engine. The cylinder firing order was rotated rather than sequential. This was accomplished by some complex mechanical calculations regarding the crank and cam shafts.

Frank Johnson, a brilliant design draftsman and University of Michigan graduate, actually made most of the working drawings for the new Lincoln. He later became head of engineering and worked at Lincoln for many years. Advertising claimed the accuracy and fit of Lincoln parts to a hair's breadth. Take a human hair, they suggested, slice it into ten equal parts and one of these parts is how tight the tolerances on three-hundred individual manufacturing operations was held. The crankcase on the Model-L engine was cast of solid aluminum. The pistons were alloy and not cast-iron. Aluminum pistons had previously proven successful in aircraft engines. The block was made in two halves and bolted together. Cylinder heads were interchangeable and the valves were made of tungsten steel alloy. The crankshaft had five main bearings, each two inches in width, which meant that there was over seventy square inches of main bearing surface.

Leland was always pleased to demonstrate that after tightening it to running clearance; you could spin the crankshaft with one finger. The connecting rods were twelve and one-half inches long, reducing the side-thrust on the cylinder walls, greatly reducing wear. Their design incorporated a new concept referred to as Fork-And-Blade, which acted like a counter balance. The Model-L eight-cylinder engine had a three-inch bore and a five-inch stroke, giving it over 350 cubic inches of displacement (85x122 mm; 5.8 liters).

The Lincoln engine's combustion chamber was of the L-head type, which meant that the valves were mounted to the side of the piston and opened upward into the chamber. This allowed the cam and the valve stems to remain within the block for better lubrication. Ford stayed with this design into the early 1950s.

The Model-L engine was a massive and durable engine that developed 81 brake horsepower at 2600 RPM. At higher RPM, the engine developed 90 bhp or better. Innovations in engine accessories were a multi-barreled updraft carburetor, circuit breaker electrical system and automatic spark advance. The electrical generator was shaft-driven off the back of the water pump. A device called the Electrofog generator operated when the choke was pulled out. The device electrically preheated the gas-air intake mixture and cut itself off after fifteen seconds.

The transmission was a standard H-pattern floor shift with three forward gears and one reverse. The cooling system was sealed and had an overflow tank. When the engine cooled, boiled-over water was siphoned back into the radiator, which eliminated the need to stop and replenish the coolant frequently. Most modern cars are equipped with overflow tanks, but this was innovative for the Model-L's time.

Engines at Lincoln were assembled under the supervision of engineer William Guy. They were then turned over to Charles Marten's group where each engine was placed on a dynamometer and ran under a load. As the load was increased from ten to twenty horsepower, each engine was checked for overheating and roughness. If these occurred, the engine was rejected. The transmission parts were machined with great precision. This, coupled with a multi-disc clutch, gave the Model-L an incredibly smooth pull away. The basic Leland engine design remained unchanged until 1931, attesting to its fine design.

About a dozen original designs for the new Lincoln had been looked at seriously. After the two development models were built, the first production prototype rolled out in June of 1920. The chassis was oversized and rugged and the body was distinguished by its quality construction rather than by innovative styling. The drive shaft was a torque-tube design and stressed the rear suspension under engine load to provide a smooth ride. Double-shackled rear springs, used by car manufacturers until the 1950s, were installed.

1920 Early Leland Built Model L 7-pass Touring winter test car.

1921 Leland-Built Model L Phaeton, Summer.

How Lincoln Cars are Leland-built

Since the making of motor cars began and passing time saw the advents of new creations, it is doubtful whether there has ever been an achievement of which so much has been expected as of the Leland-built Lincoln car.

Quite naturally should this be true, because—as has been so aptly said—this car has practically the entire automotive industry as its legitimate ancestry; and because—as also has been aptly said—if the achievements of a Leland organization are to be surpassed, it is only logical to look to a Leland organization to surpass them; again, because the Lincoln car is produced by men now equipped to turn vast experience to best account, by men devoting their every effort and their every talent to making a car such as has never been made before; in fact, to making a car such as motordom perhaps has never expected to enjoy.

To accomplish this, we have what is deemed advanced design, re-enforced by unusual precision in the making of the parts.

This is only logical to expect of men who, the world over, are recognized as pioneers of advanced ideas, and as foremost exponents of precision methods.

As a symbol of fineness, "hairsbreadth" is the term most frequently applied, yet "hairsbreadth" in a Leland-built Lincoln car symbolizes merely one of the coarser measurements.

Take a hair from your head (the average is about 2½ thousandths of an inch in thickness) and if you could split that hair into ten strands of uniform dimensions, just one of those strands would give a fair conception of the closeness to a mean standard prescribed in more than 300 operations.

In the Leland-built Lincoln car, there are more than 5,000 operations in which the deviation from a mean standard is not permitted to exceed the one one-thousandth of an inch; more than 1,200 in which it is not permitted to exceed a half of one-thousandth, and more than 300 in which it is not permitted to exceed a quarter of one-thousandth.

The illustrations herewith represent mere examples of the literally thousands upon thousands of devices, tools and gauges employed to insure these Leland standards of precision.

If the entire contents of this publication were devoted to a description of the seemingly limitless number of fine and close mechanical operations, the story even then would not half be told. If you were personally to inspect and have them all explained, it would require months to do so.

But precision, for mere precision's sake alone, means little. It is only when that precision lends itself to some practical benefit that it becomes a virtue.

To cite an extreme example; it would be absurd to prescribe that a running-board, or a fender, be held within a hundredth of an inch limit; yet a limit so liberal in thousands of essentially accurate parts would be fatal.

Precision, mis-applied, is unwarranted and wasteful, and lends itself to no advantage.

Precision, un-applied, means harshness, vibration, rapid wear, disintegration and expensive maintenance.

Precision, skilfully and scientifically applied, comes only from knowing where and knowing how to apply it.

Then, and then only, can it express itself in greater smoothness, in greater power, in greater comfort, in longer life, and in minimum maintenance.

Then, and then only, can it make for the supreme delights and for the consummate satisfaction in motor car possession.

This, briefly, is how Lincoln cars are Leland-built.

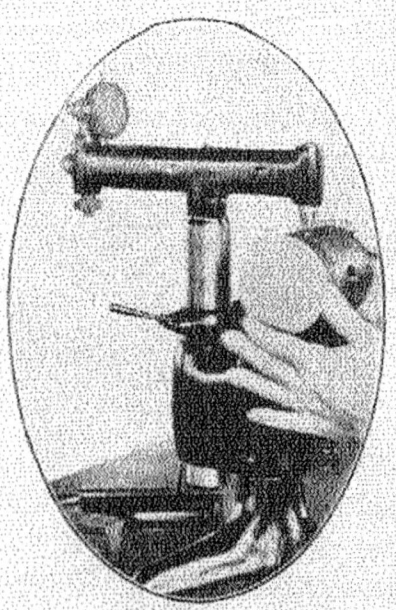

By the Amplifyer, which registers the one ten-thousandth of an inch, every piston is tested for diameter and concentricity to one-thousandth accuracy.

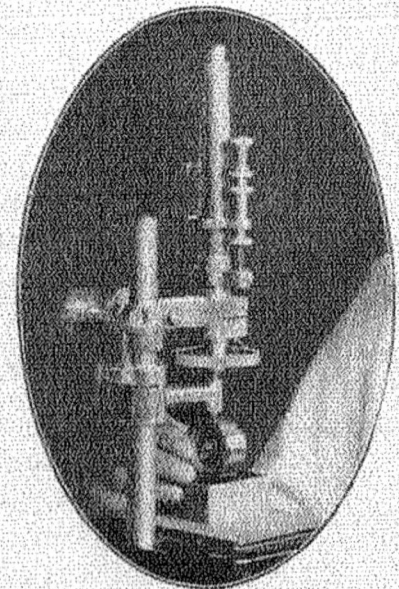

By the Comparator, which registers to the one twenty-thousandth of an inch, this plug thread gauge is held to three ten-thousandths accuracy in pitch diameter.

LINCOLN MOTOR CAR COMPANY   DETROIT, MICHIGAN

In Anticipation of a Motor Car

Almost 2,000 Distributors and Dealers apply for Sales Franchise, and more than 1,000 individuals place orders for Lincoln Motor Company's new Leland-built car

Henry M. Leland
President Lincoln Motor Company

Wilfred C. Leland
Vice-Pres. and Gen. Mgr. Lincoln Motor Company

It is doubtful whether any event in motordom has ever created such profound interest as the mere anticipation that a new motor car would be built by the Lelands and their splendid organization.

When, after the armistice was signed, and the Lincoln Motor Company—of which Henry M. Leland and Wilfred C. Leland were the chief executives—was completing its contracts with the government for the production of Liberty Aircraft Motors, it was only natural for the world to assume that these men would re-enter the field as makers of motor cars of the finer sort.

Notwithstanding the Lelands had made no announcement—in fact themselves had not determined upon their future activities—the offices of the Lincoln Motor Company became the Mecca of motor car distributors from all over the world.

These Distributors, most of whom were already handling cars of the better class, insisted upon filing applications for sales franchises and binding them with deposits.

Incidentally, one Distributor tendered a certified check for one million dollars ($1,000,000.00) as a deposit, to evidence his good faith.

From one city there were 61 applications; from another 38; from another 37.

There is scarcely a city of size in America from which there have not been from one to a dozen or more Distributors' applications. From cities in the United States and Canada up to June 1, 1920, the applications totaled 1252.

And from across the seas, from nearly every country in the civilized world, the applications aggregated 123.

Of these, 13 were from England—where the esteem in which Leland standards and Leland ideals are held, is second only to the admiration in which those qualities are held in America. 8 were from Cuba; 9 from Argentina; 6 from Australia; 5 each from France and Spain; 4 each from New Zealand, Sweden, Norway and Hawaii. And they came from Russia, China, Japan, Straits Settlements, Union of South Africa, and from the uttermost corners of the earth.

To June 1, 1920, the Distributors' applications had reached the impressive total of 1375, not taking into account hundreds received since that date, nor the hundreds of applications made direct to Distributors by dealers in the smaller cities.

It will be seen therefore that we have been in position to select as our Distributors, the very cream of the trade, and to embark with a field sales organization in every way in keeping with the car itself, with the organization which produces it and with the class of citizenship to whom a car of the Leland-built type must naturally appeal.

And in not one single instance did the Lincoln Motor Company solicit a Distributor.

Nor was this all.

In addition to the Distributors' applications, more than 1,000 individuals have placed orders with deposits, despite the fact that the Lincoln Motor Company had made no announcement concerning the details of its car, and, too, despite the fact that the Company had not encouraged advance orders. There are also, in the hands of Distributors, hundreds of orders of which the factory has not been advised in detail.

Imagine, if you can, the attitude of these Distributors, who, solely through their faith in the Lelands, deliberately obligate themselves to merchandise millions of dollars' worth of motor cars.

Imagine the attitude of these clear-headed business men, representing the best citizenship of the land, who, with confidence in Leland ideals and standards as their sole incentive, coolly affix their signatures and place deposits, in order that they may be among the early ones to possess the new Leland-built cars—cars of whose price and details their knowledge was nil.

No matter whether it was to have one cylinder or ten; no matter whether its price was to be six hundred or six thousand dollars, these seemed to be of secondary importance.

But they knew the history of the men; they knew their records. They knew the Leland traits; they knew the Leland traditions—never to retrograde, never even to pause; they knew that the Leland vision was always forward.

So of one thing they were supremely satisfied. They were sure that if the Lelands built a car, it would be a car such as the Lelands know how to build; plus Leland progressiveness; plus what might logically be expected of Leland determination and Leland ability to achieve—and to surpass.

LINCOLN MOTOR CO., DETROIT, MICH.

The Seven-Passenger Touring Car

Large mechanical brakes, capable of stopping the Lincoln effectively, were installed on the rear wheels only. Rear axle options were available in either 4.58 to 1 or 4.2 to 1 ratios. Wheels were 23-inch, wooden-spoke with bolt on rims, commonly referred to as artillery wheels. The cord tires were five inches wide and 33-inches in diameter. The front and rear treads were 60 inches.

Aesthetically, the new Lincoln disappointed many potential buyers. It looked much like a pre-World War I Cadillac. What would you expect from a mechanical genius, anyway? Styling was not particularly the conservative H.M.'s forte. Leland's son-in-law was tasked to look into this problem. Experienced as a millinery merchant, he lacked any coach design experience and his efforts produced few results. He did, however, retain Brunn & Company of Buffalo to restyle the Model-L. Brunn subsequently designed several fine Roadster and Phaeton bodies, but too late to stop many of the negative comments.

Designers like Ray Dietrich referred to early Model-L coaches as Noah's Arks. The new Murray body Lincolns were built to the highest quality standards and soon much of the criticism would fade. Walter Murphy, a successful West Coast car dealer would take a production model Lincolns and chop five to six inches out of the roof line. This gave his Lincoln coaches a much lower and more attractive silhouette.

Even back then, Californians were big on custom cars. The Murphy cars gained in popularity and the company soon moved into custom coachbuilding in a big way. The J.B. Judkins Company and the Fleetwood Metal Body Company also came up with custom coach designs for the early Lincoln Model-L chassis.

1921 Model L custom body Coupe by Murphy of California.

The second problem with early Lincoln production is the corollary that everything takes longer than you think it will. Leland's constant insistence on quality slowed down production. "Build it right the first time," Leland would often say. Henry disliked the Go-NoGo gauges, which were popular with machine builders of that time and he preferred to have parts measured with a micrometer.

CHAPTER TWO — THE LELAND LINCOLN

The Five-Passenger Sedan

Manufacturing tolerances were held to five thousandths of an inch on many parts. This made chief inspector Archer's job more difficult, particularly in view of the fact that his previous work experience had been as a choir director at the Presbyterian Church.

Leland had a statue of Abraham Lincoln placed in front of the administration building. The Lincoln factory was renowned for its upkeep. At the factory, the tools and machinery were kept spotlessly clean. A team of forty painters constantly repainted the facility Lincoln green. At least once a week, maintenance crews with long-handled mops dusted the rafters. Leland imported a set of Johannsen gauge-blocks that were stored in an air-conditioned room to maintain them at a constant temperature year-round.

The Abraham Lincoln statue that Leland originally installed was of a seated president. The local children liked to sit on the statue at Abe's feet, so Abe's shoes were always shiny. This statue was replaced with a standing Lincoln after the Ford takeover. A local joke was that Henry Ford could not abide anyone sitting around at one of his plants. This standing statue appeared in many early Lincoln advertisements and was subsequently donated to the Detroit Public Library, where it still stands.

The Model-L engine and chassis assemblies were test-driven on the factory's test track by Henry Marchand's group. The cars were tested by driving them first in low and then in second gear with the hand lever brake applied. Next, they were driven in high gear at speeds from four miles per hour to full throttle.

The Model-L was capable of cruising at speeds in excess of 70 MPH without strain. These tests, plus continual adjustment and tuning, constituted the break-in period for all new Lincolns.

Owners of new Lincolns were instructed to operate their cars normally from the time they were picked up at the dealer's showroom. No break-in period was required on the Lincoln, even though custom dictated it on most automobiles. One of the things often overlooked when describing the early Lincoln was its quiet operation. The car was built tight and massive enough to absorb considerable road pounding. Viewed from the top or bottom, the frame formed a giant H.

Coincidental to being called the Model-L Lincoln, the early Leland Cadillac used an L-frame type chassis assembled with L-brackets. It is possible they were down to the letter L with the designs before settling on a final design, but it's more likely it simply stud for Leland built.

The Literary Digest for September 11, 1920

Where Lincoln Cars are Leland-built

In one of America's most modern factories, here Lincoln Cars are Leland-built.

Originally planned for the production of that marvelous mechanism—the Liberty Aircraft Motor—here produced in largest volume in the shortest time, that wonder workshop turns to peacetime occupation.

Here now is found an almost limitless array of new equipment, representing added millions of investment and more suitably adapted to the new pursuit.

Here is machinery of the most modern kinds, seemingly more than human in its ingenuity; and literally thousands upon thousands of the most scientific and accurate tools and devices which genius has yet conceived.

Here the guiding hands rank with the world's most adept in their respective callings—men who have devoted their arts, their talents, and their skill, to designing, developing, refining and building cars and motors of the finer class.

Here pervades the spirit of cooperation, and of harmony, and of fellowship—a spirit which has its source in the administrative offices.

Here is found ideal environment, that which appeals to men's better selves.

Here too are means for healthful recreation.

Here men are encouraged to develop the best that is within them; and here honest effort does not go unrewarded.

Here is seen the atmosphere of inspiration; and here is seen incentive to achievement.

Here men of the serious minded type seek affiliation, not alone for the creature comforts, but for the skillful training they acquire, and the prestige which that training wields in the world mechanical.

Here men, and methods, and machinery; here inspiration, environment, and "knowing-how" work hand in hand for a common purpose—the production of the highest type of motor car that man has yet evolved.

Here it is that Lincoln Cars are Leland-built.

LINCOLN MOTOR CO.   **DETROIT, MICH.**

Looking Northeast   *Administration Building*   *Looking Northwest*

Composite View of Lincoln Motor Company's Main Plant in Detroit

Organization — Equipment — Knowing-how Produces the new Leland-built Lincoln Car

In this day of big things, what more magic words than these: 'Organization,' 'Equipment,' 'Knowing-how'?

Without them is nothing great accomplished.

With them, nothing seems impossible.

Many are the stories of vast achievement in the world mechanical; among them is a story not widely known, yet a story for whose parallel you would seek far to find.

In order to understand the possibility of that achievement, let us hark back some thirty to forty years.

Then, Henry M. Leland was a conspicuous figure in New England's higher Craftsmanship.

Some years before, he had left his boyhood home on the farm in Vermont, and gone to Worcester, Mass., where he engaged as an apprentice. He became a workman at the bench, but not for long, because he soon compelled recognition as an artisan of an uncommon kind. He showed an ability to do things—to do them differently, and to do them better than they had been done before.

He became a machinery salesman, and an unusual one, because he was more than a salesman.

He knew, too, how to install and to teach the operating of the machines he sold.

Manufacturers sought his counsel. They engaged him to re-organize their equipment and their men.

He knew how to increase production, not by oppressive, but by progressive methods. He did two more things, which to those who do not know him and his methods, may seem anomalous or impossible—yet he did them.

Besides increasing volume, he actually reduced production costs, and at the same time bettered infinitely the quality of the things produced.

He had a knack and a penchant for doing things while others were saying they could not be done. His was supreme delight to bring order out of chaos.

Many are the great establishments today which owe the foundation of their prestige and their success largely to the organizing, producing and quality-building genius of Henry M. Leland.

He is credited with a multitude of 'crowning achievements,' because he has made it a life principle always to do things better than they had been done before.

His generalship in organization is strikingly exemplified in that of the Lincoln Motor Co., although he maintains that Wilfred C. Leland who has been his mainstay and close associate for many years, assumed a large share of the responsibilities; and to its success he also attributes the loyal, skillful and effective co-operation of his thousands of other associates.

In the year 1890 the Lelands came from New England to Detroit, where for a number of years they engaged in the manufacture of the finer kinds of machinery and precision tools. They were among the pioneers in the making of gasoline, marine and automobile engines; and after eighteen years, many of those engines are still in service—a tribute to the Leland ways of doing.

Henry M. Leland, Wilfred C. Leland and some of their Chief Associates, viewing the 6500th Lincoln Liberty Aircraft Motor

Of these nine men, seven have been in continual relation for 12 years; five for 21 years and three for 27 years

A Duplicate of this Motor is now in the Smithsonian Institution at Washington, D.C., where it will stand for all Time, a Monument to and an Example of the world's finer Craftsmanship

Shortly after our country became involved in the world conflict, the vital need for aircraft so forcibly impressed itself upon the Lelands that they severed their many years' affiliation with the motor car industry in order that they might undertake the production of Liberty airplane motors for the allied fighting forces. This they did in July, 1917.

With absolutely nothing in the way of plant or equipment, they received the government's first award for the building of these motors—and faith in the men and their ability was the government's sole assurance.

Capital was interested, and much volunteered. The Lincoln Motor Co. was formed. Fifty-two acres of land were acquired. An adequate plant was erected and equipped in record time. A vast amount of machinery was designed, built and installed. Tools to the extent of 6,522 separate and distinct designs, aggregating 91,807 in number, were made.

Thousands of America's most skilled craftsmen tendered their co-operation and their services. Many of the men, particularly the executives, were men whom the Lelands knew and who knew them, through many years' association; and they were anxious to enlist under their banner.

Never in their lives, say the Lelands, have they seen such a vast organization get into working harmony with so little delay and so little friction.

The efficiency of that organization can best be appreciated when it is realized that in seven months and three days after starting with nothing, they assembled their first motor. In ten months thereafter, and with 6,000 employees, the Lincoln Motor Co. was producing at the rate of 50 motors per day. In contrast with these Leland methods, the leading English manufacturer, with three years aircraft experience and 10,000 employees, had required a week to produce the quantity of motors which the Lincoln organization had produced in a single day.

Within eleven months from the day production of completed motors began, the Lincoln Motor Co. had established the record of producing the largest number of motors in a day, the largest number in a month and the largest total produced by any manufacturer from the beginning; and those who know the story of Liberty motor building know the rivalry for that record.

The quality of Leland-built Lincoln Liberty motors has been attested by tributes and in ways which could not be misunderstood; and, too, the Lincoln Motor Co. was able to render assistance of immeasurable value of those less favorably schooled.

Assembling and harmonizing an organization expeditiously, for doing things in a big way and doing them right, is, like everything else—no matter how difficult it may seem—a plain, simple matter of 'knowing-how.'

This is simplified when the executive and his chief assistants in things mechanical, can go into the shops, and with their own hands perform practically every task and operation, from the ground work to the finished product.

Such is the skill and genius; such is the organization that is producing the new Leland-built car—the car destined to chart the future course of fine car making—the car destined to prove another 'crowning achievement'—the car destined once more to demonstrate Leland determination and Leland ability to surpass.

LINCOLN MOTOR CO., DETROIT, MICH.

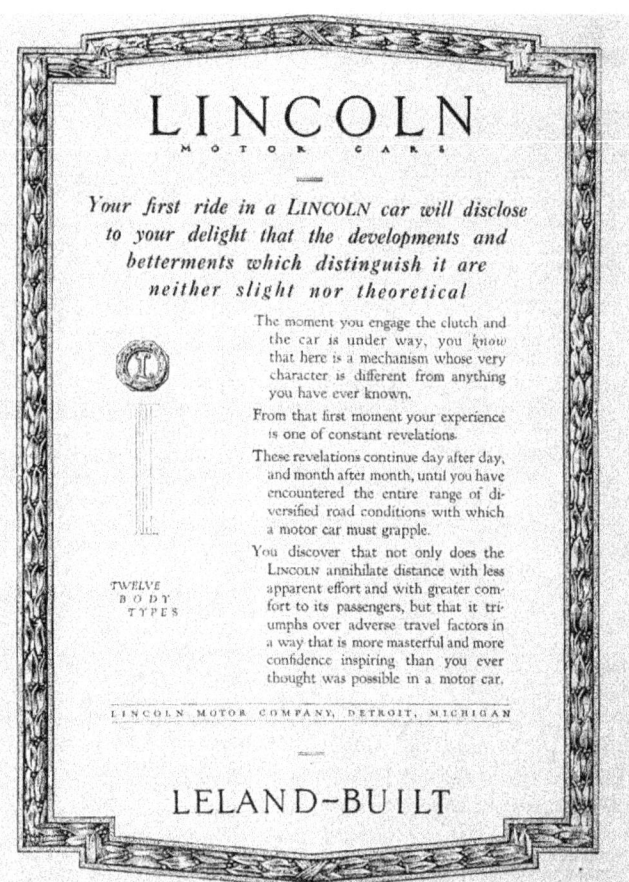

NINETEEN-TWENTY - The year was 1920 and the first Lincoln production motorcar was finally ready. It was completed on September 14th and was delivered two days later. By that time, over $4 million dollars had been expended on new production machinery, almost $2 million of it for tooling alone.

Originally, eight different body styles were chosen for the Lincoln. These were offered in the short 120 and the long 130 inch wheelbases. Lincoln chassis and drivetrain units could be purchased individually for custom building. Of these early Leland-built production models, 253 were delivered as chassis assemblies.

The September 1920 issue of Motor Age devoted three pages to the mechanical wonders of the new Lincoln. They cited features like the Alemite lubrication fittings, which replaced old-style grease-cups and the thermostatically controlled shutters that varied the air flow over the radiator coils.

Only one paragraph was devoted to Lincoln's styling. It stated simply that, "The styling is characteristically straight-line." Other journals were less kind, saying its styling was prewar (WWI) Cadillac and not modern in appearance. In retrospect, when cars of this period are viewed as a group, the Lincoln seems neither ahead or behind its time in style. The new Lincoln was, without question, mechanically superior to the current Cadillac models that Leland had earlier helped to design.

Of the eight original body styles, three were open body types and five were closed body types. Unique among these was the four-passenger Coupe. Its large rear fenders sloped forward gradually to meet the running boards following the same curve as the front fenders, only in reverse.

Standard options included an air pump for inflating tires was driven by a power takeoff from the transmission. The courtesy light, called a Tonneau Lamp, was operated by a manual switch and a door-opening switch. The large steering wheel folded to the side for easy entry. One might consider it a luxury option, but for a large driver it was a virtual necessity.

Easy-to-access tool drawers were located below either end of the front fenders. The air vent door covers and cowl-mounted clearance lights all helped to create an overall posh appearance, but what really made the Lincoln really stand out, though, was its ride and performance.

Henry Leland recorded his thoughts on this subject stating, "Let me sight my own experience. Our engineers and experimental drivers had been telling us what an unusual car they had, but frankly I was a little inclined to discount their enthusiasm. I had occasion to go to Defiance, Ohio, some 125 miles from Detroit according to the blue book. I thought, here would be a good opportunity to see for myself.

LINCOLN
MOTOR CARS

Of the many things which evidence the rare measure of approval conferred upon the LINCOLN car, there is one whose significance can scarcely be over-estimated.

Lincoln Eight Cylinder Motor Cars comprise a wide and varied range of open and closed Body Types, eleven in all — two and three-passenger Roadsters; four-passenger Phaeton; five and seven-passenger Touring Cars; four-passenger Coupé; four, five and seven-passenger Sedans; seven-passenger Town Car; seven-passenger Limousine.

Some are types of quiet, conservative mien, while others are of more imposing aspect; yet all reflect the air of elegance and true refinement.

So many motorists accustomed to owning several fine cars, after having purchased a LINCOLN and come fully to appreciate its character and its charm, have supplanted their equipment exclusively with LINCOLNS.

There are literally scores who have purchased the second LINCOLN, many the third, several the fourth, and by two families the fifth has been installed.

Would this be true except for some sound and substantial reason?

And could there be a sufficient reason other than the LINCOLN car itself?

Does it not indicate conviction that the LINCOLN is a superior car—a car of higher character and finer qualities?

Does it not indicate that the LINCOLN is a car of greater ease and comforts, of wider capabilities and more captivating action?

Does it not indicate that the LINCOLN more nearly measures up to the ideals of what a motor car should be?

And when to these is added that rugged stamina which has its source in LELAND-BUILT, constancy and endurance of the LINCOLN'S qualities are ensured for many years to come.

LINCOLN MOTOR COMPANY
DETROIT, MICH.

LELAND-BUILT

To see just what the car would do. There were five of us. The top was up. We were on a fine stretch with no other vehicles or crossroads in sight, bowling along serenely at about 40 miles per hour, so I judged. I am constitutionally opposed to speeding, but my interest and curiosity; I suppose it was, got the better of me. 'Step on it and let's see what she can do,' I said to Harry the driver. 'She is doing her best now,' he answered. Doing her best at 40? I was keenly disappointed. My hopes were fast fading when Fred, who sat beside the driver, called back, 'Why she is hitting 76, Mr. Leland,' he said laughingly. 'You know this isn't an airplane with a Lincoln Liberty motor.' Perhaps I should have known better had I observed how swiftly the scenery was passing. My hopes rose. There that car was running just as sweetly and with as little fuss and vibration and with as little apparent effort at 76 as it did at 30 and there was none you could notice at 30. Periodic vibration, which is something that engineers have tried for years to overcome, was at least absolutely unapparent to me at any speed. There seemed to be an unusual harmonizing of the various functions. The car was so steady it seemed to hold the road as if it were in a groove. I might add in passing that this elimination of the vibration period was not an accidental accomplishment. On the contrary, it was achieved only after much research, experimentation and money outlay.

Leland continued, "Elimination of engine vibration, practically to the zero point, is without question a great stride toward prolonging the life, not only of the engine itself, but of the entire car. As I said before, I am opposed to speeding, but when a car is made to possess the many other essentials to a real performer, power, acceleration and facile control, then speed is a natural consequence. You might call it a by-product, the use of which is entirely at the option of the driver. A little further on the trip, we came to another stretch, it was pretty rough, several miles of what you might call de-macadamized road. It was a stretch that ordinarily you would not want to take faster than about 15 miles per hour, but at 41 we were not uncomfortable. The situation was more like sailing in a yacht as compared to a canoe on a choppy surface. There was a most agreeable absence of side-sway and violent bouncing, no tendency to throw the passengers up and about. From a standstill, the car seemed to get away with grace and ease, but with the swiftness of a thrush, rather than the flutter of a partridge. I believe I have ridden in or on almost every kind of conveyance from the ox cart to the airplane. Even with all my fond hopes and anticipations, never did I expect to ride in anything that comes so near to what I imagined would be the sensation of flying through space without mechanical means."

1920 Traffic along Chicago's Michigan Avenue. The age of the metropolitan motorcar had arrived.

The first Model-L Tourings sold for around $4,600. By the following year, certain custom body styles would reach into the $7,000 price range. This was at a time when Fords and Chevys were selling for under $1,000.

Early Lincoln ads stated only that, "Prices are based upon the highest class of materials and workmanship and upon scientific and economical manufacturing methods made possible by tremendous preparation in labor saving machinery, tools and devices, plus knowing how to use them. While these involved a vast initial expenditure of time and capital, they lend themselves to minimum production cost in large volume. There will be a legitimate margin of profit, no more."

The Men who Distribute the new Leland-built Lincoln Car

Those who know motor cars, know that high character and soundness in the organizations which produce them, should be paralleled by like character and soundness in the organizations which distribute them—the men who form the connecting links or points of contact between the car owner and the manufacturer.

The distributing organizations of the Lincoln Motor Co. are in fifteen cities, including a factory sales branch in Detroit.

As production increases, additional distributors will be selected from the nearly 2,000 applicants already in waiting. Many of these, even now, have lists of priority orders and orders conditional upon their appointment.

In the fourteen cities where sales franchises have been granted, selections were made from among 416 applicants.

In not one single instance was it a matter of soliciting a distributor, nor of accepting whomsoever could be obtained. In every case it was one of our own choosing—of selecting those who we believed to measure up to the standards we had established, and whose high standing in their respective cities had been abundantly tested.

Nor was this a simple procedure, because most of the applicants were distributors well established, of high repute, and already handling cars of the better class. They were men who have made it their business to know motor cars and motor car builders.

With this type of applicants it was a matter of carefully choosing those best qualified.

Most of them have had sales franchises continually thrust upon them for consideration, and could obtain almost any franchise merely for the asking.

We have selected organizations and men accustomed to contact with the highest type of citizens—the class to whom the Leland-built Lincoln car will naturally appeal.

They are men cognizant of their responsibilities; men who are not unmindful that upon delivery of a car to the purchaser, their duty has just begun.

These men have shown the faith that is in them by coolly and deliberately obligating themselves to merchandise millions of dollars' worth of motor cars—cars of whose features, and details, and price they were wholly without information.

And their faith is further evinced, in most of the cities, by the erection of modern and adequate structures, quite in keeping with the product and with the clientele.

Their faith in the car, and in the organization which produces it, is confirmed by the faith of more than one thousand of the best citizens who, likewise without definite knowledge of the car, its features, its details, or its price, insisted upon filing priority orders —without encouragement from the factory, and seldom with encouragement from the distributor.

Their faith, too, is not without judgment. They know the organization behind the car. They know the character and the accomplishments of the men behind that organization; they know their works and their record; they know their ideals in motor car engineering and motor car construction; they know their forward vision.

Above all, they know the Leland determination and Leland ability to achieve — and to surpass.

Distributors

ATLANTA — Lifsey-Smith Co.
BOSTON — Puritan Motors Corp.
CHICAGO — Allison-Rood Co.
CLEVELAND — The Fitzgerald Co.
DALLAS — Fosdick-Hawley Company
DENVER — Rouse-Stephens Co.
DETROIT — Lincoln Motor Co.
KANSAS CITY — Weaver Motor Co.
LOS ANGELES — Walter M. Murphy Motors Co.
MINNEAPOLIS — A. C. Templeton, Inc.
NEW YORK — Milton J. Budlong
PITTSBURGH — Robert P. McCurdy Company
PHILADELPHIA — Sweeten Auto Co.
SAN FRANCISCO — Walter M. Murphy Motors Co.
ST. LOUIS — McNiece-Hill Motor Company

Henry M. Leland
President

LINCOLN MOTOR COMPANY, DETROIT, MICHIGAN

Wilfred C. Leland
Vice-Pr. & Gen. Mgr.

The previous two years in the auto making business had set records, but by 1920 even Pierce-Arrow and Cadillac were experiencing seriously declining sales. Leland was organizing new dealerships against these established car companies.

The Lincoln dealerships were: in Atlanta, Lifsey-Smith on Peachtree Street; in Boston, Puritan on Commonwealth Avenue; in Chicago, Allison-Rood on South Michigan; in Cleveland, Fitzgerald on Prospect Avenue; in Dallas, Fosdick-Hawley on Main Street; in Denver, Rouse-Stephens on Thirteenth at Broadway and also in Colorado Springs; in Des Moines, Consigny on Walnut Street; in Detroit, Lincoln Motors on Woodward at Palmer; in Kansas City, Weaver on Grand Avenue; in Los Angeles, Walter M. Murphy on South Hope and also in Pasadena; Minneapolis, Templeton on Hennepin; in New York, Milton Budlong on Fifty-seventh Street; in Philadelphia, Sweeten on Broad; in Pittsburgh, McCurdy on Baum at Craig; in San Francisco, Walter H. Murphy on Van Ness and Jackson and also in Oakland; in St. Louis, McNiece-Hill at Delmar and Clarenden.

Originally there were fourteen groups in fifteen cities and the factory sales branch in Detroit. Walt Murphy, a Cadillac dealer in California, had spoken for two dealerships. These prospective dealers were summoned to the Lincoln manufacturing facility where the actual negotiations for dealerships took place. Each prospective dealer was required to put up a substantial financial deposit and to prove that they either had or would build adequate facilities for a Lincoln dealership. All of this was done on good faith and their confidence in Leland's reputation for quality. As Henry put it, "There would evolve an extraordinary motorcar, the kind the world had long hoped for."

The fourteen original dealerships were selected from over four hundred applicants. Additionally, some two hundred applications arrived later, many with orders attached. There were over a hundred applicants from foreign countries. Lincoln Motor Company claimed not to have solicited any dealer, stating that the company had been sought instead.

Leland tried to select and franchise experienced and responsible businessmen. He was looking for dealers who would cater to the more affluent buyer. The new dealers were asked to obligate themselves to a $1 million order before they even saw the Model-L Lincoln.

This early Model L five-window coupe showed a definite lack of creative styling. It was, however, mechanically advanced and comfortable riding.

The LINCOLN COUPE
Seating four persons in consummate comfort, and with facility for easy entrance and egress

The LINCOLN SEDAN
Seating five persons, and with Emergency seats for two

Many months ago, fourteen groups and individuals entered into sales agreements and placed substantial deposits.

Most of them arranged to erect fine structures; others made long term leases for business quarters.

All upon faith, and confidence—nothing more.

Upon faith and confidence in two men and their associates—faith and confidence that they would evolve an extraordinary motor car, a car of a kind which long the world had hoped for.

All upon faith and confidence that they would evolve a car which even in the face of existing fine creations would, by sheer superiority, force its way to leadership.

These groups and individuals were not novices. They were men who had known motor cars and motor car makers since the inception of the industry.

But of the car itself they knew nothing, neither its details nor its price. They knew only of the men behind it and their records for achievement.

Then they waited. After some twenty months' development and proving-out, the car was ready for their verdict. Then these distributors were invited to Detroit.

There they saw one of the world's wonder work-shops, equipped with the finest machinery, tools and devices ever conceived by man, and designed especially for this Leland-built Lincoln car.

They saw the car—sturdy, dignified, and impressive to look upon.

And they rode in that car.

They skimmed smooth stretches at express train speed—and even faster.

They bowled over hills and swept thru valleys that seemed almost to flatten into a level plain.

They traversed secluded, scraggy highways where motorists hesitate to go.

They rode in a manner they never rode before.

And among them was not a man who did not marvel.

They marveled at its fleetness and its seeming limitless power.

They marveled at its superlative ease and comfort.

They marveled at its quietness—its close approach to silence.

And they marveled that it was possible to evolve a car so wondrous in its action, so rarely fascinating and of such consummate charm.

Distributors of Leland-built Lincoln Cars, at the Administration Building in Detroit

Many of the dealers had been in the automobile business since its inception. They signed up and waited. Twenty months later, they were summoned to Detroit to inspect and drive the new Lincoln.

The Touring sedan remained the most popular body style for all makes of automobiles well into the 1920s. Lincoln was no exception.

The new Model-L Lincolns had matching serial numbers in three locations. The serial number placard was located on the engine firewall, under the right-hand hood. This location can also be referred to as the dashboard under the right cowl. The second serial number was located on top of the transmission bell housing, also referred to as clutch cover and may be read by removing the interior floor plate. The third number was located on the left side of the engine block just below and between cylinders one and two. Oddly enough, the chassis frame was not serial-number stamped. Coachbuilders often installed a body style type number placard under the right front passenger seat.

There was generally a serial number on this placard, but it was the coach body serial number, not a Lincoln chassis serial number. During the 1920s, Lincoln delivered to various coachbuilders some fourteen hundred chassis assemblies including the engine, hood, drivetrain and frame. Matching serial numbers on these drivetrain assemblies was usually adhered to, but not always. Lincoln was known for the interchangeability of its parts. This may have been only a habit carried over from Leland's days at Colt Arms. The old Colt revolvers had matching serial numbers on cylinder, frame and butt; and were generally interchangeable.

Lincoln's 1920 model year production was 834 automobiles, types 101 through 150, plus the 122 chassis. Some Lincoln purists claimed that the September through December models were really 1921 models introduced early and they were actually the cars that had been promised for delivery since early January. There is conjecture as to the exact number of cars produced in that first production run. Some estimates are as low as 672, but if the serial number is below 835 it should be considered as produced in 1920. During the next calendar year, just over 2,100 Model-L Lincolns were produced. The actual figure was probably 2,123.

There are several reasons for the uncertainty in these early production numbers. It depends on what you call a model year, i.e., introduction or calendar. It also depends on whether you are working from the chassis serial numbers or actual body number count. The Leland people admitted to some bookkeeping errors. Quality inspection and rejection of various subassemblies occasionally messed up the matched serial number system causing some numbers to be skipped. A few cars were tested and disassembled and some company and family cars were not recorded.

NINETEEN-TWENTYONE - By early 1921, Lincoln assemblies were moving like a well-oiled machine. The Lincoln engineers and dealers had an exceptionally fine automobile in their hands, so they went looking for ways to get publicity. In April, a Model-L won the Los Angeles to Phoenix Road Race. That summer, a seven-passenger Touring was entered in the Tour Around Lake Superior sponsored by the Good Roads Association.

The Literary Digest for May 7, 1921

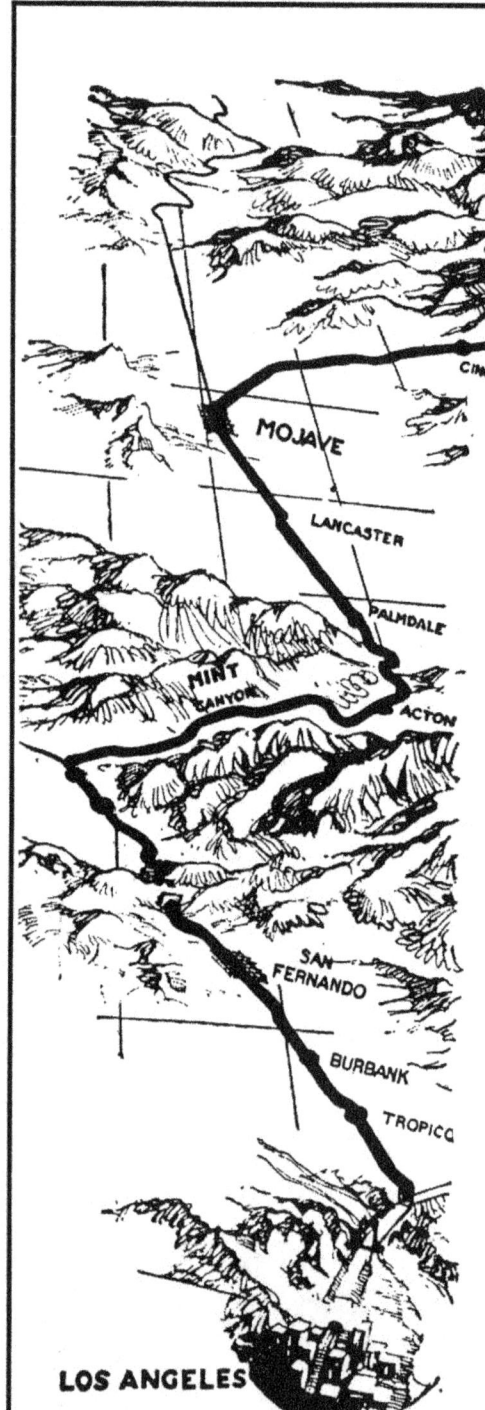

LINCOLN
MOTOR CAR

Shatters one of Most Coveted Records in California

Stage-coach time, 9 days   Train time, 14 hrs. 30 min.
Former motor car record, 9 hrs. 37 min.
Lincoln record, 6 hrs. 40 min.

From Los Angeles to Bishop, 285 miles, a rise of nearly 4,000 feet over mountain roads and rocky trails, thru desert sands and gumbo, a Lincoln seven-passenger touring car, driven by W. W. Bramlette, reduced the former motor car record by 2 hours and 57 minutes.

The Lincoln performance takes on added significance when you know that the former holders of, and the later but unsuccessful aspirants for the record, are numbered among the world's most notable roading cars.

And this new achievement, therefore, can mean but one thing—*the superior capabilities of the Lincoln car.*

"LELAND-BUILT"
What it Meant

LINCOLN MOTOR COMPANY   DETROIT, MICHIGAN

The most notorious of rugged road races was the Los Angeles to Bishop, California Stagecoach Trail Run. The standing record for stagecoach travel over this route was nine days, for train fourteen hours thirty minutes and for motorcar nine hours twenty seven minutes. The route began at the Los Angeles dry river canyon bridge. It proceeded out Tropicana Boulevard to Burbank and on to San Fernando, climbing up through Mint Canyon Pass. Next, the route traveled through Acton, Palmdale and Lancaster, crossing the Mohave Flat to Cinco, then on to Red Rock Canyon through Little Lake, One Pine, Independence and Big Pine in the shadow of Mt. Whitney, passing Owen Lake and ending at Bishop. The route was 285 miles long, climbed to four thousand feet and took the Lincoln over rocky trails through desert sand and gumbo mud. The time for the new Lincoln Model-L was six hours, forty minutes flat out.

The driver, W. W. Bramlette, wrote this account in May, 1921. "In making the record, I used a standard Lincoln Touring car. I consider this course, especially under the weather conditions as they were the hardest test of man and car that I have ever turned. The car did everything I asked of it. The engine always had something in reserve. The chassis was capable of standing any road shock I put on it, over bumps that compelled the car to bounce from wheel to wheel, placing side loads on the running gear. I have had a lot of road experience and this car performs far better than any other car I have ever driven."

Kind of sounded a little like one of those old John Cameron Swayze watch commercials, "It takes a licking and keeps on ticking."

Fine coach bodies were now available on the Lincoln and that summer prices were reduced slightly to attract more buyers. The Anderson Electric Car Company and the Towson Body Company later became Murray. They built body types 101 through 105 and the type 107 on the short wheelbase chassis. These body styles included the seven-passenger Touring, of which most had folding tops and a few had the permanent hardtop or California Top.

There was a massive three-passenger Roadster, a five-passenger Phaeton, a four-passenger Coupe and a five-passenger Sedan Brougham. On the long wheelbase, there was the seven-passenger Limousine, a Town Car, a Berline and a five-passenger Brougham. All of the latter had chauffeur partitions, a rear passenger compartment with divider glass.

Coachbuilt Landaulet Brougham.

Model L Coachbuilt Sedan.

Coachbuilt Model L Town Car.

There was also a popular long wheelbase two-passenger Roadster with a single auxiliary jump seat. Lang Body Company also built one hundred of the two-passenger Brunn designed Roadsters.

The American Body Company built a popular four-passenger Deluxe Phaeton by Brunn that had no trunk. The J.B. Judkins Company built three different types of Sedans and a Berline. Murray and Lang introduced two new Lincoln custom bodies, the Sedan Suburban and the Fleetwood Limousine

AUTOMOTIVE INDUSTRIE
THE AUTOMOBILE
January 26, 1922

Government Sets Lincoln Tax Due at $610,000

DETROIT, Jan. 25 — Lincoln Motor Co.'s tax obligations to the Government have been definitely set at $610,000. Official confirmation of the amount was received to-day from Washington by Fred L. Woodworth, Collector of Internal Revenue. The Government originally had entered a claim of $4,500,000.

Judge Tuttle, at the request of counsel for the Detroit Trust Co., receivers for the company, to-day issued an order making the back taxes a preferred claim. He also issued an order permitting the Detroit Trust Co. to issue receiver's certificates, not to exceed $500,000, to operate the Lincoln plant.

MOTOR WORLD
April 12, 1922

FORDS AND LELANDS INCORPORATE COMPANY

DETROIT, April 8 — The Lincoln Motor Car Co. has been incorporated in Michigan as a successor to the Lincoln Motor Co. It is capitalized at $15,000,000, all in common stock, of which $250,000 have been subscribed and paid for in cash.

All but three of the 2500 shares of stock already issued are held by Edsel B. Ford. The other stockholders are Henry Ford, Henry M. Leland and Wilfred C. Leland, each holding one share. The directors are the Lelands and the Fords. The Lelands continue in the position they held in the original Lincoln company, as does Nash. Craig is secretary of the Ford Motor Co.

It is understood that it has not been determined how the stock of the new company finally will be distributed between the Ford and Leland families.

AUTOMOTIVE INDUSTRIE
THE AUTOMOBILE
February 23, 1922

Ford Fixes 50 Cars Daily As Limit of Lincoln Output

DETROIT, Feb. 21—The following copyrighted interview with Henry Ford is carried by the International News Service:

"Some people seem to have the impression," said he, "as the result of the taking over of the Lincoln Motor plant that I intend to be sort of a bull in the china shop in the automobile world. They are wrong. In taking over the Lincoln plant, my son and I agreed before we started that we would restrict output. The Lincoln plant is now making fifteen cars a day. As orders are running, we could sell 200 a day. But we shall never make more than fifty Lincoln cars a day.

"The rumors that connect your name with negotiations to buy the Wills St. Claire and other plants are not true then?" he was asked.

"Absolutely not a word of truth in any of them," he replied. "Nor is it true that I am negotiating for the purchase of any railroad. The one railroad I have is all I want."

AUTOMOTIVE INDUSTRIES
THE AUTOMOBILE   *March 2, 1922*

Ford Buys Lincoln Co.

Henry Ford came into possession of the Lincoln Motor Co. on February 4, and on February 6 the concern began operations as a Ford company under Leland direction. No changes will be made in the executive personnel of the company, it is stated. Following the sale a substantial cut was made in the prices of Lincoln models.

Henry Ford's earlier disclosed bid for the Lincoln property was the only one actually presented at the sale. Thus the Ford interest took over the business at the upset price of $8,000,000. There had been two other bids in prospect, each variously attributed to powerful eastern interests that either control or are allied with equally important productive groups in the industry. One of these was disposed of later to the satisfaction of those who like to speculate on things, by the identity of its representative as vice-president of the Detroit bank of which James Couzens, former Ford treasurer, is president. Both of these, after the legality of their bids, on account of the time of their filing, had been questioned, refrained from going on with their bids.

The Two Passenger Coupe

The Seven Passenger Sedan

The Four Passenger Phaeton

Model and Style terminology was as confusing then as it is today. In general, Sport meant that the top was canvas and it usually had detachable windows called side curtains and Touring referred to a four-door open body style. The term Phaeton applied to a deluxe body Touring model, often with a second cowling ahead of the rear seat. Roadster was the term used for a two-door two-seater with collapsible top. Coupe was often pronounced Cou-pay.

Dual side-mounted or sidemount spare tires inset into the front fenders were optional and included tire covers of canvas or leather. Many early Model-L Lincolns were produced with single rear-mounted spares. It was also common to see dual rear-mounted spare tires. The sidemount option became more popular in the late twenties.

Standard factory color choices were Cobalt blue, Brewster green, Thistle green, marine blue and Athenian green. The interior for open cars was buffed black leather. Purchasers of a closed body style could select from several broadcloth options.

The standard equipment list consisted of speedometer, transmission theft lock, tool kit, power tire pump, hydraulic shock absorbers, combined tail stop and backup lights, inspection lamp with cord, rearview mirror(s), cowl ventilator, clock, cigar lighter, front bumper, rear fender guards and spare tire with cover.

After World War I, there had been general euphoria, a utopian image of world society and a belief that the League of Nations would prevent future wars. Women had cropped their hair and raised the hemline of their skirts. Men had gotten rid of high collars and high-top shoes. Automobile sales had reached an all-time high. But the post-war boom wound down rapidly

Many who could afford fine cars had already purchased them and Lincoln was a little late arriving on the market to get a share of the post-war sales. The company's goal of selling three hundred cars a month couldn't be achieved. The best month's production was in April of 1921 when four hundred cars were produced. The real problem with their goal was the limited number of buyers in the Lincoln's price range.

> **MOTOR WORLD**
>
> **OPERATIONS RESUMED AT LINCOLN FACTORY**
>
> November 30, 1921
>
> DETROIT, Nov. 26—Manufacture of cars has been resumed at the plant of the Lincoln Motor Co. by the Detroit Trust Co., the receiver, upon completion of the physical inventory. Shipments for the month of November are expected to run about 100 cars and operations, pending final reorganization, will be conducted strictly on a sales basis. Details of the inventory are not available. The work of pricing the equipment and material at figures which the receiver considers fair is now in progress. An announcement on this subject is expected within a week.
>
> Operations at the plant for the present will consist mainly of completion of cars which were in process at the time the receivership action was taken and which were held up pending the inventory. Dealers and distributors are placing orders and the receiver reports approximately 100 since the court action was taken.
>
> Through the collector of internal revenue in this city, the United States Government has filed in the office of the clerk of the district court, in which the receivership proceedings are pending, the claim of the Government for $4,500,000 additional income and excess profits taxes growing out of the construction of the Liberty airplane engines during the war.

Packard, Cadillac, Duesenberg and Lincoln were all getting some stiff competition from foreign coachbuilders. Customer desires were less influenced by salesmanship and marketing than they are today, the well-to-do demanded and got what they wanted. In Lincoln's favor was the trend toward larger and more powerful cars.

Several years, however, would pass before America would export more luxury cars than it imported. Even with Lincoln's sagging sales, they were selling more automobiles than Peerless, Pierce-Arrow, Cunningham, Daniels, LaFayette, Locomobile, McFarlan and Winton combined.

In spite of Leland's reputation for manufacturing, a large number of body parts and electrical supplies were purchased from independent vendors. Problems with these vendors slowed production. There was a strike at the Mullins plant in Ohio that supplied fenders. Lloyd Blunden was commissioned to set up a new shop in Detroit to supply fenders, but this took precious time.

The development of American automobiles would now be more gradual. The era of startling new innovations was over. It is ironic that two of the greatest luxury car innovators, Fred Duesenberg and Henry Leland, were never greatly rewarded for their efforts.

Fred T. Murphy, nephew of William H. Murphy, held a seat on Lincoln's board of directors. He became the leader of a dissident group proposing corporate dissolution of the Lincoln Motor Company. Leland insisted that the company had turned the corner and he went to New York in the fall to obtain additional bank financing. Board members Henry Nash, Lincoln's corporate treasurer and Herman Kinnicutt who represented the stock-offering firm, were opposing Leland.

The federal government entered the fray on November 4, 1921, their timing could not have been worse. They claimed that the Lincoln Motor Company had evaded payment of the War Profits tax. The tax bill was for $4.5 million. It was a shot in the last good leg Lincoln had left. Wilford Leland was convinced that this tax claim was instituted by Fred Murphy's group to further drive the price of the stock downward. The venture had never really shown a profit. Out of that year's production, only 675 Lincoln motorcars had been sold and delivered. The beginning of the end was in sight for H.M. and Wilford.

There was little doubt that, had the company been refinanced and expenses cut, that the Lincoln Motor Company under Leland could have survived. However, many of the investors now felt that a redistribution of stock should be made and this became even more cause for the stockholders to favor a possible offer for from Ford favorably. This was not in the Lelands' best interest as it would cause him to further lose control of the company. After November 21st, the firm operated in receivership with a fight for control in progress.

At the purchase of Lincoln Motor Company by the Fords. Left to right standing, Henry Ford, Henry Martyn Leland; seated, Edsel Ford and Wilford Leland.

AUTOMOTIVE INDUSTRIES
THE AUTOMOBILE

February 16, 1922

Ford Dealers Will Sell Lincoln Cars

Branches Investigating Field Possibilities—Factory Methods Being Surveyed

DETROIT, Feb. 15—Official announcement of its sales and manufacturing policies under the Ford regime has been deferred by the Lincoln Motor Co. pending the working out of a few remaining details, but it is evident from the results thus far accomplished that sales in the larger cities of the country will continue to be through the present distributor organization.

In the smaller cities the Lincoln dealers and the Ford dealers who will be authorized to sell Lincoln cars will operate directly under factory control through the medium of the branch plants. In the big cities the present distributors will conduct retail salesrooms and will distribute to Ford dealers, whom they authorize in their cities.

Investigations are now being made by the 35 branch Ford plants of the possibilities for the sale of the Lincoln cars in their individual territories and their recommendations will play a large part in the dealer authorizations. Changes will be made in many localities, but the efficient dealers will continue to function.

Production Methods Studied

Much of the detail of the sales plan was laid before a meeting of prominent Lincoln distributors at the factory this week, which was attended and presided over by sales executives of both the Lincoln and Ford organizations. For the time being, apparently, the Ford sales organization has been allowed to function by itself, while the executives give all their study to the Lincoln problems.

Manufacturing at the plant is under the observation of Charles C. Sorensen, the Ford chief of manufacturing operations, and changes which will be made in production methods will follow his recommendations. For the present the plant is working on a schedule of 20 to 30 cars daily, which will be continued until the production changes are fully determined.

LINCOLN DELAWARE ASSETS

WILMINGTON DEL. Feb. 15—James I. Boyce of this city and the Detroit Trust Co. appraisers of the Delaware assets of the Lincoln Motor Co. have appraised the notes, drafts and accounts receivable of the company at $54,775 although their book value is $354,171. The shrinkage is the result in part of failures by dealers. No valuation has been placed on the patents and trade marks.

MOTORIZING POLICE

INDIANAPOLIS, Feb. 11—A thorough motorization of the Indianapolis police department will be sought by Mayor Lewis Shank.

> **AUTOMOTIVE INDUSTRIES**
> *THE AUTOMOBILE* — 1922
>
> # $8,000,000 Offered for Lincoln Plant
>
> ### If Accepted, Lelands Will Continue in Charge and Receivership Be Lifted
>
> DETROIT, Jan. 3—Lincoln cars will continue to be "Leland built" under the plans of the group which offered $8,000,000 for the Lincoln Motor Co. property in Federal Court here this week. The offer was made by Harold H. Emmons, attorney for the company, who said he was acting for "persons interested in getting the company back on its feet."
>
> The first offer of the group was of $5,000,000 for the unencumbered property of the company and this was increased to $8,000,000 following the fixing of this figure by the court as the upset price. Date of sale was set for Feb. 4. The appraised value of the company is $11,000,000 and its liabilities approximate $10,000,000.
>
> **Original Offer $5,000,000**
>
> The original offer of $5,000,000 caused such a storm among attorneys representing different classes of shareholders and creditors that Judge Tuttle decided to raise the upset price to $8,000,000.
>
> One attorney asserted the $5,000,000 would pay only half the debt and wipe out the shareholders of the "A" and "B" classes. Another contended that $5,000,000 would pay only about 22 cents on the dollar to creditors. He estimated the liabilities at $9,000,000 and said that when preferred creditors were paid there would remain only about $2,000,000 for the remainder.
>
> If the group, represented by himself, is successful in acquiring the property, Emmons said, the Lelands will be continued in the active management of the company. Speedy lifting of the receivership and the continuance of manufacturing by the company is important to keep the sales organization intact, he said. With the company again in control, the impression is that an early revision in prices may be expected which would place the Lincoln in a much more active selling class.
>
> The slash in assets made by the appraisers has had the highly desirable effect of placing the company on a strictly present day valuation basis.
>
> Officials of the Treasury Department at Washington will be asked by the receiver to consider the writing off of the $500,000 balance remaining on the original $4,500,000 claimed for unpaid taxes. This will not be a formal appeal from the decision reducing the claim to $500,000 but the writing off will be presented as greatly facilitating the recovery of the company. Stockholders and creditors considered the offer of $8,000,000 for the company made by Emmons at an informal meeting to-day, with a view to determining their attitude on the proposed purchase. There is a likelihood of another bid being entered from this quarter.

Henry Ford had viewed Leland's Lincoln with some interest. Ford always was one for a bargain and Lincoln looked like a good buy. The entire company could be bought for less than the car's engineering design cost. Ford liked the idea of producing cars at both ends of the market spectrum. Edsel Ford got on the Lincoln bandwagon in a big way because he always appreciated fine automobiles.

Without Ford, the Lincoln Motor Company could only have survived by one of two scenarios. First, if the Lelands had obtained needed financing or, second, if the Murphy group had been able to assume the company's debt. Thus, Ford was the only real player in the game. No one else with enough money was even remotely interested. The nation was in the grips of an economic recession that would culminate in the crash of 1929. Ford and General Motors would weather the storm and prosper, but Billy Durant and Henry Leland would not.

CHAPTER THREE

LINCOLN SURVIVES

A Chrome Greyhound Leads The Way

Edsel Bryant Ford was fifteen years old when he and his friends, Charles Van Auken, William Theisen and James Smith began research on building an aero vehicle. At a barn near Woodward Avenue in Detroit, they constructed a single-place high-wing monoplane. It was powered by, what else, a twenty-eight horsepower Ford Model-T engine. Their airplane first flew from what is now the sight of the Dearborn Country Club and once again from historic Old Fort Wayne. It was damaged during a hard landing on the second flight and was not rebuilt. Edsel never actually flew in it.

As a teenager, Edsel Ford was encouraged by his father to tinker with mechanical things. At age sixteen, he built his first hot rod from a Model-T Ford; in those times referred to as a Speedster instead of hot rod; hot-rod being more of a 1940s-50s terminology. The finished speedster looked a lot like an early Stutz Bearcat and was powered by a six-cylinder engine. Edsel lost a fingertip to a machine lathe during its construction.

Years later, E.T. Gregorie designed two custom speedsters for Edsel, one of which the Model-40 Speedster he held onto the rest of his life. In 1923, Edsel received a letter that read simply, "I should like a thousand dollars and I can only promise you one thing, you'll never see the money again!" It was signed William B. Stout, Inventor.

The Fords received thousands of such requests and rarely responded. Edsel did answer this letter and enclosed two one-thousand dollar checks, one each from himself and his father. Thus began Ford's association with W. Bushnell "Jackknife" Stout and his all-metal airplane company. Stout was the grandson of David Bushnell who is credited with having perfected the modern naval submarine.

In 1927, three months before Charles A. Lindbergh flew nonstop from New York to Paris, the first all-metal Ford Tri-Motor was completed. Pilots nicknamed it the Tin Goose because it boasted an all-metal construction at a time when most aircraft were constructed of fabrics and woods and because of the Tin Lizzie, a nickname given its distant cousin the Model-T Ford. The Ford Tri-Motor was one of the most reliable and efficient transport aircraft ever built. It saw service throughout the world and a few are still flying even today.

The Ford Motor Company purchased the Stout all-metal airplane company and later built engines for the deHaviland aircraft. Technically, however, Woodward Avenue and Edsel's monoplane would remain the first Ford aircraft facility.

NINETEEN-TWENTYTWO - On June 10, 1922, the new president of Lincoln Motor Company was twenty-eight-year-old Edsel Ford. At twenty-one, he had become a director and the treasurer of the Ford Motor Company. After Henry Ford's scrape with the stockholders in 1919, Edsel was elected to the Ford presidency. Henry still owned enough stock to remain firmly in control and it was well known that he still ran things.

The original Lincoln Motor Company was a Delaware corporation. After Judge Tuttle's ruling, Lincoln was reincorporated as a Michigan corporation. The officers of the new company from February through June were Henry Leland as president, Wilford Leland as vice-president and general manager and Edsel Ford as second vice-president. William T. Nash was secretary-treasurer and B.J. Craig assistant secretary-treasurer. Both represented the Fords' interest.

In June, shortly after he became President of Lincoln, Edsel selected Ernest C. Kanzler as his vice-president and general manager. The Lincoln Motor Company was discontinued as an operating corporation and the Ford management people moved in to handle all matters from purchasing of parts to marketing and distribution. Production was at an all-time high. Ford sent quality control inspectors to work with Brunn Body Company in Buffalo, New York. Brunn had been commissioned earlier by Leland to improve the Lincoln's esthetic appeal. Edsel was very much interested in continuing along these lines.

Lincoln Model L Touring.

Model-L Lincolns were shipped in enclosed railroad cars and wrapped in protective paper. Dealers were instructed to have at least seven men ready to carefully unload and unpack each new automobile. One hundred and fifty Ford dealers were given immediate appointment as Lincoln dealers. The Ford Motor Company subsequently restructured their dealership plan in the metropolitan areas to create Lincoln only dealers. This concept of organization remains largely intact to this day and in small towns Ford-Mercury-Lincoln dealerships are still overseen by the regional Ford district office.

The following story was related in Floyd Clymer's Motor Scrapbook. Seems an individual had purchased an early Leland Lincoln from a dealer in Colorado. The distributor in Denver became a Peerless dealer after the Ford takeover of Lincoln. In the meantime, this particular Model-L seven-passenger Touring developed problems with rear springs and the engine continually overheated. Contacting the district manager of the local Ford facility, the owner found them very willing to make good on any defects in the car.

The manager suggested he bring the car into the nearby Ford assembly plant as they would need to keep the car for several days to make the necessary repairs. After about three days, the owner decided to see how the work was progressing. When he looked in, there was his Lincoln, jacked-up, with its engine out and surrounded by thirty Model-T Ford mechanics from various Colorado Ford agencies. They were being trained on the borrowed Model-L.

As mentioned before, the Ford Motor Company quickly dropped the price of new Model-L Lincolns. The cylinder heads were redesigned for better cooling and cast-iron pistons replaced the aluminum ones. By the end of 1922, the 136 inch wheelbase chassis became standard, as did Handaille hydraulic double-action shock absorbers and were commonly referred to as Ho-Dye shocks. An optional 4.90 to 1 rear axle ratio was available and was termed the Mountain Rearend. The engine was officially rated as ninety horsepower at 2800 RPM. The new radiator badge reading FORD above the LINCOLN name and DETROIT below replaced the LELAND-BUILT shield and cluster. An optional Moto-Meter radiator cap, which had also displayed the Leland logo on earlier models, was discontinued.

Most 1922 models were carry-overs from the 1921 models and many were assembled from parts already manufactured. Twenty-five different body styles were produced, but only about a dozen were built in any volume. The American Body Tourings and Phaetons were the most popular body styles, with the Murray and Lang Sedans close behind. Probably the two most photographed Lincolns of this era were the 130 inch wheelbase five-window coupe, with its large rear-seat passenger window and the rather standard Touring model.

A Phaeton is, for the most part, simply a deluxe version of the Touring. The original Lincoln sedans were about as close to a shoe box as can be built and still have an engine hood and wheels. This style had been the industry standard for some years, but newly designed less boxy styles were beginning to appear on the market.

The tire rims on the Model-L unbolted at the outside edge of the spokes, so the traditional rear mounted spares were hollow rims without wheels. The rear of the top on the open Touring sloped up and rearward, giving the appearance of being nearly ready to collapse backwards at any moment.

A large sideways V cutout in the top was beside the rear-seat passengers, who rode uncomfortably above the rear axle. The top required a supporting post, an unattractive feature common to many period designs.

The Brunn Cabriolet Town Car with an open chauffeur's compartment was traditionally styled, but a nevertheless impressive automobile. These body styles were referred to by other designers as Sedanca DeVille that simply means Sedan of Town. Lincoln called them Town Cars.

The Sport Roadster model utilized a sloping windshield and a California style top with coach bars. Its trunk was about as long as the hood and slopes sharply rearward housing a large rumble seat. Dual rear-mounted spares were optional.

Walter M. Murphy of Pasadena, California, was one of the first independent coachbuilders to recognize a golden opportunity for styling improvements on the mechanically excellent Model-L. He advertised and displayed a four-passenger Coupe with carriage roof and a long-bodied custom Sedan with dual side-mounted spare tires. Murphy thought that whitewall tires greatly improved the looks of the Model-L and he used them extensively.

In early production when they were available, use of the longer wheelbase chassis facilitated the rear seat being placed forward of the rear axle. This allowed a slightly more comfortable ride and provided more space for the traditional footlocker trunk or dual rear-mounted spares.

External wind wing-windows began appearing on Tourings and Roadsters. The Phaetons had adopted the full body beltline mold, that was used on many popular models in the early 1920s. It extended the hood mold line through the cowl and around the body. Metal disc wheels were another popular new option. Late in the model year, the Judkins Coupe was introduced.

Model L 7-passenger Limousine

AMONG the most expensively engineered cars in the world you will invariably find those equipped with HOO-DYE Hydraulic Shock Absorbers as stock equipment.

In this endorsement the Lincoln engineers have added their approval to the judgment of European engineers, who have equipped the majority of Europe's finest cars with Hoo-Dyes.

HOO-DYE
Shock Absorbers
Hydraulic

THE HOUDAILLE CO.
1416 West Ave., Buffalo, N. Y.
Houde Eng. Corp. Mfr's

LINCOLN IS BUILDING NEW DE LUXE MODEL

Shipments Will Begin in June — Company Sets Price at $3,800

DETROIT, May 19—Lincoln Motor Co. will make first shipments of a new model de luxe touring car in June, the price of which has been fixed at $3,800. The new model is a companion to the phaeton and roadster de luxe on which the company has been in production since last summer and the prices on which are also $3,800. This line is independent of the regular production model, the price on which remains at $3,300, as fixed immediately after the sale to the Ford interests.

Producing 30 Cars Daily

Production at Lincoln is now approximately 30 cars daily, dependent on the receipt of materials and bodies, the latter being still a heavy drawback to a steady flow of cars. Lincoln is served by a number of body makers, according to model, but because of the semi-custom nature of the work, it is difficult to get deliveries in the quantity required.

Henry Ford is spending much of his time at the Lincoln factory consulting with the Lelands, in whose hands the active management remains. Changes in the layout and arrangement of factory equipment are continuing, and some new equipment is being added with an eye to facilitating output.

LONGER LINCOLN WHEELBASE

DETROIT, MICH., July 17—The Ford Motor Co. announces that the length of the wheelbase of all Lincoln cars has been increased to 136 in., with the exception of the coupe which is still being built on the 130 in. wheelbase. A price change has been announced both on the 7 passenger and sedan. The seven passenger is raised from $3,300 to $3,800.

LINCOLN AT HIGHEST POINT

DETROIT, May 10—Production and sales of Lincoln cars continue at the highest rate in the history of the company, with enough orders on hand to keep the plant at capacity for three months. Body makers are unable to keep up with orders which are coming in three times as fast as the output capacity.

Ford Shifts Departments to Help Lincoln Factory

DETROIT, June 2—Sales and service offices of the Ford Motor Co. have been moved to the Lincoln Motor Co. plant, and the purchasing department of Lincoln has been moved to the Highland Park plant of the Ford company. The relocation of the departments is declared by executives to be of an experimental nature, and part of the plan is to familiarize the members of the Lincoln departments with Ford policies and methods.

There will be no consolidation of the departments of the two companies, it was declared, as it is the Ford plan to maintain them as two entirely separated divisions, each with its own executive staff.

Ford Men Selling Lincoln Everywhere

DETROIT, July 24—Lincoln cars will be sold abroad just the same as in this country—by Ford dealers, that policy having been decided upon by the Ford company. Shipments already have been made to Ford representatives in Manchester, England; Copenhagen, Denmark; Antwerp, Belgium; Bordeaux, France, and Cadiz, Spain, as well.

An initial shipment already has been made to Havana and two Lincolns are on their way to Manila. Shipments soon will be made to China and Japan. The Lincoln will be introduced to Brazil at the Brazilian Centennial, which will be held in Rio de Janeiro in September.

1922 Model L Cabriolet. Early coachbuilt body by Brunn.

During the 1922 model year, no major changes in design were made to the Lincoln, which continued to be referred to as the Model-L. The changes that were made were logistical in nature, mainly directed toward more efficient production. The engine blocks, for example, were now cast at the Ford facility in Rouge. At serial number 6030, larger brake bands were installed. As always, an effort was made to make the new parts interchangeable with the old ones. Minor changes in block and cylinder heads were made at serial number 7820 and a new quieter timing chain was installed at serial number 8500.

Emphasis was placed on producing the larger body styles like the seven-passenger Sedans and Limousines. H.H. Babcock Company was added to the list of custom coachbuilders. The most notable change in Model-L marketing strategy was the August announcement of an even lower price for the seven-passenger Touring. Other across-the-model-line price reductions followed. Between February and year-end, over five thousand new Model-L Lincolns were produced

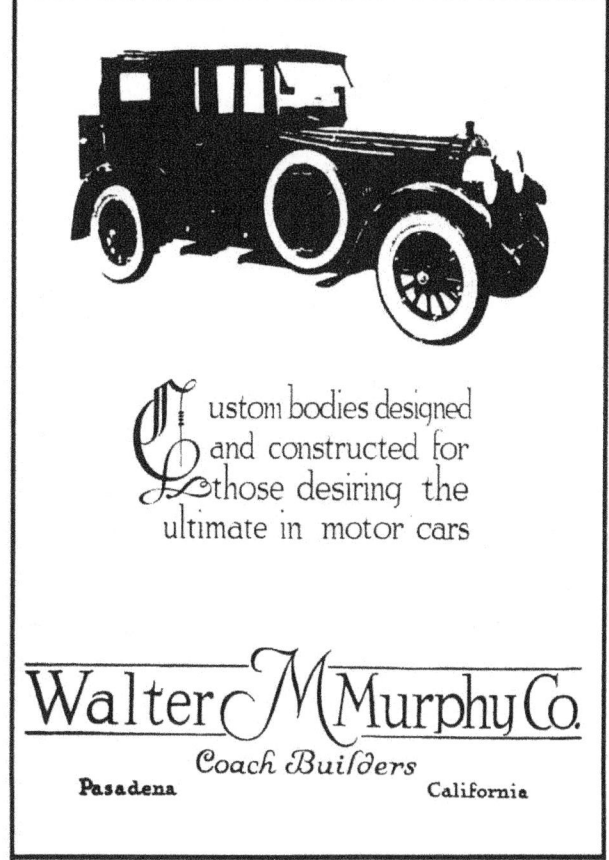

Custom bodies designed and constructed for those desiring the ultimate in motor cars

Walter M Murphy Co.
Coach Builders
Pasadena   California

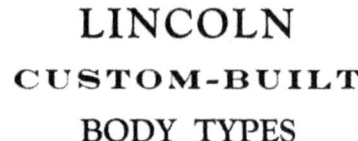

LINCOLN
CUSTOM-BUILT
BODY TYPES

Insert to
LINCOLN
SALES MANUAL

Issued July 31, 1922

LINCOLN MOTOR COMPANY
Division of
FORD MOTOR COMPANY
Detroit, Michigan

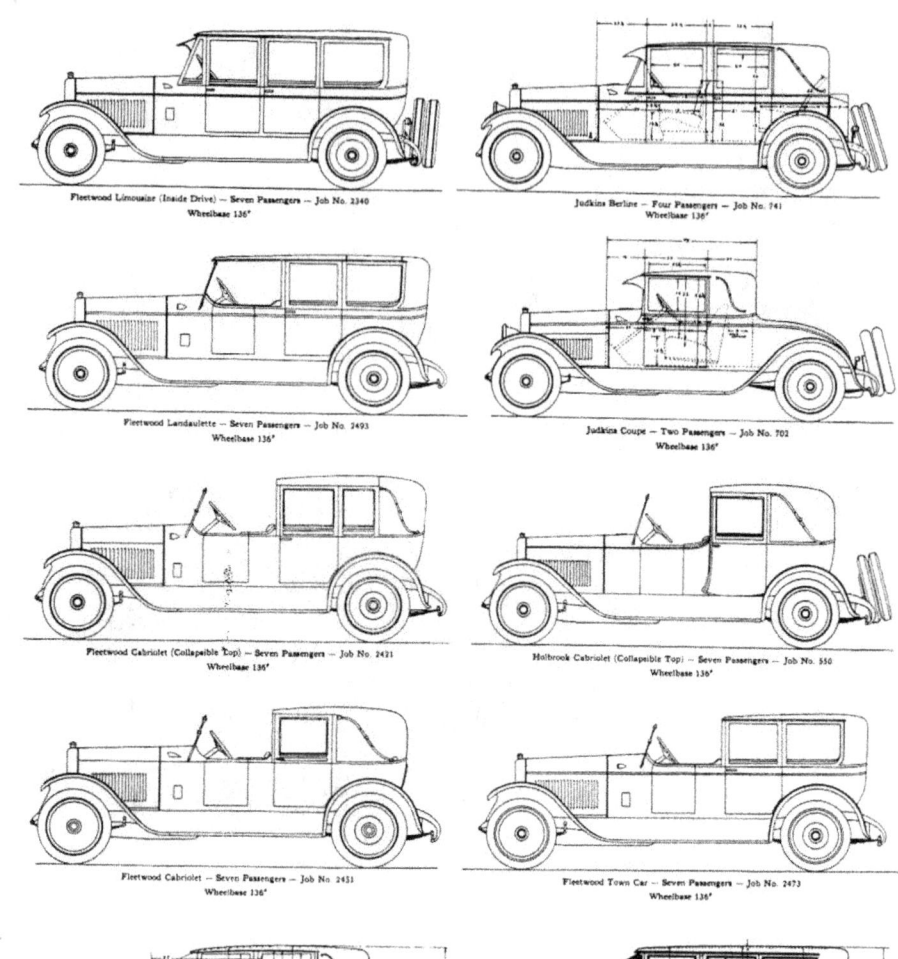

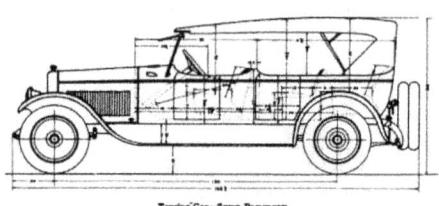

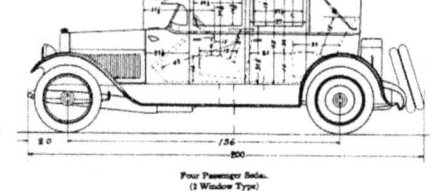

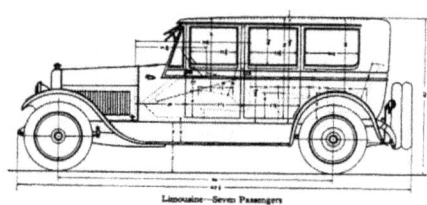

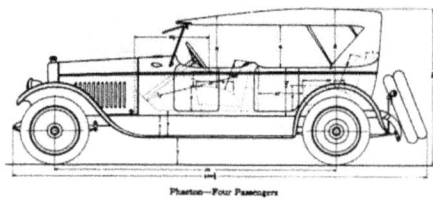

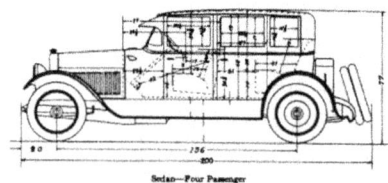

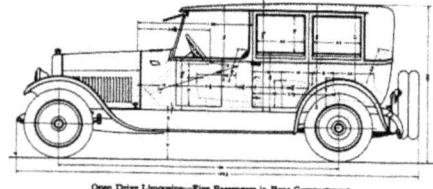

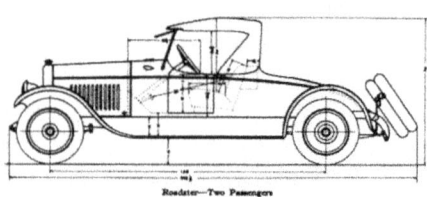

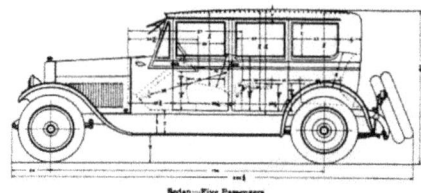

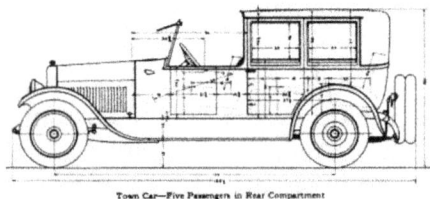

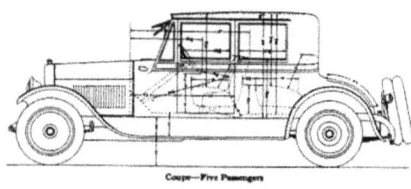

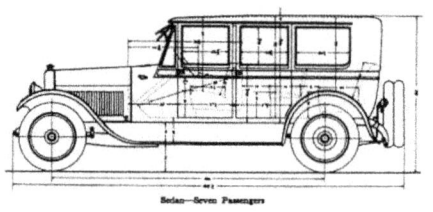

The bodies have been designed and will be produced by Fleetwood Metal Body Company, Fleetwood, Pennsylvania; The Holbrook Company, Hudson, New York; and the J. B. Judkins Company, Merrimac, Massachusetts. These concerns represent the foremost custom body builders in the country and enjoy national reputations for the exclusive designs, quality of workmanship and interior appointments of their creations.

NEW CARS AND MODELS

New Lincoln Models and Improvements

IN all, three new body styles were introduced recently by the Lincoln Motor Company, of Detroit, together with an improvement to facilitate starting and operating a cold engine. The bodies were the 4-passenger sedan, the 4-passenger phaeton, and the 7-passenger enclosed drive. The first-mentioned is illustrated herewith.

The 4-passenger sedan is of the 4-door type. The body is aluminum, and is mounted on the standard chassis of 136-in. wheelbase. The body is low. The windshield also is low and inclined, and equipped with a permanent leather visor. Just forward of the double tire-carrier at the rear of the car is a large leather trunk, which furnishes storage space and adds to the appearance. This body comes in the two and three-window types, in the former case the rear quarter being in leather.

The 4-passenger phaeton model was recently announced and has low lines and excellent appearance. The body panels are hand-hammered aluminum, and standard color is Cobalt blue, with hood and radiator shell to match. Upholstery is Spanish leather.

March 2, 1922

New Lincoln Model
This is the 4-door sedan, introduced at the shows this year. It was formerly custom-made only, but proved quite popular, and is now introduced as a standard model.

AUTOMOBILE TRADE JOURNAL

Leland's Lincoln was believed to have failed because of its pre-World War I Cadillac styling, but the real problem was far more complex. Sales manager Getsinger's advice to Henry Leland to engage professional coachbuilders to improve the styling on the Model-L proved sound. It later made Lincoln an innovator in the coachbuilt field and put them on the road to better styling.

One British automobile journal ran a picture of a Leland Lincoln Coupe with the caption, "Pleasantly Ugly!" If the Leland Lincoln was ugly, but mechanically superior, then for Edsel Ford it was a marriage made in heaven. Styling was what he wanted to do most and he did it in spades.

Whether or not Lincoln had become the luxury car of the Ford line because of the series of events between the two Henrys cannot be determined. One thing seems certain, however, had Edsel Ford never gained control of Lincoln Motor Company, he would have surely started a luxury motorcar line of his own. The Lincoln was simply a good buy on a good design.

Some months after the Ford takeover, Henry Leland was reported to have asked Ford to allow him to repurchase Lincoln for the bankruptcy sale price. Henry Ford was said to have replied, "Not for ten times what I paid for it!" The Leland family's side of this story is chronicled in the book Master of Precision by Mrs. Wilford C. Leland and Minnie Dubbs Millbrook.

NINETEEN-TWENTYTHREE - The early 1923 model Lincolns had painted bell-shaped headlight and taillight housings. Earlier models had painted drum-type light assemblies. This was further confused by the fact that in April of 1923, they returned to the chrome-plated drum type lights and chrome bells was optional. The windshield frames were redesigned to reduce vibration because these parts were interchangeable from model year to model year.

They were, however, of very little help in trying to identify a particular vintage. Sixteen different body styles, types 111 through 133, were now made available. These were produced by Lang, American, Judkins, Fleetwood, Brunn Anderson and Towson. The latter two companies were subsequently merged into Murray Corporation of America. Edsel Ford directed LeBaron of New York to create a series of custom bodies for the Lincoln. Edsel's personal one-off turret body Coupe was built this year. It had a convertible cloth top with coach bars. The Coupe's body resembled a rocking chair; the trunk deck was low and flat. Accessories included wire wheels, rear-mounted spare and whitewall tires.

For the most part, Edsel had a free hand with styling design at Lincoln. Mechanical engineering design was primarily the responsibilities of Charles Sorensen. Edsel was, however, directly responsible for bringing Clarence W. Avery to work for Ford at the Highland Park plant. Avery had been Edsel's manual training instructor at Detroit University and eventually masterminded many of Ford's mass production concepts.

Edsel Ford had a flair for styling and good taste. Why not? He was raised in affluence and had circulated with the crème de la crème of society in the U.S. and abroad. Edsel was to give Lincoln that touch of class, conceive the original Continental, introduce the Mercury and generally influence Ford styling for the next three decades. Whenever possible, he hung out with the styling design group at Ford. Unlike his father, he was characterized as easygoing and diplomatic.

The Lincoln legend would now grow and mature. When referring to an old Lincoln sedan, you may have overhead someone who did not even know the make, refer to it as gangster cars. The Lincolns were popular among rum runners and police squads alike, but Hollywood was largely responsible for this image.

Picture, if you will, the speeding black sedan with a guy leaning out of the window, firing his pistol to the rear. Close behind, in hot pursuit, comes the law in an open Touring model with the officer in the right seat firing away at the escaping sedan with his Thompson submachine gun.

This era for the Lincoln was right out of a Damon Runyon short story. One can almost imagine the "Three Wise Guys" speeding through the Jersey countryside in a Model-L sedan. It may have been the gangster Al Capone of whom it was related that, upon being involved in an accident in his large sedan, paid the driver of the other vehicle for the damages on the spot. Bizarre, indeed, for a man who was a crook to pay an automobile accident claim, but those were the times.

According to an old axiom, "the road to hell is paved with good intentions" is a good way of explaining the era into which the Lincoln automobile was introduced. From January, 1920 until 1933, when the Eighteenth Amendment was repealed, the Volstead Act had fostered Prohibition. This was the golden age of crime in America. Illegal booze became the country's number one industry. Without modern radio communications and other law enforcement aids, it was easy for rum runners to escape capture in high powered automobiles.

Lincoln Model L, turret body All-Weather Coupe. Custom built for Edsel Ford.

by WALT WILLIAMS

GRINNIN'

Over the top we went at 75

Ford Owner's Introduction

I'VE been busy the last couple of days—grinnin'.

Quite a bunch of fellows were down there and they were all cluttered around a big stripped car which was taking a bath over in the corner. I didn't ask them. Then we went for a ride.

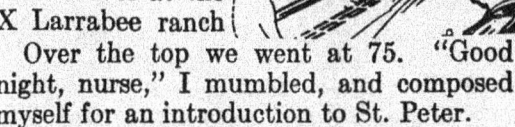

Oh, baby! I saw that downward gap in the pavement and my thoughts flew back to the days when I twisted broncs over at the X Larrabee ranch.

Over the top we went at 75. "Good night, nurse," I mumbled, and composed myself for an introduction to St. Peter.

But I am a changed man. No longer do I envy the birds with the six-cylinders and the noisy cut-outs. Not me. I've driven a Lincoln and done 80 miles without making enough noise to frighten a sparrow.

And so when I hear these sixes coming and they whiz by me at their measly 45 I just draw off to the side and grin. I'm driving a car made by the same man that makes a Lincoln, and that's good enough for me.

The City of Detroit authorized its Police Patrol Squadron to upgrade its motorcycles to some type of high performance automobiles so the police could chase down affluent mobsters driving Packards and Lincolns. The police department staged a competition for prospective patrol cars. Ten automobiles entered in the trial. On the half-mile and two-mile runs, the Lincoln bested all entries with an average top speed of eighty miles per hour. From a running quarter mile, the Lincoln finished second. Without exception, police test drivers selected the Lincoln for its superior cornering ability.

The Lincoln became the official car of the Detroit Police Department's Flying Squadron. Lincoln engineers fine-tuned the engine and installed four-wheel brakes, but otherwise the cars were stock. Mostly, the Brunn designed Touring models were used for the Police Flyers. Front wheel brakes did not become standard on the Model-L until 1927. Upon delivery, the Police Flyers were equipped with a bulletproof windshield, special spotlight and gun rack. These cars were renowned by assailants and law officers nationwide. This kicked off a sales and marketing campaign by Lincoln based on its new found high-performance reputation.

The styling plan for 1923 was centered around dropping the less attractive models and developing those that showed some promise. The seven-passenger, seven-window Sedan with sun visor and crank-out divided windshield had triangle wing-windows ahead of the front doors.

The door arrangement was of the unique front-front type. Fancy double-rail bumpers, lots of chrome and a contrasting pinstripe accented this stately Sedan. The top on the Touring model was modified to break slightly in the middle, eliminating the leaning-back-look. Support posts on the Phaeton and some Tourings were moved rearward, forming an inverse V coach bar.

The Sedans received larger windshields for better visibility, but retained their crank-out ventilation feature. A slimmer, more graceful exterior sun visor was added. Metal disc wheels were optional. In addition to their utility, they looked very good on certain models. Judkins had earlier introduced the Model-702 Sport Coupe that was selling well and continued to do so through 1928.

Henry and Edsel Ford with Charles Sorrensen entertaining the Prince of Wales in November, 1924.

They also introduced a Sedan Cabriolet with a carriage-style padded roof over the rear compartment. It had wires, canvas covered dual sidemounts and was nicknamed the Opera Coach. It could be best described as a pumpkin coach motorcar worthy of a Cinderella.

Guider-Sweetland custom coachbuilders of Detroit, Michigan, offered a pillarless four-door Sedan with three rows of seating, much like a modern Suburban or station wagon. Omitting the pillar, a center roof and door-frame post between the rear and front doors that reflected this coach shop's work as ambulance builders. Many of their models were patterned after the work of designer Lancia Augusta.

Inventor Thomas A. Edison purchased a Model-L Touring and fitted it with a special type of headlight that he felt worked better. The Highland Park Police Department had several long wheelbase chassis models built into paddy wagons Their front ends' back to the windshield were standard Lincoln. These wagons were equipped with dual sidemounts and used the traditional oval centered Lincoln front bumper.

NINETEEN-TWENTYFOUR - For 1924, the bell or tea cup-shaped headlamp assembly was dropped in favor of a raised drum style and had the effect of straightening out the hood and cowl lines. This greatly improved the looks of the Model-L's front end. By comparison, it is similar to the familiar change that would occur between the 1929 and 1930 Model-A Ford's radiator shell. The new radiator shell was nickel-plated. The thermostatically controlled radiator shutters or louver veins were positioned vertically in the grill. The new fenders were now full crown and wider. The molded border around the fenders was eliminated on all models except the Judkins Coupe.

The familiar LINCOLN oval emblem replaced the FORD-LINCOLN-DETROIT radiator badge. Cowl lights were smaller than earlier models and painted. Disc wheels, rear bumpers, Rudge-Whitworth wire wheels, side-mounted spare tires, dual rear-mounted spare tires, spare tire covers and painted radiator shells were optional. The wooden artillery wheels were painted to match the body color with a contrasting pinstriping.

LINCOLN AND CONTINENTAL

Wood grain finish was optional. Drivetrain improvements were made to the camshaft, clutch, flywheel and valves. A timing mark was added to the engine.

Prices were slightly increased in July and ranged from between fifty-five hundred and eight thousand dollars per automobile. It is questionable whether Ford ever made money on the Lincoln. The actual facts are denied us because of the company's crude to nonexistent methods of cost accounting. On occasion, receipts were literally weighed on a scale to determine the approximate cost of producing a given model. Many man-hours were spent finishing and testing the Lincolns. Models were more likely to have been priced rather arbitrarily by the market that Ford wished to target, than by the actual cost of production.

In November, the Prince of Wales came as a guest of the Fords to tour the Highland Park facilities. The chauffeur-driven Brunn seven-passenger open Touring was pulled right up on the loading dock. Ford czar Charles Sorensen sat in the jump seat with Edsel, Henry and the Prince seated aft. It was an opulent day. The escort caravan included a Fleetwood Town Car and a Brougham Limousine.

Henry Ford always enjoyed hobnobbing with the rich and famous. One testament to this was the Chuckwagon Cook Truck that Henry Ford had built on a 1921 Lincoln chassis. It now resides in the Henry Ford Museum in Dearborn, Michigan.

Henry Ford. Harvey S. Firestone, Thomas A. Edison, John Burroughs used it on many of their famous camping trips and on occasion President Warren G. Harding went with them. Mr. Burroughs, a famous naturalist and author was known for his long white beard.

Marvin Arnold

1925 Lincoln Dealership showroom, Louisville, Kentucky. Model Ls and oriental carpets.

An untrue but humorous story about one of these trips goes like this, while passing through a small town, Henry's Lincoln Chuckwagon started to run rough. Pulling into a local garage, he asked the mechanic to have a look at the car. As Henry Ford and his three famous friends looked on, the mechanic indicated that it might be mechanical trouble.

"I'm Henry Ford and I build these cars. It is not mechanical trouble," explained Mr. Ford.

"Well," said the mechanic, "I believe then, it must be an electrical problem."

"No," said Mr. Edison, "I am Thomas Edison and it is not electrical in nature."

The mechanic, a little confused at this point, said, "I guess I better have a look at the tires."

Mr. Firestone said, "I am Harvey Firestone and my company makes those tires. It's not the tires."

The mechanic stepped back, removed his hat and scratched his head.

"What are you waiting for," said Henry Ford, "fix the car."

"Well," said the mechanic, "I was just waiting for one of you fellers to tell me that gentleman over there with the white beard is Santa Claus."

The first presidential Lincoln was also built in 1924. It was a LeBaron sedan Touring. An order was placed with Ralph Roberts of LeBaron for a design to be approved by Henry Ford. President Calvin Coolidge, it was said, was an admirer of Henry Ford. Actually, the car's specifications were approved for production by Edsel. The car was pretty much a standard Lincoln Touring right down to the artillery wheels, but did have whitewall tires. The new Lincoln was delivered for service in December of 1923.

David Lloyd George, then Prime Minister of Britain, was one of the first dignitaries to ride in this Lincoln with President Coolidge, ol' Silent Cal, whose campaign slogan was, "Keep Cool with Coolidge" seldom allowed his driver to exceed eighteen miles per hour. The car remained at the White House when Herbert Hoover took office and thereafter became better known. Lincoln became the Marque motorcar of American presidents for the next six decades.

The original California style Sport Roadster was advertised with disc wheels, dual rear mounts and a Moto-Meter.

The California Roadster has a low sloping enclosed trunk in the rear made this Coupe resemble an animal weak in the flanks. Styling errors like these are surely what caused Edsel, a decade and a half later, to insist on a high trunk line for the Continental.

The Judkins California Coupe had not made this styling error. It sat very high in the back end and the top was chopped slightly, giving the whole car a more massive appearance. These features, combined with the newly restyled standard Lincoln hood, made the Judkins two-passenger Convertible one of the early style leaders. Also offered was a five-window Coupe that resembled the Sedan. Many of the Lincoln body styles had triangle wing-windows and built-in exterior sun visor.

Custom coachbuilder Guider-Sweetland produced a Phaeton with a hard top, curved third window, small coach bars, oval rear window and rear-seat windshield. It sported disc wheels, dual sidemounts and snap-on canvas wheel covers. The Judkins Berline had a front-front door and moved the entire rear passenger compartment forward, leaving more space for an add-on trunk or dual rear mounts.

NINETEEN-TWENTYFIVE - By 1925, coachbuilders like Brunn and Judkins soon learned that Edsel Ford was both a generous and demanding client. Edsel was at least honest with himself about the fine-performing, quality-built, less-than-beautiful Model-L. He took positive action early in 1925. While visiting New York, Edsel offered to relocate the entire LeBaron carrossiers to Detroit. The company did not accept, but their top designer Raymond H. Dietrich did. Dietrich referred to himself as an automotive architect.

Ford set Dietrich up in business and later gave him a contract to build Lincoln bodies. In Dietrich's own words, "It was like receiving a bouquet and the vase to put them in."

The addition of Dietrich and Holbrook brought to seven the number of authorized coachbuilders designing bodies for the Model-L. Carrossier is a European term for a custom coach body houses and was a posh name used for referring to early U.S. coachbuilders as well.

Edsel was now firmly in control of the Lincoln Motor Company. Until now, the standard Lincoln bodies were being contract-built by Murray, American and Babcock. The Murray Corporation of America would remain as the prime Lincoln body builder for ten more years until outside coachbuilding was discontinued completely.

Lincoln opened its own fine custom coach facility in 1925, but not because Edsel was less than satisfied with the contract builders. Indeed, the Lincoln chassis had become the first choice in America for custom fitting. The old-line custom houses had lofty standards and considered artistry their primary function. They had not yet grasped Edsel's perceptive view of the coming importance of styling.

The new popularity of the Lincoln increased demand for delivery that the coachbuilders were simply not equipped to meet. But, the Ford industrial complex was so equipped. Very few industries matched their capability in mass production. Additionally, Ford management supported the concept of more in-house control over body manufacturing.

The first Lincoln factory-built, a type 152 Sedan, was introduced in 1925. It was soon followed by the type 156 Coupe. The new Lincoln bodies used only number-one-grade select hardwoods in their framework. Parts were cut from a single piece of wood, not steam formed or joined. Body panels were hand-hammered aluminum and bronze or aluminum-cast body fittings were used. Die-cast iron or steel fittings were not used due to rusting. Interior trim wood was often meticulously inlaid with diamond patterns. To keep pace with a growing production schedule, the Lincoln factory and plant facilities were increased in size and improvements were made to the assembly areas.

LINCOLN

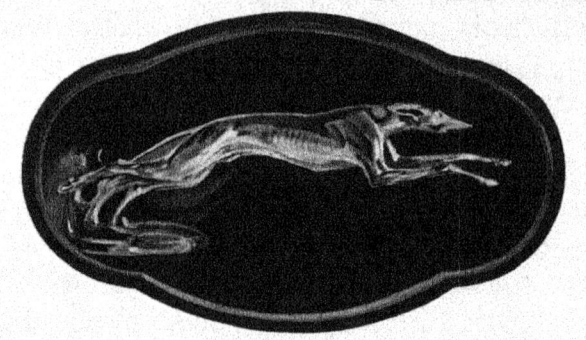

This year saw the introduction of the famous Gorham designed chrome greyhound radiator cap ornament. Edsel felt that the greyhound represented speed, grace, beauty, and endurance. He selected the Gorham Company of Providence, Rhode Island, to produce the new mascot. At first, the greyhound ornament was to have been only an option, but it quickly became standard on all Lincolns. It even became common to see replicas of the Lincoln greyhound on Fords, which people called, "Baby Lincolns." Auto accessory suppliers made cheaper versions of the chrome greyhound that could be bolted onto the hoods of almost every make of automobile built. (Hood ornaments today are carry-overs from these old decorative radiator caps.)

1925-26 American body 5-window Coupe with Rudge-Whitworth wire wheels installed.

1925-26 Touring with disc wheels. Chauffeur driven lady picks gentleman up at railway station.

This year saw the introduction of the famous Gorham designed chrome greyhound radiator cap ornament. Edsel felt that the greyhound represented speed, grace, beauty and endurance. He selected the Gorham Company of Providence, Rhode Island, to produce the new mascot. At first, the greyhound ornament was to have been only an option, but it quickly became standard on all Lincolns. It even became common to see replicas of the Lincoln greyhound on Fords, which Ford loyalists referred to as Baby Lincolns

Auto accessory suppliers made cheaper versions of the chrome greyhound that could be bolted onto the hoods of almost every make of automobile built. Hood ornaments today are carry-overs from these old decorative radiator caps.

Mechanical changes implemented in 1925, included a smoother emergency brake with longer handle and a 12.6 to 1 steering ratio and replaced the 15 to 1 ratio. Front and rear bumpers became standard and 7.00x21 balloon tires were now optional. Standard wheels were 6.00x21 with overall dimensions of 33x5. The absence of cowl lights helps to distinguish this year's models. Padded roofs and coach bars on hard top sedans were carried over from carriage styles. There were other options and trends that came in style for the same reason. Fold down center door pillars were one such example. With door windows rolled down and pillars folded out of sight, a sedan provided the same open-air feeling of a Phaeton with a hardtop installed.

Production included a 150 inch wheelbase chassis, referred to as the type 150A. Nine of these were used in the assembly of burial coaches. type 150B chassis were used for commercial delivery vehicles.

Other models produced were the Locke type 151 Roadster with auxiliary seats, the type 157 Berline Landaulet six-passenger by Willoughby, the Holbrook and LeBaron Cabriolets and a gross of factory-built five-passenger Sedans type 152. A dozen different custom coach styles were built by LeBaron and about the same number by all other custom builders combined.

American Body Company produced a little over one hundred type 123D Tourings and the last of the ABC coaches. Holbrook introduced a Cabriolet that not only provided for the usual chauffeur's all-weather top but also had a partially collapsible rear coach top for the passenger compartment like a Landaulet. California independent coachbuilder, Walter Murphy offered the first can-you-top-this carriage look-alikes. On this design, the driver's compartment was an open buggy seat with lantern style coach lamps mounted on either side.

LeBaron built a custom body Lincoln this year, which was to become one of the rarest and most distinctive of all the Model-L Lincolns. Its hood mold line continued unbroken the full length of the car body. This was a styling concept used in Europe, but not yet adopted in America. Piano hinges were secured to the hood with exposed polished rivets, a method often used by Rolls-Royce coachbuilders.

The low profile of this LeBaron was made possible by tunneling the drive shaft through the car, allowing for a step-down rear seat, a method used later on modern cars. Only two were ever built and are prized collector cars. These automobiles are benchmark examples of this period's fine coach workmanship.

Ray Dietrich described Edsel Ford as, "A generous and sensitive man whose grasp of styling and understanding of the creative mind made him a genius of the automotive art."

Ford designer Walter Teague, came to know Edsel well and further expanded on this by saying that, "Edsel was a great soul. He was wise, generous, strong and simple, a combination of qualities that mark the greatest of men. In him an extreme sensitiveness was united with an unselfconscious modesty that left no need for the kind of compensations publicity has to offer. By choice, Edsel worked behind the scenes where public eyes could not follow. Few except those privileged to work with him knew that among his many qualities, Edsel was also a great designer."

Ralph Roberts of LeBaron claimed that during work sessions with Edsel, a coach design was sometimes firmed up in a single afternoon. With other custom coach clients, this might take days or weeks of meetings. Referring to Edsel, Roberts said, "He never interjected alien preferences of his own, but could put his finger on key elements of a design and point out what did not seem to fit. The design would improve and grow in these sessions and at the end the designer would feel assisted by a master and not criticized."

NINETEEN-TWENTYSIX - The year 1926 would prove to be the best of all production years for the Model-L and Model-K Lincolns. The preceding year had been very good and during this year the Lincoln motorcar had come of age. LeBaron, Locke and Willoughby were added to the approved Lincoln custom builders' roster. Several of these coachbuilders had begun by outfitting custom order Fords with special interiors. Except for an occasional one-off and custom builds, these were the last of the coachbuilders to furnish bodies for the Model-L.

Ray Dietrich had left LeBaron and was now heading Dietrich Custom Body Company of Detroit. In the beginning, Dietrich was more of a creative designer than a coachbuilder for the parent company, Murray Corporation of America. Murray, of course, had built Model-L bodies from the outset. Edsel asked Dietrich to enter a design in the Concours d'Elegance for the 1927 Paris competition.

This Concours traditionally made awards for all types of creative designs from jewelry to architecture. Dietrich entered a Convertible Coupe with dicky and it was awarded a gold medal for excellence. At Milan, in competition with seventy-two other designs, the Dietrich Lincoln received the top award for the World's Best Design.

In Monte Carlo, it took another gold medal and in Dietrich's words, "A loving cup big enough to go swimming in." In 1926, exterior changes were nonexistent. Several interior changes and engine modifications were made. The eighteen-inch tilt steering wheel was replaced with a nineteen-inch diameter wheel that had finger grips and no longer tilted. These changes made the Model-L slightly easier to steer, even when stopped. The high beam tilt lever was no longer located just below the horn button and the steering wheel itself was black walnut.

The easier steering characteristics and the new practice by Lincoln of picturing women behind the wheel in their advertisements was a strong indication of their growing awareness of the influence of the woman buyer in the automobile marketplace. After all, these were the Roaring Twenties and some women were even beginning to smoke in public as well as drive themselves about. Heretofore, Lincoln had mostly pushed their chauffeur-driven Town Cars and Cabriolets indirectly at the female market, suggesting that a successful man's lady was driven around in luxury.

Now, not only a few successful women like movie stars were buying and driving their own automobiles, lots of women were doing so. The Judkins two-passenger Coupe was pictured in the Salon Catalogue with disc wheels, two-tone paint and a woman in a man's style tailored suit and hat behind the wheel.

Advertising in 1926 continued mostly along the society theme, using pastel watercolor drawings of various body styles in austere prestige settings.

A new, more efficient, centrifugal-type air cleaner was installed under the hood. For better high-speed performance, a flapper valve provided bypass air to the carburetor. Modifications to the distributor cam slightly improved the Lincoln's performance. The optional wire wheels were now produced by Buffalo, replacing those made by Rudge-Whitworths. Balloon tires and black walnut wheels became standard.

The factory-built coach bodies quickly gained a reputation as being even sturdier than those of many coachbuilders. It became increasingly difficult for the Lincoln coachworks and all of the coachbuilders together to keep up with the new public demand for these fine motorcars.

In all, Lincoln Model-L coaches were built under fifteen different names and by a dozen different companies. The Lincoln Catalogue was a commercial work of art in itself and read like a Who's Who of coachbuilders. Lincoln coachbuilders as we refer to them here were those commissioned by the Lincoln factory to build bodies. Additionally, there were other custom coach shops building one-off custom bodies for Lincolns

Shops like Walter P. Murphey's in California continued to do beautiful modification work and to build custom coach bodies for the Lincoln. Guider-Sweetland built limousines and ambulances on the Lincoln chassis. The early Model-L chassis were used to construct tow trucks as well as being popular chassis for commercial delivery vehicles and ambulances.

Edsel Ford perfected the Custom Body Catalogue concept from which a prospective Lincoln buyer could select a design. The Lincoln factory then subcontracted these bodies to be built in lots of ten or more, thus creating volume buying power for the custom coach automobile purchaser.

This practice also had the beneficial effect of preserving many unique body designs, unlike other manufacturers whose one-of-a-kind designs have been lost forever. It often guaranteed that a hundred or more of a given style would be built. This was especially true if a particular design happened to personally appeal to Edsel who would simply place an order for an even hundred.

The Ford people were beginning development work on the new Model-A Ford and were now thinking of phasing out the Model-T. The beautiful, ageless styling of the Model-A can be directly attributed to Edsel Ford and his coachbuilder associates. The styling design influence of Raymond Dietrich is very evident in the classic lines of the Mode-A Ford.

In terms of styling, the Model-A body was the Ford Mustang of its time. It reflected the downsizing of the classic styling trends of that period. The 1930 Model-A Ford Roadster bears a strong resemblance to the Lincoln Sport Roadster by Locke.

LeBaron introduced a Dual-Cowl Touring, on which the rear cowl closed over the back doors, placing the windshield tightly in front of the rear seat passengers. The term Dual-Cowl is slightly misused here, as this open sedan was technically a Phaeton with Tonneau cowl and rear windshield. The LeBaron design had a little less classically styled than the Dietrich Phaeton introduced later that year. Both, however, were impressive automobiles.

Prices for the Model-L Lincoln began at $4,500 with various custom bodies ranging upward to double that amount. Thirty-two different options ranged in price from $500 for a monogram to a $4,000 on the tonneau cowl and windshield option. To put this in prospective, one could purchase a new Model-T Touring for under five hundred dollars at this time hundred patents on inventions. He left Ford in 1927 to become head of engineering for Marmon.. Lincoln's chief engineer after Frank Johnson left the first time in 1922. Little held more than three went into the Lincoln. Little had also been at Cadillac with Leland and had taken over as

Marvin Arnold

NINETEEN-TWENTYSEVEN - In the year 1927, Babe Ruth hit sixty home runs for the Yankees, the bestselling book was The Bridge at San Luis Rey, Al Jolson was starring in a new talking movie The Jazz Singer and the automobile was beginning to be thought of as a dependable means of transportation. Motor oil was selling for twenty cents a quart, so Pennzoil sponsored a transcontinental run from New York to California and back.

The best time to date had been just under 168 hours. The distance was 6,721 miles and was accomplished at an average speed of 40 MPH with no major breakdowns. Model-L Lincolns were still popularly referred to as Leland Lincolns. However, this was the year that Ford engineers began increasing the number of minor changes.

Edsel, unlike Henry, was no local country boy. He had traveled Europe and owned cars like Hispano-Suizas, Bugattis and Rolls-Royces. He knew the features he wanted designed into a motorcar. Even today in Detroit, a manufacturer will go out and purchase a competitor's car in order to study what might give their competition more market appeal. Edsel had mastered the art of recognizing the best qualities of other designs and was now attempting to incorporate them into the Lincoln.

Chief engineer for Lincoln, Thomas J. Little, Jr., was responsible for much of the forward looking mechanical design work that or the Model-L, the major mechanical news this year was the installation of front wheel brakes as standard equipment. The new four-wheel brakes could be retrofitted onto the earlier models. This had been the practice on most Lincoln factory improvements to date. The implication here was that the Lincoln was so well designed that it needed only minor updating and even then your older model was not obsolete.

Until now, a Lincoln owner could purchase a factory-exchange engine for $100 plus installation labor. A statement by the Lincoln Motor Company claimed, "There are no yearly models. The Lincoln has reached a stage of development where changes are neither necessary nor desirable. Whenever it is possible to achieve an improvement, it is made interchangeable with the previous design. This protects the Lincoln owner against artificial depreciation resulting from the announcement of new models."

The installation of front wheel brakes as standard equipment was promoted by Lincoln as the Six-Brake-System. The new large front brake drums can be seen through the wire wheels in many Lincoln photographs of this year. Some coachbuilt bodies listed as 1927 models will still not have them as chassis were shipped earlier to the coachbuilders.

The six brake system meant that the internal brakes were now on all four wheels, plus an extra pair of rear brakes. The hand brake operated independently of the foot pedal brakes, controlling external contracting or band-type brakes. The hand lever also actuated the rear drum brake

1927 Lincoln Imperial Victoria Touring by Fleetwood, with LeHurleur radiator cap ornament. Owned by T.L. Osborn of Tulsa, Oklahoma.

Lang-American Touring body Type 123B displays many of the traditional options: 1. Trunk rack. 2. Trunk installed on rack. 3. Tonneau cowl option, open. 4. Canvas tonneau (tarp) installed. 5. Rear windshield and tonneau cowl closed.

The brake system, however, remained mechanical rather than hydraulic. Most Model-L Lincoln owners reported very satisfactory braking from the mechanical system. The new front wheel brakes had been perfected during their use on the Police Flyers and had been a special order option since 1923.

Hydraulic brakes were sometimes referred to as airplane brakes due to their early use on aircraft. They were also referred to as Lockheed brakes, probably for the same reason many people use to refer to a refrigerator as the Frigidaire. Hydraulic brakes had been used by car makers like Isotta as early as 1910, but Henry Ford mistrusted them. It was not until the late 1930s that Ford products would make the changeover.

An improvement to the drivetrain was a smaller, lighter-weight, clutch. This modification reduced the inertia when the clutch was disengaged and resulted in smoother gear meshing. The 1928 Cadillac introduced Synchromesh, which was not adopted by Lincoln until 1931.

The Lincoln version of the famous Ford ignition and steering lock was installed this year. Called the Coincidental Lock, it was intended as a theft deterrent device. The idea behind steering wheel locks was the known fact that most ignition and starter systems of this era were very easily wired around.

Another change for this year was a new instrument panel that grouped gauges and dials into a single oval cluster. The speedometer and clock were separated and the clock was increased in size.

The appearance and operation of the headlights and taillights were modified.

Marvin Arnold

LINCOLN and CONTINENTAL CLASSIC MOTORCARS

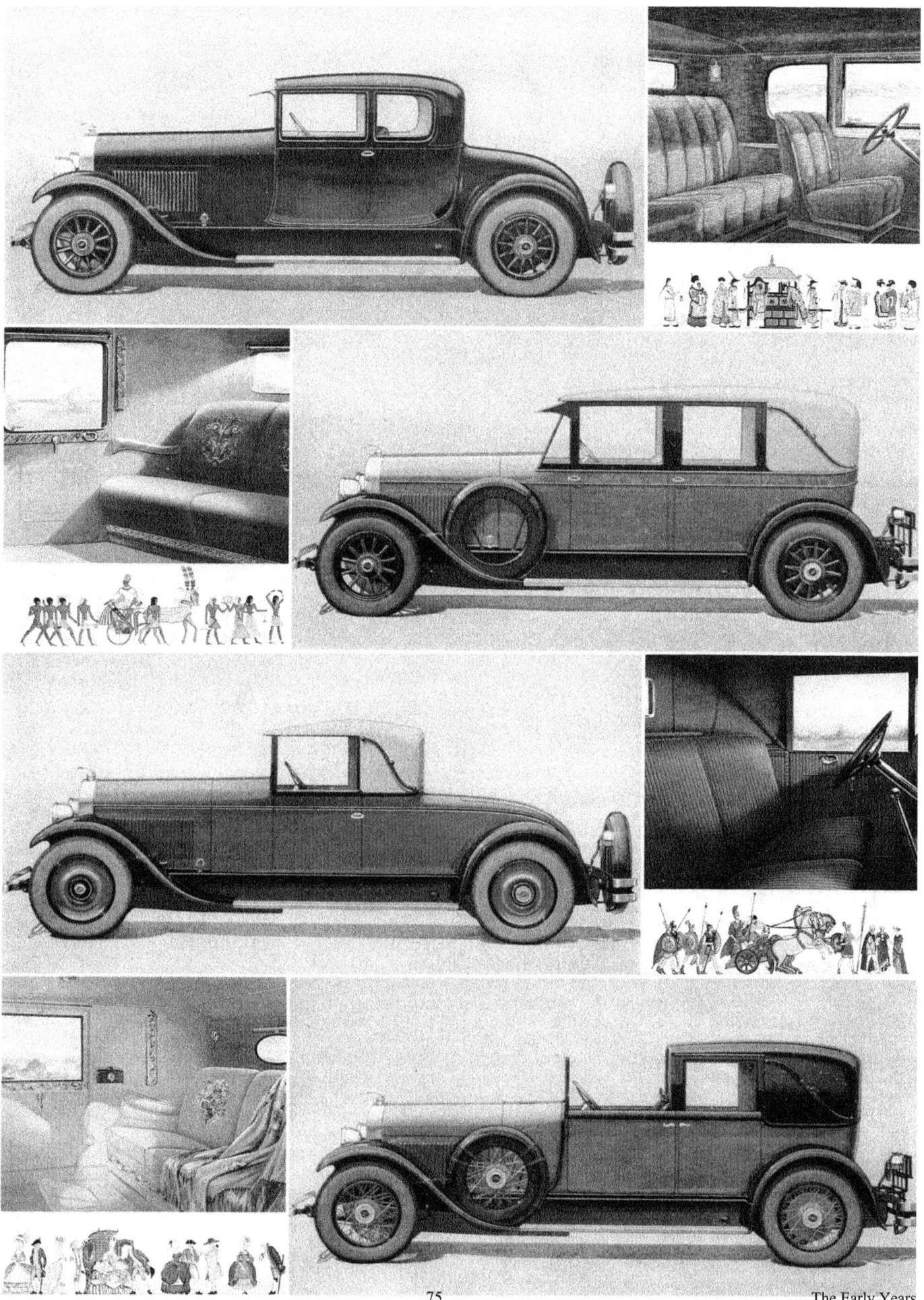

Marvin Arnold

CLASSIC MOTORCARS

The headlight bulbs now had dual filaments for high and low beam, replacing the mechanical lamp tilt arrangement. The headlight control remained on the steering wheel hub. The taillights had three lenses and bulbs. They were red for rear illumination, amber for brake warning and clear for backup. More conical-shaped lamp housing replaced the bell-style and the smaller cowl lamps were shaped to match.

The linoleum used on the running board was replaced with molded black ribbed rubber. The linoleum had always tended to curl after extended exposure to hot and cold weather. Fenders were formed with a one-inch deeper crown. This change had the effect of making the fenders more solid and less susceptible to vibration.

The Electro-Fog generator was discontinued late in the model year. The whole car sat a little lower this year due to the changeover to 32x6.75 tires and a half-inch reduction in the spring camber. As Lincoln professed no model-year changes, many of the late 1927 cars incorporated engine and accessory modifications generally associated with the 1928 models. Lincoln sales were beginning to lag and factory production rates were declining sharply. Prices were cut several hundred dollars in an effort to attract marginal buyers.

By midyear, new emphasis was placed on interior coordination. Lincoln's strong affiliation with the custom coachbuilders made this a logical evolution in styling. Until now, traditionally closed and formal body types had been upholstered in neutral colors like gray and taupe. An open Roadster or Touring usually got black or dark brown leather upholstery.

These new custom interiors were magnificently finished, but still without regard to the exterior scheme. The vogue period of transportation decor had come and gone with the luxury ocean liner and the railway passenger car, but it was alive and well in the coachbuilt automobile. Infatuation with decor and motifs is so much with us today that it seems inconceivable it did not always exist.

NINETEEN-TWENTYEIGHT - In 1928, the first major changes to the Leland V-8 engine specifications were made. Whether or not the return of Frank Johnson as chief engineer from Cadillac had any bearing on this is only speculation. This Johnson is not to be confused with Carl Edward Johansson, inventor of the Jo-Block gauges who came to work at Lincoln after Ford's acquisition of Johansson's company in New Jersey. Johannson remained on the Ford payroll at the Rouge plant in Dearborn until his retirement.

The original Leland engine was specified as an eight cylinders, 60-degree V-opposition, L-head, with cast iron block. It had a 3.375 (3-3/8) inch bore, 5.0 inch stroke, 357.8 cubic inch displacement and a 4.8 to 1 compression ratio. It developed 90 brake horsepower at 2800 RPM, a taxable horsepower of 39.2. The engine had three main bearings, mechanical valve lifters and a Stromberg 03 updraft carburetor.

The displacement of the new engine was increased to 384.8 cubic inches (6.3 liters). This was accomplished by increasing the bore to 3.5 inches. The compression ratio was increased slightly to 4.81 to 1. Intake valve diameter was increased from 1.75 inches to 1.875 (1 7/8) inches.

The combustion dome was reshaped for a more even burn. Lincoln claimed no increase in the rated 90 horsepower, but clearly these changes increased the performance of the engine. Unofficially, the modified engine produced about five more horsepower.

A few months after the engine was introduced, conical valve springs were installed for more uniform tension. Operators who were familiar with the old engine, however, complained that the new engine ran rougher. Lincoln mechanics felt that greater wear was now occurring on the crankshaft and other mechanical parts. Counterweights were added to the crank to dampen the vibration. An oil filter became standard equipment.

The Model-L had a top speed of 90 miles per hour even though the speedometer only registered up to 80 MPH. In April, a new muffler system was introduced. It was considered so superior to the old system that component parts were made available for dealer retrofits, particularly on those cars experiencing exhaust system problems. Exhaust pipes had been enameled for some time. Engine heat on the front seat occupants had long been a problem, so a new laminated wood firewall insulator panel was installed. A new, lighter axle with one less grease fitting was now being used. Oil-less bearings replaced the old-style tube bearings in the steering assembly to reduce the rattling noise. The wheelbase remained at 136 inches and the tread at 60 inches.

Styling on the Lincoln was becoming a little more progressive, influenced by the many one-off customs. The exterior was dressed up with chrome plated bumpers, front and rear. New standard wire wheels had chrome hubcaps and the hubs were of the five stud type. The wheels were drop center," meaning that the outside rim no longer bolted onto the hub.

Lincoln was one of the early, if not the first, American manufacturers to go to this type of wheel. The spokes on the new wheels were welded in place. These were superior in strength to the threaded-in spoke wheels, which had been known to collapse during a hard turn. Lincoln promoted this change by pitching, "The safety of steel from toe to wheel." The new wheels were size 7.00x20 and the tire size was now 32x6.75. Artillery and disc wheels remained options.

Cowl lights were installed again this year on most body styles. Headlights, cowl lights and taillight assemblies all matched and had returned to the semi-acorn shape. They were all chrome plated. Certain features had become Lincoln hallmarks, such as the round clutch and brake pedals, steering wheel lock, a tall emergency brake lever, windshield sun visor and a large flattened oval front bumper configuration. Time has borne out that the most popular of the collector cars among the Model-L Lincolns would be the 1928 through 1930 models.

By 1928, most of the horizontal, two-piece, middle-opening windshields had given way to one-piece, straight, slightly rearward-sloping ones. If they opened at all, it was from the bottom with a screw lock on either side. Notable exceptions were the Willoughby seven-passenger three-window and two-window Limousines.

THE ALL-WEATHER BROUGHAM

Outstanding among all fine cars on famous avenues and boulevards, Lincoln appearance unmistakably suggests Lincoln quality and fineness. Lincoln character and reputation do not need the emphasis of showy embellishment—that which is genuinely fine wins universal recognition without display—those who design Lincoln bodies—famous custom body designers—seek with beautiful body lines to express the innate fineness of Lincoln quality and performance.

A glance at this beautiful Brougham (by Brunn) reveals Lincoln distinction—it is as perfect in line and form as a sculptured masterpiece—its simplicity and genuine elegance appeal most invitingly to the educated tastes of people who invariably buy the finest things.

On these models, the windshield came to a V-shape in the middle. On each side of the windshield was a half-diamond window, forward of the front door where the old-style triangle windows had been located and were referred to as an Obtuse Angle Windshields. The doors on these models were the front-front arrangement. These models were produced in fair numbers through 1930.

Using a similar design was the Judkins two-window Landau Berline Sedan. Being listed in the Lincoln Salon Catalogue did not ensure any given number of models being produced. The term Production Model-Had a very general meaning in Lincoln's case. It indicated those designs that could be repeatedly delivered during a model year. As a rule, these were the rather average-looking Sedans and Coupes in the lower price range. This holds true, even today.

Most if the rest of the cars sold were custom and semi-custom cars from the Salon Catalogue. Some semi-custom and one-off body styles never appeared in any catalog. This may be confusing until one considers that the average annual production of Lincolns was only a little over six thousand cars. In late 1928, two new models were introduced at the New York Auto Show, Ray Dietrich's new Lincoln and the all new Model-A Ford.

Starting in late 1927, artistic bird ads ran in popular magazines like Country Life and Home and Garden. Lincoln had typically used black and white or color ads with serious and mundane aspects. Thus, the colorful Audubon series by artist Stark Davis was a major departure for Lincoln advertisements.

One of the most beautiful of these famous ads was of a peacock with the LeBaron five-window Coupe in the foreground. There was also an ad displaying a crane in flight behind a Willoughby Semi-Collapsible Cabriolet that had a landau leather top and, although not shown, armchair occasional seats. A pair of black faced gulls framed the ad for the Locke Sport Phaeton. The Lincoln Bird series was discontinued by 1929.

In other ads of this series, a LeBaron Town Car called an All-Weather Cabriolet was pictured in front of a colorful condor on a tree branch. A giant red stork with black wing tips flies through green foliage behind a Dietrich Convertible Sedan. This Lincoln was a progressively modern, five-window Sedan with a rear-rear door combination, it was the ultimate Touring. The front brakes are visible through the red wires. This new-style Sedan Convertible used a glass window insert between the front and rear roll-up door windows. It sported dual sidemounts, vertical windshield, pull door handles and roof coach bars.

The Lincoln Club Roadster type 165 was dominated over by a golden bird perched amid violet foliage. This two-passenger Roadster sported disk wheels, rear-mounted spare, coach bars and a two-passenger rumble seat. A distinctive feature was the decorative fashion in which the cowl and lower mold lines met, then curved upward just forward of the front doors.

The Five-Passenger Sedan

The compact 60° "V" type motor and the long chassis provide luxurious room for five people in this most popular of all closed car body types—room for wide, deep seats and seat backs as comfortable as arm chairs. The doors and windows are exceptionally wide—there is full vision for every passenger. There is Lincoln power for capacity loads, steepest grades and sustained high speed mile after mile—there is wonderfully easy riding comfort for trips across the continent, if need be. Lincoln craftsmanship, custom-designed beauty and the never-failing dependability of Lincoln service and performance make this, of all fine cars, the family car supreme!

L I N C O L N   M O T O R   C O M P A N Y
Division of Ford Motor Company

This body style was a continuation of the popular Locke type 151 Roadster and the Dietrich type 154 Coupe Roadster. A wide-eyed red bird of paradise provided the background for the Brunn All-Weather Brougham whose features included a removable panel above the driver with slide-up side windows, pull door handles, dual sidemounts and a rear-front door arrangement. This seven-window Town Sedan also showed its front wheel brakes through the wires and had a Gorham Greyhound on the hood.

Using the same bird of paradise, but this time in turquoise was an ad for a Limousine by Dietrich. It was a large five-window Sedan featuring forward triangle window and a roll-down interior glass partition plus two fold away cushioned axillary seats.

The Lincoln coach works five-passenger Sedan is featured in BRG with black accent. The car is parked below a long-beaked green bird with royal blue wings. The ad copy promoted the compact 60-degree, V-type motor, long chassis, Lincoln craftsmanship and service. A companion seven-passenger Sedan in royal blue sits below a perturbed peacock. Its ad copy states, "The distinguished Lincoln clientele includes many who prefer the popular Sedan body type so admirably adapted to family use."

A departure from the bird theme, but in exactly the same colorful Stark Davis style, was a blue butterfly ad. It promoted the, seven-passenger Sport Touring by Locke in black with red wheels and a red mold line accent. Long, "Low and Graceful" was used in the slogan ads.

Its interior was saddle tan. The custom sales features that promoted this aluminum-bodied Locke Touring were: "Hand crushed Moroccan leather; sport top of finest Burbank cloth, mahogany finished bows, nickel trimmed hardware; folding trunk rack and six wire wheels, spares at the side or rear optional.

Marvin Arnold

Seven-Passenger Sport Touring—by Locke

LONG, low and graceful in every line and curve, beautifully expressive of great power and inexhaustible speed... A motor as quiet and vibrationless as it is possible to make a superb piece of power machinery... Complete safety and effortless control even at the highest speeds... Equipment and appointments as fine as the quality-markets of the world affords... Spacious room for seven—even for the two passengers in the auxiliary seats. Restful touring comfort even across a continent. These are definite Lincoln qualities that make this a master-car among all fine open cars!

Aluminum body custom-designed by Locke—upholstered in soft, hand crushed Morocco in color to blend with the finish—a sport top of finest Burbank cloth with mahogany finished bows, nickel trimmed, compactly folding. Unlimited selection of color combinations. Six wire wheels—spares at the side or rear. Folding trunk rack.

CLASSIC MOTORCARS

1929 Dietrich Convertible body Sedan.

NINETEEN-TWENTYNINE - Officially announced on New Year's Day of 1929 that the new model Lincolns had completed their first decade. This year, Lincoln Division would report earnings of over two million dollars. Sales had rebound slightly after a steady two-year decline.

The exterior changes to this year's Lincoln were centered on a new sturdier grille and a radiator shell that was higher and narrower. The number of cowl louvers was increased from twenty-six to forty-two on each side. Twenty-six had been the standard number of vent louvers since the first Leland Lincolns. The radiator filler neck was now threaded on the outside and the cap was larger around with a lower profile.

The contour of the hood intersected the new squared-off radiator shell so as to carry through the body's molded beltline. Later in the year, the front fenders were shortened slightly and followed the curve of the wheel line a little less. Almost all models went to the dual side-mounted spare tire arrangement. Options were few and consisted of spare tire covers, monogram, tonneau cowl and rear windscreen. Popular accessories were the rearview mirrors that strapped onto the dual sidemounts. Large wing-windows were often added to the front and rear windshields on the Touring and Phaeton. Four-wheel brakes and welded steel wheels were due to growing interest in automobile safety.

A factor getting considerable attention by conscientious motorists was driver visibility. This had a noticeable effect on many body styles. Windshield posts and door pillars were made stronger and narrower. Safety glass was provided on all windows of the Lincoln. Many earlier cars had safety glass installed on the windshields only and still earlier models did not use it at all. Triplex, as it was called, consisted of a plastic film laminated between two glass panes, which prevented shattering. It derived its name from the words triple and plexus.

All models now had twin windshield wipers. Many body styles had gotten rid of the traditional windshield visor altogether or replaced the leather-covered ones with a dark green glass. The instrument panel was modified to include an engine oil temperature gauge.

The cigar lighter was relocated from the dashboard to the instrument panel. Old-style lighters were the type in which the cigar was inserted into the hole and a pull-down switch turned the heat coil on; unlike the modern pop out cigarette lighters. An electric clock replaced the old spring wound one. However, many coachbuilders had installed electric clocks earlier. The beveled dial speedometer was now supplied by a different vendor.

Still chasing that elusive vibration problem, Lincoln engineers installed rubberized motor mounts this year. A crankshaft damper had been added earlier with minimal results. The engine oil pressure pump now produced 50 psi, an increase of 20 psi and provided much better engine-parts lubrication at higher speeds. Some minor relocating of engine components was done so as to allow easier servicing. An improved starter generator had shown up late in the year. Brake shoes were now graphite-impregnated to reduce squeaking. The parking brake linkage between the rear wheels of the foot brake pedal was eliminated.

1929 LeBaron Aero Phaeton.

In this era of the Ford Tri-Motor and the knee-high hemline skirts, something impressive was needed in the way of automotive styling. Such a coach was provided by LeBaron. A one-off custom called the Aero Phaeton was constructed and shown at the New York Salon. It caused a sensation. The body was polished aluminum and its dual-cowl cockpits had padded and combed upholstery like an open cockpit airplane.

LINCOLN AND CONTINENTAL

A Lincoln all-weather cabriolet, with body by Le Baron, specially designed and built for H. E. Mansville, Esq., of New York, photographed at "Hi-Esmaro," his estate at Pleasantville, New York.

A Lincoln sport roadster, with body by Locke, the property of George U. Harris, Esq., of New York, photographed on his estate at Tuxedo Park, N. Y.

The windshields folded forward like a British racing sports car. The instrument panel had a built-in altimeter, tachometer and compass. There was a small rudder fin attached to the rear of the car. Fenders were more open and straight-lined, simulating wings. Parking lights were styled to look like navigation lights and were located on the fenders. Cowl louvers were horizontal instead of vertical. This custom body creation sold for a little over ten thousand dollars.

A new model of note was the Dietrich Victoria Convertible Coupe that eliminated the sun visor completely. Another desirable collector Lincoln of this year was the Locke Touring, last of the big Sport Phaetons. White leather upholstery was a popular selection on many of these cars. Locke was still using aluminum-skin bodies, but many builders were now switching to steel and some were experimenting with all-metal construction.

The Lincoln factory coachworks now produced the Phaeton type 176. This open car was very reasonably priced in comparison to the more expensive Cabriolets and Broughams. There was one Sedan Convertible body style by Dietrich that, like a few other designs, had removable windows between the door windows. As far as window pattern count, this window should be ignored as in the case of the forward triangle window configurations.

FORD RESOURCES SAFEGUARD *your* LINCOLN

Ford owned sources of supply include iron mines, coal mines, timber tracts, power plants, wood distillation plants, silica beds—in fact, all materials which in any way enter into automobile manufacture

LINCOLN MOTOR COMPANY

The Early Years

Marvin Arnold

CLASSIC MOTORCARS

1929-30 Locke Club Roadster with dickey.

These body types were rare, to say the least. This was the last year in which the type 702 Judkins Coupe and the type 151 Locke Roadster were built. In fact, it was the last year for all of the 150 series and many of the early 160 series. The Dietrich type 171 was fitted with forward opening doors and a sloping windshield to return as the type 181. Approximately seventy one-off customs were produced; this in contrast to the fact that none at all would be built in 1930.

Behind the scenes, change was in the air. Most of the original design work for the Model-L had been accomplished in 1919. As superior and well-engineered as it was, Ford people were now making plans to design a new V-8 engine and develop a more modern chassis. The new chassis would adapt itself to all metal coach work and provide a longer wheelbase on which to install larger custom bodies.

The October issue of the British magazine Autocar said of the Lincoln, "Such a superb motorcar that it is difficult to realize that Henry Ford is associated with it. The new style of coachwork is extremely smart in appearance, but has simple businesslike lines. The Weymann Salon, built by the British Bodyworks sells for about fifty thousand pounds sterling."

The following year, Autocar tested a Lincoln five-passenger Limousine and reported, "A ten to thirty miles per hour time of 5.2 seconds and fuel consumption of twelve miles to the imperial gallon.

Opposite page: 1929 Locke Sport Phaeton, painting by Leslie Saalberg from the Henry Austin Clark, Jr., collection; 1929 Judkins Club Roadster, painting by John M. Peckham from the Behr-Manning Division Norton Company.

The Lincoln makes an interesting comparison to the Hollywood glamour cars like the Isotta-Fraschini." Cadillac and Packard proponents are quick to point out that both were outselling the Lincoln by the end of this decade. Lincoln, however, was only competing at the upper end of the fine car market. This year, for example, Packard produced four times as many cars as Lincoln, but eighty percent of them were sold below the Lincoln's price range. The Cadillac LaSalle was targeted at a market even lower than Packard's market. Thus the Lincoln had reasonably maintained its relative position in the luxury car market.

NINETEEN-THIRTY - In 1930, Lincoln had the lowest production run of any year other than the first year Lincolns were produced. The new body styles offered were types 185 thru 191. As mentioned earlier, if Edsel liked a design he would order an even hundred. This was exactly the number of LeBaron (Detroit) type 185 Convertible Roadsters produced.

Above: 1929 Judkins 2-window Berline, 6-passenger with obtuse windshield. Below: 1930 Judkins 2-window Berline. Many of the cars were shipped to Europe, both to be sold and to be used by their American owners.

Marvin Arnold

The same was true of the Judkins type 186 Berlines and Sedans. The remaining coach orders were sparsely divided among Willoughby Broughams, Derham Phaetons (one was a Roadster), Judkins Coupes and Locke Sports Roadsters. Some of the Willoughby Sedans were called Landaulets. There was at least one Holbrook type 550 Cabriolet built. The balance and by far the bulk, of the year's production were carry-over designs from the previous year.

The Model-L line ended after a total of 65,149 automobiles were produced. These Lincolns represent as diverse and interesting a collection of coachbuilt bodies produced anywhere in the world and are a tribute to the automotive engineering and coachbuilders' craft of this era.

Until now, unless the customer had them refinished, Lincoln fenders were always painted black. For the first time, matching or contrasting fender colors were available. The trend early in this year was to use natural-colored canvas top covers on closed models with matching canvas spare tire covers. Black leather tops and leather spare tire covers were also popular options on closed models.

Pinstriping was used extensively for decoration. There was no real standard for paint striping. It generally followed the mold line or fender lines of the car. Component body structures of metal formed over a wood frame still comprised the bulk of coach construction, but all-metal units were becoming more and more commonplace.

Mechanical changes were headed up by a new Free-Wheeling unit added to the drivetrain. Great volumes have been written on the dubious advantages of this mechanism, which was offered on a variety of makes during this era. The graphite brake shoe inserts were dropped. The change from a roller-type steering gear to a worm-type was heralded as a great improvement. It also reduced the tendency of the Lincoln's front end to shimmy slightly as wear occurred.

By 1930, the embittered Lelands had lost all their court cases and appeals against Ford. Leland's reputation was fading into automotive history. Edsel Ford and the Lincoln people had turned the ugly duckling into a swan. The Lincoln motorcar was now respected on its own merits. If the "L" had originally stood for Leland, it now clearly stood for luxury. The Roaring Twenties were over, a more austere mood had fallen over the land. The Model-L would take its final curtain call this year.

There were still holdouts in the Leland camp who felt that Henry Ford had deliberately set out to cheat Leland and his original stockholders out of the Lincoln Motor Company, but two points help to prove that this was not true. First, Henry Ford did not need to hire the Lelands when he purchased the Company from bankruptcy. Second, the Lelands' claims were based on alleged verbal promises between the two Henrys.

Opposite page: Left to Right: 1930 Judkins 2-window Berline; 1929 Lincoln factory Limousine; 1930 LeBaron Roadster; 1929 Lincoln factory 5-window Coupe; 1930 Limousine; 1930 Sport Phaeton; 1930 Landau Berline. Above: 1930 5-passenger Sedan. Below: 1930 7-passenger Limousine. Right: 1930 LeBaron All-Weather Cabriolet.

That Lincoln would not become part of Ford Motor Company and that the original stockholders would be reimbursed for their lost investments. Henry Ford was often a poor communicator and sometimes a vindictive man, but dishonesty was not inherent to his nature. Obviously, each man felt he had made a different agreement. Henry Ford was powerful and rich enough to make his viewpoint prevail and Henry Leland was no longer the automotive giant he once was.

As a result of Ford Motor Company stockholder demands, Henry Ford withdrew as president of his own company, but he still very much controlled things. This new decade would belong to other men of vision. By far the greatest tribute to Henry M. Leland is the long time his automotive design endured and the decision by Ford not to tamper with the basic design until it was well established in the marketplace.

It was now the height of America's great economic depression, but through it all the Lincoln motorcar endured as a symbol of prestige and luxury. The Lincoln Motor Company goal stated that, "The ideal Lincoln owner is a man of means who enjoys economics. The Lincoln owner usually has both town and country homes, moving conveniently among them. The Lincoln owner considers the world his playground and his base of operations. His Lincoln carries him far, swiftly and luxuriously.

The ideal Lincoln owner has exceedingly high standards of taste. He enjoys the faultless upholstery, fittings and furnishings. An owner does not have to be an engineer to appreciate his Lincoln, although such authorities throughout the world proclaim the Lincoln as fine a motorcar as it is possible to produce."

Lincoln achieved its goal of becoming a fine American motorcar and this was effectively carried out by the same company, which gave us the Model-T Ford. Lincoln historians A.T. Heinsbergen and T.L. Powels observed that, "We cannot help but look back at the great Model-L, it was the car that became the prestige car of America to discriminating European buyers. The car whose bodies were designed by the most talented men in a talented time, it is the Lincoln that is most often found still in the hands of the original owner, perhaps on blocks in his garage. Explained simply by, it's been part of my life."

Those who are Lincoln motorcar enthusiasts are much like train buffs, airport bums, or antique collectors. They may not own their original Lincoln, but may now own that Lincoln they could not afford in their youth and always wanted. Whether original owners, collectors, restorers, historians, or just plain Lincoln watchers, that favorite model is still up on blocks in the garage of their memory and imagination.

CHAPTER FOUR

THE LINCOLN COACHBUILDERS

An American Carrossiers Who's Who

Although custom coachbuilding came into its glory in the 1920s, the 1930s were to be its finest hour. The coachbuilding art form was to all but fade away by the end of that decade as the large auto makers recognized the need for appealing to the buyer through coach styling.

In years past, automobiles were purchased on their reputation for dependability. By the mid-1920s, most manufacturers were building reliable and well performing motorcars. Custom luxury coach body building merits a separate chapter in the automotive history. Indeed, whole books have been written on some of these legend-makers. Americans in general love to tinker and have produced over four thousand brands of automobiles.

Automobile coachbuilding clearly evolved from the craft of carriage building. The pioneer coachbuilders who made the greatest impact on automotive body styling were, however, the younger and more creative newcomers to the art form. The custom hot rod builders of the late 50s, like George Barris of California, were probably the end of this era. Now, the kit car craze has brought auto building full circle, once again returning to thousands of different makes and styles of custom automobiles.

There were about one hundred coachbuilders of any notoriety in the 1920s and early 1930s. Many survived in business for only a brief period and few ever really produced any volume of auto bodies. Of course, anyone could build a custom body on a Lincoln as they can today. However, only a select few coachbuilders were engaged by the Lincoln Motor Company to do so.

Builders contracted directly by Lincoln were American Anderson, Babcock, Brunn, Derham, Dietrich, Fleetwood, Holbrook, Judkins, Lang, LeBaron, Locke, Murray, Towson and Willoughby in the 1920s. Murphy, Rollston and Waterhouse were added in the 1930s. Anderson Electric Car Company along with the newly formed Towson, were originally contracted by Leland to build the Model-L bodies. The Towson Body Company of Detroit, Michigan, became known for their work on Packards and built medium-priced bodies for the Velie and Davis automobiles.

Anderson did business under the Towson name after 1922. Both companies, by 1925, became part of the Murray Corporation of America, which had been founded in Detroit in 1912. The J.C. Widman Company was also merged into Murray in 1925. During its five-year existence, Widman originated the custom two-door sedan called the Earl Brougham and built bodies for the Jewett, Chalmers and Franklin.

The C.R. Wilson Body Company in Detroit had built carriages since 1873. In the early 1920s, they began building high-priced automobile bodies on Packard and Lincoln chassis. Wilson was purchased and became part of Murray in 1927. Murray also absorbed several smaller firms to become the third largest coachbuilder. Murray had one of the first automobile coach design studios, headed by Amos Northrup, who came to Murray from Wills Sainte Claire in 1924. Northrup collaborated with Ray Dietrich the following year to produce bodies for the Packard, Hupmobile, Jordan, Reo and Lincoln. Murray Corporation still produces automobile components.

LINCOLN

Salon Favorites

Among the finest motor cars of this country and Europe exhibited at the New York Salon, high favor was given to Lincoln. Four distinctly different Lincoln body types were favorites—a seven passenger Limousine, a Convertible Sedan, a Convertible Coupe, and a five passenger open Phaeton.

To win popular favor in so wide a range of appeal, is a sweeping endorsement of the custom body policy of the Lincoln Motor Car Company.

Every Lincoln body model is the creation of a master custom body builder. It is not merely a passing sensation, but truly artistic and correct in line and proportion—lastingly beautiful. Its finish, appointments and upholstery are rich in quality but in every detail the restraint of good taste and simplicity is evident. Color combinations, in wide variety, sparkle with beauty and originality, yet never offend by too obviously seeking attention.

Lincoln custom bodies are designed to emulate the well balanced excellence of the Lincoln chassis. It is not enough that Lincoln shall be outstanding in any one feature; but rather it must be so outstanding in every feature of fine car quality and performance that it will satisfy every requirement. With brilliant speed, acceleration and beauty, there must also be smoothness of operation, stamina, long life, riding luxury, ease and sureness of control, safety, and economy.

Each and every feature must contribute its full part to the perfection of the Lincoln car as a whole.

This is the ideal of Lincoln builders—and back of Lincoln are all the resources of the Ford engineering and manufacturing organization.

The Convertible Sedan as a beautiful open Phaeton—note the fleet trimness of the lines and the unusual arrangement of the plate glass in the doors now converted into front and side windshields.

LINCOLN MOTOR COMPANY
DIVISION OF FORD MOTOR COMPANY

Lincoln cars range in price from $4600 to $7300, completely equipped at Detroit

1932 Model KB Rollston Town Car

American Body Company began in 1919 in Buffalo, New York. They produced Model-L bodies and other medium-priced auto bodies, specializing in open Tourings. American was out of business by 1926. The H.H. Babcock Company had started as wagon builders in the 1890s. From their facilities in Watertown, Massachusetts, they built light delivery trucks and Town Cars on long wheelbases. They built chassis for Dodge and Franklin until going out of business in 1926. Babcock built a few Model-A Duesenberg and Model-L Lincoln bodies.

Rauch & Lang of Cleveland, Ohio, was founded in 1899. They began building electric cars in 1904. In 1916, they merged with Baker Vehicle Company who built electric car parts and car bodies and manufactured the Owen-Magnetic car. Baker, Rauch & Lang then purchased the Leon Rubay Company of Cleveland at bankruptcy in 1922. The company was also known as Baker-Raulang.

At the 1929 Auto Salons, they displayed their Ruxton Town Car. A few quality custom bodies and production bodies were built by them for Stearn-Knight and Peerless. Baker-Raulang ceased auto body production in 1939, but remains in business as suppliers of body parts and electronic equipment. The Lang Body Company of Cleveland, Ohio, sold their interest in Rauch & Lang Carriage Company and began building semi-custom bodies for

Dodge. Several early Model-L Lincoln bodies were built by them. It was a family owned business started in 1920 and was out of business by 1924.

Holbrook Company was founded by H.F. Holbrook in West Manhattan, New York City. It was moved to Hudson, New York, in 1921. They were best known for their Phaeton and Town Car bodies on Packard and Crane-Simplex chassis. They built several of the first Duesenberg Model-J coaches and various Lincoln custom coaches in 1925 and 1926. The most popular Lincoln body style that Holbrook built was the Collapsible Cabriolet. It was first shown at the 1925 New York Automobile Salon. About forty of these cars were built through 1929. On this Cabriolet, the chauffeur's top snapped off and the rear compartment could be folded down like a Landaulet. Its predecessor was the Holbrook Brougham, produced in 1925.

R.L. Stickney's drawing of this motorcar appears in the November 1924 issues of The Lincoln Magazine, Salon Issue. These two designs are excellent examples of the terms Brougham and Cabriolet. In this case, however, the Brougham lacked the all-weather driver's tarp. Harry Holbrook left his namesake company in 1927 to build cars with Henry Brewster at the old Blue Ribbon Carriage works at Bridgeport, Connecticut, for two years. The original Holbrook Company went bankrupt in May of 1930 and many employees including Hjalmar Holm, the sales manager, went over to the Rollston coach works. Holbrook had, for some time, been sending its repair business to Rollston.

Marvin Arnold

CLASSIC MOTORCARS

The Rollston Company of New York City was started in 1921 mainly to provide wealthy Easterners with custom bodies for their imported Rolls-Royces. The firm quickly expanded into other expensive bodies like Packard and Stutz. Rollston built the famous Duesenberg Convertible Victoria and several custom Lincoln Town Cars.

Drawings of these designs by George Hildebrand remain valuable collector items today. Rollston's founder retired in 1939 and the company relocated to Plainview, New York, continuing to build bodies for Packard until the beginning of World War II. It remains in business today, fabricating galleys for aircraft.

Budd Manufacturing Company, on occasion, has been listed as a Lincoln coachbuilder, but very few Lincoln bodies were ever custom produced by Budd. Edward G. Budd was actually more famous as a railroad car builder.

Top: Early Model L Willoughby Town Sedan. Bottom: 1932 Brunn Cabriolet. Opposite page: Left to Right: 1936 Willoughby Convertible Sedan; 1932 KB Willoughby Limousine; 1930 Willoughby Model L; 1933 Model K Brunn Victoria; 1934 Judkins Limousine; 1935 Brunn Convertible Sport Sedan; 1930 Brunn All-Weather Brougham.

He designed and built rail cars of lightweight riveted aluminum for the M-10000 and the Pioneer Zephyr. Budd was one of the first coachbuilders to produce all-steel coach bodies for automobiles.

A company occasionally listed as a Lincoln coachbuilder was Guider-Sweetland and its surviving company of Sierers & Erdman were founded in Detroit in 1913. Guider-Sweetland built ambulances and burial coaches on Lincoln chassis until the late 1930s. Central Manufacturing Company of Connersville, Indiana, is also sometimes mentioned but they too built only a few customs. Central was absorbed into Auburn-Cord.

The original Central Manufacturing complex operated almost continually for forty years and even built Jeeps during World War II. One additional company, Cunningham Sons of Rochester, New York, built a few one-off Lincolns. Founded in the 1890s, they manufactured their own V-8 engines from 1916 through 1934. During the mid-thirties, they also built custom bodied cars on Ford chassis.

The Derham Body Company of Rosemont, Pennsylvania, was founded as a carriage builder in 1884. They were known in the 1920s for their Lincoln, Packard and Pierce-Arrow Town Cars. In 1928, the Floyd-Derham Company was formed to build custom bodies at the old Alexander Woflington's Sons Company facility in Philadelphia.

This operation was short lived. Derham Body Company was famous for their Chrysler convertibles in the thirties. Today, Wolfington builds school buses and the Derham company custom builds expensive limousines.

Locke & Company began in 1902 as a quality body builder in New York City. They were known for their exquisite finishes and distinctive Town Cars. In 1926, the company relocated to Rochester, New York. Increasing numbers of orders were placed by the Chrysler, Franklin and Lincoln companies. Locke was best known for its early Lincoln Phaetons.

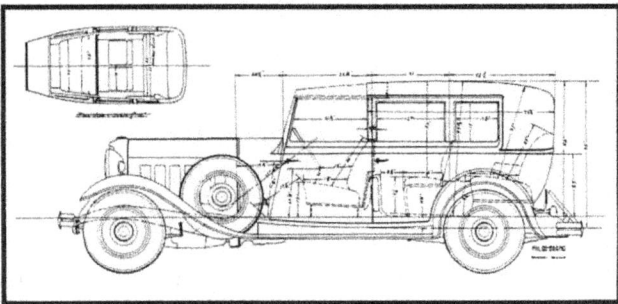
Rollston drawing by Hildebrand.

Roadster by Locke.

Derham Sport Sedan.

Derham Roadster.

In November of 1929, at the 25th Annual Chicago Automobile Salon, Locke displayed a five-passenger Sedan on a Ruxton front-wheel-drive chassis. The design was unusually low in profile while still providing ample headroom, had no running boards and was all black without body molding or striping.

The following year, a similar design was built on a Chrysler convertible. The Locke 1930 Lincoln Roadster had a totally disappearing top that folded into a recess behind the seat and was covered by a deck panel. Locke & Company was, however, out of business by 1933. Walter M. Murphy was related to Henry Leland and had been authorized as one of the original Lincoln distributors. Located in Pasadena, California, the Murphy Company began modifying the early Model-L Lincolns from the outset.

Murphy also built custom coach bodies on the Rolls-Royce and on the Model-J Duesenberg for the West Coast elite. The firm was an unauthorized Lincoln coachbuilder until 1932, when Lincoln contracted with them to build type 43 Phaetons and three different types of Sport Roadsters. Shortly afterward, Murphy Company ceased to do business. Former Murphy employees Bohman & Schwartz continued the business under their own names until 1938.

The Lehmann Manufacturing Company started building wagons in Indiana one hundred years after the American Revolution. They evolved into Lehmann-Peterson Company at Indianapolis by 1925, producing replacement bodies for the Model-T Ford. They also built ambulance bodies and other commercial vehicles, including several White House Lincoln limousines. The firm is still in business today as an automobile alteration facility.

The name Fleetwood is generally associated with Cadillac but it originated in 1905 with the Reading Metal Company, servicing companies like Duryea and Chadwick. In 1912, the officers of the company started a new operation at Fleetwood, Pennsylvania, about twenty miles from Reading. They built coaches on most of the major U.S. chassis including Daniels, Lincoln and Packard, as well as on imports such as Isotta-Fraschini and Maybach.

Fleetwood Metal Body Company became famous for all-metal coach designs and was

1932 Murphy Roadster.

purchased by General Motors in 1925. A facility was set up for Fleetwood in Detroit, as a division of Fisher Body and they began building Cadillac bodies in 1933. The older Pennsylvania facility continued to build coaches for Stutz and imported luxury cars until 1931, after General Motors had acquired ownership. The Fleetwood's New York sales office was opened in 1918 at 2 Columbus Circle, the same location that LeBaron had begun business in 1923.

An example of a Fleetwood built LeBaron design was the 1923 Roadster for Rudolph Valentino. The actor was also an accomplished auto mechanic and ordered a full-length running board tool box. Fleetwood built several hundred custom Lincoln Model-L coach bodies. A few of these coaches were not delivered until after Fleetwood's merger into Fisher Body of GM. This may have been the closest General Motors and Ford ever came to becoming co-manufacturers.

The Utica, New York, building where the Willoughby & Company coach works was located is still used as a machine shop. Francis W. Willoughby and J. Vinton Locke both attended school at Hamilton College. In 1908, Willoughby set up his company to serve the new wealthy industrialists in and around the Mohawk Valley. The firm built semi-custom bodies for Lincolns on the order of twenty-five to one hundred per run. Willoughby coaches were best known for their conservative lines and fine workmanship. They also built bodies for the Cole and the Wills Sainte Claire automobiles. Willoughby coach craftsman were exceedingly accomplished at building to a standard chassis. Packard and Lincoln bodies built by Willoughby would quite often interchange.

In some cases, a Touring body could be detached and the particular chassis fitted with a new Town Car body. Willoughby was best known for producing fine Town Cars. With the decline of chauffeur-driven cars in the thirties, their market was particularly hard hit. Willoughby had done very well in 1932 with new designs for the Lincoln Model-K. Afterward, they suffered some decline.

Judkins' 1929 Model L 2-window Berline; 1932 Model KB Coupe; 1935 Sedan Limousine; and 1936 Berline. Note that all have front-front doors.

1932 Model KB by Judkins.

Willoughby managed to stay in business until 1938. When, they closed, chief designer, Martin Regitko, went to work at Ford's Lincoln design facility in the styling section.

Herman A. Brunn had worked in his uncle's carriage shop as a young man in Buffalo, New York. Many, if not almost all of the successful carrossiers and great coach designers had served an apprenticeship in a good coachbuilding shop. Brunn worked briefly for Babcock Company in Watertown and then took over management of the Andrew Joyce Carriage Company in Washington. He returned to Buffalo and founded Brunn & Company in 1908.

Through the twenties and until they closed in 1941, Brunn enjoyed a fine reputation. It was only natural that Edsel Ford, after acquiring Lincoln, would turn to LeBaron and Brunn for creative designs. Edsel would approach each one separately with similar suggestions and they would work independently until their design concepts were completed.

At the 1927 New York Automobile Salon, Brunn displayed a yellow and brown Convertible Victoria, one of the earliest built in this country. They also displayed a Phaeton painted aluminum and black, a favorite Edsel Ford color scheme.

Another interesting Lincoln custom was built for a physician friend of Herman Brunn and shown in 1931 at the last New York Auto Salon. It was a double-entry two-door Sedan, with doors that opened from either end and had a special latching mechanism, which had been first tried on the European Pinin Farina. Only a few were ever built.

Many of the Brunn Model-L Lincoln designs were reproduced by Towson, American and Lang. A Lincoln factory photo shows a Brunn Town Cars in front of the Buffalo Fine Arts Museum, a favorite photographing location.

Brunn built many of the LeBaron designs, including the Ford family's personal cars. The friendship and personal ties between the Brunn and Ford families grew. The last Lincoln and Packard custom bodies built by Brunn & Company were the 1938 and 1939 models. They were of the Landaulet styles on which the aft part of the passenger compartment had a convertible top. In 1940 and 1941, Brunn custom built the Buick series 90 Limousines at the request of Buick's president Harlow Curtice, who had been unable to get them from Fleetwood. In 1942, the youngest brother, H.C. Brunn, went to work for the Lincoln styling section at Detroit and became one of Lincoln's most innovative interior designers.

The Judkins, Merrimac and Waterhouse Companies were loosely related. The John B. Judkins Company was founded in 1857 at West Amesbury, Massachusetts. The municipality of Amesbury was later renamed Merrimac and known as Carriage Hill because so many coachbuilding shops were located in that part of New England. Judkins' partner was Isaac Little. His two sons joined the company, Frederick B. in 1883 and Charles H. in 1891. About five years before the turn of the century, Judkins began building automobile bodies for Colonel Pope of Hartford. The firm built luxury Brougham horse carriages until about 1910, at which time they went exclusively to automobile coachbuilding.

1932 Model KB Coupe by Dietrich.

In the early years, Judkins built over a thousand bodies for the Winton Motor Car Company. In 1918, Stanley L. Judkins opened Merrimac Body Company to handle the overflow work from the main Judkins plant. It mostly produced Packards and DuPont bodies and was closed in 1933. Sergeant and Charles Waterhouse worked for Judkins prior to forming their own coachbuilding company in 1928.

Waterhouse custom built several styles of Lincoln coach bodies until 1933. The famous Ford stylist John F. Dobben worked at Judkins in the 1920s and designer/artist R. L. Stickney went to work at Judkins when LeBaron closed its New York offices to avoid a move to Detroit. One of the notable designs built by Judkins was the Lincoln Coupe deVoyage. It was a personal favorite of Mr. Judkins and was drafted by Herman A. Kapp and Hugo Pfau of LeBaron.

The famous 1926 Lincoln Model-L Coaching Brougham, based on the Concord stagecoach, was built by Judkins. This rare coachbuilt was on display at Henry Ford's Wayside Inn for years. Judkins also built the custom body coach for cowboy movie star Tom Mix's, a Pierce-Arrow Club Coupe. The main Judkins facility continued to build auto bodies until 1938.

The coachbuilder's story that most profoundly impacted the early Lincolns was that of Raymond H. Dietrich. Actually, the story begins at Brewster and moves through the LeBaron, Murray and Briggs companies. As a youth in New York, Ray Dietrich worked as an apprentice engineer. He was inclined to study art, but instead was attracted to the automobile trade and interviewed with Brewster & Company at Long Island City.

Henry Cresilius, chief engineer for Brewster, introduced Dietrich to William H. Brewster. Cresilius would later go to work for the Ford Motor Company. Brewster & Company built Ford Town Car coach bodies into the 1930s under the supervision of J.S. Inscip. Inscip also worked on the English Jensen design. During the early development of the original Lincoln Continental, both Brewster and Derham were considered as body contractors on the project. As it turned out, both facilities combined could not have handled even the relatively small number of Continentals eventually produced.

Dietrich had graduated from a design course given by Andrew F. Johnson, a carriage draftsman and soon became one of Brewster's most progressive designers. Ray Dietrich left Brewster for a short period to work at Chevrolet, but returned to work on the new Brewster-Knight automobile project.

It was during this time that he and Thomas L. Hibbard became friends. Hibbard went to Europe during World War I. He wanted to stay and work at the Kellner studio in Paris, but was shipped home with the rest of the Dough Boys after the Armistice.

Hibbard and Dietrich were planning to start their own company and Brewster fired them both when he found out they were peddling their own designs on the side. They selected the name LeBaron Carrossiers, Inc. and moved into 2 Columbus Circle. LeBaron was the French-sounding name of a doctor friend of Dietrich's family and Carrossier is French for coachbuilder. The building on Columbus Circle conveniently housed the New York offices of Fleetwood.

Ralph Roberts, a young Dartmouth graduate, joined LeBaron as the business manager. When Al Jolson came to order a coach design at LeBaron, he gave Roberts complementary tickets to his New York show and that night, while on stage, wisecracked that his performance should be worth a discount on his new LeBaron. Jolson loved fine cars. When taking the train into New York or Boston he would have his chauffeur make the trip by car to meet the train and drive him around town.

Jolson was a perceptive man and decades ahead in his automobile tastes and he asserted, "Make it low and sleek, so low I have to bend over to get in," he would tell the designers of his cars." Since they had no facility of their own, the LeBaron staff worked as contract coach designers.

Marvin Arnold

They sold prospective drawings for $25 apiece to Manhattan auto dealers like Captain D'Annunzio, son of the poet Gabriele and the local Isotta representative. Other customers included Milton Budlong of Lincoln and Paul Ostruk of Minerva. Ostruk resold the LeBaron-designed coachbuilts under their own logo, Body by Ostruk. New York Governor C. Parvis, the Packard coach body purchasing agent, commissioned LeBaron to design a limousine that became the benchmark for many subsequent Packard limousines. From their proposal drawings, Tom Hibbard and Ray Dietrich often got the job of providing the working drawings. Thus, an additional and larger fee could be charged.

Early techniques that gave these coach bodies lower and more flowing lines were methods like lowering the headlight mounting and incorporating the famous LeBaron Sweep. The LeBaron Sweep was a manipulation of the body's visual focal point. It basically centered on a flowing mold line, which formed over the cowl and around the top of the doors. Two-tone paint schemes were also used to break up the appearance of body size and accent the LeBaron Sweep.

Milton Budlong who operated York Motors, the Lincoln dealership, told Ray Dietrich, I can't sell the Model-L. They are too conservative up against the three Ps (Packard, Peerless and Pierce-Arrow) and the imports. I'd like you to build me a sport Phaeton for the New York Salon."

The custom Lincoln Phaeton was built at the Smith-Springfield body works in eighteen days. Milton was delighted, as was Edsel Ford, when he saw the car. Raymond Dietrich and Edsel Ford met for the first time in the fall of 1922 at the 23rd New York Auto Salon. It was about this time that Frank deCausse from Locomobile and Roland L. Stickney arrived on the scene at LeBaron. R.L. Stickney's watercolor drawings of this periods coach designs have become collector's items.

Opposite page: Left to Right: LeBaron KB Convertible Roadster; 1930 Model L Dietrich Convertible Coupe; 1930 Model L LeBaron All-Weather Cabriolet; 1935 LeBaron Coupe with padded roof; 1936 long wheelbase LeBaron Convertible Sedan; 1936 Briggs Zephyr.

Art work by Stickney and Hibbard appeared in popular magazines of the time like Town & Country, Vanity Fair and Country Life. Thomas Hibbard departed for Paris in March of 1923. He eventually started a business there, as he had wanted to years before, with Howard A. "Dutch" Darrin. Early Hibbard-Darrin coaches were built at the Van den Plas facility in Belgium. Darrin returned to the United States in 1938 and set up a custom shop on Sunset Strip in Los Angeles. After World War II, his shop built the Kaiser prototype. Today the shop custom fits Rolls-Royce bodies for West Coast dealers.

By 1924, LeBaron had become the most successful new group of designers in the coachbuilding industry. LeBaron was now a major supplier of custom coach working drawings and Ray Dietrich personally supervised the work on many of the projects, traveling from shop to shop and spending a great deal of time at Bridgeport, Connecticut. Bridgeport Body Company merged with LeBaron after the failure of Locomobile. The former owners of Bridgeport built custom station wagons and Packard coach bodies until the mid-thirties.

The A.T. Demarest & Company, an old New Haven coachbuilder, moved to New York in the early 1920s. They built several different LeBaron designed bodies for Locomobile and Sportif. The Clayton Company of New York also built several custom LeBaron bodies. The Humer-Binder Company built early LeBaron bodies and is still in business in New York. They were the main service and repair center for early LeBaron coach bodies.

One of Ray Dietrich's favorite stories was of an attorney who owned a Renault coachbuilt. The counselor complained to Ray that the body always squeaked. Dietrich had the attorney take the car in to one of the local coach shops. Dietrich used an old trick of shooting the inner body with graphite to stop the squeak; it always worked, at least for a while. Later, during a luncheon, Ray asked the same attorney to look over a contract he was considering signing as a personal favor. The attorney did and later sent Ray a bill for $400 with a note saying that one cannot use a professional's time for free. Ray replied with a $500 invoice for the coach repairs and a similar note.

1932 Lincoln Coachbuilts (left to right): Waterhouse Convertible Victoria; Judkins' Coupe; 3-window and 2-window Berline; Dietrich's Convertible Sedan and Sport Berline; Brunn's All-Weather Brougham and All-Weather Cabriolet; Willoughby's Panel Brougham and Limousine. Lincoln Twelve Cylinder Motorcars all had long hood with cowl doors. Judkins and Dietrich offered V-windshield, most body style had front-front door arrangements. The body styles shown were offered on the Model KB long 145 inch wheelbase, although a few were also offered on the Model KA shorter 136 inch wheelbase.

By 1925, Edsel Ford was prevailing upon Raymond Dietrich, mostly through Allen Sheldon the president of Murray Corporation, to open a design shop in Detroit. Larry Fisher of General Motors was also after Dietrich. Ralph Roberts, now half-owner of LeBaron, was against the move entirely, but this new challenge was just what Ray was looking for. Besides, Edsel had agreed that Dietrich could continue doing independent designs and consulting.

Ray was set up in Detroit as the Dietrich Custom Body Company under Murray Corporation of America. Before long, Ray wanted to do more than concept work and so Dietrich, Inc. was founded. During this period, some of the finest luxury car body designs were created. The last Raymond Dietrich Lincoln production design built was a 1934 Model-K.

Dietrich himself lost a personal fortune with the decline of the Salon Catalogue market. He was even more vulnerable than most of the coachbuilders as he had less of customizing trade to fall back on. He left the company he had founded in 1932 and the following year Dietrich, Inc. was merged into Murray Corporation. In addition to his friendship with Edsel Ford, Ray Dietrich also had a friend in Walter P. Chrysler and worked at Chrysler as a design consultant.

Walter warned him, however, that Chrysler was ruled by iron-willed mechanical engineers and that all work would be on cars planned for mass production. Dietrich took the job anyway and remained until Walter Chrysler, his champion, died in 1940. The Chrysler LeBaron today is named more in honor of Raymond Dietrich than for his former design company.

While at Chrysler, Dietrich upgraded the modeling procedures, taught at the Chrysler Institute of Engineering and influenced design concepts for years to come. In semi-retirement, Dietrich created one last custom-designed coachbuilt for the Ford family and designed the 1950 Lincoln White House parade car. The American motorcar industry was made a better place because of Raymond H. Dietrich.

Ralph Roberts ran LeBaron after Dietrich left, but was not well known for his design talents. However, Roberts had some very talented people working under him. People like R.L. Stickney, Hugo Pfau and Ray Birge were still at LeBaron. Ray Birge was the former manager of the Bridgeport facility. After Ray set up business in Detroit, Roberts contacted him explaining that he was having difficulty managing LeBaron as a minority stockholder. Dietrich agreed to sell his interest in LeBaron to Roberts. Edsel Ford had been pushing LeBaron, Murray and Briggs for greater Lincoln production quotas.

The Briggs Manufacturing Company of Detroit had been founded in 1909 by Walter Briggs, a former Ford plant manager. His company specialized in high-production, inexpensive closed coach bodies and had been a major Ford Motor Company subcontractor for years. LeBaron had lots of luxury car experience, but in low production numbers.

Briggs had the opposite experience and both wanted Lincoln's business. It was a shotgun wedding at best. Imagine Ray Dietrich's surprise in 1926 when Ford vice-president, George Walker told him that LeBaron had been purchased by Briggs for a considerable sum.

In 1928, Briggs acquired the Phillips Custom Body Company of Warren, Ohio. It was an old family owned carriage company that had turned to auto body building in the early twenties. Phillips' general manager Ed Carter became a major asset to the Briggs organization. Briggs of Detroit should not be confused with the Briggs Carriage Company of Amesbury, Massachusetts. The latter was founded in 1876 and began building automobile carriages as early as 1908. They built the early steam Locomobiles, but ceased auto production altogether in 1920.

The new LeBaron-Briggs company was called LeBaron-Detroit Company and operated under that name until 1941. The Lincoln Model-K bodies by LeBaron were built at Detroit and totaled 412 Coupes and 413 Convertible Sedans. The body building facilities were purchased and most of the talent was absorbed, by Chrysler in 1948 after Walter Briggs' death. LeBaron, Inc. maintained a New York office until 1930.

During the mid-thirties, Briggs became well known for their streamlined Airflow and Zephyr designs. One of the last LeBaron-Briggs designs was Alex Tremulis' Chrysler Thunderbolt and Arrow.

S. A. E. Standard Names for Body Types

MOTOR AGE
May 4, 1922

The Society of Automotive Engineers committee on body names has reported to the parent society and the names given below have been adopted as standard by that organization.

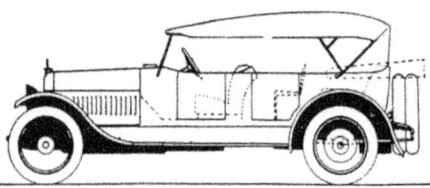

PHAETON
An open type body with two fixed cross seats for four or five passengers. Folding seats in the tonneau for two additional passengers are sometimes used. The conventional body has four doors and a folding top with removable side curtains. This car is commonly known as a touring model, but it was decided to call it a phaeton, as all types of cars are now used for touring purposes.

COUPE
An enclosed single compartment body with one fixed cross seat. This seat may be straight and accommodate two persons, or be staggered and accommodate three persons. With the latter arrangement, a folding seat may be placed beside the driver's seat. The conventional body has two doors and two movable glass windows on each side. The roof is permanent and there is a luggage compartment at the rear.

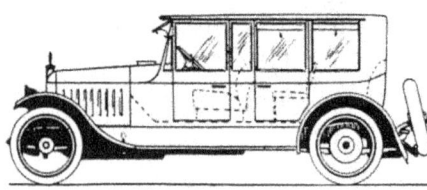

BERLINE
A body of the same general description as the sedan, except that there is a partition at the rear of the driver's seat that makes it an enclosed two-compartment body. Generally one glass window in the partition is made so that it can be moved horizontally or vertically.

ROADSTER
An open-type body, having one fixed cross seat for two passengers and a space or compartment at the rear for luggage. Folding seats fitting into the luggage compartment are sometimes used. The conventional type has two doors and a folding top with removable side curtains.

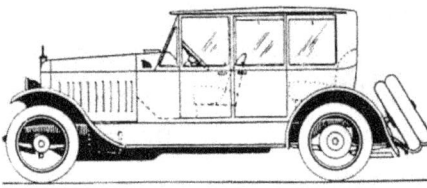

SEDAN
An enclosed single compartment body with two fixed cross seats for four or five passengers. Sometimes the front seat is divided by an aisle. Folding seats in the tonneau for two additional passengers are sometimes used. The conventional body has four doors, but some models have only two. There are three movable glass windows on each side and the roof is noncollapsible.

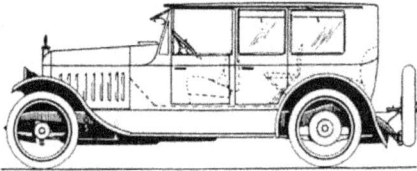

LIMOUSINE
A partially enclosed body with a non-collapsible roof that extends the full length and is attached at the front to the windshield. Only the rear portion of the body up to the partition at the rear of the driver's seat is fully enclosed. There are two low doors and one fixed cross seat for two in the forward section. Folding seats for two additional passengers are sometimes used. There are two doors and two movable glass windows on each side.

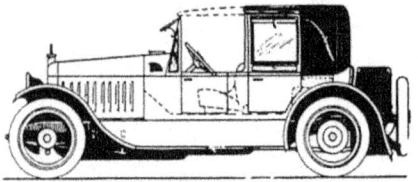

CABRIOLET
A body similar in appearance to the brougham and having the general characteristics of the landaulet, except that the falling pillar hinge is set back from the pillar line. The rear section is, therefore, longer than that of the landaulet. The body has one fixed cross seat for two or three, and folding seats on the partition for two additional passengers. Doors in the rear section are made with either flappers or hinged upper parts, and there are glass windows in the doors only. The top is fully collapsible, including the partition at the back of the driver's seat. The upper rear quarters, the back and the top are covered with leather or fabric and, in the conventional design, the top quarter at both the sides and the back have larger radii than other types of closed bodies. There are outside joints to support the top.

SEDAN LANDAULET
A body of the same general description as the sedan, except that the top back of the rear doors is collapsible.

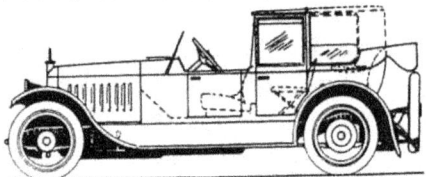

BROUGHAM LANDAULET
A body that bears the same relation to the brougham as the sedan does to the sedan landaulet.

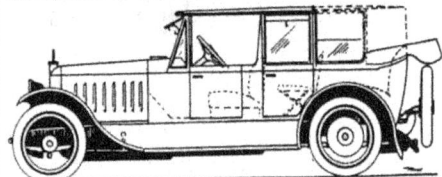

LIMOUSINE LANDAULET
A body that bears the same relation to the limousine as the sedan landaulet bears to the sedan.

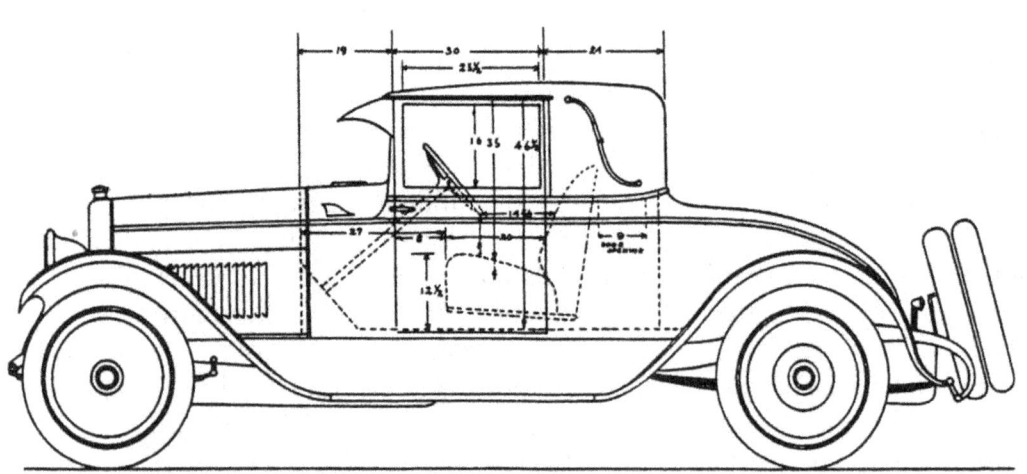

JUDKINS COUPE, TWO-PASSENGER, TYPE 702

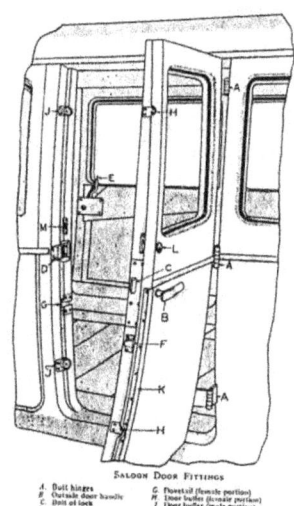

LINCOLN AND CONTINENTAL

Mrs. Morgan Belmont and friend egress her custom coach body sedan with rear-front doors. Lowering the coach top too much sometimes caused stepping onto a runningboard to become a less than graceful feat.

AUTOMOBILE SALON
Presenting the Aristocracy of Motordom

COMMODORE HOTEL, New York
Auspices Automobile Merchants Ass'n of New York, Inc.
November 29—December 5, 1931

DRAKE HOTEL, Chicago
Auspices, Chicago Automobile Trade Ass'n.
January 30—February 6, 1932

HOTEL BILTMORE, Los Angeles
February 13-20, 1932

PALACE HOTEL, San Francisco
February 27—March 5, 1932

THE AUTOMOBILE SALON presents annually to a discriminating and distinguished clientele, all that is really meritorious in high-grade motor cars, custom coachwork, and the various accessories thereto, admirably staged in a beautiful and appropriate setting and on a scale commensurate with the importance and character of the products exhibited.

The world's foremost carrossiers will present a brilliant ensemble of new creations in custom coachwork. Six nations, England, France, Belgium, Germany, Italy and the United States are represented this season.

On Exhibition

CADILLAC	FRANKLIN	MAYBACH	PIERCE-ARROW
CHRYSLER IMPERIAL	ISOTTA FRASCHINI	MARMON	ROLLS-ROYCE
DELAGE	LANCIA	MINERVA	STUTZ
DUESENBERG	LINCOLN	PACKARD	

Coachwork Exhibits by

AMBI BUDD	FLEETWOOD	LE BARON	WALKER
BREWSTER	HAYES	MURPHY	WATERHOUSE
BRUNN	JUDKINS	ROLLSTON	WEYMANN
DIETRICH			WILLOUGHBY

The World's Finest Motor Cars

The new president of Chrysler was K.T. Keller. Like Edsel Ford, he always tried to encourage talent. Keller remarked one time that the Thunderbolt looked like a streamlined Budd train. It was modern with straight slab fenders,

pre-World War II, pre GM future car and ten years ahead in styling.

LINCOLN COACH BODY TERMS - The Lincoln Model-L and Model-K coachbuilts followed the traditional luxury body styling of the 1920s and 1930s. The French term Cabriolet originally applied to a collapsible top carriage with doors, usually two. Most early motorcar Cabriolet styles had a rag top over the first two-doors or driver's compartment only. In later years, the term Cabriolet was used for several classically styled four-passenger, three-window Convertible Coupes.

Whether coupe or sedan, a true Cabriolet style is an automobile that has the ability to open partially over the driver's area and also to be fully opened. The term All-Weather can mean almost anything, but it generally applies to the ability of the vehicle to carry its own removable top. Many terms are used interchangeably in describing model and body styles Refer to the glossary in the back of this book, which will provide some general definitions.

There are no precise rules on the use of many of these terms. For example, a difference that is generally accepted between a Roadster and Convertible Coupe is that the Roadster has sidecurtains and the Convertible has roll-up windows, although many models of Convertibles are referred to as Roadsters.

The large rear compartment lids on Coupes and Roadsters usually had an auxiliary seat called a dicky (or dickey) being an early name for the rumble seat. Auxiliary seating is a more general term that might also refer to the small rear bench seat in a coupe or the foldaway seats in a limousine.

Another commonly used term was Victoria and describes a deluxe two-door sedan. It later became the proper name for a given body style like the Convertible Victoria. An earlier popular name for a single bench seat coupe was the Doctor's Coupe and sometimes a Business Coupe for the long trunk that would hold sample cases.

A Berline is a style of closed sedan named for the capital of Germany, but pronounced Bur-lean. Use of this term was dropped as America entered World War II. Another term for an often unclear body style is that of Brougham. It was named after Henry P. Brougham, a carriage builder of the early 1800s and refers to a closed carriage with an open driver's seat.

Brougham is sometimes confused with Herman Brunn, a contemporary coachbuilder. Brougham is really a better term than Cabriolet for an open driver Town Car, but the terms were used interchangeably throughout the 1920s. In today usage, Cabriolet is used for cars like the Rolls-Royce convertible that's top can be opened part way. Body styles like the new Locke Sport Phaeton were referred to as four-passenger and five-passenger because of their adjustable hideaway rear seat center armrest.

A distinctive bar located at the rear of a convertible top or padded roof is called a Coach Bar or a Landau Iron, functional on early model folding tops for both carriages and automobiles and were later used as decorative items on closed sedans and coupes. The term Closed in early model automobiles refers to its not being a Touring or a Roadster with soft top. Later, however, the term closed also applied to the omitting of the last window in profile on sedans and limousines.

In window counting, there is a different rule for coupes than for sedans. On a coupe, all windows are counted except the windshield and the wing-windows. The rear window, the one that you look through the rear view mirror towards, is counted as one window even if double. Thus, a closed coupe might be referred to as a five-window or three-window coupe. Sedans, both two-door and four-door styles, use only the profile windows in counting. Here again, the forward triangle or wing-window is not counted. Thus, sedans are either two-window or three-window.

The two-window style affords more privacy for the rear passengers and was sometimes referred to as a closed sedan or limousine. It is perfectly workable to use the same window count method for sedans as Coupes. In doing so, a two-window sedan would be a five-window and a three-window sedan would be a seven-window. Anything less would by default been a sedan delivery or a hearse.

Doors on most four-door sedans and Tourings are positioned adjacent to one another. The exception to this is on a Dual-Cowl Phaeton, where a center section or second cowl separates the side doors. Doors on coupes were either forward (front) opening or modern standard (rear) opening. Doors on sedans are either of the front-rear, rear-front or rear-rear opening arrangements. The rear-front was very popular on Town Cars due to the ease by which the chauffeur might open the rear door for his passengers. Lincoln was the last of the sedan builders to depart from this arrangement, but did so finally in the late sixties.

Front-opening doors were nicknamed Suicide Doors. Hugo Pfau wrote that in all his years at LeBaron, he had never heard of an accident involving such doors in spite of their reputation. The front-opening doors were popular in early years as they were particularly useful if one had to crank start or adjust something in the engine, then run and jump in.

The rear-rear door arrangement was finally adopted for safety in modern family sedans. When unlatched, the airstream aids in holding the door shut on the rear opening arrangement. The terms Model, Style, *Series* and *type* are often used interchangeably. Most of this nonstandard terminology arose from the methods used by various coachbuilders and from Lincoln's own catalogues.

In referring to the Lincoln make in general, the term Model applies to a specific design and not a year, i.e., Model-K or Model-L. The term Style refers to body styling, i.e., Roadster or Touring. A type number is that particular number within a series assigned to a given body design.

Series refers more often to the years in which a group of body styles were built, i.e., 201 series indicates body types 202 thru 221 for 1931. The term *Series* can also be used interchangeably with Model Years, to refer to a given year's chassis design.in production; for example, the years that the Model-K was built.

The 231 series began with the 1932 Model-KB. The 501 series began the 1932 Model-KA and so on. Prior to that, the Model-L had only two chassis types, the 122 and the 150B. The Model-H could not be separated from its chassis so a year code was devised.

MOTOR AGE

BROUGHAM

A body of the same general description as the limousine, except that the non-collapsible roof extends only over that portion of the body that is entirely enclosed.

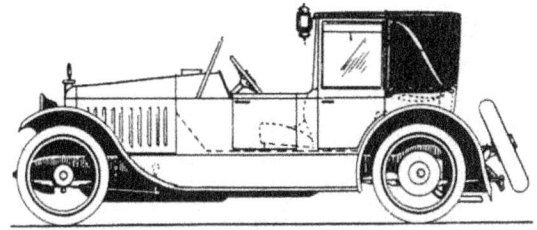

LANDAULET

A body similar in appearance to the brougham, except that the enclosed section is shorter from back to front and the roof is fully collapsible up to the partition at the back of the driver's seat. The body has one fixed cross seat in the rear section for two or three passengers, two doors made with either flappers or hinged upper parts and glass windows in the doors only. The rear quarters, back and top, are covered with leather or fabric. There are outside joints to support the top. This body is similar in some respects to the cabriolet. The enclosed portion is somewhat shorter and consequently there is no room for collapsible seats.

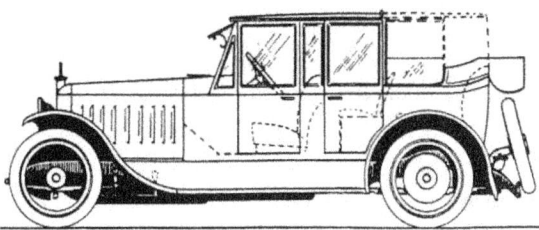

BERLINE LANDAULET

A body that bears the same relation to berline as the sedan does to the sedan landaulet.

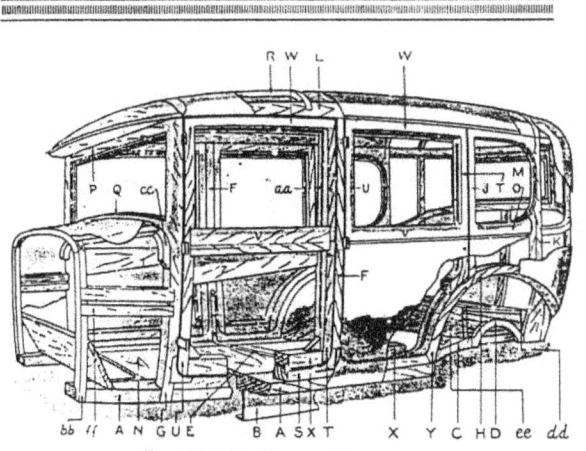

FRAMEWORK OF A FOUR-DOOR SALOON WITH THE PANELS PARTLY REMOVED

A. Bottom side	J. Hind standing pillar	R. Hoopstick	Z. Garnish rail
B. Chassis	K. Side light pillar	S. Door rocker	aa. Glass run
C. Bottom side connecting piece	L. Cant rail	T. Lock door pillar	bb. Front scuttle arch
D. Drum arch	M. Side light	U. Hinge door pillar	cc. Rear scuttle arch
E. Body Plate	N. Floorboard	V. Door rail	dd. Seat frame
F. Middle standing pillar	O. Elbow	W. Door top	ee. Heel-board
G. Front standing pillar	P. Front top rail	X. Door bottom	ff. Scuttle battens
H. Wheel-arch	Q. Middle top rail	Y. Quadrant piece	

EARLY LINCOLN ADVERTISING -

The best word to explain early Lincoln advertising is that it was institutional in nature. Under Leland, advertising promoted quality and reputation. The first graphics of a Coupe and Touring were done rather crudely in pen and ink. Ford's advertising moved toward what might be called stately advertising. The Model-L was pictured in front of various monuments and government structures.

Very early Lincoln ads stopped short of being depressing, but they were a little drab. These pen and ink drawings improved in quality and by 1922 some were also appearing with pastel watercolor tints. There is an old advertising idiom that says that if you repeat something often enough people may start to believe it. Thus the phrase Beauty That Lives was often repeated in the Lincoln ads.

By late 1925, Lincoln discontinued the stately advertising approach and went in for society themes like a day at the hunt, the dog show, on the golf course, or a night at the opera. The same ads were often printed in pastels as well as in black and white. Their focal point was always an austere and tasteful artist's rendering of a particular Lincoln body style. Above the pictured scene, a decorative oval or block bore an inscription relating some kind words about the particular automobile in the drawing.

In general, at the top of the ad in large standard typeset was the word LINCOLN and bore the signature line Lincoln Motor Company Division of Ford Motor Company. Through 1925, Lincoln used the letter L in an octagon seal as its logo. Advertising also appeared in foreign magazines like the French L'Illustration and promoted the style and grace of the improved Model-L. The word Lincoln had a greyhound dashing through the center of the logo in the foreign and some domestic ads of the late 1920s.

Advertising in popular magazines for 1929 began using actual photographs of Lincoln body styles in natural settings. These photos were of excellent clarity. During the 1930 model year, a switch was made back to artist's drawings, which were now very detailed and included intricate background scenes. The people in the scenes were almost cartoon-like, but the drawings represented restraint and artistic taste.

Many of the latter were drawn by James Williamson and appeared in the Saturday Evening Post. The coachbuilders themselves, on occasion, ran separate advertising of notably different layout. The coachbuilders, however, mainly confined their promotions to brochures and prospectus to be given away at salons and showrooms.

THE LINCOLN SALONS - The Salon of choice for prestige coachbuilders was New York City. During this era New York, not Detroit, was the auto capital. These New York Auto Salons were the custom coachbuilder's showrooms. The first was held in 1905 and was a competitor to the New York Auto Show founded a few years earlier. The New York Salon was held in the fall, usually in October in the Grand Ballroom of the Hotel Commodore. In addition, special salons at the Astor Hotel were held by various manufacturers.

Seven years after the New York Auto Show's beginning, an American car was finally admitted for exhibit. Bodies on American chassis by established coachbuilders were admitted if they were $3,000 or higher in price and until its conclusion in 1931, European chassis dominated. The New York Auto Show exhibited mostly imports and is often confused with the New York Auto Salon, which exhibited mostly American coachbuilts.

By the late 1920s, a Chicago Salon at the Drake Hotel was added in January. A few years later, a Los Angeles Salon was begun in February at the Biltmore Hotel and, still later, at the Palace Hotel in San Francisco the following month. The New York Salon was by invitation only, but the western Salons were generally open to the public. These exclusive Salons were different from the Automobile Show, which was open to the public. In New York City, the public shows were held at Madison Square Garden. In Los Angeles, they were held in circus tents. They were open to all manufacturers and were more for the ready-built models than the custom coach designs. In fact, these early public shows were not much different from the auto shows conducted today at municipal auditoriums and state fairs.

At the New York Auto Salon, a typical program would list four groups of exhibitors; they were "Exhibiting, Exhibited by Coachmakers, Coachwork Exhibits and Accessory Exhibits." The Lincolns were shown in the Exhibited by Coachmaker group. Automobiles shipped by rail could be brought into the Commodore Hotel via an elevated railway running from Grand Central Station to the hotel. Other cars were trucked in. Many coachbuilders like LeBaron would build a special custom show car each year for the event. On occasion, identical designs and color schemes would show up. Admittedly, this was as embarrassing a situation as two ladies wearing identical designer gowns to the same formal ball.

However, due to concern for the expensive oriental carpeting and the city fire codes, the gas and oil had to be removed from all the show cars. This is not an altogether great solution in that a caped full gas tank is far safer than an empty tank full of gas fumes.

On a good show year, cars would overflow into the lobby and onto the terrace outside the hotel's Grill Room. Most of the coach bodies displayed were Town Cars and Limousines because, after all, this was the Carriage Trade.

At the 1925 Salon, LeBaron displayed their design number 1331, which later became the Lincoln type 155. As a forerunner to the tropical bird advertising theme, this Sport Cabriolet had a rather gaudy decor. It was painted Parqouet green with a black top and reddish-brown pinstriping. Holbrook displayed their Lincoln Cabriolet and Dietrich's entry was a Convertible Sedan. This was Dietrich's first show separate from LeBaron. Brunn presented a pair of Lincolns, a Town Car and a Sports Sedan. In all, six different Lincoln body styles were on display.

A Lincoln est une voiture qui complète et qui consacre le luxe. Elle s'harmonise avec l'existence la plus raffinée et non pas seulement par son élégance et sa beauté proverbiales, mais par sa qualité. La Lincoln, grâce à une perfection technique sans cesse maintenue en tête du progrès, est le véhicule qui dispense à son possesseur le plaisir total auquel il est possible d'atteindre aujourd'hui avec une automobile. Quitter le yacht le plus somptueux pour une Lincoln c'est vivre dans le même cadre, c'est tracer le même sillage, c'est goûter un plaisir de même qualité.

Automobiles Lincoln, 245, quai Aulagnier, Asnières (Seine).

CABRIOLET BY BRUNN ON LINCOLN CHASSIS
Recently exhibited at the New York Automobile Salon and purchased by Cornelius Vanderbilt Whitney

BRUNN & CO., Inc.

HERMANN A. BRUNN   WILLIAM J. WEEFNER

980 ELLICOTT STREET

BUFFALO

AUTOMOBILE
REPAIRING   PAINTING

Coach Builders

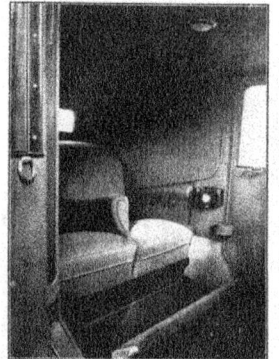

Interior View of Brunn Cabriolet

LINCOLN AND CONTINENTAL

In the 1927 Lincoln Salon Catalogue, one finds the Renaissance Semi-Collapsible Cabriolet by Brunn. The driver is in the open but has a large side window independent of the chauffeur's top. The passenger compartment is closed, with a padded roof and decorative coach bars. Variations on this body style were the Eighteenth Century All-Weather Convertible by LeBaron and the Colonial Semi-Collapsible Cabriolet by Willoughby. The latter had a bellflower pattern woven broadcloth interior. All had dual sidemounted spare tires. Their paint schemes and lower headlight mountings gave them the illusion of having an extra-long hood and lowered cowl.

The Custom Salon Catalogue business in the mid-twenties was in full bloom. In fact, these publications were so artistically done that most are sought after collector's items. The 1927 full-color Lincoln Salon Catalogue illustrated a LeBaron five-window, four-passenger Coupe in an oriental motif with gold, ebony and red trim. There was also a Judkins closed Sedan Berline with landau bars called the Egyptian. Its upholstery was done in lotus blossoms and papyrus pattern.

The triangle windows located either side of the windshield were retained from an earlier body style. The Dietrich Convertible Club Roadster was finished in ribbed broadcloth. The Willoughby seven-passenger Limousine appeared as the Gothic style and was rather plain except for an odd windshield design with hand-carved interior window arch garnitures.

The Georgian Landau Limousine by Locke was much like the Judkins Berline, except that it was a three-window sedan. The Empire Cabriolet two-window sedan by Holbrook was devoid of any streamlining. The most modern offering of this 1927 Salon Catalogue collection was Dietrich's Dual-Cowl Sport Phaeton. A boat-tailed open Touring, it was equipped with a rear-seat passenger compartment windshield and dual sidemounts. The exterior was BRG with dark orange wires and accent pinstriping just below the coach sill. The interior was two-tone green handcrafted leather with orange piping.

In 1927, both Locke and Judkins, built carriage replicas. Locke's offering was the Louis XIV French Brougham.

LINCOLN MOTOR COMPANY   DETROIT, MICHIGAN

*Leland-built Lincoln Motor Cars will be exhibited
at The National Automobile Show,
Chicago, January 29 – February 5, 1921*

The Leland-built Lincoln Eight-cylinder Motor Cars Comprise Eight Body Types

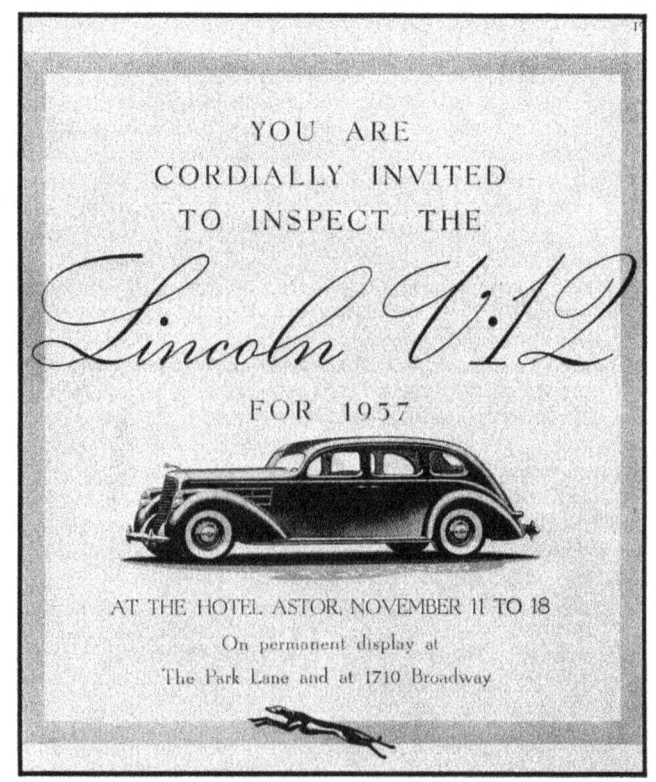

The Coaching Brougham offered by the John Judkins Company was designed by their chief engineer and closely resembled a European stagecoach. Much research had been done for this design at the carriage-building facility of Abbot and Downing in Concord, New Hampshire and it survives as a unique example of the coachbuilder's art.

The Coaching Brougham was sold to Miss Ethel Jackson in Hollywood It may have been too gaudy to sell elsewhere. On one occasion, it was used to promote a W.C. Fields movie. In the 1960s, MacMillian Company used it as a publicity device for the television show "The Beverly Hillbillies." The Coaching Brougham was painted traditional English coach colors of yellow and black with red accent striping. The interior was dark green Moroccan leather with plush red trim like the early Concord coaches. This car went to Tokyo, Japan, on tour with the Harrah's Collection in 1971.

The 1928 Salon Catalogue promoted designs like the Cabriolet Brougham by Brunn with phrases such as, "The rear compartment offers drawing room comfort with two occasional seats. A trunk rack is provided for those who prefer this type of body for touring."

The Locke Sport Touring boasted, "Yacht-like length and beauty." The Sport Roadster pitched, "Large luggage compartment with a curb-side access door."

The New York Salon often failed to draw good western attendance. Thus, the Chicago Salon followed the New York Salon, with only a week between the Chicago and Los Angeles Salons. The show automobiles were placed on railway cars attached to the regular express passenger trains. Beginning with the 25th New York Salon, the Chicago Salon preceded it.

At the 29th New York Salon, Lincolns were represented in every major corner of the Grand and West Ballrooms. On display were two Brunn Town Cars, a Derham Convertible Phaeton, a Convertible Coupe, a Sedan by Dietrich, a Berline and Coupe by Judkins, a LeBaron Roadster and Town Car, a Panel Brougham and Limousine, a Landaulet by Willoughby and a Locke Roadster. About the same numbers of Packards, Pierce-Arrows and Cadillacs were on display.

In 1929, the Chicago Salon preceded the New York Auto Show by almost a month. Many manufacturers of luxury cars took advantage of this earlier opportunity to introduce their new designs. As these Salons were by invitation only, dignitaries including Henry and Edsel Ford often attended. Famous designers such as Amos Northrup of Murray and Walter Briggs also came. Security was provided by the same Pinkerton men who manned the gates at the Belmont Park club house during racing season.

Many Detroit designers and other automotive notables received invitations from more than one major company and so were able to bring along staff members. The Chicago Salon became a place for the exchange of innovative engineering and body design ideas. Custom firms, however, could not keep up the pace with the new and less expensive production techniques of the mass manufacturers. The 27th New York Auto Salon held in 1931 would be the very last.

The standing joke among coachbuilders was that if you designed and built something too wild for Yankee conservatism, you could take it to Hollywood to sell. They found that Beverly Hills celebrities, starlets and promoters would buy anything flashy. Thus, the Los Angeles Auto Shows were always popular and generally successful. None, however, had quite as spectacular a finish as the 1929 show. The many tents that shaded the cars caught fire and hundreds of show cars from Fords to Duesenbergs were incinerated.

During the 1920s and 1930s, the railroads were the land cruisers, the caravan hotels of Pullman sleepers with dining cars and lounges. They were the links between major cities and resorts. The well-to-do shipped their motorcars by express railways on trains with romantic names like Overland, Dixie Flyer, Empire State, Santa Fe Chief and the Crescent Limited.

The men who debated Lincoln versus Packard also debated the New York Central versus the Baltimore & Ohio. Ocean cruisers no longer placed passengers at peril on the sea. Trains no longer passed through hostile savage territory. Risk had given way to luxury. For the coachbuilt motorcar, this was the age of opulence.

More than ability to purchase enters into the ownership of any fine thing—seaside home, or sloop, or motor car. Taste and judgment must play their part. They are reflected clearly by those who choose the Lincoln. And they guide unerringly all those who design and build it. . . . There need be no mystery about the position that this motor car holds in the American scene, and throughout the world. It has only one standard of engineering, of designing, of workmanship — and that the highest. In its building there is no hurry, no straining. Every last detail shows finished, patient workmanship. No appointment, however small, that can contribute to luxury or comfort or safety is overlooked. Sweeping, graceful lines heighten that distinction which is Lincoln's tradition. . . . The famous V-12 cylinder engine welcomes every test of the road. . . . There are twenty-one body types, including custom designs by Brunn, Judkins, LeBaron and Willoughby. Lincoln Motor Company, builders of Lincoln and Lincoln-Zephyr motor cars.

THE WILLOUGHBY LIMOUSINE

THE Lincoln

CHAPTER FIVE

THE CLASSIC SERIES

"K" Is For King Of The Road

Why the new Lincoln model moved up the alphabet instead of down, leads to interesting conjecture. Obviously, the L in Model-L stood for Leland, but for the new luxury Ford, the alphabet was ascended to the letter K. The real reason was simply that Edsel Ford decided to call it the Model-K. There were several logical reasons for this choice. First, the Model-L designation had not been determined by descent as had many other automobile models. The Ford automobile and Leland's Cadillac began with Model-A, but there were no A, B, C Lincolns.

The most popular speculation centers around the fact that the new Lincoln was named for the early Model-K Ford that Henry had produced in 1905. Only a handful were ever built and sold. This large Touring was in the line that preceded the 1908 Model-T. Those early models bore almost no resemblance to the famed Model-T Ford, the Tin Lizzie of later years. In these early years, Henry Ford had shown little interest in pursuing the large car market and had focused on developing a car for the masses.

The new Model-K was promoted as a Ford Lincoln and no longer a Leland Lincoln. In the early days of large chassis automobiles, the frames required more bracing than smaller cars and thus a K-member was added to provide extra support. This factor might or might not have had some bearing on the choice of the model's name.

The English language K is truer to the verbal sound made for the words car, carriage and coach than is the C sound. Indeed, it is a guttural Germanic sound, which connotates power and force, as in the words like king and kaiser. So if nothing else, it sounded good. The reasoning behind Chrysler's return to the term K-Cars in the seventies had nothing to do with series either. The body bridges used for mock-up, buck and layouts are sized by letter. Thus, when a modern car is referred to as a J-Car or K Car, this indicates the approximate body size.

NINETEEN-THIRTYONE - The 1931 Model-K Lincoln was a classic example of this era's transition in automotive design. It retained the massive antique appearance of the Model-L while incorporating smoother, more modern body lines. It was the last Lincoln to use the trade-style, open-center-oval, two-piece bumper. It was also the last flat front radiator shell and grille. The large, flat, tubular veins in the grille were carried over from the Model-L and were thermostatically controlled to open and close as before. The cowl vents were stamped metal louvers. This style of louver would be used one more time on the 1933 Model-K cowls and then phased out for good.

The 1931 Lincoln was a hybrid. One might equate it to a Ford that was midway between the design of a Model-A and Model-B. One of the reasons for the chassis redesign was coachbuilders had for years complained about the Model-L chassis being on a 136 inch wheelbase. It was too short for some of the more extensive limousine coach bodies. The new Model-K Lincoln, introduced in late 1930, had a 145 inch wheelbase. This new chassis was designed with flexibility in wheelbase and engine compartment size. The competition now offered V-12 and V-16 engines and Lincoln was planning to follow suit. The V-8 engine for the new Model-K underwent some major redesigns and many of its parts were not interchangeable with the V-8 engines used in the Model-L.

The design, however, was still generally based on the old, smooth-running Leland engine. It remained a sixty degree V with a 3.5 inch bore and a 5.0 inch stroke. When Frank Johnson returned to Lincoln from Cadillac in 1927, many improvements were made to the Lincoln LV-8. The new KV-8 engine, redesigned by Johnson, was about the maximum extent to which this engine could evolve.

The fact that the basic LV-8 design had survived eleven years of automotive development speaks highly of the engine's advanced concepts. Lincoln LV-8 and KV-8 engines have electrical and other systems that are more akin to GM engines of this era than to the Ford and Zephyr power plants.

Lincoln had enjoyed a reputation for high performance from its inception. In later years even the words of a popular song lamented, "Son, you're gonna' drive me to drinkin' if you don't quit racin' that hot rod Lincoln."

The new Model-K engine was rated as 120 horsepower at 2800 RPM (some specs say 2900 RPM) or 39.2 rated horsepower. This was an increase of 30 horsepower over the Model-L. Engine displacement remained unchanged at 384.8 cubic inches with a compression ratio of 4.95 to 1. The standard of quality and care to which the LV-8 and the new KV-8 engines were built remained the highest in the industry.

For example, the cam shaft was subjected to no less than two hundred tests during manufacturing. Starting with a 37-pound bar of special alloy steel, the cam weighed only ten pounds when completed. Fifty-four mechanical operations were followed by fifty inspections. A hole was drilled the full length of the shaft and then the adjoining oil ports were drilled.

Processes included hardening, grinding and polishing. Every cam and every bearing was tested for hardness. Parts were sometimes tested with several different tools to the same specifications and the tools themselves were tested for accuracy.

The new KV-8 cylinder block was cast-iron. The intake manifold was greatly improved over the LV-8. The redesigned intake manifold went into the engine block and not through the head as on the LV-8. A dual throat, downdraft Stromberg carburetor was installed. Although common today, it was considered very innovative at the time. The DD3 Stromberg had two 1.5 inch venturi with two fixed jets and a seasonally adjustable jet built into the accelerator pump. The throttle incorporated a hydraulic return check action to prevent stalling when the engine returned idle.

This was important due to the new freewheeling drivetrain mechanism. A wet-oil-bath air cleaner replaced the old style turbine type. An intake silencer was installed, as was a new smoother-flow exhaust manifold system. These innovations made the Model-K engine very quiet, as a luxury car should be. Fuel pressure was maintained by a new mechanical AC fuel pump that replaced the vacuum gravity feed system. Many small engine parts were chrome plated. The engine itself was painted a silver gray. Internally and externally, all cast aluminum parts were polished. The Electro-Fog generator had been discontinued earlier and this was the last year for the Kellogg tire pump accessory. The starter and new independently belt-driven generator were now Auto-Lite instead of Delco.

The Model-K engine to transmission coupling uses a double disc dry clutch. The transmission was synchromesh in second and third with the lower gear ratios changed only slightly. The freewheeling mechanism, mounted behind the transmission, was operated via a pushbutton on the gearshift lever. When engaged, the freewheeling allowed the engine to idle and the car to coast when the accelerator was released and permitted shifting from second to third without depressing the clutch.

Photo, page 105: At the 1932 Indianapolis 500 Speedway are from left to right, Eddie Rickenbacker, Henry Ford, Edsel Ford. Seated in Model K, Harvey Firestone, Jr., Henry Ford II, Benson Ford, and Harvey Firestone. Above, left to right, 1931 Model Ks: Willoughby Panel Brougham; Short body Sedan with trunk; Lily Pons, the singer, beside her Lincoln Limousine during Detroit Opera tour; Governor Rolph in California Lincoln number one (Union 76 Oil Company); Phaeton; Sport Touring. Below, 1931 Model K LeBaron Convertible Roadster designed by Raymond Dietrich.

1931 THE ALL NEW MODEL K LINCOLN

Motor Magazine rated the new KV-8 powered Lincoln as superior to its predecessor. It was reported that the acceleration to 25 miles per hour was 12 percent better and to 60 miles per hour even better yet. Their road test also reported that the large Lincoln would coast (freewheeling) almost a mile on level terrain from 50 miles per hour.

Lincoln and many of the luxury car manufacturers seemed to lag behind public demand. The interest in large motorcars had peaked in the late 1920s, but Lincoln was still increasing horsepower and extending its wheelbase. The public's requirements in personal transportation were moving in the opposite direction.

True, those who could afford the comfort of a Lincoln were certainly not going to give up this luxury. However, many traditional large car buyers were purchasing Buicks and the like for about half the cost. The new Fords and Plymouths were now reasonably dependable transportation. Lincoln would downsize slightly in a few years, but for Lincoln it was "damn the torpedoes and full speed ahead." The Lincoln Model-K attacked the Depression head on.

The new Lincoln chassis used a massive channel section structure that was 9.5 inches deep. It had a double drop with six heavy cross members called Cruciform Bracing. The central K-structure was a principle that would be used on Lincoln chassis for the next three decades. The wheelbase was extended nine inches. The hood and the overall profile of the car was lowered. Its large classic, chrome radiator shell came slightly to a point. The bowl-shaped headlamps mounted on the fender crossbar with a fluted oval Cloisonné emblem in red in the center. Cowl lamps were standard equipment. Bumpers were stronger.

The dual trumpet horns were externally mounted below the headlamps on the cross bar. It could be sounded high or low depending upon the direction in which the horn button was depressed and was known as a Town and Country horn. The walnut steering wheel was replaced with a new 19 inch hollow steel wheel with four spokes. Better steering was provided by a new Gemmer worm and roller bearing gear box.

Houdaille double-acting hydraulic shocks became standard equipment. The old rod and pivot brake system was replaced by new Bendix Duo-Servo brakes. Front brakes were operated by cables and the rear by rods. The high carbon steel drums were ribbed for better cooling.

The separate rear wheel parking brake mechanism was eliminated. The wider, lower balloon tires used 19 inch wheels. The last Model-L had used 20 inch wheels. The tire size was 32x6.75 by the old method of outside diameter dimensioning or optional 32x7.00. The move to 19 inch wheels and later to 18 inch wheels greatly improved the looks and ride of the Model-K.

These cars were being driven less and less on rutted dirt roads, so a high center was less important. The new Lincoln was very stable and comfortable. The Model-K was road tested by Autocar in May of 1931, which rated it as impressive and advanced. In fact, the article declared, "The Model-K is so outstanding in performance as to be well within the category of a sports car."

When attempting to reconstruct the production figures for the early Model-K, the totals are nearly as unclear as they were for the Model-L production runs. However, somewhere between 3,311 and 3,592 Model-K Lincolns were manufactured in calendar year 1931. In all, 3,466 were shipped to Lincoln dealers in the United States. A new Model-K Lincoln sold for between $4,500 and $5,500 with some special coach body styles selling for $2,000 higher. For 1931, the 201 series body styles were types 202 thru 221.

This 1930s advertising art depicts a lady driving a Model K Lincoln Sedan, meeting a gentleman who has just arrived by train.

Special orders included sixty-one bare chassis, twenty-one RHD chassis and twenty-six Special chassis. In addition, Rollston ordered three each of the 150 inch and 155 inch wheelbase chassis. Contract coachbuilders this year included Brunn, Dietrich, Derham, Judkins, LeBaron and Willoughby. Body styles included Dual-Cowl and Sport Phaetons, Tourings, Town Sedans (two-window and three-window), Coupes (two-passenger and five-passenger), Limousines and Cabriolets. A chassis without coach body weighed thirty-five hundred pounds and the average completed Lincoln weighed about five thousand pounds. A custom Derham Phaeton weighed six thousand pounds.

One of the most beautiful Lincolns ever produced was this year's two-passenger Convertible. It was designed along the lines of a Dietrich and Judkins Roadsters, but was a one-off custom built by Murphy. Its rising cowl and low profile windshield set it apart from other body styles. Famed cartoonist Rube Goldberg purchased a new Model-K Lincoln, stating that he was most impressed with the car's long, powerful-looking hood and cowl. When Walter Chrysler heard this, he promptly extended the hood of the Chrysler Custom Imperial, due out the following year.

Many of the coachbuilders continued to list in their catalogues the body styles previously sold on the Model-L, but only a few were ever built. One of these was the Locke Model-K type 191, a stylish Sport Roadster. Factory built body styles were types 202 thru 207.

1932 Model KA Touring. Opposite page: KA 3-window Sedan; 2-window Sedan; 5-passenger Coupe; and 3-passenger Coupe.

An extensively photographed body style was the Dual-Cowl Phaeton type 202A with rear-front doors and large curved wind wings. This car is most often held up as a typical example of the Lincoln's Model-K styling. Even though Roadsters and Phaetons received most of the publicity, sedans and coupes always outsold the sport body styles by more than five to one. The coachbuilders had a field day with the new long chassis, turning out no less than 265 individual custom designs.

The new longer Model-K chassis had a lower center of gravity and gave passengers a feeling of riding in an even larger machine. Although Cadillac had almost doubled its horsepower and gone to a 148 inch wheelbase, the new Lincoln held its own in the luxury car market. Cadillac was outselling Lincoln two to one but, for the model year 1931, Lincoln sales were off only slightly over the preceding year. Lincoln design engineers were hard at work meeting the challenge of the Cadillac and Packard initiated multi-cylinder race.

N.W. Ayer & Son, Inc., publicity managers for Lincoln at the time touted the new Model-K as, "Low slung and Rakish, expected to be a popular sight around country clubs and fashionable beach and mountain resorts this coming summer." The Lincoln marketing slogan was, "As nearly perfect a motorcar as it is possible to produce."

Advertising illustrations were pen and ink line drawings of various Lincoln coach styles in rustic or scenic settings. Some had pastel overprints. A typical lead in one of these ads read, "When Wheels are Wings."

The 1931 factory brochure was entitled "The New Lincoln." It displayed twenty standard and custom body styles, had forty pages and measured 14x10 inches. The art work was printed in color with a black background. An eight-page version was printed with only four styles represented. The Salon Catalogue had twenty pages and featured twelve different body styles. The first edition had a Murphy Sport Phaeton illustration and the second edition was identical except that the Phaeton was replaced by the Locke Sport Roadster.

In 1930, Ford Motor Company profits had exceeded $40 million. When 1931 ended, the Company had lost over $50 million. Lincoln division losses were $4,615,464 for the year. It may not be fair to blame all of these losses on poor sales figures. Development costs were up. The new KV-12 engine was just being completed and the Lincoln chassis had been especially redesigned the preceding year to hold the larger engine. The Ford line was introducing a new V-8 engine and the new Model-B body style.

NINETEEN-THIRTYTWO - The year 1932, was to be the year of the Classic Lincoln, with a capital K. There was a dramatic change in the Lincoln model lineup this year. Models were divided into KA and KB. The Model-KA continued to use the V-8 engine on a 136 inch wheelbase chassis. The Model-KB used the new V-12 engine on a 145 inch wheelbase chassis.

Both models shared major upgrades in styling. Louvers on the engine cowl were replaced with vent door panels, five on each side with a matching cabin vent door on most body styles. The new cowl doors were controlled by their own thermostat, independent of the original thermostatically controlled radiator vanes.

Eighteen inch welded steel wire wheels with matching chrome hubcaps and a chrome radiator shell was standard. The hubcaps bore the fluted Lincoln oval emblem. The two-piece bumper with the traditional open oval gave way to a straight, ribbed one-piece bumper. The cowl lights were relocated to the top of the front fenders.

Often the Model-KA is thought of incorrectly as the continuation of the 1931 Model-K because it offered the same V-8 engine.

Its downsized chassis, lower price and limited choice of interior options, however, introduced it into a new market stratum. The improved Leland V-8 engine was now rated as 125 brake horsepower at 2900 RPM or 43.2 rated horsepower, primarily due to an increased compression ratio of 5.23 to 1. The second ear in the transmission was upgraded to a helical gear. This, it was claimed, made the Lincoln run as quietly in second gear as in third. The freewheeling unit, mounted behind the transmission, was retained. The Model-KA used size 7.00x18 tires.

There were nine factory standard Murray-built bodies offered, plus the standard bare chassis and the RHD chassis. The factory offerings were the two-passenger and four-passenger Coupes, Town and Victoria Sedans, a Phaeton, two Roadsters and two variations on the Sedan Limousine. The Model-KA Lincoln 501 series body types were numbered 502 through 510. The Model-KA radiator shell was a carry-over from last year's Model-K. A dual marketing approach was begun, similar to the practice followed on Fords throughout the 1930s.

The grille work was comprised of long, vertical tubes. The Model-KA Lincoln emblem differed only in color from the Model-KB emblem. These oval emblems were mounted on the headlight bar and the hubcaps. The Model-KA interior appointments were rather plain. Prices started at $2,900, an obvious response to slow economic conditions and stiff competition.

These Model-KA Lincolns would be the last Leland based V-8 engines ever built. This engine design was completing a twelve-year production run. Cadillac and Packard had now developed smoother running eight-cylinder engines. Engineer Peter Heldt, in 1915, had theorized that a sixty degree V-8 engine with an uneven firing order would run more smoothly than those in production at the time.

Leland had proved this theory and Ford had perfected the design with quality and excellence, but the LV-8 engine always had a mild secondary imbalance. The unique fork-and-blade connecting rods did, however, offset this problem to a great extent. The roller-type valve lifter concept had been used on aircraft engines before being adapted to the LV-8. All of these engine refinements were implemented to overcome early, crude manufacturing techniques.

To produce a two-plane crank, the shaft has to be forged in a flat plane and while the metal is hot, the two throws must be bent exactly into place. All of this is a tricky process even with today's modern equipment.

By May 9, 1931, Ford engineers Jack Wharam and Fred Wilborn, under the supervision of Frank Johnson, had tested the first Lincoln KV-12 engine over a year. Six days after the static run, it was installed in a test car. The new Lincoln KV-12 engine was introduced to the luxury car buying public in November of 1931. It was called the Lincoln Twelve Model-KB for the 1932 market promotion.

1932

In his biography Frank Johnson related how decisions were often made at Ford, "Edsel and Henry Ford would walk through the shops with men hard at work. They occasionally stopped to sit down, prop their feet up and talk over something. Edsel generally had a good idea of what he planned for the Lincoln and, of course, Henry was more preoccupied with the Ford product line."

At any rate, the decision was made to go with two series of Lincolns for the model year 1932. The new Model-KB was on the longer 145 inch wheelbase and powered by the newly designed massive V-12 engine. Weighing in at over a half ton (1,070 pounds), the engine had a displacement of 447.9 cubic inches. It developed 150 brake horsepower at 3400 RPM, which translated into a 50.7 license horsepower rating or 292 foot pounds of torque. The cylinders were cast at a sixty-five degree V angle.

The material chosen for the engine block was a close grained gray iron alloy. This iron alloy contained 15 percent steel, 1 percent nickel and a .5 percent of chromium. The 3.25 inch bore was held to a machine tolerance of .0005 of an inch. The stroke was 4.5 inches. The polished and balanced crankshaft weighed ninety-one pounds when completed. There were seven bronze Babbitt main bearings and eight cam bearings. The four-ring aluminum pistons were matched to within .25 ounces per set. The combustion chamber was 1.875 inch diameter.

In many ways, the new KBV-12 was an enlarged and updated LV-8. It still used the fork-and-blade rod design. The compression ratio matched the current KAV-8 engine at 5.25 to 1. Stated in Ford terms, this is 103 PSI.

The Lincoln Twelve was superior to those engines being used on current model Duesenbergs and other luxury cars. The KBV-12 engine was supported at three points by large rubberized motor mounts and equipped with torsional vibration dampers at the front of the engine. The exhaust manifolds went forward, then under the engine for quietness and with less heat transmittal into the driver compartment. The Model-KB was equipped with a 28-gallon fuel tank. The crankcase held 12-quarts of oil as compared to the V-8 engine's 10-quarts. The cooling system on both engines had a 34-quart capacity.

Both of the Lincoln Model-K engines used dual ignition systems. The 135-amp 6-volt battery was relocated to the engine compartment. There were, however, a few drawbacks to the new KBV-12 engine's design. For example, due to the placement of the valve lifters, the manifold had to be removed in order to adjust the valves.

Manufacturing problems and increased costs were caused by the shear physical size of the engine. The multitude of steps in its manufacture and testing made these engines costly to produce. Large displacement engines require greater gas-air velocities through the venturis, ports and valves to assure good throttle response under a high-torque, low-speed condition. Big valves and large carburetors only help at high speeds.

The brake system was vacuum assisted as well as being adjustable from the steering column for summer and winter driving. The Bragg-Keisrath vacuum brake unit had been especially designed and produced for the Lincoln. Standard tire size on the Model-KB was 7.5 by 18. The 145 inch wheelbase had a turning radius of approximately 26 feet. The semi-elliptical suspension springs were 42 inches long in front and 62 inches in rear. The average body's overall length was 214 inches. Rear axle ratios were 4.23 to 1 standard with optional 4.58 or 4.90. An average Lincoln, when completed, weighed between 5,600 and 5,900 pounds.

The radiator shell on the Model-KB was more massive than the one on the Model-KA. Its crown was rounded and the grille came more to a forward point. In overall styling, however, the Models KB and KA were very similar. There were two large trumpet horns faced forward under the headlights. Model Kb and KA both used the same thermostatically controlled cowl doors and radiator louver vane arrangement.

CYLINDER GRINDING

BALANCING CRANKSHAFTS

GRINDING CAMSHAFTS

ENGINE "BLOCK TEST"

MACHINING CRANKCASES

WEIGHING AND MATCHING CONNECTING RODS

TRANSMISSION TESTING

PRESSING FENDERS

This giant press with a single downward motion of the huge die forms a front fender for Lincoln cars. The metal as a flat sheet is placed between the moving and lower fixed die and emerges instead almost ready, after painting, for application on the car. An idea of the size of the machine may be gained from the height of the man operating it.

ATTACHING AXLES TO FRAME

PLACING ENGINE IN CHASSIS

SPRAY PAINTING CHASSIS

VIEW OF PARTLY ASSEMBLED CHASSIS

MOUNTING THE BODY

COMPLETION OF ASSEMBLY

TEST OF COMPLETED CAR

LOADING DOCK

Marvin Arnold

The two piece V-type windshield was used for the first time on many of this year's new body styles. On the grille bar was mounted on an oval Lincoln emblems with the background blue on the new Model-KB and in red on the new Model-KA.

The body styles offered for the new Model-KB were types 231 through 250. The Model-KB body serial numbers started approximately where the previous year's Model-K had left off. There was no Lincoln body type numbers 222 through 230.

Murphy of California had been building fine custom bodied Lincolns for several years and was now recognized as an official factory coachbuilder for the type 232 Dual-Cowl Sport Phaetons. There were 2,132 Model-KA and 1,515 Model-KB produced in 1932.

The infamous Red Journals are hardbound hand-posted ledgers that were maintained from the very beginning of the Model-L. For the record, this author (while researching this book) personally and privately reviewed these journals at the Henry Ford Museum & Greenfield Village Archives in Dearborn, Michigan where they are now stored.

The Red Journals show that Model-KA and KB Lincolns were not always shipped with matching serial numbers. When a given power plant did not perform to certain road test standards, it was recycled or scraped.

For example, Model-KB serial number 1630 had engine case number 1469 and Model-KA serial number 72004 had case 49607. Lincoln Model-KB serial number 1014 had its engine replaced with serial number 1633, Model-KB serial number 1325 was replaced with 1636 and so on. The last Model-KB with the large V-12 engine was completed in late June of 1932 and was shipped in early July. Partially completed Model-KB chassis were quickly modified to begin the 1933 model production.

For the model year introduction at New York's Commodore Hotel, the Lincoln brochure had not promoted the new Lincoln as a Model-KB. Instead, the brochure was entitled Lincoln Twelve Cylinder Motor Cars. The model lineup was officially described by the Lincoln Motor Company, a Division of Ford Motor Company, in their tan and gold catalogue for 1932. It stated, "A brilliance, comfort and luxury with twenty-five body types ranging from $4,300. This motor car establishes more than ever the preeminence of the Lincoln name."

The type 234A two-window and the type 234 three-window Town Sedan versions had sweeping, flowing lines with V-windwhields, long hoods and low bodies. The five-passenger Coupe type 236 offered wide doors for ease of rear-seat entry and individually adjustable front seats. The five-passenger Sedan type 235 had a center rear-seat armrest and two fold-out opera seats. The type 237 seven-passenger Limousine's rear passenger compartment, with partition glass, had hideaway rear auxiliary seats and a robe rail. A reading lamp was provided for the chauffeur's compartment. All of these body styles used rear-mounted spare tires. A rear facing front door arrangements soon became a Lincoln tradition. The body type number 231 identified a chassis only.

For the more sporting, there was the Sport Phaeton four-passenger type 232 with a rear-seat compartment inlaid with pewter. It offered upholstery of hand-buffed leather and was available in brown or black. The tonneau cowl on the Sport Phaeton was optional. The door windows form a large quarter circle mating the front and rear windshields, as in the earlier type 202. These body styles were originally offered by the factory and subsequently contracted out to Murphy. Only forty-three were built, but the Sport Phaeton remains one of the finest examples of classic Model-KB body styling.

The seven-passenger Sport Touring was designed for long distance touring. A large family with luggage could travel comfortably in it. Seven-passenger seating meant two in the front, two in the rear auxiliary seats and three in the rear seat. As with the Phaeton and the Sport Touring, most Model-KB body styles featured dual sidemounted spares. Thus, a large travel trunk could be mounted on the rear bumper rack.

LeBaron's Convertible Roadster with coach bar top irons was a sleek, streamlined design for its time. The manual folding top mechanism operated easily, folding away to a very low profile so as not to obstruct the rear view. A small curb side door accessed the large trunk for easy stowing of items such as golf clubs.

This type 248 Roadster was listed as a two-passenger or four-passenger body style. Actually, the second two seats were the rumble seat. This body style was a continuation of the previous year's very popular type 214.

The Convertible Victoria type 247 by Waterhouse was a five-passenger Continental style coupe. Its large rear-mounted metal chest (trunk) was finished in the body color.

With its low profile top design, it converted quickly from a dashing open Phaeton into a snugly enclosed Victoria. This popular Victoria design was the first Lincoln factory-recognized Waterhouse custom body. The Roadster type 249 by Murphy had a completely concealed top, which hid away under a hinged lid. It combined streamlined appearance with the protection of an enclosed coupe and a low center of gravity.

Above: 1932 Model KBs Dual-Cowl Phaeton; Lincoln factory Limousine; Coachbuilt Cabriolet with V-windshield and landau bars; coachbuilt Convertible Victoria. Below: 1931 Model K and 1932 Model KA Mechanical; 1932 Dietrich Convertible Sedan.

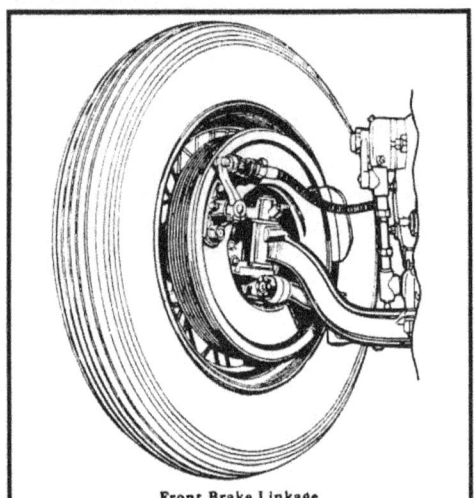

Front Brake Linkage

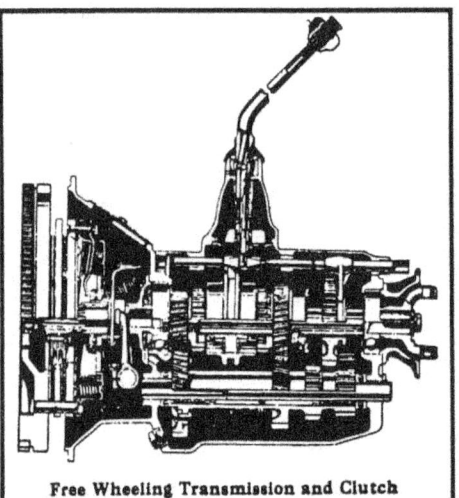

Free Wheeling Transmission and Clutch

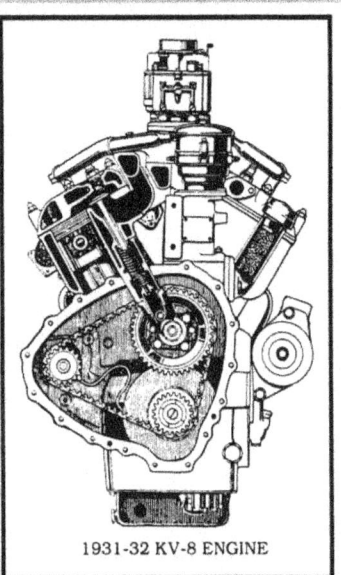

1931-32 KV-8 ENGINE

Dietrich produced three Salon offerings for the Model-KB. The Convertible Sedan type 241 five-passenger combined the luxurious comfort of a closed body and the flashing grace of an open Touring. It can be transformed into a chauffeur-driven formal car with closed rear compartment or used as a dashing family sedan. The windshield was of the V-type, set at a rakish angle parallel to the lines of the front door. The top on this Convertible Sedan could be folded completely below its belt line. The center posts between the windows were detachable. The Sport Berline type 240 was a formal closed body design of the non-convertible style that had a padded roof simulating a convertible top. Its windows were encased in frames, which dropped out of sight and covered by automatic lids. The Sport Berline's interior trim was severely tailored. The rear passenger area had moldings of rare wood, built-in toilet cases and a smoking set. The rear seat back folded forward for access to the rear deck compartment.

Both of these Dietrich sedans had front opening doors (suicide doors) in the front. The Dietrich Coupe offering also had front opening doors. The four-passenger Coupe type 242A and the two-passenger Coupe type 242B had graceful airflow lines with V-type windshields. The front pillars were cast of manganese bronze, small sections of great strength that allowed minimal restriction to forward viewing. These body styles were offered with a rear luggage compartment or rumble seat. This basic Dietrich coupe design was carried over into the 1933 Chrysler coupes.

The Judkins Coupe type 244 was a distinctly personal car for the owner driver. The inclined single-piece windshield was free from rear window headlight glare. This coupe was especially boxy for a Dietrich design. A rumble seat was optional. The other major Judkins Salon offering for the Model-KB was the Berline, which was available in two and three-window sedans. These body styles, unlike the coupes, featured the V-type windshield. The two-window Berline type 243A was an ingeniously designed motorcar that could be driven daily or on formal occasions like a limousine.

The sedan featured the new Coach Sill lines, which continued the high beltline styling and give the appearance of added length. The Judkins three-window Berline type 243B was a highly desirable motorcar due to its smartness. Both sedans had padded roofs and the two-window body style had added decorative coach bars. Door arrangement was front-front. The interior glass partition could be cranked up or down and the interiors offered novel extras such as a hand mirror, a notebook holder a wireless (radio), cigar lighter and map pocket, bookshelves, center armrest and auxiliary seating.

Brunn and Willoughby each had two offerings for the new Lincoln Twelve Cylinder Salon. The all-weather Brougham type 239 by Brunn was a finely developed line of motorcars worthy of their high tradition. This Brougham could be converted into an open drive by lowering the front windows and folding the canopy top out of sight behind a panel in the roof above the partition window. The all-weather Cabriolet type 238 by Brunn was featured simplicity of line, dignity and exclusivity, marking it as a formal Town Car. Its rear quarter leather top could be lowered and the front compartment converted into an open drive.

The Limousine type 245 by Willoughby was in keeping with the formality of its function. It was elegant equipage being dignified and conservative. Curved coach sill, slanted windshield and sweeping lines created an impression of long, low luxury. An impression reinforced by the wide, deeply cushioned, seven-passenger interior. The Panel Brougham type 246 by Willoughby was a four-passenger coach. Elegant sweeping downward-curving sill was the distinguishing characteristic and was reminiscent of carriage days. The door arrangement was front-front and the open drive Panel Brougham's was rear-front.

There were eighteen type 231 chassis, three specials, ten RHD and one 150 inch Model-KB chassis shipped in 1932. The latter was probably a Silver Knightstown Hearse. The April 13, 1932 issue of Business Week reported, "The 1932 auto battle will be fought on a price basis. The May 25th issues also carried an article proclaiming the 1931 automobile year was better than expected." The luxury car market had peaked in the late 1920s. Fifty percent of the Big Iron on the road was now over five years old.

Marvin Arnold

CLASSIC MOTORCARS

The headlines on most Lincoln display ads read; "The Lincoln 12" with a scroll border. Simple pen and ink drawings of a single body style remained the vogue. Six major factory brochures were offered for 1932. The two-color (two-toned) Model-KA catalogue was sixteen pages long and featured seven body styles, its second edition added a Roadster to the lineup. A smaller Model-KA catalogue was twelve pages.

The Model-KB had three catalogues: a gray hardcover edition with forty-eight pages and illustrations of twenty-one standard and custom body styles; a blue hardcover Salon catalogue was thirty-eight pages long showing sixteen custom designs; and a black and white version showing four popular body styles.

A manufacturing brochure describing many of the techniques used in building the Lincoln was also printed this year. It was very similar to the one printed three years before for the Model-L. Several pamphlets described various options and features.

Autocar and Motor magazines reported that the new Lincoln KB Twelve had been road tested at the Brookland track in England. This banked oval track was similar to the old brickyard race track at the Indianapolis Speedway in that it was rough and demanding. The magazines reported that the Model-KB cruised easily, almost hands off around the course. Top speed was recorded at 95.74 miles per hour. Best lap speed was 89 miles per hour. Low gear was found to top out at 31 MPH and second gear at 51 MPH. The zero to sixty run was accomplished in 26 seconds flat. One of the reports went on to comment that the suspension and vacuum boosted mechanical brakes were totally adequate for the heavy Lincoln KB.

The Soviet government reportedly ordered four hundred Model-KA Lincolns, for use by tourists and foreign dignitaries. It was, however, reported that Stalin himself preferred Packards. Whether these units were included in the type 505 and/or 507 production figures for this year is not clear.

The Model-KB is considered by many collectors to be the most truly classic motorcar of all the Lincolns. For the total two-year run, there were 2,132 KAV-8 and 1,515 KBV-12 door-cowled models produced. The lower priced KAV-8 had proved the more popular model. Ford engineers were already hard at work designing a new V-12 engine for the Model-KA. It was the end of an era and the Leland V-8 passed into the annals of automotive history. Ironically, Henry Martyn Leland died on March 26th of this year. He was age eighty-nine.

NINETEEN-THIRTYTHREE - In 1933, the development of the Model-KA and KB was the result of two familiar market forces. The Model-KA had been developed as a result of economic pressures and the Model-KB as a result of pressure being brought to bear by the competition. Ford engineers developed an all-new 381.7 cubic inch V-12 engine for the 136 inch wheelbase Model-KA. The Model-KB remained on the longer 145 inch wheelbase and retained the 447.9 cubic inch V-12 engine.

The oval Lincoln cloisonné emblems continued to identify the Model-KA with red and the Model-KB with blue backgrounds. This large and small concept is not unlike the marketing lineup used with the 1980s Lincolns, i.e., Town Car and Continental. The new Model-KA met the competition head on. Lincoln now had a V-12 model on the market at $400 less than the Cadillac V-12 and $700 less than the Packard V-12. The Model-KA and KB Lincolns both had V-12 engines, but Cadillac was now offering a V-16 engine. Ford engineers may have considered a V-16 engine on the drawing board, but there is no indication that such an engine was ever seriously looked at for production.

Left to Right: 1933 hood ornament; Lincoln KB Twelve advertising logo; Model KBs seven-passenger Limousine; Town Sedan three-window; Brunn Brougham; Town Sedan two window; Model KA four-passenger Phaeton; KA five-passenger Coupe; Model KBs Cabriolet; Willoughby Limousine; Sedan seven-passenger; Sport Phaeton.

The logical extension of the V-8 engine would be a V-16 engine instead of a V-12, but it never evolved. The Leland V-8 had been too massive for extended cylinder development. The KBV-12 would be the last Lincoln engine to use the fork-and-blade design, which permitted one rod to straddle the opposite crank throw when using an opposed rather than a staggered firing order.

The new KAV-12 used techniques pioneered on the small Ford V-8. This made the engine much lighter in weight and less expensive to manufacture. It had a 381.7 cubic inch (6.2 liter) displacement and developed 125 brake horsepower at 3400 RPM. The new design was a 67 degree V with a 3.0 inch bore and a 4.5 inch stroke. Valves were smaller than the earlier V-8 and V-12 engines. The cast-iron blocks were bored with the cylinders offset. There were only four main bearings compared to the seven on the big Twelve, a main bearing between every other crankshaft journal instead of between every one.

The engine was thus shortened to about the same length as the KV-8 that it replaced. The double-sided rod bearing used with fork-and-blade were no longer required. Ford did not go to the poured Babbitt rod bearings, which were now being used by most engine manufacturers.

Instead, they used the more advanced concept of replaceable insert bearings. Designer Johnson kept much of the rest of the engine old-fashioned and conservative. The timing chain still operated the accessories, the crankcase and cylinder block remained separate pieces.

Auburn, Packard and Pierce had abandoned these design concepts several years ago. Cylinder heads on the new KAV-12 were cast-iron and detachable. Intake ports were smaller. The engine used a Stromberg EE22 dual 1.25 inch barrel, downdraft carburetor. The new small KAV-12 engine almost equaled the torque of the big Twelve at low RPM, but did lack the top end capability of the Model-KB engine.

Edsel Ford had instructed the sixty-one-year-old Frank Johnson that, "When you have some ideas that you think are good, call me, I will come down and we will discuss them."

The first priority, Johnson knew, was to phase out the Leland engines and was accomplished with the Model-KA. Layoffs at Ford had left Lincoln with only two engineers, Wharam and Wilborn. They went to work on a more powerful 65 degree KBV-12 engine with the objective of modernizing and downsizing it. Other engine experiments were conducted on improvements like oil coolers, aluminum heads, oxide pistons and copper plated steel bearings.

Henry Crecelius, who joined Ford in 1926, had just supervised the completion of Lincoln's own new coach works facility. Edsel had hired Crecelius from Brewster & Company saying that, "His conservative taste in coach designs parallels my own."

Herman Brunn and Ralph Roberts, however, felt that Crecelius was overly conservative. Sometimes, when trying to sell a marginal design to Edsel Ford, these designers would trim or paint their proposed automobile design in gray, which was Edsel's favored color for a large stylish motorcar.

There was a wide choice of colors for 1933. Bodies and fenders were finished with fifty-nine quarts of paint. The traditional paint scheme of colored bodies on black fenders had been discontinued and two-tone paint schemes were available. Standard color choices included Rhodenite Tan, Sunstone Brown, Paris Gray, Ascot Maroon, Jade Mint and Birmingham Green.

G. Henry Stetson, manufacturer of the famous Western style hats, had purchased a 1932 Berline Sedan by Judkins.

Marvin Arnold

In 1933, Stetson ordered a matching Model-KB Coupe. Both Lincolns were two-tone brown, light and dark. Even the chrome radiator shell was painted to match the body. Stetson lived on a sprawling Spanish estate near Salmar in California's San Fernando Valley. His Rancho El Sombrero covered much of what is now Griffith Park.

The cars were purchased through the Coberly Lincoln dealership on Vine Street in Hollywood. In those days, poor Mexican farmers still roamed the streets of what are now shopping centers and subdivisions. Stetson, like many Lincoln owners, enjoyed the finer things of life but did not want to flaunt his wealth. This was the reason for painting the grille shell and the choice of a rather drab paint scheme of Rosewood and Thorn.

Brown also showed the dirt of the ranch roads a little less. The interior of Stetson's Model-KB was tan English wool broadcloth with wool pile carpeting. The instrument panel was wood grain and the fascia was polished stainless steel. The gear shift and brake lever as well as the steering wheel column were chromed, which was standard on the Model-KB for this year. The car measured 18 feet 2 inches in length. It was privately owned in California today and was in excellent original condition.

A Lincoln Model-KA type 513A Convertible Roadster was restored by a New Hampshire collector. Finished in Ascot Maroon with black belt line and silver pinstriping, the car had coach irons on the light canvas top with matching sidemount covers. Luggage rack and dicky with steps were installed. According to an article in Cars & Parts, which featured this luxury sport Lincoln a few years ago, the car sold for $85 in 1940. It was now a show car and most of its driving was restricted to short on and off trailer trips.

At first, the luxury car manufacturers hoped that the auto market would turn around. Response varied from manufacturer to manufacturer. Cadillac, for example, dropped its open-bodied Tourings. The company soon introduced the lower-priced LaSalle and the Fleetwood was reduced in size. Packard, on the other hand, retained its expensive lineup continuing the Eight, Super Eight and Twelve for two more years.

The Dietrich V-type windshield Sport and the LeBaron Phaeton are examples of fine coach body Lincolns that fell by the wayside during this period. In fact, Pierce-Arrow at Buffalo never restocked their 1931 custom body Tourings after the supply ran out. Afterwards, Packard stayed mostly with formal sedans and limousines from that time on, offering only one soft-top body style. Even Lincoln scraped the large Model-KB the following year.

The Franklin automobile company had already gone into receivership and by May, the Marmon declared insolvency. Stutz would cease automobile production in about a year. Chrysler was selling the luxury Imperial only by special order, mostly to political personalities.

Auburn and Cord downsized leaving the Duesenberg floundering. Those coachbuilders who remained in business cut back and laid-off talented workers. The age of custom body automotive artistry was at an end and time would show that the 1920s had been its apex.

By the end of the year, successful coachbuilders like Holbrook, Locke, Merrimac, Waterhouse and Weymann-American had all closed their doors. LeBaron was doing mostly design consulting work. Derham and a few others offered budget Town Cars on Ford and Plymouth chassis. Some took on automobile dealerships.

Brunn, Judkins and Willoughby managed to keep going on Lincoln's business. The new buzzword was Alteration Custom body works and the concept remains with us today. Since the lines of most major automobiles were plain vanilla, many small coach shops sprang up to install leather padded roofs, vanities, custom seating and Cabriolet tops.

The coachbuilder's relationships with the manufacturers had been established early in the automotive era. For example, coachbuilder Angus Woodbridge was Henry Leland's son-in-law. In 1922, after Ford's takeover of Lincoln, sales manager R.C. Getsinger had continued the policy of using custom coach houses, so that even though Lincoln now had in-house coach facilities, the custom catalogue body styles were still available to prospective buyers. Eventually, Herman Brunn was hired by Ford at a salary of fifty thousand dollars a year to coordinate the entire Lincoln custom body line.

A typical Model-K body was hammered from one-sixteenth inch aluminum to fit over a complex framework consisting of no less than 250 wooden parts. The wood itself was yellow birch and white ash. Parts were cut to shape, not formed by steam heat, so they retained their shape with age. The fittings that held the wood were forged bronze that were more durable than the white cast metal used by lesser quality coachbuilders. There were over sixty cast aluminum braces within the body's framework. Some two thousand screws were hand-installed during fitting of the coach body and interior trim. Lincoln used only solid, hand-finished mahogany trim in the interiors.

The Pierce-Arrow, Packard and Cadillac Eights used stamped metal parts with artificial wood grain finish. Lincoln advertisements read, "The tap of a coin will reveal its hollow construction and a scratch will show that it is imitation."

A typical completed Model-KB coach was six feet tall, five feet wide and eighteen feet long. Lincoln ads suggested, "The rich conservativeness of the Lincoln body design does not become antiquated. The Lincoln lines remain as richly distinctive with the passing of years as those of a colonial mansion, a fine piece of Sheffield silver or well-built furniture."

Workers at the Warren Avenue plant in Detroit worked to the highest standards of their trade. A good day's production at Lincoln was about fifty cars. This did not change until the introduction of the Zephyr.

Exact production figures for the 1933 Model-K are clouded. Reports set the range from a low of 1,707 to a high of 2,210. It is possible that the Russian order of four hundred automobiles was still being filled during 1933. Henry Ford was the quintessential American capitalist, yet he had been well received by the Russian government, either for what he did or what he could help Russia do.

Henry Ford and the Ford Motor Company established a manufacturing facility in Russia in 1926. The major early output of this factory was trucks and some are operating in that country to this day. The Lincoln standard Sedans that Russia ordered were produced by Murray and were shipped by overseas freighter to Europe.

Marvin Arnold

CLASSIC MOTORCARS

The Model-KA body styles were types 511 through 520, most of which were designed and produced by Murray. Several of these models had a distinct LeBaron-Dietrich design influence. The body styles for the Model-KB were types 251 through 267, plus assorted custom builts like the types 2197 and 1308. No new Lincoln coachbuilders would be authorized from this year on. The new Lincolns had smoother, but more austere lines. Both models sported new, larger, chrome radiator shell of wire mesh grille that covered the thermostatically controlled vertical radiator louvers.

The radiator itself was more pointed and it sloped rearward at the top in a snow plow effect. The front of the fenders curved inward and met just under the radiator. The headlights were mounted between the radiator shell and fender, the badge bar was omitted and the center emblem was displaced. The fluted oval Lincoln emblem was now mounted neatly on the chrome radiator shell crown, about three inches below the filler cap. The red and blue (KA and KB) background color scheme for the cloisonné emblem was continued. The horns were moved inside and concealed behind the grille.

The Badge Bar was actually a top front fender brace used on most automobiles since 1910. In addition to stabilizing the fender, it provided for the mounting of headlamps, horns and decorative badges.

Page 130: Model K, 1934 7-passenger Sedan; Dietrich Convertible Sedan; LeBaron Convertible Roadster. Page 132: Model K 1934 5-passenger Convertible Phaeton; 1935 5-passenger, 2-window Sedan. Page 133: Model K 1935 7-passenger Touring; 1935 Brunn Convertible Victoria; 1935 LeBaron Convertible Sedan. Page 136: Model K 1936 Catalogue; LeBaron Roadster; Willoughby Limousine; Coupe 5-passenger; Judkins 2-window Berline; Sedan 7-passenger. Page 138: Model K 1936 Willoughby Limousine in Central Park; Sedan 5-passenger at Williamsburg; LeBaron Convertible Sedan at the Maryland Hunt Cup; Sedan 5-passenger, 2-window Sedan at Gloucester; 1937 Model K Sedan; 1936 Model K Judkins 2-window Berline. Page 140: Model K 1936 Brunn Convertible Victoria on the Storm King Highway; 1937 LeBaron Convertible Roadster; Judkins 2-window Berline. Page 142: Model K 1938 Berline at the Rittenhouse Square Flower Mart; 1939 Willoughby Limousine.

Oddly, the cowl vents reverted to stamped-out slotted louvers. This was, however, their last year to be used on any Lincoln.

The Gorham chrome greyhound remained as the Lincoln radiator filler cap ornament and would do so until the end of Model-K production. The one piece dual-rib front bumper now had a slight dip in the center. Early in the year, a few body styles slipped through with the old straight front bumpers. The rear-deck luggage rack was restyled. The only major body change was the conversion to valanced fenders. This style of fenders follows the curve of the tire to create a more modern looking boxed-in wheel well.

Most luxury car competitors had converted to this style of fender the year before. Lincoln switched to the valanced fender in mid-February, after the model year introduction. An offer to retrofit all of the cars delivered without them was made through Lincoln dealerships. Any owner desiring to change over would be provided the new-style fenders. A letter to dealers, however, implied that such requests should be kept to a minimum. The valanced fender style was also referred to as Skirted. A few years later, the term Fender Skirt took on a different meaning, suggesting the full covering of a wheel well.

A double drop was still built into the frame for a lower center of gravity. The gas tank capacity was reduced slightly from 28 gallons to 26 gallons. Standard tire sizes were 18x7.00 for the Model-KA and 18x7.50 for the Model-KB.

Most accessories were common to all body types, for example the Waltham speedometer and the Trico vacuum-operated windshield wipers. Other standard equipment included the Auto-Lite starter and generator, dual Auto-Lite CE-400K coils, K-S Telegage gas gauge and AC type I vacuum fuel pump. The KAV-12 crankcase had a ten quart capacity of oil while the KBV-12 held twelve quarts.

The electrical system was negative ground, unlike the Ford and Zephyr. The new Model-K instrument panel cluster was composed of three circular groups and the speedometer indicated up to 110 MPH. Freewheeling was optional this year and the control lever for it was relocated to the instrument panel.

Marvin Arnold

The often-told story that the first White House Lincoln was a 1924 LeBaron Touring cannot be substantiated. More likely, it was a Ford company car provided for President Cal Coolidge's use. The 1923 Lincoln Touring photographed with British Prime Minister Lloyd George displayed a Virginia license plate. The first documentable Lincoln at the White House was a 1933 Model-KA five-passenger Phaeton purchased by the Secret Service. President Franklin Roosevelt, on several occasions, switched from the White House Packard or Pierce to the less showy Model-KA Lincoln when riding in parades.

The economic recession was worldwide, overseas shipments were down considerably. Four of the RHD Model-KA and three of the Model-KB were exported in 1923. Seventeen Specials, including one 155 inch wheelbase were delivered. The odd numbered type 2197 was a Dietrich two-passenger Coupe similar in style to last year's type 242. Eight of these were built. Judkins also offered an out of sequence type number, the type 1308 seven-passenger Sedan Limousine. It is not certain if any of these were built.

Ads for 1933 were simple line drawings featuring a particular body style. Ad copy read, "More than you could ever expect, even of the Lincoln. A new Lincoln 12-136 with full equipment sold for $2,700 at Detroit."

The new Lincoln Twelve was on the 145 inch wheelbase and were the most luxurious Lincolns ever built. They were priced at $4,200 FOB Detroit. Like the design of the Model-KB, the quality of the Lincoln brochures reached an all-time high.

The Model-KA color brochure featured ten body styles and had twenty-eight pages. The Model-KB, also in color, featured twenty body styles on forty-eight pages. Both came in matching printed envelopes. A hardbound custom catalogue featured twelve custom body styles. A second set of smaller sixteen-page brochures was also printed. The Model-KA brochure showed ten body styles while the Model-KB contained nine. The only brochure to illustrate the valanced front fender was a color folder printed on stiff paper featuring the Model-KB Phaeton with the new fenders.

The Model-KB coach work and finishing was the finest yet, making these Lincolns possibly the most traditionally classic and elegant of all. The automotive writers used phrases like, "Cathedral hush ride… for town or touring… something out of the ordinary… and tremendous performance." However, the economy left this beautiful motorcar and its unqualified luxury waiting at the altar. These classics passed into the pages of automotive history with very low production numbers, which is one reason why they are scarce and expensive today.

NINETEEN-THIRTYFOUR - In 1934, Lincoln offered only one engine for Models KA and KB. Both were now referred to as the Model-K, there were no exterior differences between the two and for all practical purposes the two model concept had been abandoned. The new Model-K Lincolns had full skirted wheel well fenders and smaller cone-shaped headlamps. Radiator shells were painted to match the body color. Parking lights remained atop the front fenders, but were smaller and more pointed at the rear. The side-mounted spares were enclosed in a full metal case. The engine cowl vents once again returned to the thermostatically controlled doors that had first been introduced in 1932. These vent doors, sometimes referred to as hood shutters, were screened inside and the mechanical mechanism had been improved for better operation. The sloping or torpedo trunk line introduced on the sedan body styles matched the sweep of the rear fender. The 521 series was on the 136 inch wheelbase and the 271 series on the 145 inch wheelbase.

The upgraded KAV-12 engine, now used on both models, had a bore of 3.125 inches and a stroke of 3.50 inches, resulting in a 414 cubic inch displacement engine (6.8 liters or 6784 CC). This displacement was between last year's two V-12 engines. The new improved 67 degree KV-12 engine performed better, ran more smoothly and developed the same 150 brake horsepower (46.8 rated HP) as the heavier KBV-12. Rating RPM was 3800 (some specs state 3400 RPM) giving the Model-K a top speed of 96 MPH.

The new engine turned in much better fuel economy figures. Special engine features include aluminum cylinder heads with water pump-driven oil cooler to regulate engine temperature. Oil coolers were being extensively used on aircraft engines of the era, but this cooler differed in that the oil lines were water cooled. The engine's compression was a 6.28 to 1 ratio. This was relatively high for the grades of gasoline available, but a new 70-octane ethyl gasoline was introduced about this time.

The new KV-12 engine used replaceable copper-lead rod bearings on all but one of the four main bearings. The number four main bearing needed to be stronger because it takes a major portion of the engine thrust. The new bearings were more resistant to overheating and thus less susceptible to burnout. The older Babbitt metals used had a melting point of approximately 300 degrees Fahrenheit, the new copper-lead types could withstand 750 degrees.

Babbitt bearings had been used in most automotive engines from their early inception. The process of making soft bearings had been developed by Isaac Babbitt, a goldsmith, in 1853. Normal engines create temperatures very close to the 300 degree mark when overheating. The changeover to the new bearing metals greatly increased the burnout safety margin. It also allowed a reduction from seven to five main bearings on the new KV-12 engines.

Allison, the aircraft engine division of GM, had developed the steel strip bearing for Liberty aircraft engines. By the early 1930s, many automobile engines were incorporating its use. Within three years, Ford and Lincoln would combine the properties of the steel strip and copper-lead bearings to produce the first high-load-withstanding engine bearings.

LINCOLN AND CONTINENTAL

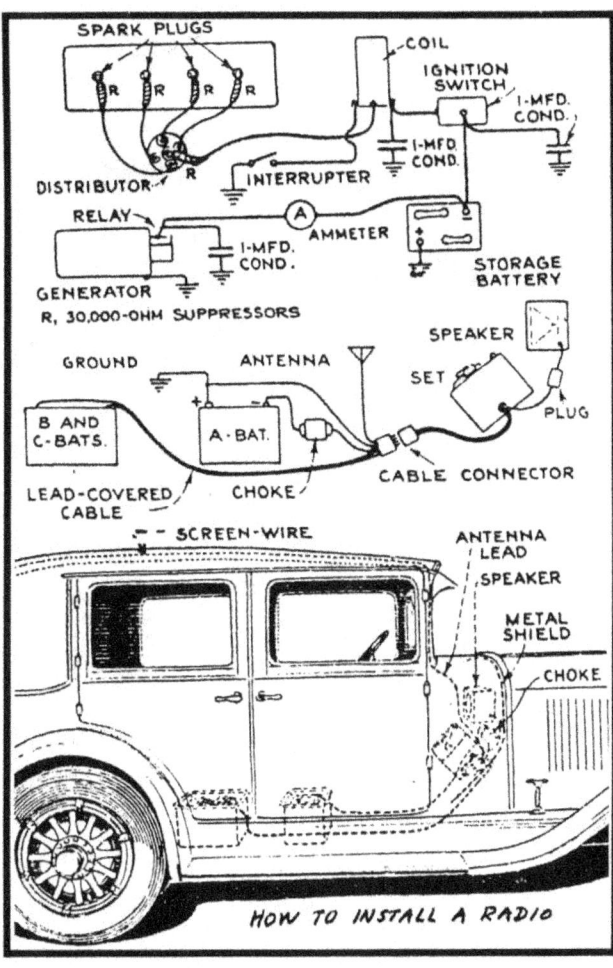

1935 saw the beginning of the more solid appearing automobile, valanced front fender wells and sweeping rear decks. The streamlined cone headlights and rounded radiator shell gave these Models Ks a new modern look. Page 144, top to bottom, 1935 V-12 Model Ks: LeBaron Convertible Roadster Type 5 2 2-passenger with dickey; Lincoln coachworks Sedan 3-window; Lincoln factory built Sedan with trunk installed. Brunn Brougham with hardtop over chauffeur, detached in this picture. Page 145 Model Ks: 1935 V-12 Brunn Convertible Victoria; Sedan 2-window; Coupe 5-passenger (2-door Sedan); Coachbuilt Brunn semi-collapsible Cabriolet Landaulet.

145 The Early Years

Top: 1934 Model K LeBaron Convertible Roadster. Bottom: 1934 Dual-Cowl Phaeton; 1934 Willoughby Sport Sedan, front-rear doors and dual sidemounts. Note the roof vent, dome light accessory.

The new KV-12 engine was 4.5 inches shorter and one inch narrower than the old KBV-12. A shroud was installed behind the radiator and filled the air gap on the longer KB chassis. Freewheeling was optional on the short wheelbase KA, but standard on the long wheelbase KB. This standardized the use of drive shafts. The same drive shaft could be used on the 145 wheelbase with a freewheeling gear box as on the 136 wheelbase without. A shorter old-style drive shaft was used on the KA chassis when the freewheeling option was installed. An extra cross tube was added to the 145 inch wheelbase chassis for extra support.

The two-shoe expanding brakes were modified to anchor at a single pivot pin. This modification and the vacuum boost system were needed for adequate high-speed braking. A shock damper was mounted forward of the left front spring. The steering linkage was increased in length and provided more leverage. The new single-plate clutch required less pedal pressure.

Engine accessories for this year's Lincoln were the Stromberg EE-22 carburetor, the Auto-Lite distributor IMG-4002A and dual CE-4001L coils. Other accessories were a speedometer by Waltham, a temperature gauge by King-Seeley and a wiper motor by Trico. The Exide-type X-21L 6-volt battery was standard. The fuel system used a type I, AC vacuum pump.

The starter and generator were built by Auto-Lite and the starter drive was made by Bendix. Original equipment spark plugs were No. 7 Champions. The engine cooling system capacity was 32 quarts, the crankcase held 10 quarts of oil and the gas tank had a 26 gallon capacity.

One might argue that the new KV-12 engine was cheaper to produce since the block was now poured like a Ford V-8 in a single cast process. True, it was less massive, but many improvements like valve seat inserts and heat exchangers tended to keep the costs high. The production of one engine instead of two was certainly advantageous, but at these low production volumes the cost savings were negligible. The new engine was simply lighter and more efficient.

NINETEEN-THIRTYFIVE - Some Model-K enthusiasts contend that the 1934 Lincoln was actually not two models, but rather a single model with optional wheelbases. This may have been Lincoln's advertising plan and management's intent. However, poor sales in 1933 had left a large inventory of Model-KA and KB chassis.

So even though both were now Model-K Lincolns using the same engine configuration, there were two distinctly different chassis. Two factors seem to confirm this: first, the gap between the KB radiator and the new KV-12 engine; and second, the 136 inch chassis serial numbers were KA1501 thru KA3176 and the 145 inch chassis were KB3001 thru KB3744. This was corrected in 1935 when the serial numbers began rather arbitrarily with K3501.

The three large instrument clusters on the panel remained unchanged, but the dial faces were new. Interior appointments were slightly better on the long wheelbase Model-KB. The Lincoln front doors did not have wing vent windows. However, the previous year General Motors had introduced their No-Draft vent window, so the Lincoln door windows were modified to move slightly rearward (vent position) before rolling down.

The deluxe interiors had a combination dome light and air vent. The asymmetric headlamps permitted the driver, via a switch, to tilt the left headlight separately for night courtesy passing. The vacuum booster for the brakes could be adjusted from a dash mounted control. Dual top-mounted windshield wipers were standard. Very few V-type windshield body styles such as the Judkins Limousine were built.

The Murray custom bodies, the lowest-cost coach bodies in the line, were dropped this year. The Lincoln factory custom coach facility was now building a greater percentage of the standard bodies produced. In fact, only Brunn, Dietrich, Judkins, Willoughby and LeBaron remained as Authorized Lincoln Coachbuilders. Of course, one could still order a bare chassis and have it custom built anywhere.

Only twelve of the 271 series and one 541 series body styles were ordered. There were seven Special coaches built at the Lincoln facility, all were short wheelbase KA. Ten RHD chassis were exported, five of each of the wheelbases. Most of the new coach body styles had less interior head clearance, which lowered the overall profile and greatly improved the looks of the sedans. Dual sidemounts were optional, but most Model-K Lincolns came equipped with them as they greatly enhanced the looks of the car. A single rear-mounted spare was standard equipment.

Literature and brochures for the Model-K were fewer in 1934. The standard catalogue was twenty color pages and illustrated eleven body styles. The custom body brochure was eight pages and had nine full-color plates of various body styles. It was printed in both glossy and matte finish versions, the latter being somewhat scarce as a collector's item.

A forty-eight page booklet on how the Lincoln was built, "The Story of Lincoln's Inevitable Leadership," was published. The style of ads that ran in popular magazines was changed shortly after new model introduction. Ads at model introduction hyped a $3,200 starting price, but quickly departed from the low-price theme of the previous year, moving toward opulence. Pen and ink drawings of various coach body profiles were shown parked in minimal but classically scenic settings.

The backgrounds often had a Roman or Greek architectural flavor. These renderings appeared in black and white as well as in pastel colors.

Body styles included the Lincoln coach works Touring type 273, Sedan and Limousine types 277A & B on the short wheelbase KA, the two-window and three-window Sedan types 543 & 544 and a Coupe type 545 on the long wheelbase KB. Brunn offered two styles of Cabriolet the type 278A & B, also a Brougham type 279 and a five-passenger Convertible Coupe type 280 on the short wheelbase chassis. Brunn built a Convertible Victoria type 547 on the long wheelbase chassis.

Dietrich's entries were a Roadster type 280 and a Convertible Sedan type 281. LeBaron's designs were the Roadster type 542 with dicky, a Convertible Sedan Phaeton type 546 and a Coupe type 548. Judkins built the Berline types 283A & B in two-window and three-window versions.

Willoughby built only a seven-passenger Limousine type 285, but it was the single best seller of the contract coachbuilts for this year. The Lincoln custom catalogue advised that Roadster and Touring styles were special order items.

At least one Henney Motor Coach conversion was built this year in Freeport, Illinois. Henney had become famous for their custom Packard coachbuilts.

The large luxury Lincolns, it is said, were more at home on Grosse Point or a Newport Estate than in Miami Beach or Hollywood. However, Fred Waring, Bing Crosby and W.C. Fields all purchased new Lincolns in 1934. Fields and Crosby both selected LeBaron type 267 Convertible Roadsters.

The successful luxury car marques were faced with one of three choices in the dwindling market. They could be carried by a large company's economy line by Ford, GM and Chrysler; they could produce a toned-down, cheaper version and ride along on their good name to impress purchasers with Packard and Cord; they could go out of business like Franklin, Marmon and Stutz.

Art Deco was in and Classic Renaissance was out. This was the year that saw the introduction of the DeSoto Airflow. The Briggs Zephyr was off the drawing board and rumors were flying about a new Baby Lincoln. Lincoln and Packard would hold onto their classic sweep fender line one more year, but the end of the large traditional luxury car was in sight.

Right column: Top to Bottom: 1936 Model K short wheelbase Convertible Sedan with top up; same with top down; Touring 7-passenger long wheelbase with top up; same with top down. Opposite page: Left to Right: 1936 Model Ks Sedan 2-window (metal roof); Sedan 3-window; LeBaron Coupe (padded roof); Limousine; Brunn Convertible Victoria; LeBaron long wheelbase Convertible Sedan; Willoughby Limousine; Brunn Cabriolet decorative Landaulet rear roof.

The year 1935 ended the classic Model-K Lincoln's sweep styling. It was the last year for top-mounted windshield wipers. The body was moved forward on the chassis. The torpedo trunk line, along with the lower windshield and headlamps, moved the focal point forward so that the Model-K appeared to be in motion while sitting still; marked departure from the heretofore, all too familiar Beast at Rest impression. The 541 series was on the 136 inch wheelbase chassis and the 301 series was on the 145 inch wheelbase.

The 500 series body style type numbering would end with this year's production. Serial numbers were K3501 through K4919 and did not denote wheelbase length. The body was moved nine inches forward on the short chassis and four-and-a-half inches forward on the long chassis.

The result was to move the rear seat passengers forward off the rear axle, providing a more comfortable ride. This also permitted a lower center of gravity and improved the Lincoln's handling qualities. Modified front springs softened the Lincoln's ride. Roadability was further enhanced by the installation of an anti-sway torsion shaft stabilizer.

The radiator cap, upon which the Gorham greyhound perched, was eliminated. The hood ornament was mounted on a chrome base. The radiator filler cap was relocated to under the hood. The grille face consisted of a chrome honeycomb mesh with a center vertical bar and a chrome bar border. A new Lincoln logo appeared for the first time this year on the upper right-hand grille. It was about three inches round and read LINCOLN V-12 with a blue background for the long and red for the short wheelbase. It became the accepted emblem for all of the later series Model-K Lincolns.

The cone headlamps and the radiator shell were painted to match the body color. The new headlights were the Hall Pre-focused type lamps. These smaller headlight shells were often referred to as Bullet styling in contrasts to drum, cone and bell styles. The cowl doors (hood shutters) were slightly larger and mechanically improved. Front fenders were larger and bumpers smaller. Two bumper guards were mounted front and rear.

Safety glass was standard in all windows. The front windshield cranked out at the bottom on most models. The instrument panel was completely redesigned with two large dual clusters located directly in front of the driver. Radios were the single most popular option after heaters, which were not standard on models of this era. This decade introduced many new developments in mobile radio receivers, particularly in DX (long distance reception). Space was now provided for a radio in the center with a newly restyled instrument panel.

A larger and deeper glove box was installed on the passenger side. The flat portion of the panel was accented by four horizontal chrome strips. The optional clock was mounted at the center of the left engine group cluster. Upholstery selections were plush and had the overstuffed appearance popular on period furniture. The steering column and hardware were highly polished steel on most interiors. The anti-theft steering wheel lock continued to be standard equipment on all Ford built automobiles. The Model-K gearshift was floor-mounted and would remain so until the end of its production in 1939. Late in 1935, however, the emergency brake handle was relocated from the floor to under the dash.

The engine received a newly designed camshaft, which improved its performance, but primarily quieted the running. A cartridge-type oil filter was installed. The manual spark control mechanism was removed. Automatic vacuum advance had proved very efficient. Needle bearings were installed on the clutch lever helping it to operate more smoothly. A complete new exhaust system was installed. Lincoln designs had been plagued with exhaust system complaints since the early Model-L days and these modifications were directed at heat dissipation and noise reduction.

The KV-12 continued to be rated at 150 brake horsepower, now officially at 3800 RPM. The 46.8 rated horsepower at the higher RPM figure was actually too conservative. Improvements to the transmission were the addition of a rear support used mainly to stabilize the drive train. Helical gears in second and high allowed them to synchronize and thus shift without a cling.

The wheel size was reduced one inch from 18 to 17. The tire size was 7.50x17 for both wheelbases. The front and rear treads continued to be 60 inches through to the end of the Model-K production.

Indicators from the year were now proving out. Lincoln was losing money and market share trying to produce a more economical Model-K. The cheaper body styles were dropped and new beginning prices were $1,000 higher than at model introduction the year before. Indications that marketing was moving in this direction had been perceived in the previous year's change in advertising approach and ads were continued along the same motif.

It was clear that the introduction of the Briggs-Tjaarda Zephyr would cause Edsel Ford and others to conclude that the big car must now make it, or fail, at the high end of the market. Unlike cheaper cars, these luxury automobiles were not traded-off every two or three years. As in Europe, these coachbuilt models might remain in a family for a decade or more. Both new demand and replacement demand for them was dwindling.

Fewer models were offered in 1935. Only Brunn, LeBaron (now Briggs), Judkins and Willoughby remained as Lincoln coachbuilders. Raymond Dietrich, whose two 1934 designs had only sold twenty-five each, also threw in the towel. His company was absorbed by Murray, but even they were no longer producing Lincoln bodies. LeBaron produced a Convertible Roadster type 542 and a Convertible Sedan Phaeton type 546 on the short wheelbase. The Convertible Sedan was also available as a type 307 on the long wheelbase. By far the largest numbers of coach bodies were built by the Lincoln factory, specifically the two-window and three-window Sedan types 543 and 544. A Coupe type 545 was also built on the short wheelbase.

The factory builts on the long wheelbase were the seven-passenger Sedan and Limousine types 303A & B. Fifteen seven-passenger Tourings type 302 were built. Brunn offered four body styles, Judkins three and Willoughby two. There were twenty-three RHD units shipped, fifteen special order coachbuilts and nine bare chassis delivered. One of the latter was used for a custom coach body by James Cunningham Son & Company of Rochester, New York. Yet, another was custom-converted into a Silver Knightstown by that Indiana body company.

Lincoln produced only 1,411 units all year, an all-time production low. Because of Lincoln's narrow upper end market appeal, literature was sparse. The forty-page color catalogue displayed seventeen body styles. Interior illustrations were rendered in a misty, artistic gray. In the second edition, the print quality was improved slightly. Two 5x6 feature catalogues were also published.

Sad but true, it was the beginning of the end for the big Lincoln. Lincoln had produced more V-12 luxury automobiles than all other V-12 builders in the world. Backed by the Ford dynasty, the classic Lincoln motorcar could have continued until today, but alas they were practical men.

NINETEEN-THIRTYSIX - In the year 1936, Streamlining was the new buzzword. The influence of the Trifon, Sterkenburg and Delahaye was apparent in automotive designs. The Model-K was no exception. The 320 series introduced a radical new fender design on the prestige Lincoln. They were known as Pontoon fenders. The headlamps were placed still lower between the cowl and fender, in an area sometimes referred to as the Catwalk. The radiator grille shell continued to be painted the same color as the body. It was rounded even more than before.

The hard-mounted Greyhound could be correctly referred to as a hood ornament instead of a radiator cap ornament. The grille mesh was coarser, with more pronounced horizontal bars. The windshield sloped backwards seven more degrees, reclining at 27 degrees.

All body styles used the swept-back rear deck. Fold-up rear luggage racks were installed on most body styles. Closed and convertible body styles had low windshield lines and flat top profiles. This, combined with the large teardrop fenders, gave the 320 series Lincolns a unique and almost cartoon-like appearance.

Windshield wipers were moved to the bottom of the windshield and were driven by single linked motor rather than top-mounted dual motors. The fluted steel wheels with large hub caps also helped modernize the appearance of the Model-K. Metal cased dual sidemounted spares, although considered optional, were installed on most cars delivered.

One would be hard-pressed to find a promotional photograph of a 1936 Lincoln without them. The emergency brake handle was located under the left side of the dash in the now familiar location. Two-door and four-door sedans had an enclosed rear trunk, accessed through the rear seat. It was referred to as a Locking Package Compartment.

The Brougham and other body styles offered a spacious tool compartment under the front seat. As in the past, interiors in the seven-passenger body styles had auxiliary rear seats. Some of these seats folded away into the back of the front seat. Heater, clock and radio were optional.

Engineering changes for the year were few, but evolutionarily functional. It has been said that early Lincoln engineers would not so-much-as move a rivet without a good reason. In the transmission gear box, the first gear was changed to a helical gear like second and high. Freewheeling was discontinued altogether. Shackles were installed at both ends of the front springs. A radius rod was used to align the front end. The steering gear ratio was increased and eased steering on the heavy cars, but made the steering less responsive.

The number of engine motor mounts was reduced from five to four. This allowed the KV-12 to absorb torque better and was the direct result of having discontinued freewheeling. Full floating axial rearend ratios were 4.23 to 1 standard, 4.58 to 1 and 4.90 to 1 optional. Engine serial numbers had stopped at K4919 last year and were now K5501 through K7014.

It was becoming an accepted practice to skip blocks of serial numbers when beginning each year's new Lincoln series. This was probably the result of the model, series and wheelbase confusion of the previous four years.

The influence of streamlining had affected everything from washing machines to locomotives. It is true that a boxy car probably has greater wind resistance than an airflow design. However, the average speeds at which automobiles of this era performed rendered the benefit negligible. The coefficient of drag (air resistance) is cubed, not squared as many believe. Thus, an airplane or automobile at 120 MPH has triples its drag at 60 MPH.

At higher speeds, these older engines developed considerably more horsepower due to the high RPM. This largely offset any economies of low drag. Thus, most streamlining was more for aesthetics than for functionality. It is doubtful that any of the streamlined automobile designs produced in the 1930s were ever subjected to serious wind tunnel tests.

Magazine advertising continued along last year's theme. It was tasteful and simple, some of the prettiest watercolors ever produced for automotive ads. The color catalogue was forty pages and featured eighteen body styles. There were several different series folders printed for mailers. Most of Lincoln's advertising centered around the introduction of the new Zephyr, but the Model-K as a result received increased attention also. A three-folder grouping featured drawings by well-known illustrators.

The series numbers began with 320 in 1936; the 1935 Model-K had ended with the type 311. type 321 was a 145 inch wheelbase bare chassis and type 322 denoted the 136 inch wheelbase bare chassis. As had become common practice, the factory coach works produced the high volume sellers, mostly Sedans and Coupes. It is hard to know whether the phasing out of the contract coachbuilders was a cause or an effect of the dwindling Lincoln production figures. In retrospect, one might conclude that having a dozen or so coach shops pushing your product line could only help sales.

Factory-built short wheelbase body styles for the year were the Coupe type 326, two-window and three-window Sedan types 324A &

B. The long wheelbase styles were the Sedan and Limousine types 327A & B, also a Touring type 323. Only a handful of these Tourings were built each year. They now had large crank-up wing windows for front and rear windshields, with side curtains that snapped in between. The Touring body styles weighed approximately 5,276 pounds. They looked much like the now-infamous German staff car with canvas and top bows folded rearward and under a boot.

The coachbuilt offerings were the non-collapsible and semi-collapsible Brunn Cabriolets types 329A & B. These and the seven-passenger Brougham were built on the long wheelbase. On the short wheelbase, Brunn designed a beautiful five-passenger Convertible Victoria. Its popularity was not reflected in sales, however, only ten units were ever built and delivered. It was one of the higher priced body styles selling for $5,500.

LeBaron, Judkins and Willoughby offered the same body styles as the previous year. type numbers for the 320 series Lincolns ranged from 321 through 341. There were fifteen factory custom orders and nineteen RHD chassis shipped. Total production was 1,514 automobiles.

NINETEEN-THIRTYSEVEN - For 1937, the Model-K was further modernized with the introduction of the 350. series Except for a few unusual offerings like the Brunn Touring Cabriolet, the Model-K Lincolns were beginning to look like a luxury Hudson Teraplane. The roof bulged up emulating the lines of the front fenders and the rear deck sloped in scheme with the lines of the rear fenders. The new top was all-metal.

The most immediately noticeable features were the headlights that mounted in the fenders like those of the Zephyr. Dual filament headlight bulbs were used for the first time. The two-piece windshield came to a point at the molded peak of the forward roof line. The grille motif was the same as last year's, but the mesh pattern was slightly different. The round Lincoln logo was about three inches round and mounted on the upper right-hand grille mesh.

All body styles had a pronounced body mold line that swept from cowl to trunk. The runningboard was enclosed by the doors coming nearly to the top of the step. The trunk opened from the rear, concealing a standard spare tire. Dual side-mounted spares were still optional, without them the new body styles looked pretty much mid-market.

Something was needed to dress up these cars, so whitewall tires became standard equipment. The interiors offered were rich broadcloths and curly maple garnished moldings. Rear seat cigar lighters were added to the options list. Model prices were increased slightly and production figures continued to decline.

The major mechanical improvement was the installation of hydraulic valve lifters in the KV-12 engine. This made the engine run more quietly, but necessitated changing the oil regularly. In the period prior to HD grades of oil, the lifters would otherwise sludge up and stick. An engine oil filter had become standard equipment a couple of years earlier.

The engine was moved further forward on the chassis and motor mounts were modified accordingly. These engines were not known for their top-end performance, even though the speedometer dial now read to 110 MPH.

Above: 1937 Model Ks Sedan 7-passenger (no trunk bulge); Judkins Berline with bulging trunk; Willoughby Limousine; LeBaron Convertible Sedan with top down, same as opposite page with top up. Below: Brunn Cabriolet with roof glass and Landaulet top; Custom coach for the King of England when he made U.S. tour.

The Lincoln's large, heavy body dictated a need for good low-speed response. In the days of no automatic transmissions, driving around town required less gear changes with good low-end power.

The 1937 Model-K can be correctly referred to as 350 series. They were offered in short 136 inch wheelbases and long 145 inch wheelbases in most body styles. The body type numbers as well as Serial numbers K7501 through K8490 became intermixed between the two chassis lengths. The 300 series Model-K began with the 1935 long wheelbase bodies and were types 301 through 311. Both chassis lengths used the same 300 series numbers the following year that were 321 through 341. This year's 350 series body types were 351 thru 375. The 1937 type number set would conclude the 300 series Model-K Lincolns.

Willoughby managed to obtain orders to build Four Panel Broughams type 373, which sold for $7,050. The Brougham had a high, squared roof, compartment and a chauffeur's compartment. The custom four-passenger Judkins Coupe used an unusual sweep on the rear passenger windows, extensively modifying the mold line. Durham made several coupes they named Town Victoria. The prominent feature of this Victoria was its curved door lines. The Lincoln factory coach works produced its usual lineup of Sedans. Brunn offered five body types, LeBaron four, Judkins three and Willoughby three. Because of the very few ordered (eleven total), the factory contracted Willoughby to build the Coupe type 356 and Touring type 353. Total production for the model year was 990 units.

The U.S. Secret Service purchased a Model-K type 302. President Franklin D. Roosevelt was photographed riding in this Lincoln during a motorcade, on the occasion of his visit to the Los Angeles Coliseum. The 1933 White House Pierce-Arrow V-12 followed the Lincoln in the motorcade. The Secret Service also purchased a type 363A LeBaron Convertible Sedan with partition, serial number 8238.

Opposite page: 1939 Lincoln Presidential limousine "Sunshine Special" as delivered with original grille; LeBaron Convertible Sedan with top up; Same car with top down. 1939 Model Ks (note wider spaced horizontal grille bars) Convertible Coupe 2-passenger; LeBaron Coupe 2-passenger; Brunn Cabriolet with sky lights and Landaulet.

There was no change in the style of display advertising that ran in popular publications. Literature was the traditional full-color catalogue, forty-four pages showing nineteen body styles. A series of smaller folders was also printed. The kind and quality of materials used in building the Lincoln were heavily advertised, for example, 60 square feet of sheet aluminum, 161 pounds of cast aluminum, 321 feet of high grade lumber, 59 quarts of paint and so forth.

NINETEEN-THIRTYEIGHT Actually, 1938 was the last year for most Lincoln Model-K production. The 400 series numbers began this year and continued unchanged through to the end of Model-K production. They were types 401 through 425. type numbers 401 and 402 were reserved for long and short wheelbase bare chassis, but none were so delivered. Early 400 series cars still had last year's grilles.

After the prior year's grills were used up, the grilles originally meant for this series were installed. The new grille had fewer horizontal bars, eighteen instead of thirty. The thermostat cowl doors were discontinued. Horizontal veined cowl shutters were fixed in place. Stainless steel moldings extended the full length of the body. Chrome door handles were replaced with stainless steel so as to better match the body molding. Larger trunks were the trend. Many sedan body types added rear bulges, a styling trait popular with other makes of the period.

These later KV-12 engines were much better performing than their predecessors of a year or two earlier. This was the result of slightly modifying the cam when the hydraulic valve lifters had been installed. Specification sheets continued, however, to rate these engines as 150 horsepower at 3800 RPM. The transmission became fully synchromatic or synchromesh via some minor modifications. It was now almost impossible to clash the gears when shifting the large Lincoln. The numbers of ribs on the brake drums were increased for better brake cooling, that helped prevent high-speed fade due to brake overheating.

An interesting custom Model-K was built by LeBaron at the request of the Knox Lincoln Dealership of Buffalo, New York. The back end and top were standard LeBaron Sedan Convertible, but the front fender headlights were fully faired-in, probably due to the Zephyr's influence, not pop-eyed like the current production models. The grille and catwalk looked very much like the LaSalle's. The stretch to the front fenders and hood resembled what later become known as the Continental Look. This custom Lincoln was featured in an early issue of Special Interest Autos. The 1937 Michigan license plate on the car bore manufacture number 30, probably LeBaron-Briggs as Ford's number was 22. A later photograph shows the car with the owner's 1938 New York license plate and a chrome nose plate with aeroplane hood ornament had been added.

Judkins offered a two-window Sedan Berline. Its rear passenger compartment was very posh and private. The Sedan's doors all opened forward (front-front). The Lincoln factory coach works produced the Sedan types 402A & B, also the Limousine types 407A & B. For the Sedan body style type 404, the "A" meant two-window and the "B" meant three-window. However, for the type 407 the "A" meant without partition, the "B" meant with partition. Brunn built four body styles, a Convertible Victoria type 408, two Tourings types 425A & 425B and a Brougham type 411.

The Touring Cabriolet had a front-front door arrangement and was not particularly impressive in styling. It and the Willoughby Brougham were the two highest-priced body styles, just over $7,000. Judkins and Willoughby offered three each and LeBaron offered four body styles. As no bare chassis were shipped, one-off customs by non-authorized coach shops were nonexistent. No RHD chassis were shipped this year, due in part to the war clouds hanging over Europe.

Magazine advertising was of the same motif as the previous several years. Except for an original design proposal and the art work of the custom coach houses, these ads were the best of all the color drawings of Lincoln body styles. This year's ads were more scenic, with detailed renderings appearing in the art work. The color catalogue was mostly an updated version of the prior year's catalog and was also issued in a special hardbound version.

The interior appointments of these cars were super plush. New selections in upholstery were offered on the standard factory body styles. A rheostat mounted on the instrument panel now operated the Lincoln's interior lighting. The serial numbers were K9001 through K9450. Prices on the average Model-K were increased $350. This was the year the archer, Pierce-Arrow, quilled his arrows. The big Lincoln had out lasted them all, but the large luxury car market itself seemed no longer to exist.

NINETEEN-THIRTYNINE - The 1939 Model-K 400 series would become known as the '39-'40 models because sales had declined so far that not all of the big Lincolns were sold until well into 1940. One factor affecting sales was that Lincoln introduced its own competition for the Model-K. The H series, types 32 and 36 the forerunners to the Zephyr Custom types 31 and 32 were offered as a luxury limousine replacement for the Model-K. The new Zephyr Continental Cabriolet, it was hoped, would also appeal to the Model-K sport style purchaser.

Edsel Ford is reported to have said, "We did not stop making luxury cars, people just stopped buying them." And if he did not say it, he should have. A popular myth associated with the end of the Model-K production was that the blue cloisonné Lincoln emblem, mounted at the upper right of the grille mesh was produced this year in black to mourn the passing of the Model-K, but it's not true.

As to production figures, the exact numbers were lost in the rush to Zephyr production. By serial number arithmetic, there would have been 223 units produced. By custom body count, the number would have been 133 units. By various other accountings, there were 120 total units produced, or 120 units each year for a total of 240 units. The 400 series type numbers were identical to the 1938 body type numbers. Only one each of seven different type numbers were produced of the thirty-three body styles offered and were rare ones-of-a-kinds indeed. The only two styles produced in any quantity were the factory built seven-passenger Sedan and Limousine types 407A & B.

A couple of minor mechanical changes were incorporated near the end of production. The pressed steel wheels were reinforced. There had been several incidents of the steel wheels bending during high-speed turns. No wonder, due to the five thousand-plus pounds of automobile. On the backside of the rim, steel spokes were welded into place. There was also a modification to the Stromberg carburetor.

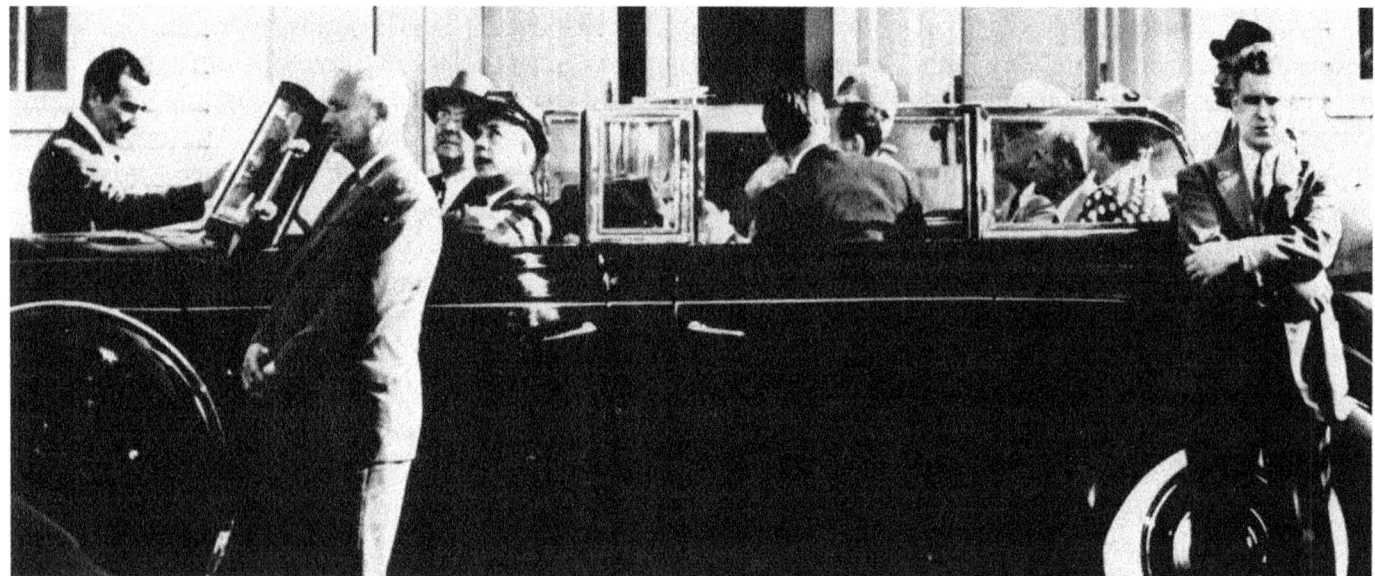

The engine maintenance manual does not record the part number of the modified carburetor, but they were interchangeable with the standard EE-22 model. Tire size on the Model-K remained 7.50x17 even though the H series had adapted the 16 inch wheel.

The most famous Model-K of all was a 160 inch wheelbase Convertible Limousine by Brunn. Its overall length was 258 inches. Officially called a parade car, it was shipped to the Ford Alexandria branch on September 29 and delivered to the White House on December 1, 1939. This Brunn Limo was leased to the government for a minimal fee, thus beginning the identification of Lincolns as America's Cars of State. A story on this Lincoln was featured in Old Cars Weekly and is also described in the book Presidents on Wheels.

The Secret Service called it 99 for its license plate number, but the world knew it by its nickname, the Sunshine Special. In his younger years, President Roosevelt had been an avid yachtsman and enjoyed the open air. This Brunn convertible was his choice during fair weather.

The Sunshine Special was returned to the Ford Rouge plant for modifications in 1942 and was extensively overhauled. Armor plate and extra-thick safety glass were installed.

Above: 1939 Model K Limousine. Seated in the far back, Franklin D. Roosevelt, Henry Ford and Eleanor Roosevelt. Seated center, Charles Sorensen and Edsel Ford. Photo taken in 1942. Below: Model K Parade Limousine the "Sunshine Special" with updated 26H (1942) grille. Opposite page: 1939 Model K Limousine; One of the last Model K ads to run; 1939 Brunn Model K.

The car weighed 9,300 pounds after modification. It was refitted with the current 26H series with an H grille, headlights and Art Deco ball and spire hood ornament. The blackwall tires were the bullet-resistant self-sealing type.

There was a 1941 Model-K on the drawing board and of course, it never produced. The drawings of a Sedan resembled a Model-H type 32 Limousine with long hood and Continental style fenders. Its wheelbase dimensions were proposed to be 145 inches.

The greyhound hood ornament crouched low and resembled a stalking panther. The factory bays used to produce the custom built Model-K were soon filled with custom Zephyr Cabriolets known as the Continentals and so a 1941 Model-K never came to be.

The last factory-produced literature on the Model-K, printed in May, 1939, was a brochure illustrating a green seven-passenger Sedan. The regular Lincoln Catalogue was the same as last year's with the date changed. One additional two-color folder was printed. There were a few early year magazine ads for the model that would be introduced, but they were identical to those of the previous year's models even though rumors were of a major change.

By spring, however, all pictorial ads were discontinued. The ads that did run were of the best quality matte background, tan on gray, bordered in silver. A small frontal silhouette of the Model-K in black with a white greyhound was the last of the Model-K Lincoln ads to ever run. One of these final ads said it all, "Here is a motorcar so distinguished for comfort, safety and dignity that it belongs with your finest possessions. It will be your pride long after far places, not yet visited, have become familiar."

Marvin Arnold

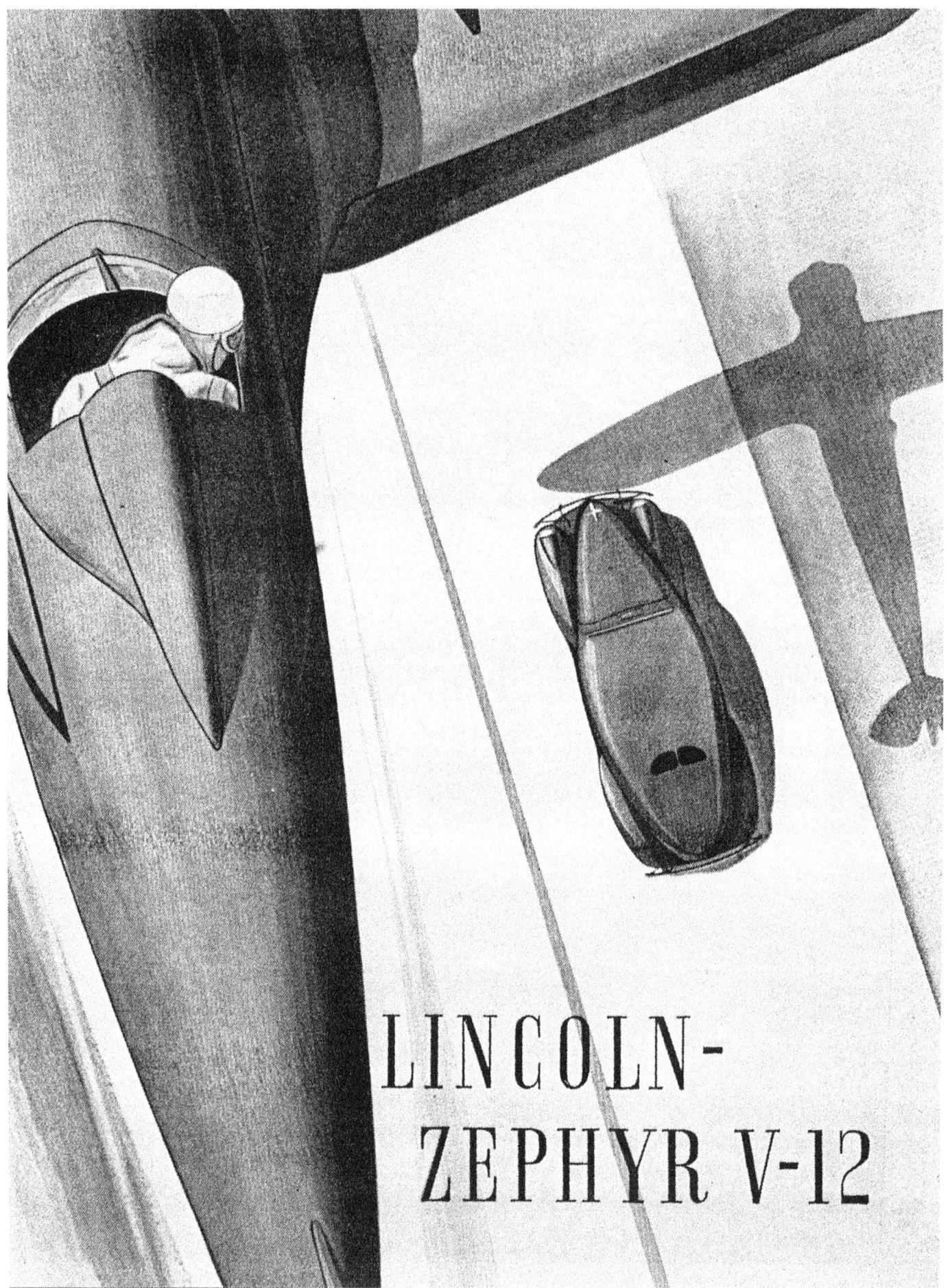

CHAPTER SIX

ENTER THE ZEPHYR

Ride Like The Wind

The story of the Zephyr, like that of all great concepts, begins with an individual and an idea. The idea was that of aerodynamic design and the individual was John Tjaarda. Born in Holland, Tjaarda was educated in England and studied aerodynamics under Dr. Alexander Klemin.

Tjaarda served as a pilot instructor in the Royal Dutch Air Corps and worked as an engineer for Fokker Aircraft. He came to the United States in 1923, where he first did custom auto body portfolios for affluent Hollywoodites.

At Locke & Company, he worked as a coach designer on the Pierce-Arrow and for a short time on the Duesenberg. Over the years, John had developed his own idea about aerodynamically clean body designs. He referred to his new designs as the Sterkenburg series, a name taken from his Friesland family home of the Tjaarda van Sterkenburg estate. The original design concept working sketch, called the Sterkenburg C-3, was drawn up in 1926. The "C" stood for Carcass, which was Tjaarda's term for a unit body construction.

In 1930, Tjaarda met and went to work for Harley Earl at the newly formed Art & Color Studio of General Motors. For the upcoming Chicago World's Fair, Earl held an in-house design contest. From this competition came the classic V-16 Cadillac, but the also-rans were Gordon Buehrig's Cord 810 and Phil Wright's Silver Arrow. John Tjaarda's forerunner to the Zephyr was also entered in the competition, but no great interest ensued.

Harley Earl showed very little interest in Tjaarda's design. After several tries at obtaining financial backing for to produces his new design, John accepted an offer to work for the W.O. Briggs Company.

By 1932, Model-K Lincoln production had fallen off to the extent that Charles Sorensen advocated closing it down. Briggs had been a major supplier to Ford and wanted desperately to retain the Lincoln business. They hired Howard Benbright, a close personal friend of Edsel Ford, to head up a new Ford Policies and Relations Department.

John Tjaarda was given the green light to secretly develop a new design for presentation to the progressive-minded Edsel Ford. Briggs believed in the unit body design concept, but wanted Edsel to champion its cause to Sorensen (Cast-Iron Charlie) and the senior Ford. (Ol' Henry) did not accept new ideas all that well.

The development at Briggs continued under wraps on the fifth floor with frequent visits from Edsel. The security problem was complicated by the fact that Briggs was also currently building parts for Chrysler.

Three proposals were prepared for the new unit body Lincoln. The first was a rear-engine car that resembled a large streamlined Volkswagen Beetle. However, the VW Beetle was not yet in production. It is likely, however, that Dr. Porsche borrowed from the Sterkenburg concepts for his Peoples Wagon.

The second unit-body design was similar in appearance to the first, but with a more conventional front engine and standard drivetrain. The third design draft was of a convertible coupe that incorporated basically the same lines as the previous two sedan designs. This convertible coupe design would ultimately become the Zephyr Continental.

The unit body concept held much promise for Lincoln. It might, indeed, enable Lincoln to produce a large luxury automobile for far fewer dollars. A full-size prototype, complete with rear-mounted V-8 engine, was constructed. This wooden mock-up was introduced to the public at the Ford Exhibition of Progress in New York City during December 1933.

The car toured the United States via Lincoln-Ford dealers and ended up in the Ford Rotunda at the 1934 world exposition held in Chicago. Called the Century of Progress, this World's Fair had opened in 1933. It stretched a half-mile along the Chicago shoreline of Lake Michigan.

Emphasis was on the application of science and industry in everyday living. Ford marketing personnel mingled with the crowd and ask questions of prospective purchasers in an effort to obtain the public's opinion of how successful a new streamlined Lincoln automobile might be.

Edsel had done a good selling job on Henry and Sorensen, but Ford engineers held out for the more conventional front-engine design. As it turned out, the public seemed to agree with them.

The Sterkenburg series was not alone in the race to streamline the automobile. Walter Chrysler had commissioned two Trifon Special prototypes in 1932. These would become the Chrysler and DeSoto Airflows. Alexander Klemin, Tjaarda's former professor, was brought to the United States to do the analytical equations on the design for the new unit body Chrysler Airflow. It was over these equations that Klemin and Tjaarda had disagreed years before. Tjaarda personally disliked complicated mathematical calculations and used a method he referred to as Guessomatics, his own version of an engineering WAG.

As it turned out, Klemin over-stressed the Airflow resulting in a much heavier body and somewhat sluggish automobile. On the Sterkenburg design, due to his past design experience, Tjaarda managed to guess pretty accurately. The result was the large and lightweight unit body chassis design that became the Lincoln Zephyr. Some areas proved to be too lightweight and would require modification.

One example is the forward floor plates that should have been of heavier gauge steel. However, better drainage of water seeping in through dried windshield gaskets might have accomplished considerably more in preserving these floor panels. It is rare to find a Zephyr or Continental without rusted-out or partially rusted floor plates.

The Hupmobile and Hudson Terraplane were early contenders in the streamline era design market. The Hup 427-T aerodynamic design by Loewy was produced in 1934. The streamlined Hup's styling was quickly changed to that of the Cord and Graham design when the companies were merged.

The 1937 Hudson was very streamlined and incorporated full rear fender skirts. The last really pulchritudinous Hudson was the 1939 model, but even it was beginning to look much like a cross between a Ford and Chevrolet.

Architectural engineer Buckminster Fuller developed a concept he called Dymaxion and applied it to everything from buildings to automobiles. Fuller made application for a patent in October of 1933 for a streamlined three-wheel car that would turn on a dime. It was powered by a Ford V-8 and had front-wheel-drive. The Dymaxion would do 120 miles per hour and got 30 miles per gallon. The third and most widely driven (some 300,000 miles) of the four Dymaxion cars built was purchased by Harrah's Auto Museum, where it remained for many years in unrestored condition.

Above: Production model Zephyrs 1936 through 1940. Left: Tjaavda's mock-up on display in 1934. Below: Instrument panel in the mock-up; Briggs prototype on test track; Scale model 1938 and last two-door sedan. Opposite page second column: 1936 Zephyr Brochure.

This author had the good fortune of viewing the Dymaxion at the Harrahs Museum years ago before Holiday Inn, who bought the estate, sold off the Harrah's car collection.

Streamlining was derived from the concept that the lines of an object should be efficient in an air stream or aerodynamically clean. There was, however, nothing much in the 1930s that moved fast enough to really require streamlining. Styling in the 1920s had been boxy. The cars looked like shoe boxes with fenders. Bi-winged airplanes resembled Chinese box kites. So the styling trend of the 1930s became streamlining.

Art became Art Deco and even static objects, from toasters to pencil sharpeners, were streamlined. This trend was inspired by the great airships of the late 1920s, the Graf Zeppelins. Those of us who saw the demise of the magnificent steam locomotives, such as the Baldwin Hudson Engines, will always associate the word Streamliner with the early diesel trains like the Santa Fe Chief.

One of the earliest of these streamline train was called the Zephyr. It may be difficult tocomprehend exactly why Lincoln would choose the same name for their new car as the General Motors designed and built Zephyr diesel locomotive. Several automotive writers and some Lincoln advertisements seem to support the theory that the new Lincoln Model-H, indeed, was named for the train itself.

Although not a Lincoln, this French design was representative of the streamline concept in styling popular in the early 30s.

This kinship certainly did not hurt the new Lincoln prototype. The new train was got a lot of publicity and it too was displayed at the Chicago Century of Progress Exposition in 1934.

The 1934 Lincoln Zephyr prototype, as redesigned by Tjaarda, used a 125 inch wheelbase with transverse semi-elliptical leaf springs. The upper independent suspension arms at each end were linked to the top of a Magnalium alloy hub carrier. Unique innovations such as a periscope rearview mirror and a cylindrical radiator were used. Two air scoops behind the rear door provided the air intake for the radiator.

The instrument panel was so simplified that it was plain. Dual glove boxes were located either side of a large, center-mounted horizontal speedometer dial. The aircraft type semi-monocoque construction was its single most outstanding feature and managed to survive through all the design changes. This made the new Lincoln Zephyr one of the strongest, lightest weight and vibration-free automobiles of its size constructed in this era.

The original prototype of the Sterkenburg Zephyr had the rear-mounted engine. A transverse engine mount was also experimented with for a short while, but abandoned. The engine used was an aluminum block V-8. The engine weighed about 300 pounds and developed 80 horsepower at 4700 RPM. Tubular wishboned frame allowed the engine and transmission to be easily dismounted for maintenance.

An automatic overdrive and Bendix-Weiss constant speed universal joint were incorporated into the drivetrain. The prototype weighed 2,500 pounds and achieved a top speed of 110 miles per hour on the test track. Tjaarda disliked engine mounts that extended outside the wheelbase. He claimed such designs just increased the number of gimmicks required to correct oversteer.

The Zephyr prototype did require one degree of toe-in to trim its handling. Proof of how correct Tjaarda was about engine location can be attested by the handling problems. General Motors experienced similar problems with the Corvair series. Additional testimony as to this concept is borne out by today's mid-engine race cars.

Marvin Arnold

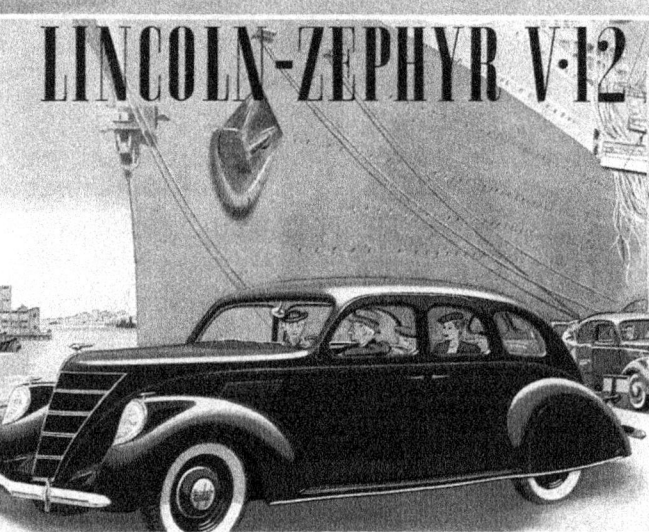

New car...old tradition

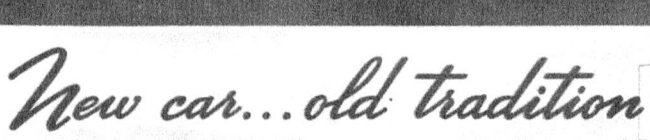

CLASSIC MOTORCARS

Sorensen, Mr. Ford and the Ford engineers ultimately prevailed and the Zephyr would be built only if it utilized existing Ford Company front engine and drivetrain technology. Two sedan prototypes were hand built and used for road tests and for unit body construction tests.

A souped-up version of the Ford V-8 was unable to provide adequate power for the large Zephyr. The final production weight was being estimated in the range of 3,200 pounds. Thus, Frank Johnson's engineering team was instructed to come up with yet another Lincoln V-12 based on the flathead V-8 Ford engine.

Ford stylist E.T. Gregorie redesigned many of the Zephyr body parts. His work accounts for much of the overall larger automobile appearance of the Zephyr versus that of the original design.

Ford designer Holden "Bob" Koto described in an article for Special Interest Autos his work on the development of the new front end design for the Briggs Zephyr. The entire front end was redesigned to accommodate a larger frontal radiator and V-12 engine. The new wheelbase was established at 122 inches and had more to do with the drive train match-up than with aesthetics.

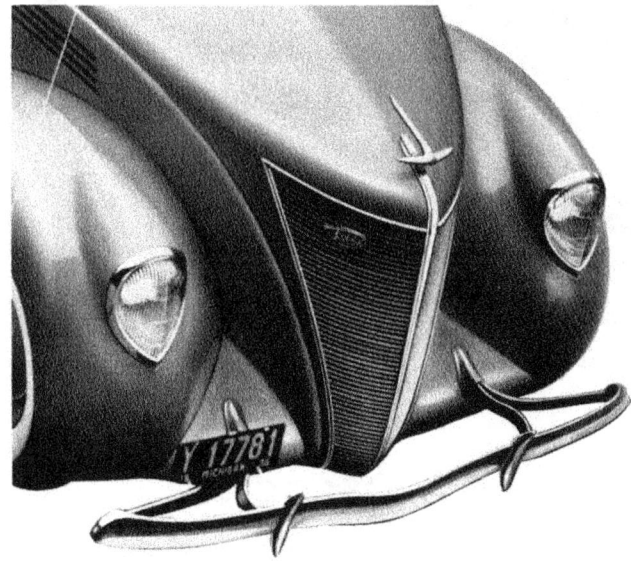

NINETEEN-THIRTYSIX – With the creation of the Zephyr, Lincoln had a very unique automobile even though Tjaarda did not get his revolutionary design in its entirety. Edsel did not get the classic and impressive coach look that he liked so well. The Ford engineers did not get just another big Ford. But the sum was greater than the total of its parts; a car appreciated even today for its forward thinking design and impressive styling. Ford sales manager William Cowling announced the Lincoln Zephyr in November of 1935 as, "A completely new motor car."

The 1936 Zephyr was called the Model-H, but some early manuals refer to it as the 'Model 901'. Actually, 901 was the series number. The practice of assigning a model year chassis number was not applicable to the unit body Zephyr, as it had been with the Model-K.

The Zephyr's final test weight with gas and oil was approximately 3,600 pounds. With a standard rear axle, the Model-H had a top speed of 91 miles per hour. This meant that the car had been geared fairly low. It could accelerate to 50 miles per hour in just under eleven seconds, very good for the times.

Autocar magazine reported an average fuel consumption of 17 miles to the gallon in their road tests. Motor magazine performed a three hundred mile test on the Model-H and also reported very favorably on the car's performance. The Model-H was an immediate success and outsold the Model-K ten to one.

The introductory price of the two-door Sedan was $1,275 and the four-door Sedan sold for $1,320. These were the only two models offered. The small Packard and the LaSalle were priced approximately 10 percent lower than the Zephyr. Slowly, the Zephyr began to outsell them and the Chrysler Airflow. European designers like Ferdinand Porsche had been interested in the car since it had gone public in 1933.

There is little doubt that the Zephyr greatly influenced foreign automobile designs of the 1930s. About a thousand RHD versions were built and shipped. There were 908 Sedans, seven Town Sedans with Deluxe interior and 25 two-door Sedans exported this first year of production. Three hundred Zephyrs were shipped in knockdown and prime coat only condition for export to France, Denmark and Holland. The next year, over two hundred were shipped to Mexico. The dual glove box dash on the Zephyr prototype was conceived for ease of installation of a RHD or standard left-hand steering column.

This original panel arrangement, in modified form, was used again beginning with the 1938 model year. The only mention the Zephyr gets in the Motor Service Encyclopedia of Automobile Facts is, "The alligator hood: Lincoln introduces first rear-hinged, front opening hood on 1936 Zephyr."

Indeed, the Zephyr did set the standard for modern hood openings. It also influenced grille design by using a vertical grille with horizontal bars. Two years later, however, Zephyr would abruptly departed from the trend it set and return to a vertical grille bar pattern, probably in an effort to be different from other auto makers who began using the horizontal grille bar arrangement.

Trunk space was a problem for the early Model-H. Access to the trunk was through the rear-seat passenger compartment. The back of the seat hinged forward to access a small luggage compartment. The streamlined rear deck lid concealed only the spare tire. The rear passenger doors opened forward, popularly known as suicide doors.

The windshield was flat and one piece. Teardrop fender skirts enclosed the rear wheel wells and were standard equipment. Other styling accents were three louver vents on each side cowl, teardrop headlamps, missile-shaped tail lights and a combination chrome hood latch and hood ornament that resembled an airplane silhouette. Large round corners on the windows retained the characterized 1936 and 1937 model years look.

Features that were down played were the floor gearshift, transverse leaf springs, solid front axle and mechanical brakes. All were carry-overs from the Ford line. Regarding the lack of hydraulic brakes, most Zephyr owners claim that properly maintained mechanical brakes stopped the car even better. Tires were size 23x7.00 on 16 inch rims. The new dropped center wheels were of fluted pressed-on steel construction.

The standard factory colors offered on the 1936 Zephyrs were: Royal and Ascot Maroons; Gunmetal and Stonington Grays; Cardiff and Meadow Greens; and Cordoba. Black was not offered until 1939. Chrome hand rails bordered the backrests on the front seats, lending an Art Deco appearance to the interior.

The headlight control was located on the steering wheel center button. The instrument cluster was similar to earlier Model-K Lincolns, basically two large round dials. The left contained oil temperature, fuel quantity and battery charging indicators. The right cluster comprised the speedometer. Both were located in front of the driver. A pullout round ashtray was located in the center of the dash. It was either removed or moved to the clock mounting hole on the left when a non-factory option round radio dial was installed.

Ignition and steering lock was on the lower right steering column. The windshield wiper control knob was at the top center of the dash. Throttle, choke, lighter and panel light control were in front of the driver. This rather plain dash arrangement was only used for this first year of the Zephyr. Options for the new Zephyr were a clock, leather upholstery and a set of fitted luggage.

NINETEEN-THIRTYSEVEN - In 1937, the Model-HB was introduced. There had been a positive buyer response to the new Zephyr Model-H 901 series, types 902 and 903. The HB Sedan became the type 730 and a Town Limousine version was dubbed the type 737. A new-style business Coupe with either a shelf or small auxiliary seat was introduced as the type 700. The two-door Sedan became the type 720. Three prototype Convertibles were produced at the end of the model year and were built on the type 730 chassis. Although the Zephyr HB differed very little outwardly from the 901 series, there were many changes.

The horizontal grille bars sported five new bright metal double bars and the side cowl louvers now numbered five. The front and rear bumpers formed a slight V. The interior underwent a major rework. Upholstery trim patterns were changed, but the material choices remained the same.

The entire instrument panel was redesigned and rounded. It featured glove boxes on the left and right sides. A large speedometer was located on the center panel and the lower center dash formed a console that went all the way down to the top of the transmission housing on the floor. The radio receiver speaker and an air heater duct could be mounted inside of this console. The console was forward of the exposed floor-mounted gear shift.

A smaller round dial containing the non-standard clock was relocated to below the speedometer. Engine gauge clusters were installed either side of the speedometer, the left ones for fuel and oil and the right for temperature and charge. The windshield wiper control, starter button, choke and throttle remained in approximately the same locations as on the 1936 model.

A major functional improvement for the Zephyr was the mounting of the spare tire on a hinged rack allowed access to the luggage compartment from the rear deck lid. The price of a new Sedan was slightly lower. A newly offered Town Limousine with glass partition between front and rear compartments was marketed for $1,425.

The Zephyr's sales continued upward and its styling was now setting a trend. Its influence was apparent on the new Ford models introduced this year.

The first production model Lincoln Zephyrs were labeled the Model-H. Here again, we ascend the alphabet moving up from the Model-K and not down the alphabet as one would assume. The second year's production became the B version of the Model-H or HB. On subsequent models, a number 6 representing the last digit of the year 1936 preceded the H, which was the first production model year for the Zephyr. Beginning in 1938, the last digit of the model year precedes the 6H. Thus, the 1938 Zephyr would become the 86H series.

LINCOLN AND CONTINENTAL

1937

The Early Years

THE LINCOLN-ZEPHYR COUPE-SEDAN

THE NEW KIND OF CAR

THE LINCOLN-ZEPHYR COUPE

...YEARS AHEAD OF THE TIMES

Its performance is years ahead. The LINCOLN-ZEPHYR has a V-type, 12-cylinder engine — designed by Lincoln engineers, built by Lincoln precision methods, in the famous Lincoln plant. It develops 110 horsepower.

Its economy is years ahead. So efficient is the engine design, so skillfully streamlined is the car, so high is its power-to-weight ratio, that owners report 14 to 18 miles per gallon.

Its safety is years ahead. Body and frame are one, inseparable. Steel paneling is welded to the rust steel framework — light, yet strong — top, sides, bottom. You ride close to the ground, enclosed in steel, protected all around.

Its comfort is years ahead. The "flowing" ride of this new car is a thrilling new experience. All passengers sit "amidships," toward the center. The car flows along like a fast ship on a calm sea — the new rhythm of motoring!

Its value is years ahead. Only the Lincoln-Ford background makes this car possible at the price. Thousands of Lincoln-Zephyr owners declare it transforms their previous ideas of motoring. Why not arrange, now, for a demonstration in the car built by Lincoln, priced by Ford.

THE LINCOLN-ZEPHYR TOWN-LIMOUSINE

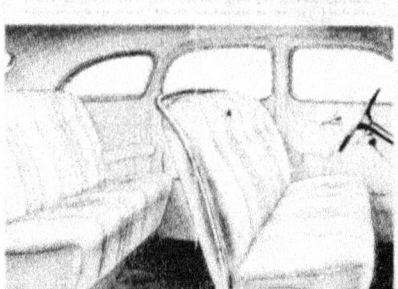

LINCOLN AND CONTINENTAL

The Early Years

Marvin Arnold

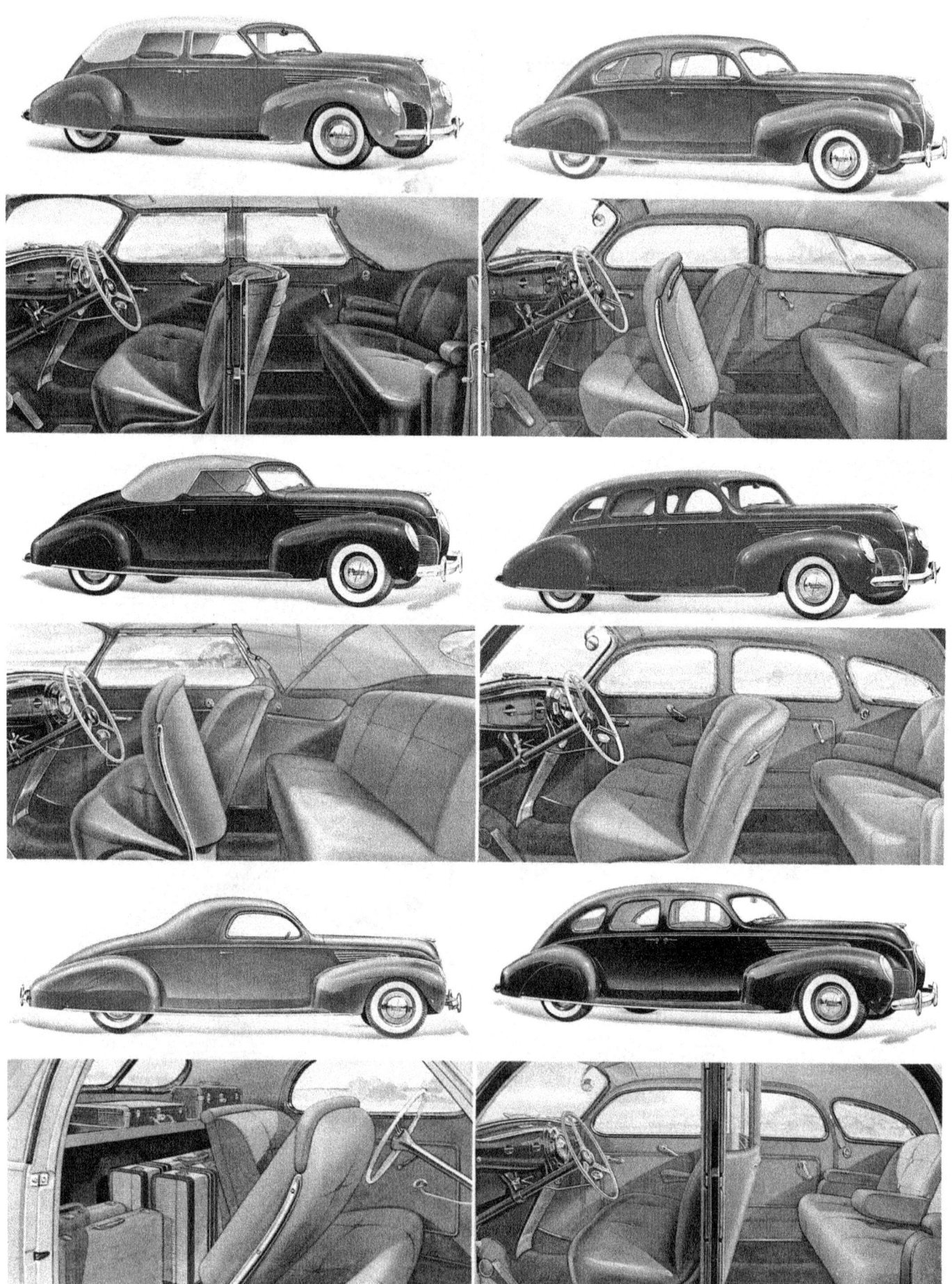

Marvin Arnold

CLASSIC MOTORCARS

NINETEEN-THIRTYEIGHT - For 1938 the Zephyr line offered a Convertible Sedan type 740 and a Convertible Coupe type 760. The s 86H series underwent a remarkable front end rework. Unlike most model updates, these modifications actually improved the Zephyr's appearance. The hood now sloped very slightly downward coming to a V and was crowned with a streamlined hood ornament trailing a chrome tail resembled a comet.

The hood release was now relocated into the interior, under the dash. Breaking with the grille design trend that it had set, the Zephyr was fitted with two large halves of a heart-shaped grille on the lower front end. Each half had a border around the outer edge and horizontal bars. The new cowl trim was a Zephyr teardrop logo trailing four chrome accented louvers.

The car now looked even more aerodynamic, although there is no record of it ever having been subjected to a wind tunnel analysis. Appearances sell cars and the automotive industry had learned its lessons well. The 1938 Zephyr was recognized in later years by the New York City Museum of Modern Art for its modernistic styling.

Mechanical changes and improvements on the 86H series included the use of hypoid differential and hydraulic engine valve lifters. The instrument panel remained generally unchanged except that the engine gauges now encircled the center mounted speedometer. Other manufacturers were converting to column gear-shift levers.

The Zephyr's gear-shift lever appeared to come out of the side of the center console. It was, in fact, a floor gear shift elaborately curved and hidden behind the dash to floor center consol. A spring action aided its shifting. The Zephyr transmission had always been synchromesh in the upper gears. This curved and balanced gear-shift lever arrangement proved to be one of thesmoothest manual floor gear shifts ever devised.

The wheelbase on the Zephyr was extended to 125 inches, Tjaarda's originally proposed dimension. The engine and transmission were moved forward slightly. The drive shaft tunnel was lowered slightly and was a direct benefit of going to the Hypoid rearend. The drive shaft actually enters the differential below the axle line on a Hypoid gear rearend.

The steering ratio of 18 to 1 was increased to 20 to 1. The large Lincoln Zephyr had always been easy to steer, due in part to the steering wheel itself. The new steering wheel was eighteen inches in diameter. Even a small woman could turn the wheel from a parked position and even more effortlessly with the car rolling slightly.

Page 152: Lincoln-Zephyr brochure for 1938. Cars and interiors are: Convertible Sedan; Coupe-Sedan; Convertible Coupe; Sedan; Business Coupe; and Town-Limousine. Page 153: Brochure for 1940. Cars and interiors are: The Sedan; Club Coupe; Coupe; Convertible Coupe; Town Limousine interior; and standard Sedan interior. Page 156: Zephyr 1940 Sedan; 1940 Convertible Coupe; 1940 Sedan; 1940 3-window Coupe; 1941 Sedan; 1941 Sedan. Page 157: 1941 Sedan, 1940 Club Coupe. Opposite page: Illustrations from 1938 brochure are: Zephyr fuel economy; Interior; New trunk area; Swing out spare tire; A Convertible Sedan; and Zephyr unit body construction.

LINCOLN AND CONTINENTAL

The accessories listed for the 86H Zephyr were washable San-Ton seat covers, lap robe, summer cushion, fitted matched luggage, wind wings, locking gas cap, fresh air heater with blower, rear heater outlets, defroster, fresh air outlets, license plate frames and center bumper guards. Also offered were two styles of outside rearview mirrors, a driver-operated spotlight, road lights or driving spots and a visor mirror. Optional bright metal wheel rings were popular on Lincolns and Fords of this era. They were the forerunners of the full disk hub caps that became so commonplace in the sixties.

From late 1938 until 1941, wheels were pin-striped in silver. There was also a less popular chrome inner hub ring that snapped behind the hubcap. A new optional radio was offered this year. It was mounted to the left of the speedometer, in the same size rectangular instrument panel hole as the ash tray on the right side. A factory-installed cowl antenna was mounted on the right-hand side by two insulator standoffs. The battery was moved from under the passenger side floor board to under the hood. A generator voltage regulator replaced the old-style electrical cutoff late in the model year.

NINETEEN-THIRTYNINE - For 1939, the 96H series was offered in types H70 two-door Sedan, H72 Coupe, H73 Sedan, H22 Town Limousine, H74 Sedan Convertible and H76 Coupe Convertible. New exterior color options included blues, tans, reds and black. The hood came to a more pronounced point with a chrome airplane hood ornament molded onto the nose. Stylists sometimes refer to this as an Inverted Prow as on the bow of a boat.

Page 166: Zephyrs, 1937 Sedan; 1936 Sedan; 1937 Sedan; 1937 3-window Coupe; 2-door Sedan and Sedan; 1936 2-door Sedan; 1936 Sedan. Page 168: Sedan 2-door with Zephyr Train in background. Opposite page: 1937 Zephyr brochure. Right: Streamline travel trailer and 1937 Zephyr.

Marvin Arnold

CLASSIC MOTORCARS

The New York World's Fair of 1939

The grille bars were now vertical and without the border trim. The result was the best looking Zephyr front end ever built.

Although it had little or nothing to do with the story in the book "Ford the Men and Machine," a 1939 Zephyr front end was used on the cover of the book.

The new Zephyr had two chrome strips decorated the side of the engine cowl meeting at the bright red Zephyr V-12 teardrop logo. This logo had been mounted on the grille of earlier models. A curved metal flange was added to the lower part of the doors so as to enclose the rubberized running boards and was a vast esthetic improvement.

The front bumper now used two bars centered in front of the grille. A small chrome strip began at the aft lower edge of the front fender and ran the length of the car to the rear of the fender skirt. This is referred to as the Rocker Panel molding. Rear fender skirts latched on and were operated by chrome lock nuts. This was the last year for the teardrop headlamps that went so well with the Zephyr's overall streamlined motif.

The story goes that Edsel had originally wanted hydraulic brakes installed on the new Lincoln Zephyr, but Henry had said no. During the Zephyr's development, Edsel had two Ford cars equipped with hydraulic brakes and took Henry to see them demonstrated. Both cars' brake systems failed during the test and Henry became even more adamantly opposed to them. Edsel, however, finally prevailed and the 1939 Zephyr was equipped with hydraulic brakes.

The instrument panel's basic design remained unchanged, but the speedometer dial was enlarged to enclose the engine gauges encircling it. For an additional cost of $150, buyers could purchase a Custom Interior in a wider choice of colors. Leather had been an option for several years and was especially popular in the convertible body styles.

The New York World's Fair of 1939 commemorated the 150th anniversary of the inauguration of George Washington. The Expo's concept was similar to that of the Chicago Century of Progress. Its theme was the World of Tomorrow and how man's accomplishments could improve the world's living conditions. The symbol for the Fair was a ball and spire named the Trylon and Parsphere.

The ramp leading up to them was called the Helicline. Exhibition buildings were on the same grand scale and included impressive pavilions by both GM and Ford. Norman Bel Geddes designed the Futurama Exhibit for General Motors. Bel Geddes' concept centered on the metropolis of the 1960s. It was a large-scale working model called Highways and Horizons. Walter Dorwin Teague, who did Ford's pavilion, used actual cars to transport visitors up a spiral ramp and over a futuristic expressway. The Ford exhibit was named the City of Tomorrow.

HE HV-12 ENGINE - The Lincoln HV-12 engine, as it was originally designed for the Zephyr, was in theory an expanded Ford flathead V-8 in production for several years. The Lincoln Zephyr twelve-cylinder engine was 75 degrees opposed versus the 90 degrees opposition on the V-8. Making these engines alike allowed many parts to be similar in design and manufacture.

Many small parts from fuel pumps to starters were of the same physical design and some were even interchangeable. The stroke on the original HV-12 engine was 2.75 (3 3/4) inches and the bore of 2.75 inches; sometime referred to as a Square engine. The displacement of the engine was 267.3 cubic inches (4387 cc or 4.4 liters). The engine developed 110 horsepower (36.3 taxable HP) at 3900 RPM as compared to the 221 cubic inches Ford V-8 and developed 80 horsepower.

Engines of the type and design of the HV-12 would produce good torque, but were generally slow to accelerate due to the mechanical friction of the twelve cylinders. Thus, the engine was coupled to a fairly low speed rearend, a ratio of 4.44 to 1.

This meant that the engine must turn approximately four and one-half times for each turn of the rear axle, assuming a 1 to 1 transmission coupling. The early Zephyrs had 4.33 to 1 rearends, a slightly higher speed axle. The clutch was of the common single plate centrifugal type.

A two-speed vacuum shift rearend, manufactured by Columbia, became a very popular option on the HV-12 powered Zephyrs. It provided a sort of fourth gear for highway cruising at lower engine RPM. It also turned in better fuel economy figures. The actual reduction in engine RPM was 28 percent.

The engine could be coupled to the optional Columbia rearend beginning in 1936. An optional electrically actuated overdrive unit, an automatic fourth gear unit mounted behind the transmission, was introduced in 1941. Engine RPM reduction was 30 percent on this unit. The Zephyr's standard transmission provided 2.82 to 1 ratio in low gear, 1.6 to 1 in second and 1 to 1 in high gear. Thus, the transmission was transparent in high gear and allowed the drive shaft to turn at the same speed as the engine.

The HV-12 engine was an L-head design, like the Ford V-8. This means that the valves set to the side of the cylinder and open upward into the combustion dome. The compression ratio remained 6.7 to 1 through the 96H models. The engine contained 5 quarts of oil, not counting the external oil filter reservoir.

Early engine specification sheets, however, stated 6 quarts. This was corrected by a Service Bulletin the second model year. Also, the original oil specified for the HV-12 was 40W below 32 degrees and 50W above. This was revised to read 40W up to 90 degrees outside temperature.

It is worth noting here that oil standards were also changing during this period. The oil quantity on the HV-12 engine was measured by a float rather than a dip stick. It was indicated by a red circular pointer on a plaquard, aft of the carburetor, when the engine was viewed over the left front fender. It worked very well, but did not allow for actual viewing of the oil. This could be done only by draining some oil from the pan.

An oil filter option was listed the second year of production. It required a drilled and tapped hole into the oil pan for a return line. Most were dealer installed. A factory installed oil filter option was offered the third year of production.

The engine cooling system contained 27 quarts of coolant. Due to front end redesign, radiators were not interchangeable between the 1938 and 1939 models. There was no radiator shroud on the engine and the fan was too small with inadequate blade pitch.

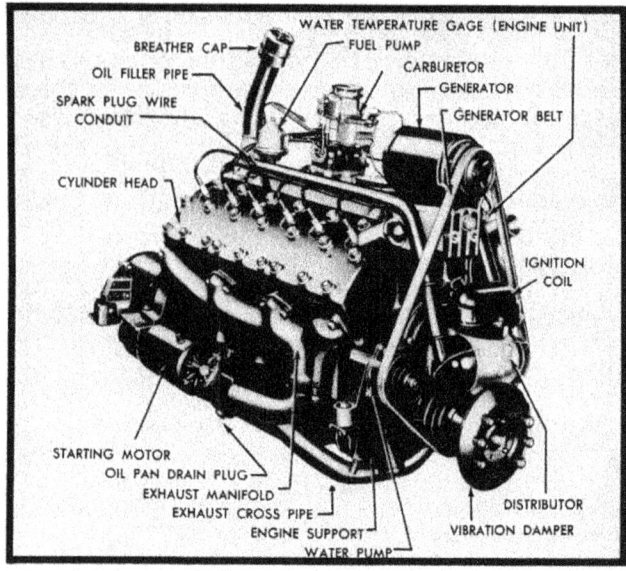

Both of these factors contributed to heat buildup at idle or low speed operation on hot days. The fan incorporated a unique centrifugal spring clutch mechanism for vibration dampening. One might assume that this allowed it to disengage at high RPM, but it did not. The twelve cylinders and the 120-degree throw on the crankshaft made the HV-12 engines smoother running than the older KV-12 engines.

A lot of design thought was put into accessory redundancy on the HV-12. The large coil mounted on top of the distributor, old style Ford V-8 fashion, actually contained dual coils. There were two independent ignition systems firing six cylinders each. The distributor caps and rotors fired three cylinders on the left bank and three on the right. The coil was, however, dedicated to left-side and left-bank or right-side and right-bank. The left-side cylinders were odd-numbered (1,3,5,7,9,11), the right-side cylinders were even numbered (2,4,6,8,10,12). The HV-12 would, in fact, run on six cylinders, although it was difficult to start.

Two independent water pumps were also used to help prevent the Lincoln from breaking down on the open road. Nowadays, one expects a car to operate trouble-free from coast to coast. In the 1920s, this was not the norm. Even into the 1930s, breakdowns were common. Like the famous Jordan Roadster advertisement entitled, "Somewhere West of Laramie." The ad's location at the time might have been fifty miles to the nearest gas stations and two hundred miles to available service for a Lincoln motorcar. It was a neat ad that implied a need for reliability in one's automobile.

There had been subtle changes and many minor improvements in the HV-12 engine over the first four years of production. Hydraulic valve lifters were installed in 1938. These made the engine run quieter, but may have added to engine problems because unless the oil was kept clean, the lifters would malfunction. In 1940, the 06H engine's displacement was increased to 292 cubic inches. On this engine, the cylinder bore was 2.875 (2 7/8) inches and the stroke was 3.75 (2 3/4) inches. It produced 120 horsepower at 3500 RPM (39.75 taxable HP).

Another change included the switching over to the Holley from the Stromberg carburetor. For the 26H series in 1942, the engine bore was increased to 2.9375 (2 15/16) inches. The stroke remained at 3.75 inches. This larger displacement engine was 305.0 cubic inches and developed 130 horsepower at 3800 RPM (41.4 taxable HP). The compression ratio was 7.2 to 1 on this larger displacement engine.

In June 1945, production was resumed on the HV-12 engines using the larger bore specifications. Early sales brochures also stated that the new HV-12 engines were 130 horsepower. After 1,797 of these engines were installed on 66H series Lincolns and Lincoln Continentals, the V-12 returned to the series 16H engine specifications with the 292-CID configuration.

On the 26H engines, there had been problems with the block castings shifting during boring causing cylinder walls to be too thin. The

76H and 876H series Lincolns all used the 292-CID engine and the compression ratio (7 to 1) was lower than that of the year before. Production of the HV-12 engine ended on March 24, 1948. A total of 182,129 of these engines were produced. Most were delivered, but a few were rejected and scrapped at the factory.

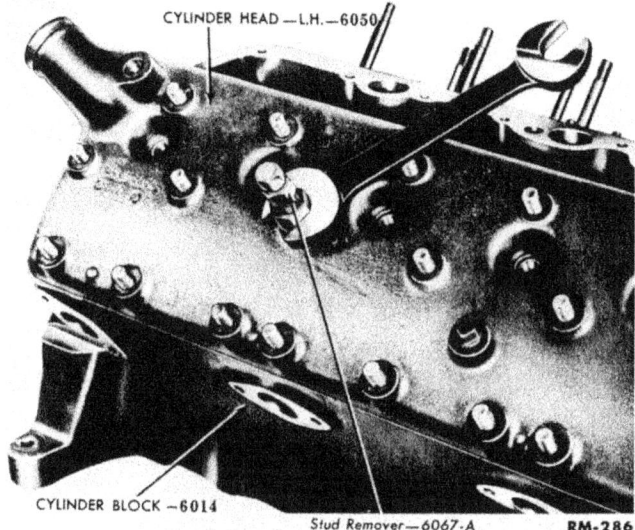

The Zephyr V-12 engine had suffered, to some extent, from a poor reputation over the years. It was only fair to state that an enthusiast of these engines will get downright upset when anyone blames these engines for what they feel is out-and-out driver abuse. Some historians tend to blame Edsel Ford who was traditionally more attentive to styling than engineering design. Actually, there is little or no basis in fact for such blame.

Frank Johnson, Ford's top engine man, had been assigned the job of designing an engine for the Zephyr. The HV-12 was not a bad design, but it was just never fully developed and tested. The HV-12 had the characteristics of a high torque engine. Such engines did not lend themselves well to stop-and-go city traffic.

Additionally, it was a large engine and this made it difficult to properly ventilate and cool. The result was a 30,000-mile engine in an era of 60,000-mile engines. Some Model-H engines have, however, logged over 300,000 miles, but not without proper and timely maintenance.

Many early Lincoln HV-12 engines were maintained by local Ford dealers who sometimes did not understand that these engines would simply not take the abuse of the little Ford V-8s.

The HV-12 engines were plagued with excessive oil burning and nicknamed Mosquito Killers. The main cause of this was that the steel alloy pistons were not compatible with the cast-iron cylinder walls. Also, the cast pistons tended to vary slightly in weight. Inadequate hydraulic valve lifter lubrication was often caused by dirty oil or the use of incorrect oil grades and the split or two-piece valve guides tended to seep oil.

Also lack of proper crankcase ventilation resulted in internal engine varnish and oil sludge buildup. The rear engine main seal would leak onto the clutch plate, producing a kind of thud upon engaging.

Early HV-12 engines had aluminum cylinder heads sealed by copper head gaskets. A bimetal dielectric action occurred around the head bolts and these heads became almost impossible for the unskilled mechanic to remove intact. Cast-iron heads were used beginning with the 26H engine and were almost always used as replacement heads.

The raised number on the engine cylinder head casting located below the forward spark plug was not a serial number, it was a part number. The first three digits of any part number indicated the correct or first model year it was used. It was Lincoln's policy to continue the prefix unchanged so long as the part was not modified from previous years.

An engine serial number on early Lincolns had been located on top of the transmission bell housing, but this was not true of the HV-12. Beginning in late 1946, however, a number matching the chassis serial number was stamped on top of the right side motor mount flange of the block. It is not likely you will ever see this on earlier model Zephyrs or Continentals. Today it is rare to find a Model-H Lincoln with its original engine, even though they might now have the correct HV-12 installed.

The present trend is to restore and reinstall these engines, but many Zephyrs and Continentals have had V-8 engines installed in them at one time or another. One of the telltale signs of such an installation are the weld marks on the frame just aft of the V-12 engine mounts. This is where the shorter V-8 engine's forward mounts were positioned. One of the reasons it was so common to replace the V-12 with a Ford or Mercury V-8 engine was that the transmission and engine bell housings mated without any modification.

The most popular replacement for the HV-12 was the 5-9AB Mercury engine. It produced excellent performance for a stock flathead engine. Lincoln Zephyrs and Continentals, because of their universal styling appeal, have undergone many extensive engine and transmission modifications. It is not uncommon to find these automobiles with late model Lincoln or Cadillac drive trains complete with automatic transmission.

The 1960s Chrysler rear axles were often used for these modifications as they had the correct tread and coupled easily to an automatic transmission, unlike the enclosed Model-H drive shaft. The Lincoln purists, however, make every attempt to return these cars to their original well-performing and nostalgic configurations. It was also popular to cannibalize Zephyr transmissions for installation in Fords with souped-up V-8 engines, because of the Zephyr transmission's higher performance.

The HV-12 was the last popular twelve cylinder used on an American automobile. Many of these engines are still operating today and they are highly prized by their owners. Many NOS or New Old Stock parts for these cars are still traded; but increasingly in shorter supply.

Dealers like Earl Eberhart of Tulsa, Oklahoma, traded regularly in used Zephyr and Continental parts. Well-known Zephyr expert Jake Fleming of Dallas, Texas, rebuilt the HV-12 dual coils by boiling out the tar and remanufacturing them.

If you liked the old flat head V-8 engines, you were destined to fall in love with the HV-12. The engine had no shortcomings that proper maintenance like correct tolerance on valve guides, proper tappet clearance and regular oil changes could not cure. Again, these were high revolution engines that should never be loped or bogged down. Skilled drivers downshifted to prevent this.

A well maintained HV-12 engine will run for 75,000 miles, burning only about one quart of oil per 1,500 miles if modified to provide adequate exhaust venting and positive crankcase ventilation. The use of studs to replace the bolts on cylinder heads also provides better head gasket seating. The engine oil pump needs greater output, but a later model V-8 Lincoln oil pump can be easily installed, remedying this problem. These and other small tricks will improve the HV-12 engine's performance and greatly increase its life span.

If it is so easy to accomplish these improvements on an HV-12 engine, why did Lincoln not do it originally? It is only supposition, but probably for lack of testing and the belief that the engine was adequate when new.

The Lincoln HV-12 was a popular racing engine. When properly geared and tuned, it was a powerful and well-performing engine for its time. Zephyrs were raced at Daytona in 1936, Monte Carlo in 1937 and Langhorne in 1939. A 76H series Lincoln finished, but was disqualified in the 1950 Mexican Road Race. In 1951, race driver Les Keeton drove a Zephyr V-12 on the Northern California stock car circuit.

The engine Keeton used was standard displacement, but had an Allard racing engine cam with adjustable valve lifters installed. The engine also had a chrome crankshaft and a greatly relieved exhaust system. Keeton's racing Zephyr was so successful that the rules were changed, limiting engine displacement on the California tracks to 267 cubic inches. This effectively eliminated all Lincoln HV-12 engines from stock car competition.

In Great Britain, Sidney Allard used the Lincoln HV-12 engine in several of his Super Sports marketed extensively as rally cars. These Allards turned in some very respectable racing records. They were three-seaters with motorcycle fenders. Later configurations were updated with body attached envelope-fenders and counter sunk headlights. Tom Tjaarda, himself a designer of high-performance cars, claims that his father's earlier rear-engine Zephyr set the trend for today's modern mid-engine race cars.

There were other Anglo-American HV-12 hybrids such as the Atlanta and the Brough Superior. Produced in Middlesex, England, the first Atlanta used a Zephyr V-12 engine. Built in 1938, they had a 120 inch wheelbase, hydraulic brakes and independent coil spring suspension all around. The first was a two-door Salon model with pillarless side windows and a drop-head coupe body style was produced later. Performance was excellent, 0 to 60 in thirteen seconds with a top speed of 101 miles per hour. These cars sold for approximately $3,500, slightly less for the sport two-seater.

The styling of the Atlanta is said to have set the trend for the Sunbeam Tiger and the AC Cobra. The whereabouts of any of these cars is unknown, although it is suspected that several survived World War II and the scrap piles. The Brough Superior's body was designed by Charles Worth. Its body lines resembled a rather low-profile Rolls-Royce. Three were constructed, but George Brough only completed one with an HV-12 engine installed and that was in 1938. The automobile was privately owned and bore British license plate FAU999 in the mid-1970s.

NINETEEN-FORTY - By 1940, the era of limited production custom bodied cars was coming to an end. The Lincoln Model-K was dropped from the production line and from prestige Lincoln now became the Zephyr-based Continental. The Zephyr was a high-production automobile by Lincoln's standards, but not by Ford's. The Zephyr's annual model changes had mostly been held to parts easily retooled like the hood, fenders, grilles and chrome trim.

This year, major changes were made to the basic Zephyr, changes that would carry the chassis through to its conclusion with the 1948 model. With these redesigned bodies, Ford was taking more and more of the production control away from Briggs. During early Zephyr assembly, Briggs manufactured fenders and even painted the cars. Edsel Ford once joked that, "The Lincoln Zephyr assembly line is only forty feet long. We might as well send the Ford mechanical parts to Briggs for completion."

The new 06H Zephyrs were introduced on October 2, 1939. The Convertible Sedan body style was dropped this year. Also dropped was the two-door Sedan. It had been one of the two original Zephyr body styles. A new body style, a Club Coupe type 77, was introduced.

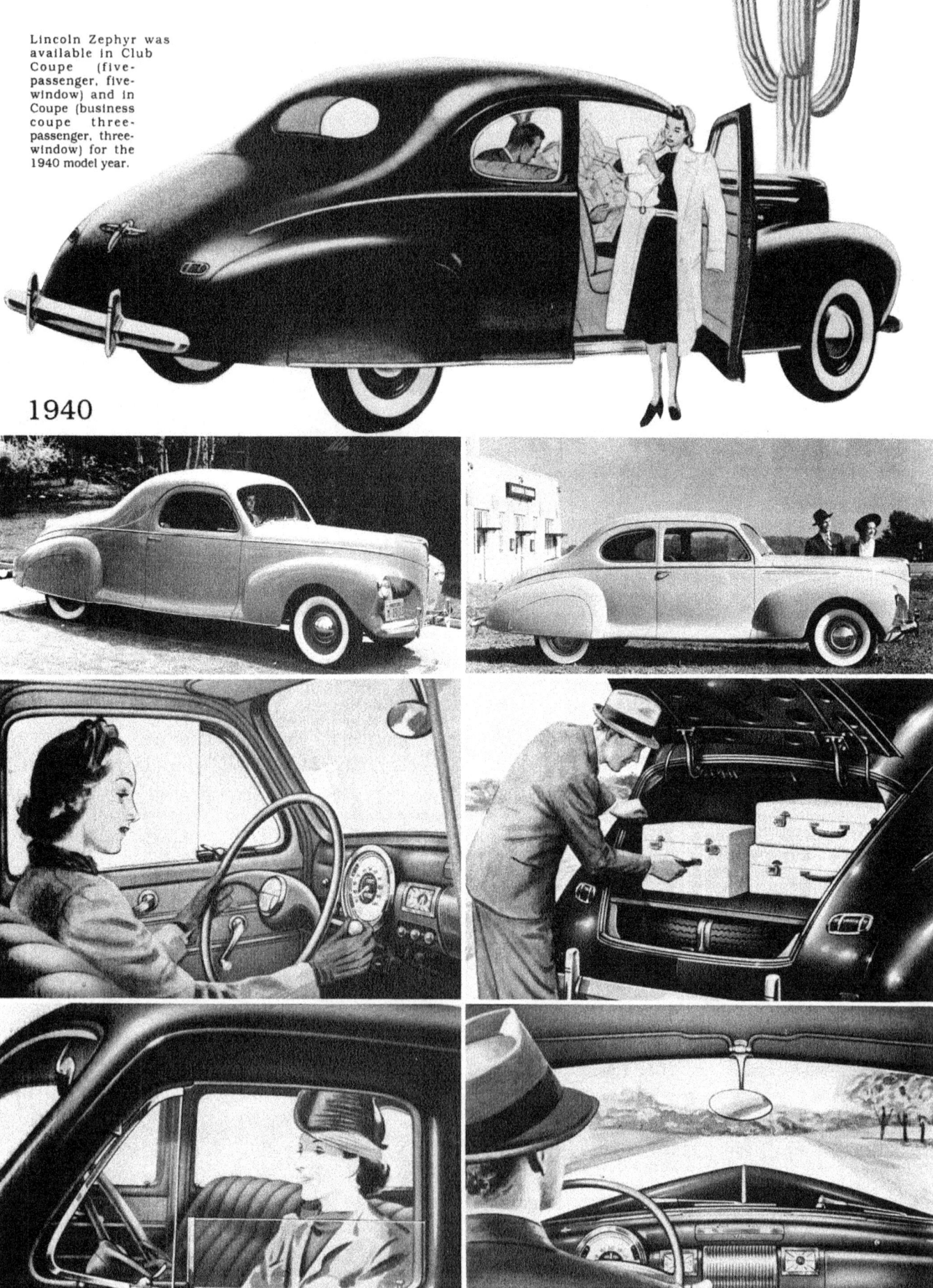

The standard business Coupe type 72 became a 72A or 72B depending on whether or not it had the auxiliary seating option. These coupes are often referred to as three-window coupes, abbreviated 3WC. The auxiliary seat configuration was occasionally referred to as type 72AS. The type 73 Sedan, the type 22 Town Limousine and the type 76 Convertible Coupe were retained. The Convertible now had a vacuum operated power top.

The restyling and re-engineering of the Zephyr's unit body actually produced a lighter-weight automobile. It also provided more interior room and about 30 percent more trunk space. The spare tire was mounted below a lift-up shelf or false trunk floor. Better safety glass was installed. The restyling also provided for about 22 percent more window area, a badly needed improvement as the streamlined Zephyrs had always been a little blind-sided. The corners of the windows were much less rounded on these models. Independent crank-out vent windows were added to the front doors.

The running boards were removed completely, although the doors and rear quarter flared out at the bottom as if enclosing a running board as had the flange on the 96H. This lower body flare actually added to the Zephyr's unique streamlined appearance. Sealed beam headlights became standard equipment and are an easy spotter's clue to a 06H over the 96H. The teardrop lights would have continued to go well with the new body styling had the sealed beams simply been installed inside of them.

The instrument panel was redesigned, deleting the dash-to-floor center console. The gear-shift lever was relocated to the steering column. The speedometer and engine gauge cluster were again moved to in front of the driver. There was a large speaker grille in the center of the dash. In general, the rear instrument panel looked like most of the standard dashes on cars of the next two decades. Lincolns of this period had two placards on their firewalls. The one mounted in the center listed several Ford patents. The other, located towards the passenger side, was the body identification plate.

The body ID consisted of three sections: the model year or series, the model style or body type and production numerical sequence. As an example, 06H-72-138 would translate into a 1940, type 72 (Coupe body Style), the 138th body built for that model year. The first digit of the prefix denoted year model, a 9 for 1939 or 0 for 1940 and so on. The second digit was always a 6 and stood for 1936, the first year the Zephyr was produced. The H denoted the Model-H Lincoln.

The serial number was stamped in two places on the frame. The first location was just ahead of the left-hand motor mount on the left side frame rail. It faced outward and could be read when looking down into the engine compartment over the left fender. The second location could be viewed from the ground looking up toward the gas tank filler pipe where it was stamped on the lower part of the frame rail. Supposedly, there were serial numbers stamped on the upper frame rails, but Lincolns, unlike Fords of the same era, cannot be unbolted from their chassis frame so it is rather academic.

The Lincoln body production rate was at an all-time high. A new Michigan plant was completed in September at a cost of over one million dollars. The mono-construction of the Zephyr required over four hundred spot welds and hundreds of inches of arch and gas welding during assembly. An average body took about twenty-five assembly line hours to produce. The flow rate was about 150 cars per work shift.

Lincoln factory, administration building and Ford Rotunda as they appeared in the late 1930s. 1941 Club Coupe; 1940 Convertible Coupe; 1941 instrument panel with radio and heater options; 1940 dimension drawing; 1941 standard Zephyr panel; 1940 Zephyr Sedan ads; 1941 Brochure cover. Opposite page: 1940 Club Coupes and 3-window Coupe. Four views from 1940 Brochure. Page 170: Magazine ads for the 1941 Lincoln Zephyrs.

NINETEEN-FORTYONE - The 1941 Zephyr was basically a continuation of the previous year's 06H series. An easy spotter's guide to the 1941 models is that the parking lights mounted on top of the front fenders and the chrome border outlining the grille. The two half-heart grilles contained vertical bars. This Zephyr did not have a hood ornament per se, but more like a heavy chrome ridge crowning the nose. There were minor trim changes to the tail lights, trunk latch, door handles, hub caps and so forth. This was the first year that the overdrive unit, manufactured by Borg-Warner, was offered. The Columbia rearend remained an option. Only on rare occasions were these options installed together.

Delivery records indicate that only two such cars were ever built. The rear tread was widened and several suspension improvements were made. Front and rear leaf springs were widened by a half-inch and the girth was increased by three inches. Minor suspension changes helped to produce a much softer ride. These changes included more efficient shocks, a change to the spring shackle angle and the addition of inter-leaf inserts.

Only one Town Limousine was built this year. The convertible body styles all came with electrically power-actuated tops as standard equipment. The body styles seemed now to settle into the more familiar forms of the Coupe type 72A & 72B, Sedan type 73, five-window Club Coupe type 77 and two-door Convertible type 76. The interior door releases were pushbutton. Outside pushbutton door releases were used this year on the Continental, but the door handles remained on the Custom and the Zephyr models. The handles were the pull-out type that operated mechanically the same as the push-button type.

The Gilmore Economy Run rules were such in 1941 that entries were graded on ton-miles. The Lincoln models won first and second place in this event. The lead Zephyr turned in a respectable 22.96 MPG. Both cars used Columbia rearends without overdrive.

Marvin Arnold

CLASSIC MOTORCARS

By mid-1941, work had already begun on the 1942 26H series. Cadillac was now taking away a large percentage of Zephyr sales. Cadillac entered the medium-price field with one LaSalle model priced a hundred dollars under the Zephyr.

The new LaSalle had a powerful V-8 engine with quiet hydraulic valve lifters. By accident or design, the Cadillac 62 series looked very much like a four-door Lincoln Continental except for the trunk. General Motors had gone to the horizontal grille bar motif. This was the style used earlier by the Lincoln Zephyr series, but some say improved on by GM and now growing popular with the automobile buying public. It was therefore no surprise that the 1942 Lincolns, now on the drawing board, were be longer and wider. They would also incorporate the new horizontal grille bar motif.

NINETEEN-FORTYTWO - The 1942 Model-H Lincolns were introduced in Dearborn on September 11, 1941. Prices were raised two hundred dollars over the previous year. However, the invoice price now included federal tax and some added delivery to the dealership charges. The 26H series Lincolns were heavier and their engine horsepower was increased slightly. They were no longer called Zephyr. The three model lineup was the Lincoln Custom and Lincoln Continental. For the new 26H series, all Lincoln hood noses were topped with a ball and single large spire. The spire looked very much like a Spartan's helmet with an extra-large plume. The Continental and Custom had shared a common hood ornament in 1941, while the Zephyr had been basically without one. Only V-12 appeared on the grille, located at the top of the center strip. The name LINCOLN in black letters on a chrome placard was mounted on the nose of the hood just above the grille.

The knight's head crest logo, in green, was mounted separately above the nameplate. The hubcaps were now barrel shaped with a rectangular LINCOLN name plate like the one located on the hood nose. All four hubcaps were the same. Like most new cars of this year, the Lincolns had stamped stainless steel grilles instead of the brightly polished die-cast chrome zinc alloy grilles.

Most of the increase in Zephyr size was obtained by the retooling of the fenders and minor body parts. The chassis remained essentially the same. The overall length of the car was extended seven inches and the width five inches done by lowered by flattening the springs slightly and by the changeover from 16 inch to 15 inch wheels. The interior dimensions remained unchanged, but more luxurious interiors were

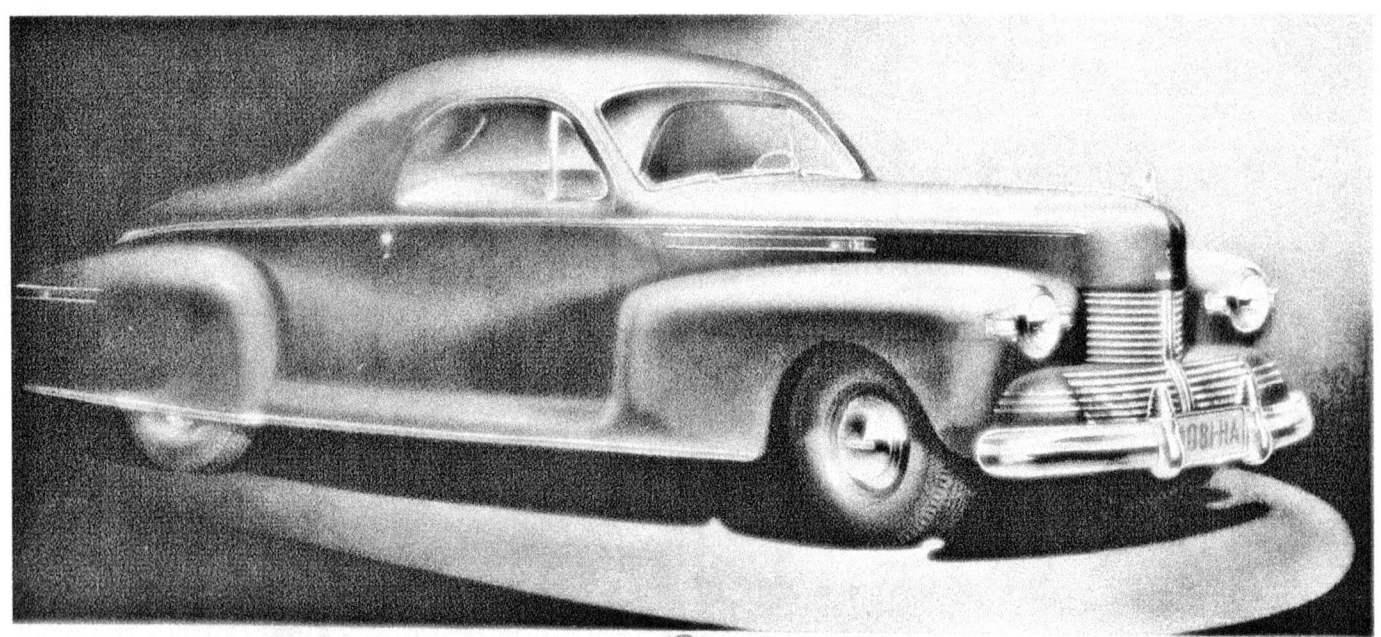

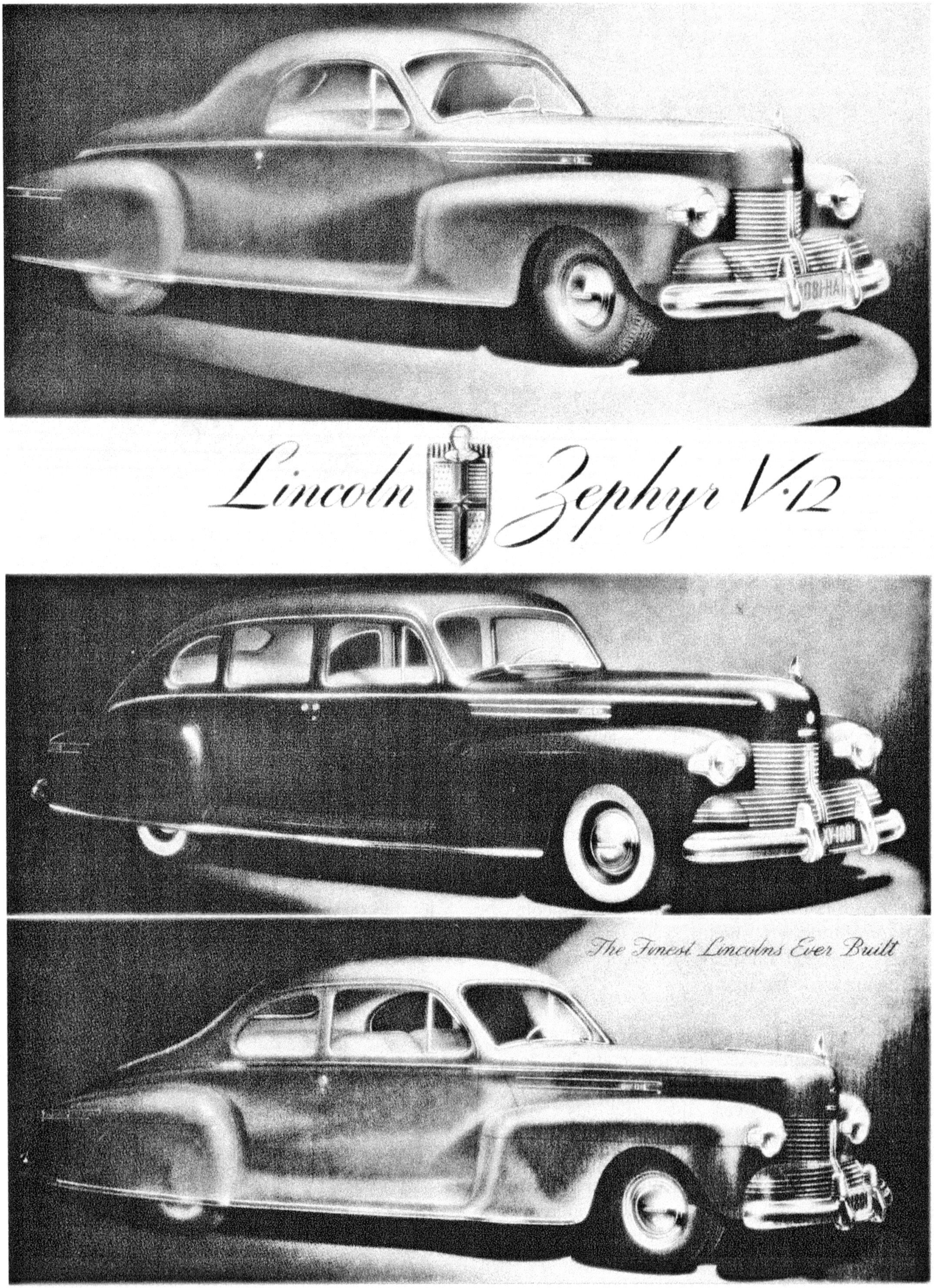
Lincoln Zephyr V-12
The Finest Lincolns Ever Built

Outside push-button door releases were installed on all models. This style of door opener afforded safety and style. One of the most now being offered
obvious components that the Zephyr did not share with the Continental was the instrument panel. The styles were basically of the same, but the control knobs and cigarette accessories border the speaker grille on the Continental while on the Zephyr, they mount below.

The Custom types 31 and 32 instrument panels were similar to the Zephyr, but with square clock and ash tray. A vacuum-operated radio antenna and power-lift windows were optional.

The Zephyr so set the trend for Ford styling that those who do not know the design chronology often refer to them as the Big Fords. However, it was the other way around. Had Henry Ford set out in 1939 to have someone design a Lincoln after the Ford, there is little doubt that the resulting automobile would have been something similar to the Lincoln Zephyr.

The word Zephyr means a light breeze or refreshing wind. The streamlined Zephyr automobile came like the wind, left like the wind and was indeed refreshing. Whether these automobiles were really fast or just look fast, we leave to conjecture.

The car was comfortable to ride in and strikingly appealing in appearance. These Lincoln motorcars passed quickly over the land, both relatively and figuratively. Like Margaret Mitchell's civilization, these fine automobiles and the men who created them are gone with the wind.

Marvin Arnold

Friends of the Wind

THERE'S true kinship with the wind in every flowing line of the new '41 Lincoln-Continental. Completely streamlined from the inside out, it cleaves the rushing currents of air cleanly and quietly in its smooth, effortless gliding flight. You seem to ride on the wings of the wind!

SKILLED craftsmen in the great Lincoln precision plant have created for the staunch, power-charged, 12-cylinder heart of the Lincoln-Continental a long, luxurious, low-slung body that surpasses all previous conceptions of automotive beauty. Here is a car almost daringly young—so decidedly *different* in design and construction you know at a glance it's styled for you who want unstinted luxury tempered with good taste...

IN PERFECT keeping with such sheer splendor—such unusual performance—is the comfort of billowy seats cradled amidships on liquid-like, slow-motion springs. And the Lincoln-Continental is triple-cushioned in rubber to block out noise and vibration...give you a ride as smooth and quiet as a glider's flight!

BEFORE you buy any car make a date with your dealer and go for a ride in the new Lincoln-Continental. See how it hugs the curves, holds snugly to the road and cuts the air like a bullet. Delight in the brilliant performance and lithe streamlining that make it truly a "friend of the wind." You'll discover, at last, the thrill of driving a car that's altogether *new* and *unusual!*

Suave, sleek masterpiece in steel and luxury, the Lincoln-Continental Coupe shown above combines a host of unusual automotive comforts, conveniences and betterments: Exclusive Lincoln V-12 engine...push-button door openers...unit body-and-frame construction. (White sidewall tires extra.) ❧ Interiors are custom-tailored. You choose from a wide range of fabrics and leathers. ❧ Smart Convertible Cabriolet also available. Every feature of the dynamic *new-and-different* Lincoln-Continental will convince you that here, indeed, is a limited edition of a fine motor car!

LINCOLN MOTOR CAR DIVISION, FORD MOTOR COMPANY, BUILDERS ALSO OF THE LINCOLN-ZEPHYR V-12, SEDAN, COUPE, CLUB COUPE, CONVERTIBLE COUPE; THE LINCOLN-CUSTOM, SEDAN AND LIMOUSINE

CHAPTER SEVEN
THE ORIGINAL CONTINENTAL

A Ford That Was An Edsel

If its father was Edsel Ford, then surely its mother was the Zephyr. The birth of the Lincoln Continental is a story that has been told and retold by Lincoln and classic car buffs alike. No other automobile has been held up to such general acclaim for its styling, as has the Continental. It invokes an aura that sets it apart from the commonplace. Its praises have been sung by admirers from Frank Lloyd Wright to John Steinbeck. Modern art museums, publications and the general public have all praised the styling of the Lincoln Continental. In 1946, it became the basis for industrial designer Raymond Loewy to create two of his dream cars.

Most automobile historians record that Edsel Ford commissioned this new design upon his return from The Continent, Europe, in September, 1938. Indeed, the go-ahead to build a one-off custom Continental automobile for Edsel was given at this time, but the story goes back much further.

The Henry Ford Museum archives at Greenfield Village have preserved many of Edsel's personal drawings and sketches. Some of these articles date back to when Edsel was only ten years old. A scrapbook, beginning with newspaper clippings from 1911, contains a brochure entitled "The Continental Pneumatik."

Other clippings are of the Austro-Daimler, the Apollo and other classic European designs. By the time the scrapbook reaches 1918, Edsel was collecting American coachbuilts like George Brokaw's Canoe Roadster Marmon, William Wrigley's Semi-Touring and the Vanderbilts' Custom Locomobile. There are also paste-ups of special coachbuilt bodies for the Model-T Ford. The useful and appealing features of these various automotive styles were measured and annotated by penciled in notes. Features like the fenders on a Vauxhall and the windscreen on Grand Prix racers, which were circled. These notes and the scrapbook represent Edsel's early interest in styling and design.

Edsel was to develop a keen eye for the classic and a disdain for the mediocre. He became not the mechanical tinkerer his father was, but a connoisseur of art objects. The establishment of Lincoln as a marque and the creation of the Continental were primarily due to three factors; they were factors being the Man, i.e. Edsel, The Idea, i.e. the gathering of creative people around him and The Means, i.e. the vast Ford industrial empire.

Walter Dorwin Teague, an independent designer who worked for the Fords and with Edsel for many years, said of him "Edsel was a truly great soul. By choice, he moved quietly behind the scenes at Ford. It was no accident that Edsel Ford, in his lifetime, would dynamically affect Ford styling and produce the world's most highly praised motorcar."

The story of the early Ford designers is really a trilogy. Ray Dietrich, John Tjaarda and Bob Gregorie were all supported and encouraged

in their work by Edsel Ford. Eugene Turenne "Bob" Gregorie, Jr., a twenty-three year old yacht designer, came to work at Ford in 1931. Bob Gregorie and Edsel Ford were kindred spirits. Sometimes they would talk for hours, seated among old dusty prototypes, about boating and things of common interest. Bob Gregorie never spokes of Edsel except as "Mr. Ford."

Gregorie and some other young designers had established Ford's first styling design department under the blessing of Edsel Ford. It was in this department that Edsel escaped from the pressures of his office. Here in 1935, Gregorie and Ford first discussed the possibility of producing a European style of automobile within the Ford line. This concept, for a completely new motorcar, was discussed off and on for several years. Edsel consistently referred to it as "the Continental."

Eugene Gregorie had been called Bob from an early age. His father was the son of a South Carolina plantation owner. Educated in New York, the senior Gregorie was an automobile hobbyist. The family owned a Bugatti, a Pierce-Arrow and other makes. Growing up on Long Island, Bob developed a keen interest in both cars and boats.

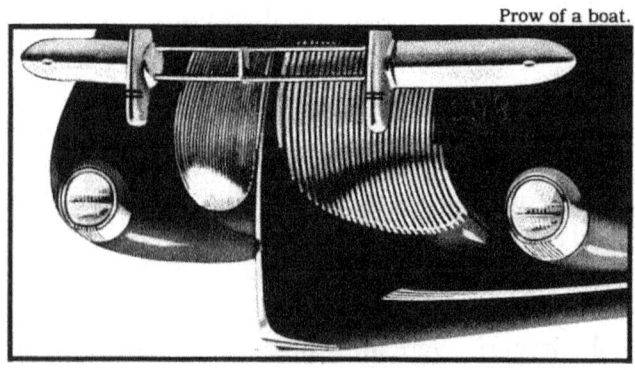
Prow of a boat.

In 1927, he went to work in Bayonne, New Jersey, for the builders of Elco yachts and a year later as a naval architect in New York. Pursuing an interest in automobile styling, his next job was at Brewster, where he was assigned to the Rolls-Royce coach design group.

On his twenty-first birthday, Bob Gregorie boarded the night ferry to Albany. He interviewed at Franklin Motor Car Company. Ken Haven, chief designer at Franklin, had no openings. He suggested that Gregorie talk with Ray Dietrich, who was there on business. The two men met and visited in the lounge that night on the return ferry to New York Central. Dietrich arranged an introduction for Gregorie at Pierce-Arrow, but the next day Bob found an opening at General Motors in Detroit. The Great Depression deepened and a series of odd, part-time jobs followed. That summer, Gregorie traveled in his father's Pierce-Arrow back to the family plantation for an extended visit.

In January of 1929, a job opened up under Henry Crecelius at Ford. Gregorie worked first on the Model-Y English Ford and then on the KA and KB Lincolns. John Crawford, a Ford shop master and Edsel's personal production advisor, rounded out this early project design team.

Crawford said of Gregorie, "He was a young man with good ideas. Edsel took Gregorie under his wing, handled him with kid gloves and gave him the freedom to be creative."

When Gregorie joined Ford, there were no clay mock-ups and body bridges were not used. Component parts were designed and built individually. The first major design task assigned to Gregorie and his new group was to restyle the front end of the Briggs Zephyr.

Bob Gregorie used to joke with Edsel about the nose of the Zephyr being just an upside down boat prow. The Continental would also later evolve from this design. Both of which resembled a sleek land cruiser with yacht-like style. Gregorie would sometimes not keep a regular work schedule, but instead drive for hours through the Michigan countryside working out an idea in his head. The concept of automobile styling is commonplace today, but in the 1920s and the early 1930s, it was a radical new idea. It was, however, a logical development in the evolution of automobile design.

The Dietrich design for the Model-L had greatly influenced the styling of the popular Model-A Ford. The Tjaarda concepts for the Model-H were affecting the styling for the total Ford product line. The new group headed by Gregorie was the first real styling and design department at Ford or Lincoln. The air in the new department was thick with foreign accents. Ford was hiring many of the laid off designers from the now defunct coach building companies.

In 1927, Cadillac experienced a rather disappointing sales with its new models. Alfred Pritchard Sloan, Jr., president of GM, retained California custom body stylist Harley Earl to design the new LaSalle. This was a calculated and direct attempt to appeal to the auto buyer's visual sensibility. It also resulted in the establishment of the "Art and Colour" section at General Motors. Lincoln and Ford followed suit. For the next eight years, Bob Gregorie would style everything from Ford trucks to a woman's dress for an automobile show.

On one of Edsel's trips to Europe, he purchased an English sports roadster. Upon returning home, he made a big fuss over its classic lines. Gregorie decided that it was now time to incorporate into a single design, many of the features he and Edsel had discussed. The "Continental look" was to be characterized by a long hood, sweeping front fenders, high narrow grille, thin bumpers and special interior trims like piping. A short rear deck and blind quarters were also very much part of the Continental look. By late 1937, a now familiar classic form began to take shape.

At first, both men had considered only that the sporty new car would be built on a Ford chassis. Neither really considered it a luxury motorcar, at least not in the beginning. Two major problems arose. First, the Ford Company resisted anyone, even Edsel and especially Gregorie, making proposals for new models. Second, the long hood effect of the new design simply would not fit on the shorter Ford chassis.

The logical choice was the new lightweight Lincoln Zephyr. Gregorie could influence the design of the Zephyr, as he was already working on the 1940 model design changes. Edsel also had a rather free hand with Lincoln he did not have with the company's main line of cars. Gregorie did some yellow crayon sketches, superimposing the new Continental's lines over a Zephyr blueprint. These one-tenth scale blueprints were commonly referred to as package drawings.

NINETEEN-THIRTYEIGHT - In November of 1938, a one-tenth scale clay model of the Continental was completed. There were some similarities to the Cord styling, particularly in the fender lines and in the boxlike body. There the similarity ended, as the Cord hood lines lacked the smooth transitional form of the Continental. The spare tire was exposed behind the trunk. This caused some of the Ford stylists concern, for they felt this was not modern. Ford designer Martin Regitko, formerly with Willoughby Coachbuilders, even made some sketches enclosing the spare. Edsel considered it briefly, but turned the idea down because he felt that it did not look continental enough.

All good designers look for styling focal points. They know that the human eye seeks a place to rest or focus when viewing an object. The Zephyr and the early Continental hoods come sharply to a point. From the front, this becomes the focal point. The spare tire hump, retained on Continentals to this day, becomes the styling focal point from the rear. One can experiment with this by glancing at various car silhouettes. View, for example, an older Cadillac attracts the eye to its tail fins. A Mark II, from the side, will focus the eye on the aft part on the top behind the rear-seat window. Edsel may have been conscious of these styling concepts. Like many good designers he may have just developed an instinct for that sort of thing.

The rear deck of the new Continental was raised as high as possible while maintaining the sleek lines of the Zephyr. On the original scale model, the grille concept looked much like the one Gregorie had designed for the new Mercury that was introduced on November 4, 1938. To retain its compatibility with the Zephyr, the Mercury grille concept was dropped. In retrospect, this was probably a very good choice. It is probable that the many early discussions on the Continental, gave rise to the concept for the midsize Mercury.

It was not unusual for Edsel to have custom cars built for his personal use each year. In fact, it was the norm. Since 1932, Gregorie had personally designed two of the specials which were built for Edsel. Neither received much acclaim or was ever considered for production and both had been on Ford chassis. The first of these Speedsters was built in 1932 and it appeared in a November 1933 issue of the English publication Autocar. The Roadster resembled a Model-B street rod. It had a boat tail rear deck, teardrop fenders and an all-aluminum body. It was started at the Dearborn engineering lab, but shuffled off to the Lincoln plant where it was completed. The car was often parked in the gardener's shed when Edsel was at home to keep it out of Henry's sight. His father disliked Edsel being involved in these types of projects.

The second car, called the Model-40 Special Speedster, sported a long hood, V-shaped rearend and motorcycle fenders. Its design was similar in appearance to the most modern race cars of this period and may have set the styling trend for the English Allard and similar sports cars. The Model-40 Special Speedster was purchased outright by Edsel and delivered to him on September 21, 1934. The car was extensively photographed bearing 1934 Michigan license plate number F988. The car was painted dark grey with a grey leather interior. It sported a machine-burnished instrument panel, a decorative finish used on airplane metals of the time. In fact, the Model-40 was assembled at the Ford aircraft factory. In 1940, a scale model of the Speedster was rendered and photographed with an updated two-part grille. FMC photo #14531, dated 3-21-40, has scrawled across it in Edsel's handwriting, "EGT, this form is very good, but wonder if the two grilles should join?" and is signed Edsel. A grille of similar design had been installed on the Speedster in 1940 and a similar grille pattern was used on the 1942 Lincolns and Lincoln Continentals.

Edsel Ford's Custom Speedster designed with Gregorie.

The Model-40 remained in Edsel's personal collection until it was sold at auction in June, 1944. It was listed in the auction brochure as "Ford Special Speedster #18-1022711, thirty horsepower." It sold for $1,000. The car surfaced for a while in Hollywood in 1952, where it was photographed by Auto Sport Review with actress Lynn Bari at the wheel and was more recently owned by Earl Pallasch.

Before leaving for Florida to winter at the family estate in Palm Beach, Edsel reviewed and approved the final designs for the new Zephyr Cabriolet. Edsel continued to refer to it as the Continental and the name finally stuck. The name Continental had previously been used in the automotive industry, but Edsel was not alluding to any of these. One such company was the Continental engine manufacturing company.

In America, there were four early companies incorporated under this name. The companies were Continental Automotive of New Jersey in 1899, Continental Motor Vehicle of New Jersey in 1903, Continental Motor Car of Illinois in 1907 and Continental Motors of New York in 1914. It is doubtful that any of these companies ever produced an automobile. In 1907, the Continental Motor Company of Chicago, Illinois, did produce a Roadster. Another company, Continental Automobile Manufacturing of New Haven, Connecticut was originally called University Automobile and was probably associated with Yale University.

UA built a Runabout and a rather large Touring model. In 1907, while on a spring tour in his Continental, C.S. Johnston was arrested in Richmond, Indiana, for speeding and later collided with a trolley car in Dayton, Ohio. The Indiana Motor Manufacturing Company built several models of Continentals between 1909 and 1914. It later became known as Knightstown and the company produced a kit called the Ultimotor for converting carriages to autos. Rolls-Royce designated one of their Phaeton II bodies as a Continental in 1931. They also used the name Continental for a series of streamlined Bentley coach bodies they produced years later.

A rather latecomer was the successor to the DeVaux-Hall Motors of Grand Rapids, Michigan, which became the Continental Automobile Company. In 1933, they produced over three thousand six-cylinder motorcars called the Flyer and the Ace. They also produced a four-cylinder Beacon and Red Seal. In 1934, only the four-cylinder version was continued and the company failed shortly thereafter. The latter is noteworthy in that some reference books state that the Continental was first produced in 1933. This, of course, was a reference to the DeVaux-Hall, not the Lincoln Continental.

Ford body engineers Henry Crecelius and Joe Galamb were asked to review the scale model and drawings of the Cabriolet to see if they felt that it could be built on the Zephyr chassis. They both agreed that it could. This may have been the first clue that Edsel was considering building more than just one or two Continentals. Work on the first Lincoln Continental proceeded from full-scale drawings. It was to be built of as many standard Zephyr parts as possible.

The car was easily lowered three inches because the original design for a Zephyr convertible had a three-inch sub-floor. A special firewall box insert was constructed to extend the hood twelve inches. The running boards were removed completely. There was much cutting, welding and a lot of lead filling. A four-inch horizontal strip was cut out of the doors and side body. Body parts were formed on wood framed dies. Small parts like windshield frames were made from aluminum castings.

Some early reports state that the instrument panel on the first Continental was a prototype planned for use on the new Lincoln Custom Limousine. In fact, the panel was a standard 96H Zephyr with the lower console removed. The clock was relocated to the center of the glove box door. The floor shift remained, but the shift lever was modified for panel clearance. A radio was installed in the standard location, but the car lacked an antenna and speaker grille.

The outside door handles were of unknown origin, but the rest of the car was basically a 1939 Zephyr. The nose plate read, "Zephyr" and the chrome nose bar.

The grille was omitted. The cloth top and bows were stock from a standard Zephyr convertible coupe. The comet, a chrome ball and spire hood ornament appeared for the first time on this car. Due to the body stretch, the steering wheel was mounted closer to the windshield and panel. Ford engineers generally referred to the firewall as a dash and the dashboard as an instrument panel.

The first Continental was very heavy. It weighed almost 5,000 pounds. It was 210 inches long and sixty-two inches high with the top up. It was built from a 96H Zephyr chassis scheduled to be a type 74 Convertible and it was serial number H74750. The car was originally yellow and was repainted Eagle Grey and trimmed with grey leather; as were many of Edsel's personal cars. It was ready on March 1, 1939 and was shipped by railway car to Edsel in Florida.

Edsel drove the car around Hobe Sound in Florida that spring and many prospective buyers, friends and acquaintances inquired as to how they might order a custom-built Continental Cabriolet by Lincoln. Edsel phoned Gregorie back in Dearborn complaining that the car leaked like a sieve and was a bucket of lead. Build two more, he told him. These cars were supposedly ordered for his sons, Henry II and Benson, according to an account given some years later by Ford Company historian Owen Bombard and quoted in a book titled The Lincoln Continental.

It is relatively certain, however, that Edsel and Gregorie had planned to build an additional engineering prototype all along. Ordering additional bodies in the family name temporarily kept the cars from being considered prototypes and might have saved some bandying about in the Ford Company hierarchy. It is not believed that the second of these two cars was ever built and it is doubtful that either son ever took delivery on a 96H Continental.

NINETEEN-THIRTYNINE - In April of 1939, Edsel returned to Dearborn having already decided to go ahead with a limited production run of five hundred Continentals. Over two hundred inquires had been made about placing advanced orders for the new model. The original Florida car was scrapped, but documentation on this is nonexistent.

This was the year of the big Ford Pavilion at the New York World's Fair. Edsel did not summer at Seal Harbor, Maine, as he usually did. He took a place on Manhasset Bay to be near the Fair. He rarely looked in on a development project once it started, but Edsel maintained a closer than normal liaison with the new Continental. It was the last personal custom sports car that Edsel would ever have built.

Above: Lincoln Zephyr Cabriolet II. Second and last Continental built from 1939 sheet metal. Right: Early 1940 Continental showing its advanced design as compared to the parking lot in the background.

In June, the second Continental was completed. The car was built on chassis serial number H82410. This second car was used extensively as an engineering prototype and test bed, according to Bob Gregorie who later purchased it. It was made from 96H sheet metal and was built on a chassis assigned to a type 74 Zephyr Sedan Convertible, as was the first Continental. The type 74 chassis used much stronger frame cross-members.

This was desirable as there was no hard top to provide additional body support. The 96H series and the subsequent 06H Cabriolets and Coupes shared many type 74 chassis parts as the 16H Continentals did not. One of the most notable changes was the reduction, by four inches, in the hood stretch on the second Continental. An effort was made to reduce the amount of lead fill and thus the weight. The front fenders were shortened for better entry access and the trunk was noticeably higher than the original prototype. Both 96H Continentals used the new dual-spoke steering wheel from the Mercury. The Zephyrs used a three-spoke style, sometimes referred as a Banjo Steering Wheel.

Only the second car used the new column gearshift lever and was the test car for this new style shift lever. Lincoln's version of the column shift was to be called Finger Tip Control. The second car used the same customized instrument panel as the original, but no radio was installed. This car was photographed, in early August, behind the old Lincoln plant on Warner Avenue. Neither of the 96H Continentals bore a body number and their production quantity was grouped in with the other type 74 Zephyrs for the year. Had they been assigned body serial numbers, they would have been 96H-56-1 and -2 respectively. It is often related that the early Continentals were built from full-scale drawings without benefit of full-scale mock-up.

This was true of the first two Special Convertibles. It was not true of the 06H series Cabriolets built in the fall of 1939. The full-scale clay mock-up was being built at about the same time as the second Special Convertible. Robert M. "Bob" Thomas, who went to work in the styling design department at Lincoln in 1927, recalls working on the full-scale clay mock-up.

Thomas related that the studio stylists and draftsmen watched in amazement as the armature for the new Continental was rolled in. What was this squared-off back end, long-hooded thing, anyway? Most had never seen the original Cabriolet that was built for Edsel. Has Gregorie finally lost his mind, they wondered. At this period in automobile body design, engineers were hiding spare tires and were moving passengers to the center of the wheel base in order to lower the car's height. Edsel was right again, Thomas recounts. After the molding clay was filled in, the car looked great.

Armature is a term used by clay modeling stylists. It is generally a metal frame with wood slats for attaching the molding clay. It is roughly the same outline as the car's body, except that it allows for a three-inch clay buildup. It is also referred to as a Buck. In the case of the Continental Cabriolet, the armature was actually a Zephyr chassis complete with suspension and wheels. The real fenders and the hood were sectioned and molded in with clay. The trunk and rear part of the fenders were wood slats. Because this buck was an actual car chassis, one was able to climb inside it.

Bob Thomas actually worked inside the armature on the instrument panel mock-up and recalls, "We used Ford instruments and any off-the-shelf parts that could be scrounged up. I remembered thinking at the time, why are we building a luxury car out of Ford parts?

The steering wheel column was pivoted downward due to the lower windshield line of the car. The instrument panel was a pretty clobbered job, at best. Everyone was surprised at how well it actually turned out."

The clay mock-up was finished in late spring of 1939. Production design work was well under way by July. Thomas recalls working among the bridges set up in the design area before his departure from Ford that summer. A bridge is a large template showing the profile of a car's body at various sections. Bob Thomas is retired now and lives in Southern California. He has written a book entitled Confessions of a Designer about his experiences at Ford and other auto makers.

In 1935, E.T. "Bob" Gregorie set up the first styling design center at Ford. In discussing those years leading up to the design of the Continental, Gregorie recalls that there were not really any executives or officials at Ford. Joe Galamb was considered head of the body engineering department. He had been with Ford since the Model-T days. John Crawford was Edsel's assistant and technical advisor and he usually followed any project that Edsel was interested in.

By 1936, Gregorie had built two different sports cars for Edsel's personal use. One was on a lowered Ford chassis with a new special type of suspension Gregorie himself had conceived. Edsel hoped to market such a car through the Ford dealers. The bodies would be contracted out to one of the Lincoln coachbuilders. Ford would supply the design, chassis and running gear, but no suitable agreement was ever reached in this regard.

Gregorie purchased and retained one of the prototype sports cars after Edsel had tired of it. On one of Edsel's trips to England, a deal was struck to build a similar sports car in conjunction with Jensen. Five prototype cars were built and shipped to England for manufacturing prototypes. Ford furnished the chassis to Jensen, who built these cars until the latter part of 1939 at which time the war in Europe halted production.

Bob Gregorie related in a recent interview, "The fact that Mr. Ford (Edsel) had just returned from a trip to Europe in 1938 had nothing to do with our starting the Continental project. We had talked about such a design for several years in conjunction with the Ford sports car projects. The Ford chassis could easily have been lengthened, but it was the suspension and weight that concerned us. General Motors had been giving Ford some real competition with a variety of midsize cars. Edsel thought that a continental-style car might fit well into the new Mercury line."

Actually, Gregorie was the first to propose that the Continental be built on the Zephyr chassis. The cost of such a car would be high and a better price could be obtained in the luxury car market.

Gregorie continues, "Mr. Ford (Edsel) was thrilled with the one-tenth scale sketches and work proceeded on a one-tenth scale clay mock-up. Most of the actual molding on the model was done by an intern named Eugene Adams. The first Continental was intended only as another hand-built custom car (for Edsel). This scale model and some drawings were what the car was actually built from. As many standard Zephyr parts as possible were used because they were readily available.

A convertible chassis was used because of needed frame bracing. As to whether it was a two-door or four-door convertible, one couldn't really tell. The Zephyr unit body was little more than a shell holding the wheels on."

Gregorie seems to remember the custom built Zephyr Cabriolet being loaded onto a Ford Company transport truck for shipment to Florida.

Gregorie said, "They had these trucks for hauling show cars around. Mr. Ford (Edsel) called from Palm Beach and instructed us to go ahead with a second car.

The rumor that Gregorie wanted to build two cars for Benson and Henry II was just another one of those tales that got started. The Ford sons had their own cars. Young Henry's car was a 1937 Zephyr Coupe. On several occasions, special equipment like dual exhausts or a custom steering wheel was installed in these cars."

Gregorie recalls that, "The young Fords would see something on one of my cars and want it put on theirs. When Mr. Ford (Edsel) called from Florida, we did discuss the Cabriolet leaking. It was more on the tone of his kidding me about it. Yes, the car was heavy, probably about a thousand pounds heavier than a regular Zephyr convertible. What else would you expect with all that solder fill? That spring and summer, we built the second prototype Continental."

With the Model-K Lincoln, Edsel had kept the coachbuilt era alive an extra decade beyond the time it would have died a natural death. His private goal was to merge the styling of a custom built automobile with the technology of a production model. The Continental would be the last vestiges of that dream.

A major factor in the decision to produce the Continental was the discontinuation of the Model-K. Its departure had left open a bay in the production line had been specially set up for custom cars. In addition, Lincoln had all these very talented custom body workers on the payroll who had worked on the Model-K. The go-ahead was given to start a limited production run of the Continental.

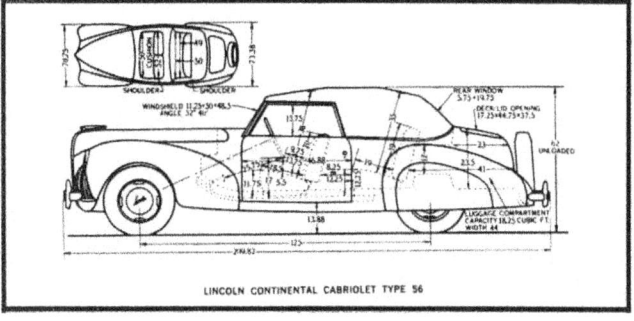

Gregorie's group got busy on the full scale clay mock-up and a set of working drawings. Gregorie explained, "The second car was extensively tested by engineering and used by my design group for dimensioning. The power plant was left up to ol' man Frank Johnson; so of course, they (Ford) stayed with the V-12 concept. Those engines and the KV-12's always had a rough spot in them. It would have been nice if we could have had something like the three hundred CID six-cylinder engine used in trucks now days. Back then, the twelve cylinders were needed for the prestige value."

The number two car, the actual development prototype, was acquired by Gregorie and he drove the car to the 1939 New York Auto Show. It was not displayed. Gregorie does not recall ever seeing Edsel's Zephyr Cabriolet after it was shipped to Florida, but it was likely returned to his home on the lake estate at Gaukler Point on Lake St. Clair. Edsel had a garage there where he kept some of the cars that were of special interest to him.

Gregorie sold the number two Continental about two years later to a used car dealer in Detroit for $800. This car was located in the early 1960s by Jessie H. Haines of California. He extensively researched the car and wrote several short stories about it. The car was recently known to be privately owned and located in Pennsylvania. This author last saw the car on display with other owner's Lincolns at the Seventy-fifth Anniversary of Lincoln celebration in Dearborn. The car had not been restored and was in fairly poor condition at the time.

A photograph dated 7-13-39 shows the first full-scale clay mock-up of the new Cabriolet. Sheet metal forms were now based on the 06H body styling. Early Continentals and to some extent virtually all Continentals, were custom built. Much hand finishing work was required. To inspect the body number on an early 06H Continental, it is found in many locations on the car; written with crayon on the inside of doors or even stamped on the inside flange of the bolt on fenders.

These early parts were fitted to a given body and needed to return to that particular car after being painted. Continental production bodies serial numbers one and two differed in many minor details from number three and subsequent cars. Some experts contend that these first two 06H prototype cars were actually the first true Continentals or they were the first two 96H production Continentals; they were neither.

By late fall of 1939, a facsimile of an assembly line had begun to take shape.

It was said that, on occasion, Henry Ford would look in on the Continental production and just walk away shaking his head. Twenty-five cars were produced by the end of the calendar year. Some Continental buffs regard these as 1939 models, but Ford considered them only as the first part of the 1940 model Continental run. This new Lincoln would have been an excellent opportunity to make some improvements to the Zephyr drive train.

Edsel was not willing it seemed, to buck the Ford people on two issues at the same time. Styling was dearer to his heart. Besides, using as many standard Zephyr parts as possible assisted in holding the development costs down.

At the Ford Rotunda on October 2, in Dearborn, the new top-of-the-line Zephyr Continental Cabriolet was announced. It is interesting to note that the first 1940 Continental (serial number H85825) is shown on Ford production records as not being completed until October 3. It was painted a Tropical Sand color with a tan cord and leather interior. Proponents of the additional cars theory concluded that the Continental shown on October 2nd was of unknown origin or possibly a Ford family car. Other possibilities are that it was the engineering prototype, or it was the car recorded as being produced on the following day, October 3rd.

The possibility also exists that no Continental was actually on display during the announcement, only art work. The most likely conclusion, however, is that production model Number One was on display for the visiting dealers and Ford Company executives who attended the announcement. Rumors persist that several other Zephyr Continentals, in the eighty thousand serial number range, were produced. Exhaustive research by automotive historians and hobbyists has failed, however, to substantiate this contention.

A week later, two Lincoln Continental show cars were displayed at the New York Auto Show and still later at the Los Angeles Auto Show; this according to a Ford promotional release at a later date The National Auto Show was held in New York from October 15 through the 22. Ford was not part of the National Automobile Association at this time, so the new Lincoln models were exhibited earlier at the ballroom in the Astor Hotel. The lavish decor adorning the automobile display was designed by Walter Dorwin Teague. The show's theme was Road of Tomorrow.

Fords, Mercurys and Lincolns were all on display at the show. Edsel Ford remained in New York and personally toured the National Auto Show on October 17. Considering that the second production car, a green Continental (serial number H86025) was recorded as being completed on October 10, it would have been a rush to get it to the New York and Los Angeles Auto Shows on time. The first two 06H models recorded on Ford production logs had no shipping destination of record. It is most likely that these two cars were, indeed, intended as show cars. Both were part of the Harrahs Automobile Collection in the early 1970s.

Lincoln historian David L. Cole of California relates that the Continental shown in New York was actually body number 06H-56-1 (serial number H85825). Production model 06H-56-2 (serial number H86025) was also shown at the Detroit and Chicago Auto Shows. No Continentals were shown in California until the latter part of the year and then only at dealers showrooms and at hotels. Cole also states, without reservation, that most of the early eighty thousand serial numbered cars mistakenly reported to be Continentals were actually convertible Zephyrs. One of the reasons for this is that researchers mistook the abbreviation of CON coupe for a CONtinental when in actuality it refers to CONvertible.

The Lincoln-Zephyr CONTINENTAL CABRIOLET

Thus, there were only two 96H series Continentals ever built and serial numbers H74750 and H82410 are listed on the 1939 production records as Special Convertible Sedans. The first two 06H Cabriolets were built in October. They were serial numbers H85825 and H86025 and were considered Ford Company cars. Harrahs has one of these cars and will not say to whom the other was sold. The first Continental to be shipped to a dealer was 06H-56-3 and was Beetle Green serial number H91688. Completed in December, it was sent to Long Beach for sale to movie actor Jackie Cooper. This car was junked some years ago and no longer exists.

NINETEEN-FORTY - Production for the model year 1940 officially began on December 13, 1939. Continental chassis and HV-12 engines were selected at random from the Zephyr production run. Thus, one can obtain only a general idea as to when a car was produced by its serial number. The chassis used on the Continental Cabriolet was similar to the type 74 Zephyr Convertible Sedan. The engine and drivetrain were identical except for some accessories. The cylinder heads on early models were brightly polished aluminum as was the intake manifold. The air cleaner was side-mounted on later Continentals and there were a variety of air cleaner styles. Hot air heaters and overdrive units also caused minor engine compartment variations.

There are a few photographs in existence of early Continentals showing certain options omitted. The story that various trim items were not installed on many early Continentals is probably without basis. In fact, there was a concerted effort to standardize these early factory options. Lower side moldings were retrofitted on 06H-56-1 in time for the New York Auto Show and a spare tire cover was added in December. The gravel shield on the rear bumper and the wider rocker panel moldings were installed from 06H-56-3 onward. The rubber boot on the lower leading edge of the rear fenders were omitted on the first twenty or so cars. Several of these cars did, however, have them added later. By April of 1940, most of the Continentals were trimmed identically. Standard Zephyr door handles were used.

Push-button outside door handles did not appear until the following year. The license plate bracket was never located on the fender as on early Zephyrs, as some reports indicated. It was always centered behind the spare tire. Originally, the license plate light and bracket mounted to the body below the spare, but it was attached to the bumper from March on. That same month, the hundred thousandth Lincoln Zephyr was produced. This honor was bestowed on a Zephyr Continental Cabriolet and publicity photos were made of the car rolling off of the assembly line.

Page 160: Continental Cabriolet from 1940 brochure. Page 178: Original Continental with Zephyr nameplate and comet hood ornament, just prior to being shipped to Edsel Ford in Florida. Page 180: Clay mockup. Page 181: Prototype Continental, 1939. Page 182: Interior of 1939 prototype Cabriolet with center console removed and column gear shift installed; 1940 Zephyr Cabriolet. Page 183: Three pictures of early 1940 production Continentals with various options like gravel shield and spare cover not installed. This page: Actor Randolph Scott takes delivery of his 1940 Zephyr Continental Cabriolet; ad for chrome restoration; Continental V-12 engine compartment distinguished by step on firewall, 1941 shown, with hot air heater. Beginning in 1942, air cleaners were sidemounted; 1940 Continental drawings from brochure top down and top up. Opposite page: Early 1941 Continental Coupe; dimension drawing; interior; and press release photo.

Henry Ford had been a close friend of Thomas A. Edison, the inventor. Ford held Edison in great esteem, so much so that the grounds on which the Ford Museum is located are named Greenville Village in his honor. Actor Mickey Rooney made a movie titled "Young Tom Edison." Some of the scenes were filmed on location at Greenfield Village. This pleased the Ford family very much. In February of 1940, Mr. Rooney was invited to Michigan for a world premiere of the new movie. Rooney, Edsel and members of the Ford family rode an old Civil War train, the Sam Hill, to Port Huron

Edsel's childhood home had been chosen as the site for the movie's premiere. Henry Ford presented the young actor with a new Continental Cabriolet, or at least the keys to one. Publicity billed the car as the first production Continental, although it was body number 134 (serial number H98800). For many years it was assumed that this car, presented to Mr. Rooney, had been the rather ornate Los Angeles show car, 06H-56-2. More recent information indicates that Edsel personally issued the list of specifications for this car, ordering it especially for this occasion.

The interior, including the panel and the steering wheel, was blue. Those attending remember the car as having been light green. This, however, was not the car actually delivered to Rooney in March of 1940. The car and Mr. Rooney parted company about the time of his divorce from actress Ava Gardner. Four other Continentals, with body serial numbers under fifteen, are shown as having been shipped to Dearborn. This sometimes meant that these cars were intended as Ford family or Ford Company cars, but not always. Continental body number 20, like number 134, was marked Home Office and Continental 06H-56-20 was, in fact, Edsel Ford's personal car.

The first Continental Coupe was completed on April 3, 1940. It was body 06H-57-1 and was installed on chassis serial number H101742. More so than the Cabriolet, the Continental Coupe would set the trend for Marks to follow. It was painted Bennington Gray, a light gray. It was and Eagle Gray was the rather darker gray used on Continentals. The interior was tan whipcord and leather. This car was extensively photographed and used for promotion of the 1940 Coupe. Continental Coupes are sometimes called hardtops due to their being first produced as Cabriolets. In view of the fact that it was designed as a hardtop version of the Cabriolet, this might be the most nearly correct term.

A sad footnote to the first Coupe comes from its original factory data card. It reads, Date Shipped: (blank), Shipped To: (blank) and scrawled across the card was written "Salvaged see blanket work order."

The new Continental Coupes were introduced to the public in May. Less emphasis was placed on the word Zephyr and this was an insight into the fact that the Continental would become a line unto itself when the 1941 models were introduced in the fall.

About one-third of all Continentals were black. Other popular colors were burgundy, red, Capri blue, tan, green and gray. Special paint colors could be custom ordered.

The most popular leather was a dark red and was installed on slightly over half of all the cars. About one-fourth of the cars had tan interiors.

The majority of the convertible tops were tan, with black making up most of the balance. Regarding accessories, many Continentals had factory options not recorded on their data cards. It was a widespread practice during the forties for dealers to complete the cars with options requested by the buyers.

Factory available accessories were radio with cowl mounted antenna, hot air heater, Columbia rearend, chrome wheel rings, road lights, side view mirror and extra bumper guards. Standard tires installed at the factory were mostly Firestone and some Goodyear. White sidewalls were more frequently installed than black walls, except right after World War II when they were hard to get.

These were to be the motorcars of ranking dignitaries and movie stars. The Continental was sleek and modern. It had a classic dignity, something that the streamlined Zephyr had never seemed to have up against the Packards and the Cadillacs. The classic lines of the Continental were to influence the design of automobiles for years to come. Lee Iacocca related that, after taking over as vice president of the Ford Division in the early sixties, he gathered a group of planners to come up with a new European style design. The Fairlane group, as it was called, was instructed to design a car around an existing Ford running gear in order to save on development costs.

Does that statement seem to have a familiar ring? The running gear was the Falcon and the ratio of long hood to boxy trunk was taken from the styling of the Continental. Ford stylists Dave Ash and Joe Oros originally called their design the Cougar. This name was later used on the similarly-styled Mercury. The new car introduced in mid-1964, at the New York World's Fair, was the very popular Ford Mustang.

Lee Iacocca said, "I used to sit and look through picture books of world automobiles searching for an impressive design. The one that I always seemed to return to was of the original Continental."

The new model year, 1940, saw just over four hundred Continentals produced. It was obvious by its popularity that the production run would continue past the originally planned five hundred units. Continental type 56 and 57 were never set up to be mass produced as the Zephyr had been. Between its inception and its discontinuation from production in mid-1948, just over five thousand Continentals were ever produced. The public demand was there and had the cars been available, far more might have been sold. The sales numbers might even have been respectable enough to have interested Ford's upper management.

The dealer organization was probably one of the keys to the Continental's low sales figures. On occasion, a remote dealership would be assigned a Continental and it would be shipped to them. He would sell it as quickly as possible, even at cost, to get it out of his inventory. One Continental represented his ability to inventory three or four Fords. Most dealers did not have the type of clientele to whom they could market a luxury car and many Ford dealers did not even have the trained staff to service Lincolns at all.

There were other changes in the Lincoln model lineup during 1940. It was the last year for type 22 Zephyr Town Limousines. These standard sedans had deluxe interiors and a partition window between the driver and the passenger compartment.

The big Lincoln Model-K was also dropped from production. Three chassis were called Specials and were sent to Brunn for construction of custom coach bodies for the Ford family. Brunn also purchased four long wheelbase chassis on which to build type 36 Limousines. These Specials and Brunn Town Cars were probably the forerunner to the types 31 and 32 Customs that would be introduced in the fall. For 1940, there was only one line of cars and they had all been called Zephyrs.

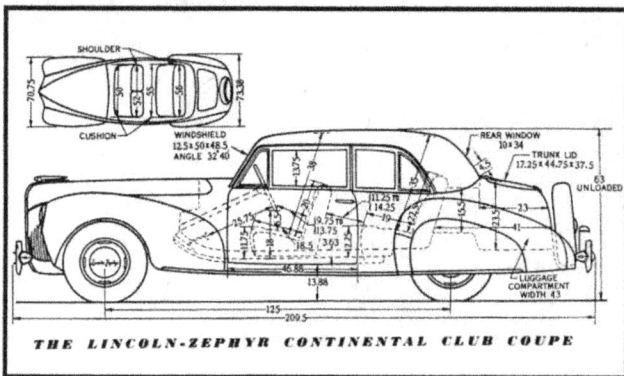

THE LINCOLN-ZEPHYR CONTINENTAL CLUB COUPE

NINETEEN-FORTYONE - For the year 1941, the Lincoln model lineup was divided into the Zephyr, the Continental and the Custom. It was hoped that the Continental would replace the sporty Model-K Roadster and that the Custom could fill the market void left by the large Model-K Sedans. The new Custom provided competition for the Packard 180, Cadillac 75 series and Buick Limited, as well as the Chrysler and DeSoto limousines. All were on stretched wheel bases of the standard models. Hudson was building a seven-passenger sedan called the Big Boy. The Lincoln types 31 and 32 Customs were offered for the first time this year and are often confused with the custom ordered Specials built by Brunn Town Car.

Because of its unit body construction, the Zephyr chassis was not well suited for custom coach rework. Ross Cousins supervised custom design and construction for Ford and built by Brunn for outside customers. These coachbuilt Specials were originally 06H and 16H series, but several were later updated with 66H grilles and trim. An oversimplified explanation of
how to tell a coachbuilt Special from a Custom is that if it looks like a Zephyr with a Model-K passenger compartment it is probably a Brunn-built Special and if it looks like a long-bodied type 57 Continental with four doors, a not-so-long hood and no outside spare then it is most likely a Custom.

The Lincoln Custom Sedans were very large cars with roomy interiors. They were advertised as eight-passenger, compared to their contemporary competitors who promoted seven-passenger Limousines and Town Sedans. The wheelbase of the Custom was 138 inches and the body itself was over eighteen feet long. The wheelbase dimension was arrived at by a rather interesting method. The Lincoln overdrive unit measures thirteen inches in length and the Zephyr with a standard drive shaft had a wheelbase of 125 inches. The sum of the overdrive unit and the standard drive shaft produced a resulting 138 inch wheelbase automobile. Thus all Customs were equipped with overdrive.

The primary difference between the Limousine type 32 and the Sedan type 31 was that the Limo had a partition window between the driver and the passenger compartment and the Sedan did not. The wider front doors for the Custom were taken from the Zephyr Club Coupe. The rear doors were four inches longer than the Zephyr Sedan's and had to be fabricated especially for the car. The spare tire was enclosed inside a nearly vertical trunk. A 06H series chrome belt line trim molding was used on the sides of the hood so as to omit the word ZEPHYR that appeared on the 16H series Zephyr trim.

About fifteen Specials were built and there will always be some conjecture about the number of Brunn Specials and Town Cars built, due to their confusion with Brunn's work on the Custom. The Lincoln Continental was now being no longer being considered as part of the Zephyr line up; it had come into its own.

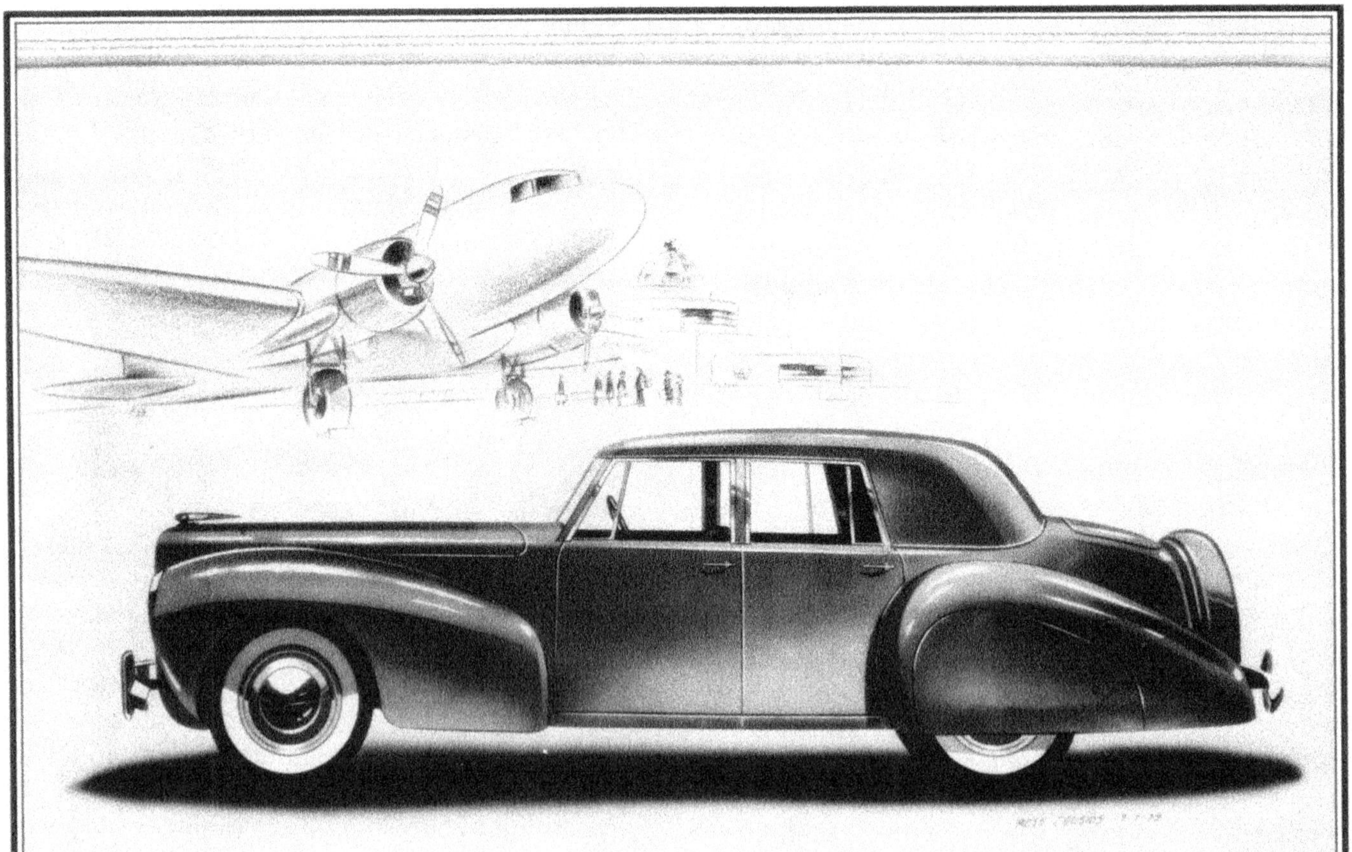

Thirteen different interior appointment options were available for the Custom Town Car Sedans. Hydraulic power windows were also offered. The Duro power window pump was mounted under the driver's seat and displaced one of the two under-seat heater units.

The divider window was also hydraulically powered, as was the front seat. Brunn, who had done much of the coach work on early Customs, usually installed padded roofs. Thus, such an option was offered on the Custom. The Formal Sedan, as it was called, omitted the rear passenger side windows and on occasion Coach Bars or Landau Irons) were installed in this location.

By mid-1941, all Customs were built at the Lincoln factory and Brunn, Inc. ceased building Customs in September of that year.

t came into its own as the Continental, offered in type 57 Coupe or type 56 Cabriolet. The Continental, like the Custom, shared the Zephyr running gear and there were only minor mechanical differences between the model lines. The new models were announced on September 20, 1940. Continental now had its own tooling, but changes were limited since the Continental's design had been based on the 06H series sheet metal from inception.

Like the Zephyr, there were numerous small trim modifications to headlight rings, tail lights and the addition of a chrome border around the grille bars. The parking lights were now mounted on top of the front fenders and turn signals were standard equipment. Turn signals were not offered the year before, even as an option. A LINCOLN CONTINENTAL logo was added to the sides of the hood and to the spare tire hub cap. The exterior and interior door releases were both pushbutton. The hood ornament looked the same as before, but no longer operated the hood latch. The hood unlatched by a pull cable and knob located under the left-hand side of the instrument panel. The ball-and-spire hood ornament was changed to a single chrome plated bronze casting instead of two pieces.

Interior changes were limited to cloth and color options. Selected interior options cost $100 extra to special order. The instrument panel had an artificial mahogany finish and the plastic hardware was a dull gold. Parts like the ring around the door pushbutton were aluminum, finished in gold plastic coating called Plastine.

A vacuum-lift window system was optional, but was installed on many Cabriolet and Coupes. The instrument panel differed from the Zephyr, although not drastically.

Marvin Arnold

CLASSIC MOTORCARS

Two large dials faced the driver. The left one was the engine gauge group and the right one was the speedometer. A large radio speaker grille was centered on the dash and the radio dial was mounted just above. Matching round clock and ash trays were mounted on either side of the speaker grille. To the right of the speedometer were three small indicator lights for turn signals and high beam. They looked more like an add-on option, but were standard equipment.

The 16H series came equipped with some positive suspension improvements, including longer, wider springs and rubber interleaf inserts. The rear tread was increased by two and one-half inches; a dimensional change that had been long needed on the model. Shocks were improved and the mounting angle for the spring shackles was changed.

A Borg-Warner overdrive unit was introduced, which allowed automatic shifting to a fourth gear With the exception of the air cleaner mount and extended firewall box, the under hood arrangement on the Continental was essentially the same as the Zephyr.

To dress up the Continental's V-12 a little, chrome acorn-nuts were used on the cylinder head bolts. The Continental body serial number placard was located in approximately the same place as on the Zephyr. The body number of Continentals was also stamped on the inside flange of the rear trunk lid. There was also a body serial number located under the windshield seal on the passenger side. The year 1941 was the last in which even the standard Lincoln was called a Zephyr.

Page 212: Brunn custom Zephyr Town Car Type H-36; Drawing made in late 1939 of proposed Continental Sedan, DC-3 airliner in background. Page 211: Lincoln Custom with capital "C" was not considered a Zephyr, and was available in Sedan or Limousine version. Opposite page: Three views of a 1941 Continental Cabriolet; 1941 Continental instrument panel; 1941 ad announcing the three lines of Lincolns; 1941 award winning Continental Coupe owned by Wendell Mathis; Continental Coupe; 1941 Cabriolet with top up; 1941 Custom. Above, left: 1941 Cabriolet drawing from the Mark Series, a dealer gift packet. Top: Press release photo 1941 Continental Coupe. Page 214 Model year 1942: Continental Cabriolet, with top down; Liquamatic transmission drawing; Continental instrument panel with standard Zephyr panel below; 1942 Brunn Special with 1946 grille originally owned by Mrs. Ford and presently in the Imperial Palace Auto Collection at Las Vegas. 1942 Continental Coupe advertising art; 1942 Cabriolet Convertible with top up; and advertising logo from 1942.

NINETEEN-FORTYTWO - The 1942 Lincolns had longer and wider bodies. A new major grille redesign was installed on all three lines. The hood and grille were more massive. The fenders had a horizontal mold line and were squared off at the back. The fender skirts now fastened over the outside of the rear fenders instead of inside. These larger cars were equally attractive without their fender skirts in place, unlike the old rear wheel-well design. The grille was stainless steel instead of the zinc chromed alloy casting, due to material shortages caused by the war effort. This unique horizontal grille bar design was used only for the short five-month production run of the 26H series.

All lines now used the exterior push-button door openers. The headlight rings had wings on both sides. The outboard wing now contained the parking and turn signal lights. The matching inboard lenses were dummies. These cars were about eight inches longer and wider than their predecessors. The front tread was fifty-nine inches. The suspension was beefed up and the gross weight was increased by over 200 pounds. The engines were bored to a new larger dimension that produced a 309 cubic inch displacement engine and developed 130 horsepower.

The 1942 26H series were viewed by many Continental and Zephyr watchers as ugly ducklings. In the case of the larger Custom, they became the swans of the fleet. The 26H grille and wider fenders were very impressive on these types 31 and 32 Sedans.

The 1942 models had been introduced on September 30, 1941. After the attack on Pearl Harbor, the government ordered all U.S. auto manufacturers to conclude civilian production and prepare to support the war effort. In an attempt to meet the competition, Lincoln introduced the all new Liquamatic automatic transmission.

There are two common misconceptions about this early automatic transmission. The first is that it was a two-speed transmission and the second is that it had no manual clutch. Neither is true. In fact, the only outward clue to its installation was the LIQUAMATIC LINCOLN emblem in place of the standard Lincoln emblem on the glove box door.

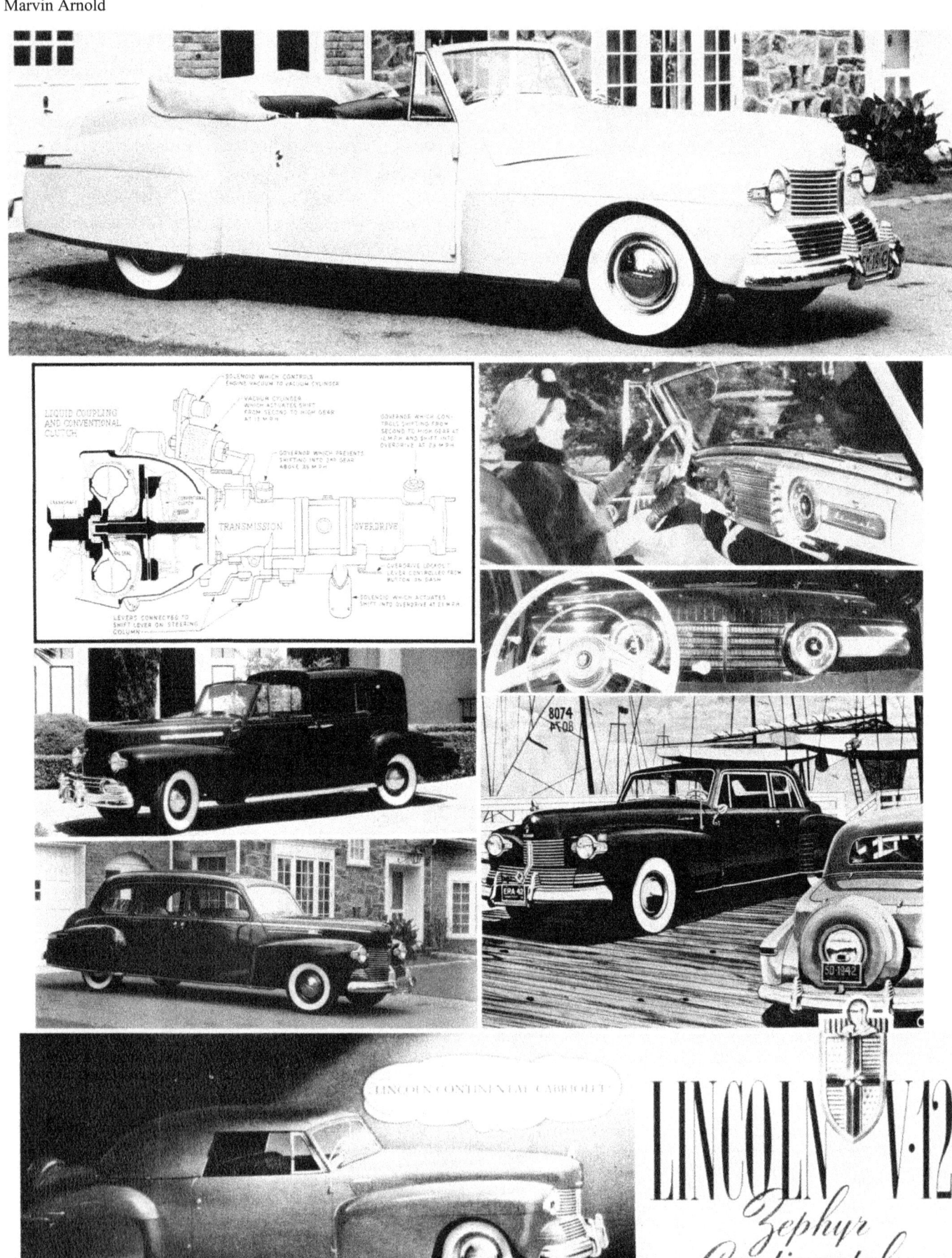

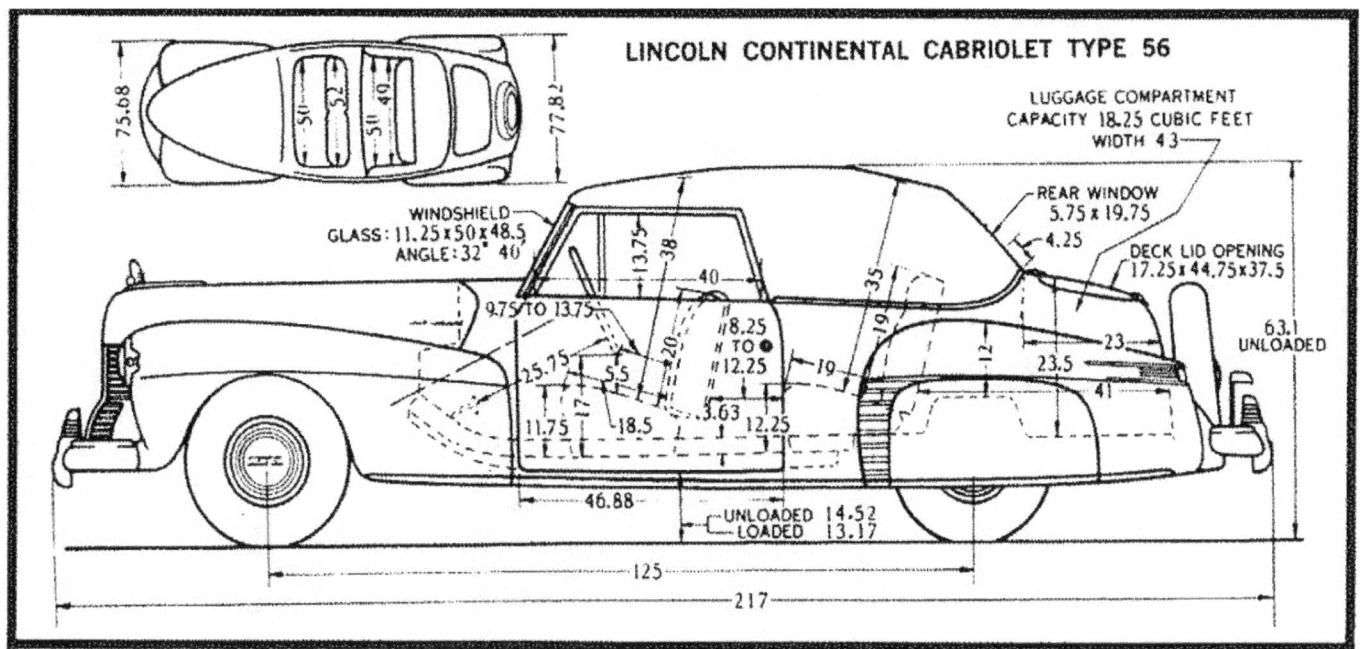

Liquamatic automatic transmission had a fluid coupler as part of the transmission that incorporated a unique countershaft arrangement. It allowed second and third gears to run at the same speed. Low gear or first and reverse could not be engaged except by using the manual clutch. Low gear was used for steep grades or pulling loads.

When placing the gearshift selector in the second gear position, the transmission would not shift into high. This position was adequate for most in-town driving, but a little hard on the V-12 engine. The overdrive unit came standard with the Liquamatic and could be engaged in second or third gears. A governor operated vacuum valve and holding coil circuit provided automatic shifting from second to third gears at approximately thirty-five miles per hour and explains why the Liquamatic is often referred to as a two-speed automatic transmission.

The Liquamatic Lincoln transmissions required accurate adjustment to operate properly. Most units were replaced with standard transmissions by a dealer at under ten thousand miles in service. The dealers were instructed to also remove the glove box emblem. Thus, only the factory data card gives a clue as to a car's that had been equipped with a Liquamatic.

The panel and instrument cluster were completely redesigned for the 26H series. It featured a large radio speaker grille in the center, bordered by matching control knobs. Down the driver's side were the headlight switch, choke, throttle and ignition. On the passenger's side were matching cigars lighter and pullout ashtray. Plastics were popular in the early forties, so the glove box logo was edge-lighted to glow with the panel lights on. A new fold-down rear-seat center armrest was added.

The Ajust-O-Matic Radio and the vacuum-powered fender-mounted antenna were optional. The radio could be tuned to the next station signal by means of a touch bar or foot switch. A way for Lincoln drivers to amuse kids or impress a new passenger was to wave their hand magically toward the radio while secretly depressing the floor mounted foot switch to change the station. If artfully accomplished, one could get by with it several times before the passengers being entertained caught on.

The Custom was not continued after the war, but did appear in an early 1946 Lincoln brochure. By February 10, 1942, most of Ford's quota for Lincolns had been produced. The last Lincoln to come off of the assembly line was a Custom Sedan, shown as completed on the 27th of February. Part on 26H series interchanged and some postwar Lincolns were updated with new grilles after the war. Cars from this short production year remain among the rarest and most interesting of all the modern Lincolns. Ironically, they were destined to be the last Lincolns ever produced under the guiding hand of Edsel Ford.

CHAPTER EIGHT
THE LINCOLN LIBERATORS

Into The Breech With Henry II

From 1931 on, General Motors overtook Ford in numbers of cars sold. The Mercury, introduced in 1939, had failed to put much of a dent in the GM and Chrysler middle car market. Only in light truck sales had Ford maintained a respectable lead. The recent economic depression had driven down the automobile market. Not until 1949, did the industry as a whole equal its 1929 production figure of 5.3 million cars.

It has been suggested that Henry Ford initiated the five dollar per day wage so that common workers could afford to purchase an automobile of their own. He felt that the auto market would always remain limited unless working people could afford to purchase automobiles. He hoped other industries would be forced to follow his salary lead.

After the stock market crash of 1929, Henry Ford again applied the principles of a true capitalist. The price of a Model-A was lowered, wages were raised and branch factory construction was begun even though Ford Motor Company was steadily losing market share. The main product line, the Ford, was suffering from declining sales. Many automobile historians conclude that this was due, in part, to factors other than the Ford automobile itself. Henry Ford had a poor reputation in labor relations and was very outspoken on controversial political matters. These attributes may have indirectly affected the buying public's attitude toward the Ford product.

The early organizing of labor unions had little impact on the automobile industry as a whole. However, in May of 1939, Walter Reuther of the United Auto Workers singled out Ford Motor Company to protest working conditions. The UAW began by handing out leaflets, but violence erupted. The incident became known as the Battle of the Overpass. It occurred at the Rouge plant and was widely reported in the press. Chief of Security Harry Bennett headed up a group at Ford called The Service. They provoked, then beat up Reuther and several of his supporters. This was the beginning of a rather lengthy period of adverse relations between Ford and the labor unions.

Henry Ford was also opposed to America's becoming involved in the expanding war in Europe, just as he had been to this country's involvement in the First World War. Maybe in principle his pacifism was correct, but it was perceived by the American public as unpatriotic. This and his anti-unionism hurt the Ford Motor Company as a whole. Even worse, it curtailed car sales and hurt the Ford dealership network. To add to these problems, Henry Ford suffered a stroke in 1938. Edsel Ford was now president, but he and Ford's general manager, Charles Sorensen, never really acquired full control from the senior Ford.

Harry Bennett had been hired when Edsel was a youngster. Henry Ford had become keen on bodyguards and had developed a fear of kidnapping after the Lindbergh baby incident. Bennett, however, was not Edsel's friend. He intimidated the young Ford and even fantasized about becoming president of Ford Motor Company himself. In the end, it was Edsel Ford who convinced his father to make peace with the labor unions.

After the strike on the Rouge Plant in April of 1941 was settled, Henry steadfastly refused to sign the new labor agreement. He had still not done so by June. Mrs. Clara Ford intervened and told Henry that she would leave him if he did not do so and prevent further violence. "Don't ever discredit the power of a woman," Henry is quoted as saying.

In the summer of 1939, Edsel's son, Henry Ford II, had toured Europe in a Lincoln Zephyr with two college friends. A short time later, the world was engulfed in a European war. By early 1941, Nazi Germany was overrunning industrial Europe. General Chennault's Flying Tigers had been fighting the Japanese on the coast of China for two years. While it seemed clear to many Americans that a world war was a real possibility, it never actually sank in. As to suspending civilian automobile production, the thought seems never to have entered the automaker's minds. Events in Europe and the Hawaiian Islands soon brought most Americans to the startling realization that the free world was now fighting for its very existence.

In December of 1941, the Office of Production Management, which later became the War Production Board, shut down all automobile exports and established production quotas. Those cars not delivered by March of 1942, went into military service or were stored in warehouses. Ford Sedans painted olive drab, grille and all, became staff cars. Police departments and taxi cab companies drove Hudsons. Individuals bought Nashs who never had before and never would again. Chrysler began building tanks. Willys-Overland was already producing Jeeps and Ford's new khaki painted Jeeps were nicknamed Blitz Buggys.

The war effort had already affected the 1942 cars themselves. Most chrome parts were now stainless steel or painted metal. The effect of the military buildup was also showing up in the automobile advertising campaigns. Chevrolet called their engine the Victory Valve-in-Head. Chrysler named their engine Spitfire after the British fighter plane. Oldsmobile celebrated its forty-fourth anniversary in automobile making with a B-44 grille medallion. The "B" stood for Better-built, but it didn't hurt that it also sounded like an Army Air Corps bomber designation.

The last Lincoln sedan was photographed rolling off of the assembly line with two American flags tied to the front bumper.

The Lincoln ad campaigns through 1943 and 1944 pictured scenes of empty, lonely stretches of road. Lincoln retained the "Nothing Could Be Finer" slogan throughout the war years. The cross crest and knight's head logo, introduced with the 26H series, was now the official Lincoln emblem. Only one of these ads depicted the Lincoln automobile.

In a scene along a Rocky Mountain ridge road, a Lincoln Sedan is viewed at a distance. The ad read, "Someday a rendezvous... When it's over, the open road will again challenge... A new motor car, the smartest and finest ever built, will be the answer to your dreams."

On an Arizona dirt road bordered by Saguaro cactus the ad says, "The gray years will end with brighter days. And a new Lincoln motorcar will be waiting to get under way..."

Down an Indiana country road the ad laments, "Remember how the highways use to beckon? They will again. In the coming days of peace, a new Lincoln motor car will be waiting to satisfy your travel urge."

Thus, the ad campaigns continued, never giving the slightest hint of what the new Lincoln models might look like. There was good reason for this because no one really knew.

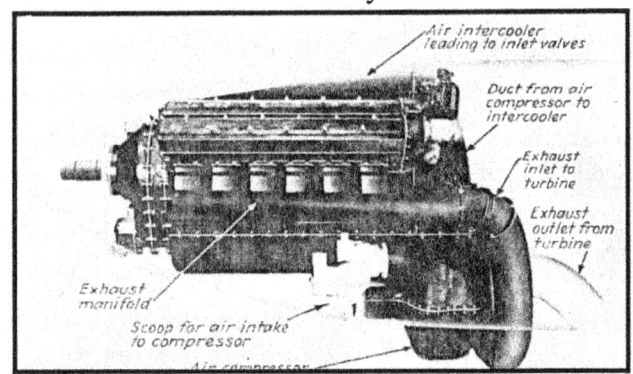

Ford's powerful V-12 aircraft engine developed during WWII.

William S. Knudsen had been appointed by President Roosevelt to head the U.S. National Defense Commission. Knudsen had been the chief executive officer of General Motors after Alfred Sloan had left in 1937. In his new capacity with the N.D.C., Knudsen offered Ford a plum. It was a contract to produce Rolls-Royce Merlin aircraft engines.

When the press picked up that Ford would build war supplies for the British, Henry pulled out saying that Ford would manufacture war goods for the U.S. Government, but would not be part of arming any foreign power. Once again, Henry Ford's position was popularly perceived as unpatriotic. Consider for a moment how much safer the world would be to live in if all industrialists today took that same position.

Major Jimmy Doolittle, who became General Doolittle after his famed Tokyo raid, remarked that the Automotive Committee for American Air Defense was like a bad wedding without the benefit of a shotgun. Pressure on Ford from Knudsen and the government continued. In November of 1940, fearing a government takeover of the company, Edsel and Sorensen finally persuaded Henry to commence military production.

The first project undertaken was the manufacture of Pratt & Whitney airplane engines for the Army Air Corps. Next Ford converted the Willow Run and Ypsilanti plants to be used to assemble B-24 Liberator bombers. In September of 1942, the first Liberators were completed.

Ford was slow getting started, but once into war production the company became a major contributor to the U.S. war effort. At its peak, there were 42,000 employees working at Ford bomber plants. Many were women and regardless of their tasks, they were all nicknamed Rosie the Riveter. Slacks and hair nets became fashionable because of their obvious safety advantage.

The Ford facilities used in aircraft production totaled three million square feet. Of the 18,188 Consolidated Aircraft designed B-24 Liberator four-engine bombers produced, Ford built 8,685. The last aircraft rolled of the assembly line in June of 1945.

Ford was America's largest glider aircraft producer. The gliders were built at the Iron Mountain complex. Used primarily for producing wood auto body parts since the 1920s, the plant had been closed early in the war effort. This complex was reopened in March of 1942 and ultimately produced 4,205 of the fifteen-seat CG-4A cargo gliders and 87 of the forty-two seat CG-13A combat personnel gliders. These aircraft were built of wood and tubular metal covered with cotton fabric. Many new production processes for bonding were developed at this facility. After the war, the plant resumed building component automobile items like station wagon woods until 1951.

Albert Kahn, the son of a German rabbi, had designed a reinforced concrete factory for the Packard car company in 1905. In 1907, Henry Ford hired Kahn to design and build a new Model-T factory on the site of an old race course at Highland Park. Henry always wanted the biggest and best, so for the next thirty-five years, architect Albert Kahn gave the Ford Motor Company just that. Kahn designed the Rouge River plant in 1918, the Engineering and Research facility in 1925 and Edsel's manor home in 1929. The Willow Run factory had been Kahn's last project before his death in 1942.

It is ironic indeed that Henry Ford, who outwardly spoke against the Jews in the banking business, should hire a Jew of German descent to design a facility that would ultimately play a major role in the defeat of the German Nazi war machine.

Page 220: Wartime ad, Lincoln car set into a famous postcard scene. 12,000 foot pass on Trail Ridge Road above Timberline, Colo.
Page 118: Wartime Lincoln ads. Page 221: Ford developed V-12 aircraft engine in 1941 superior to the Rolls-Royce. Above: B-24 Liberator bomber; and Jeep built by Ford. Page 223: Loewy Cabriolet custom built by Enos Derham in 1946 on a 1941 Lincoln Continental; and a customized 1942 Continental Coupe.

All Ford facilities were now either manufacturing for the defense effort or shut down. Jeep engines were mass produced by Ford. It is claimed that the Willys designed Jeeps built by Ford were better than the originals. The Lincoln plant produced thousands of amphibian bodies, Jeep parts, tank engines and nacelles for the B-24.

So efficient was the Ford industrial complex at producing aircraft parts that some aviation manufacturers feared that Ford might try to stay in the business after the war ended. The demand for new automobiles after the war was so great that most automakers, including Ford, returned to their original endeavor and never looked back.

One of the wartime casualties was "Cast-Iron Charlie" who had run Ford for forty years. In September of 1943, Sorensen faced a management showdown with Larry Sheldrick of engineering. Several of Ford's top engineers and design people, including E.T. Gregorie, resigned. During Gregorie's absence, Tom Hibbard filled in and continued what little wartime civilian design could be accomplished.

Photo of Whiz Kids taken in 1946. (Front row, left to right) Arjay Miller, Francis Reith, George Moore, James O. Wright, Tex Thornton, Wilbur Anderson, Charles Bosworth, Ben D. Mills, F. Edward Lundy, and Robert McNamara.

Additionally, Sorensen managed to cross the Air Corps and the Consolidated Aircraft people. Harry Bennett had also been working behind the scenes to discredit Sorensen.

On March 3, 1944, Charles Sorensen resigned from Ford. E.T. Gregorie and several others were rehired by Vice-President Henry Ford II. Sorensen became president of Willys-Overland Company for a short period and then went into retirement.

Due to their ability to retool rapidly, the auto industries had been able to quickly get into production of already designed military equipment. They greatly contributed to the Allied war effort. During the war, civilian automobile parts support would have been abandoned completely except for the fact that cars were badly needed to get workers to and from the defense plants.

Rubber and petroleum were in short supply. If a 55 MPH speed limit seems worrisome today, consider that during the war the speed limit was lowered to 35 MPH. In addition to saving fuel, the lower speed limit decreased tire wear. Tires were retreaded, engines were rebuilt and gasoline was rationed.

Auto dealerships that managed to stay in business became used car dealers. It might be hard to perceive a four-year-old automobile as a current model, but this was the American public's view of the 1941 and 1942 model cars until 1946. There were some less-than-scrupulous dealers willing to sell a late model car for twice its prewar value.

A Lincoln Continental that might have sold new for $3,000 could now bring as much as $10,000. A few California traders would go back East and buy up convertibles by convincing the seller that rubberized material for tops would be impossible to obtain. They would then transport them to the milder climate of the West Coast and double their money on these automobiles. Often workers going west to work in the defense plants that were now hiring would drive the cars for free transportation to deliver them.

To get around being accused of black marketing or excess profit-taking, a salesman might sell you a pet dog or something else for part of the purchase price. The problem lessened after the war ended, but automobiles were still in very short supply. Cars were starting to wear out and the young servicemen returning home to start families wanted new cars to drive. Through about 1948, there were waiting lists at most dealerships. When the cars came in, purchasers would pay the full retail price and also take whatever accessories the dealer chose to add on.

It was not uncommon to pay a couple of hundred dollars extra to a salesman who might get you moved up on the waiting list a notch or two. Many volumes have been written about the mystique of the Ford family and the intrigue surrounding its constant struggle for control of the Ford Motor Company. Edsel Ford respected his father greatly, but at best the relationship between them was strained. Edsel's health was failing. A nervous condition had manifested itself in the form of a chronic stomach disorder and other complication.

Edsel Ford died at 1:10 A.M. on May 26, 1943, in the upstairs bedroom of his home at Grosse Point Shores. His father was a grand and power American industrialist, but he, Edsel, would be remembered for his creativity and gentleness. One thing was certain, that was the Lincoln and Continental automobile would not exist today had it not been for Edsel Bryant Ford.

Henry Ford once again became president of Ford Motor Company. Lincoln was wholly owned by Ford and had for some time functioned more as a division than as an independent company. Clara Ford and Edsel's widow, Eleanor, made it known that they would sell their voting shares of Ford Motor stock if Henry Ford II was not installed as president.

Young Henry II had enlisted in the Navy and was an ensign assigned to the Great Lakes Training Station. Had he chosen to do so, he might have been exempted from military service altogether due to the family business. There were two younger brothers, Benson and William and a sister, Josephine. Edsel's eldest son, Henry II, had been made a Ford Company vice president on December 15, 1943. On January 23, 1944, he became executive vice-president. Still, this office was ineffectual against what Harry Bennett continued to imply were the wishes of the elder Ford. Henry Ford II became president of Ford Motor Company on September 21, 1945. Harry Bennett was given one month to get his affairs in order and leave.

The Ford Foundation had been given most of the stock in Ford Motor Company, but these were nonvoting shares. Five percent of the stock and most of the voting shares were retained by the Ford family and they had always controlled the company. Henry Ford had set up the Ford Foundation in February of 1936 to avoid Roosevelt's inheritance tax.

When Henry died on April 7, 1947, this strategy saved the Ford family $321 million in taxes. In 1955, two-thirds of the Ford Company stock would be reclassified to voting common and sold by the Foundation. One of the largest family-owned businesses went public less than a decade after its founder's death. Lincoln Motor Company remained a wholly-owned subsidiary of the Ford Motor Company.

By the early 1940s, most of the custom body coach builders were out of business. Because of this, Ford was able to hire fine designers like Tom Hibbard, Charles Waterhouse and Herman Brunn, also talented commercial illustrators like Ross Cousins. As the war work began to wind down in 1944, more effort was placed on future civilian automobile design, but any hope of getting new tooling was still years away. As more free time became available to the design group, many new and different body styles were explored. Such was the pent-up demand for new cars at the close of the war that anything new on wheels would have sold.

Thus, newer versions of the old models were put back into production and retooling was scheduled for the 1949 models. Ford was the first to return to civilian automobile production. By June of 1945, Ford was well into producing the warmed-over 1942 models that would be introduced in the fall as the new 1946 models.

Postwar Ford production officially commenced on July 3, 1945 and on October 22ed Thomas W. Skinner was named to head up Lincoln. He replaced Raymond R. Rausch who was considered by Henry II to be in the Harry Bennett camp.

This change accompanied a dozen other key appointments, including Benson Ford's being named to a vice presidency. These changes were to have a great impact on the future of the Lincoln automobile. New Lincoln production officially began on November 1, 1945.

No Lincoln was ever again called Zephyr. However, some years later, the Mercury version of the Ford Fairmont was named Zephyr; for what reason, one can only wonder. Materials remained scarce and Lincoln production never reached its full potential due to these shortages. Prior to the war and just after, practice was to ship cars to dealers short of parts. Joe Wilkerson, a dealer, recalls a 66H Lincoln coming into the California dealership short of bumpers. It was an ugly sight, he explained, a Lincoln with a wood plank for a front bumper.

New Lincoln prices were increased one-third over the prewar prices. The first 66H Continental was not produced until February of the calendar year. In spite of all of this, Lincoln managed to produce over sixteen thousand units for the 1946 model year.

In late 1945, Colonel Charles Bates "Tex" Thornton negotiated a deal to bring his management team to Ford. In early January of the following year, the Whiz Kids as they became known began arriving on the scene. Henry II was faced with running a company without an established hierarchy. Not to mention the Company was losing nine million dollars a month. The Whiz Kids were former Army Air Forces efficiency experts who came to Ford as a group. A couple of them even became Ford Motor Company presidents, the most notable being Robert Strange McNamara.

Still others of this new breed of Ford executives came from the ranks of established corporations like Bendix and Borg-Warner. A few worked their way up through the ranks like Lido "Lee" Iacocca. When the 1946 Lincolns went into production, Iacocca was a journeyman engineer graduate from Lehigh University who wanted to get into marketing McNamara was a wet-behind-the-ears Harvard graduate and Henry Ford II was twenty-nine years old.

The ten original Whiz Kids went on Ford's payroll January 31, 1946. Their nickname was quickly changed to Quiz Kids. Having no authority, they mostly went around asking questions. The management hierarchy at Ford was in disarray. Money was being wasted for lack of management communication. Production was inefficient and inadequate. It seemed as though nothing that existed had been planned and there was no official strategy for the future.

In December, Lewis D. Crusoe came to Ford from Bendix as the new vice president of operations. From that time on, the changes began. Of the original ten Whiz Kids, some stayed with Ford and some left, but most had a profound impact on Ford's future. Tex Thornton left Ford in 1948 to go to Hughes Aircraft, later founded Litton Industries. Robert McNamara became a vice president and then for a short period president of Ford. He later became Secretary of Defense under John F. Kennedy. Francis C. "Jack" Reith became involved in the Edsel automobile project and advocated its being a separate division from Lincoln-Mercury. The idea was over ridden by Ernest Breech.

Reith headed up the Ford V-8 powered Vedette development for SAF. He and John R. Davis spearheaded the concept of the Lincoln and Mercury sharing body components. Charles E. Bosworth became Ford's General Purchasing Agent. A native of Detroit, George Moore left after one year at Ford to become a partner in a local Lincoln-Mercury dealership. Wilbur R. "Gene" Anderson left Ford and the industry.

Arjay Miller was president of Ford for five years before leaving to head up Federal Mogul Bearing. James O. Wright became general manager of the Ford Division. He pushed for the Falcon and headed up the Fairlane design project. The last of the Whiz Kids, J. Edward Lundy, became treasurer, then vice president at Ford and was the last to retire in 1968.

A member of this insiders group, although not one of the Whiz Kids, was Ernest R. Breech who came to Ford from Bendix in July. Breech hired Del Harder and Harold Youngren, both of whom would have important roles in the postwar Ford turnaround. Most of these men were not automotive geniuses. Only a couple had any real automotive experience. They were simply good business managers who gave the talented engineers and workers at Ford, Lincoln and Mercury the capability to produce.

NINETEEN-FORTYSIX - The 1946 Lincoln body 66H series and fender parts were pure 26H, but a new massive chromed die-cast grille was the crowning glory of the postwar Lincoln and Continental. Some non-admirers refer to these multiple crosshatched bar grilles as the Egg Crate look. Lincoln's new front end was as impressive as that of any postwar model. Both the Continental and the standard Lincoln shared push-button door latches, trim parts and hood ornament. Hood ornament on 66H and early 76H Lincolns was a ball with twin triangle wings.

Some of the Model-76H and all 86H Lincolns used the ball and long tail missile or comet style hood ornament. This ball and trailing spire hood ornament remained the Lincoln and Continental nose decoration until the end of Model-H production. (The latter's design is very similar to one originally used on Edsel's Zephyr Continental Cabriolet.)

The coat of arms medallion, a crest and knight's head armor was used initially on the 26H series hood nose was relocated to the top center of the grille. The differences between the standard Lincoln and the Lincoln Continental were the rocker panel moldings, trunk hardware, cowl logos and rear fender mud guards.

Engine changes were limited. Midyear the HV-12 returned to the 16H cylinder bore and displacement. Early 66H engines still had the 305 CID while the later year models returned to the 292 CID engines. A new oil pump with redesigned sump screen, for greater output capacity, was installed. At about this same time the practice of stamping the matching chassis serial number into the top of the right-hand motor mount flange on the cylinder block was begun. Bumpers were heavier, with two large bumper guards. The Lincoln rear bumper had left and right-side wing guards were joined to the bumper guard by upper horizontal bars.

Regardless of body color, wheels were painted black. The optional three-rib, bright metal wheel rings were larger than those used on prewar models. The taillight accent chrome was painted red in the grooves on all models. Where the cross crest and knight's head logo had been accented in green on the 26H, it was now accented in dark blue. Hubcaps were barrel shaped with a raised octagonal symbol around LINCOLN in block letters. The 66H series being the only year in which this style of hubcap was used.

Even with fender skirts installed, all four hubcaps had the octagon and logo. As on the 26H Continental, the spare tire hubcap differed from those on the ground wheels and had LINCOLN CONTINENTAL in script on the upper third. Some state laws made it illegal to have more than two headlights and one spotlight or driving lamp facing forward. Thus, an under dash switch could be wired so as to turn the headlights off when the fog or driving lamps were turned on.

This feature became standard on the following year's models. When the lamp option was not installed, two chrome grille plates were located in their place. These plates had a four-bar arrangement, reminiscent of the 26H series outboard grille's three whiskers. The driving or fog lamp option was often originally installed or retrofitted. These 66H grille end plates are very rare.

Continental body styles for 1946 were the Coupe type 57 and the Cabriolet type 56. The Lincoln body styles were Sedan type 73, five-window Coupe type 77 and Convertible Coupe type 76. This lineup prevailed through the end of this model of automobiles in 1948. The 66H series ended with the calendar year 1946 and the 76H series began with the calendar year, 1947, according to records kept by W.A. Currie of the Production Control Department.

Three body styles were dropped from the postwar model lineup. They were the two Custom Sedans and the Business Coupe known a three window coupe (3WC) even though the rear window was actually two small windows. Early 66H Lincoln brochures did, however, picture the Custom models. The Custom was not dropped because of Edsel Ford's absence as some have speculated. The demand for luxury Sedans was as strong as ever and its tooling was not dissimilar from that of the other Lincolns being produced. It was simply that due to manpower and materials being in short supply, limited production body types were the most logical style to discontinue.

Except for the back end design, there were only minor trim variations between the 70 series and the 50 series Lincoln body types. The fact that the type 56 and 57 Lincolns were the last popular motorcars to be equipped with an external rear-mounted spare tire is responsible for an automotive term used to this day. The term Continental Kit refers to an external spare tire regardless of the make or model of automobile on which it is installed.

When viewing only the front two-thirds, except for the cowl trim, it is difficult to differentiate a type 76 Lincoln Convertible Coupe from a type 56 Continental Cabriolet. The standard Lincoln had a mold line chrome strip, which ran the length of the body.

Above: Press photo of 1946 Continentals and Lincolns coming off of the assembly line; Actor Ronald Reagan driving 1946 Continental on Hollywood movie set; Henry Ford II at the wheel of 1946 Lincoln Continental Cabriolet; May 30th, 1946 Pace Car at the Brickyard (Indy 500 Race). Opposite page: 1946 Lincoln Sedan, note pushbutton doors and grille whiskers; leather and whipcord Continental interior; 1940 Club Coupe; late year 1946 Type 56 Continental with comet hood ornament owned by Ted Leonard of Rhode Island. Page 228: New 1946 model year Lincolns. Page 237: Overdrive transmission, this type offered from 1941 through 1948; 1946 through 1948 Page 231: Continental instrument panel.

Marvin Arnold

ANNOUNCING THE 1946 LINCOLN
Nothing could be finer

The cowl trim was a large square chrome plate with the name LINCOLN trailing a checkerboard pattern. The Continental cowl had a script LINCOLN CONTINENTAL nameplate. Rocker panel trim remained unchanged from the 26H through the 86H on the Continental. The rocker panel trim was not interchangeable between the standard Lincoln and the Continental.

Optional accessories included an improved AM radio, which had been introduced on the 26H. A three-section telescoping antenna, mounted on the aft portion of the left front fender, would extend upward six feet. Antennas were more critical to good reception on the old-style Heterodyne receivers, but they worked well. The radio continued the unique touch-bar station changer

LINCOLN AND CONTINENTAL

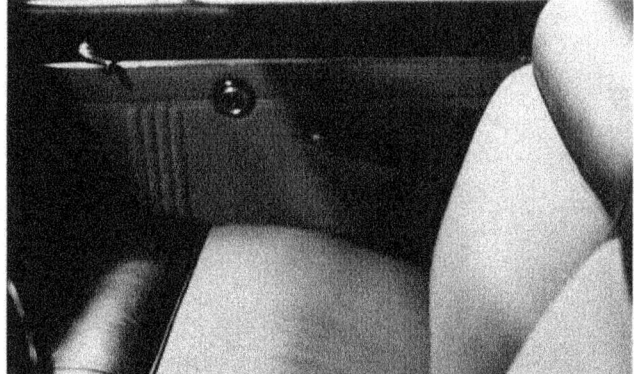

Touching the center bar or depressing a dimmer-type foot switch on the floor would cause a small electrical motor inside the radio to cycle forward to the next mechanically preset stop. The station settings were preset by the right-hand station selector knob and the bar selector. The center thumb wheel was a tone control. The knobs on the 26H had been ivory and the dial numbers were silver. All of the 26H plastic, including the steering wheel, had been ivory color. For the 66H model through to the end of model production, the steering wheel and accessory knobs were dark maroon.

A vacuum-powered antenna was optional and operated by a push-pull neutral-off knob just above the instrument gauge cluster. The windshield wiper control knob, pulled-on and rotated for wiper speed adjustment, was also located in this area. Power-lift door windows were optional. When extra vacuum equipment was installed, a large air reserve tank was mounted under the right front fender. This reserve stabilized the windshield wiper speeds during acceleration, a low vacuum point.

Chrome was used extensively on the instrument panel components. The Lincoln panel and Continental panel were similar in minor detail, but distinctly different in overall appearance. Major components like the clock, speedometer, radio and the engine gauge group were all interchangeable. On the Continental the headlight switch, choke, throttle and ignition border the left side of the large chrome center speaker grille. A cigar lighter and ashtray with matching chrome knobs were located to the right of the speaker grille.

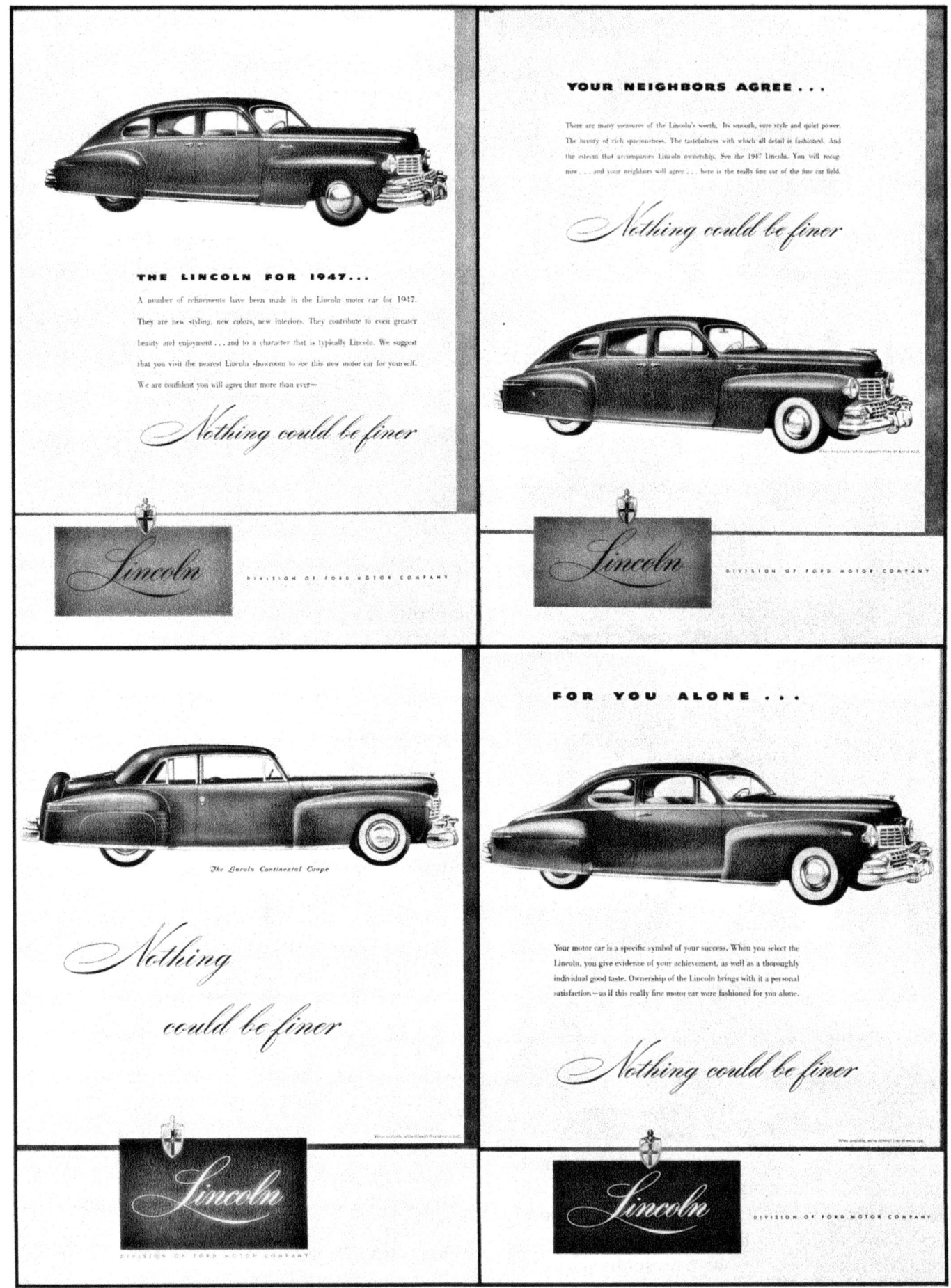

On the standard Lincoln models these controls were located along the bottom of the panel, below the speaker grille. Both models retained the top cowl vent panel that could be opened by a lever under the instrument panel near the clock.

A custom interior option costing $149 was available for Lincoln Sedan or Coupe. The Continental used leather on the forward seat and on the top of the seat back. Cord broadcloth, sometimes called Whip Cord, in the center section was standard and most often shipped on Coupes. The optional matching leather center section was shipped most often on the Cabriolet.

The overdrive push-pull knob was to the left of the steering wheel column under the dash, adjacent to the emergency brake handle. With the control knob pulled-out, the transmission operated as a standard 3-speed forward and pushed-in, overdrive engaged the drivetrain was freewheeling in all gears. This allowed the overdrive solenoid to pull in at about 35 MPH. A small electrical kick-down switch was located under the accelerator pedal for temporarily shifting down, out of overdrive. Clutch and brake pedal foot pads were round, a tradition since the Lincoln Model-L.

The under-dash defroster blower and under-seat heaters continued to be optional accessories. The control unit for them was located under the dash to the left of the steering wheel column and looked very much like an add-on accessory. The edge-lit instrument panel lighting was artfully done. A separate dash light dimmer, a rheostat switch, was under the panel to the right of the steering wheel column. Also located here was the trip speedometer reset knob.

A small key light located just below the ignition switch came on when the parking lights were turned on. The overhead courtesy dome light and under dash light were door switch operated. The courtesy lights could also be turned on by a switch located under the glove box. A dome light slider-switch, which operated the luggage compartment light was located on the passenger door post. Many is the Continental whose dome light was burned out and the battery ran down with this switch left on.

Auto restorer Walt Jenkins relates that during the repainting preparation of an early postwar Continental Coupe, the original paint scheme was found to be robin's egg blue with a black top. He called his friend, Bob Gregorie, who replied, "Oh, you've got one of those Easter egg cars." Henry Ford II seemed to take more of an interest in color schemes in the spring and would order several cars painted various nonstandard colors. Paint schemes of blue and black, gray and black, two-tone green and metallic maroon were used on these Continentals. Henry II personally drove one of these Continentals painted Chantilly Green.

NINETEEN-FORTYSEVEN - The 1947 Lincolns were just that. With minor exceptions, the 76H Lincolns were a continuation of the prior year's 66H series. The hood ornament and engine displacement had been changed midyear on the 66H. The 76H was officially introduced on January 1st and not in the fall of the prior year, as had been the prewar custom. The new ball and single spire hood ornament was installed on all models. The front grille now included as standard equipment the dual driving lights outboard. The lamps were amber and could be called fog lights.

Page 230: Four ads from 1947 and 1948, top two Lincoln Sedans, note left is 1947 with grille whiskers and black wall tires, right has fog lights and whitewall tires, both have pull door handles; 1947 Lincoln Club Coupe; 1947 Lincoln Continental Coupe, Type 57. Page 233: Press photo of 1947 Sedan; Bob Bordman's 1948 Continental in Albuquerque, New Mexico; 1947-48 Continental Coupe at Salado, Texas. This page: 1948 Continental Cabriolet; Ford Manual photo of Continental Coupe and Lincoln Convertible; 1948 Lincoln at Ford engineering facility. Page 233: Drawing from Mark II Continental story by Ford Motor Company. Page 236: Composite views of 1946-1948 Lincolns and Continentals, popular at car meets everywhere; color views from 1946-1948 Lincoln ads.

Added to the back of the trunk, just behind the spare tire, was a single horizontal chrome strip. It resembled a single luggage rack guard strip. Hubcaps were heavier looking, barrel shaped without the octagon. The front two had the LINCOLN script logo attached. The rear two were without logos as the fender skirts hide their center. The Continental's spare tire hubcap had the same script logo as on the 26H and 66H. Optional bright metal wheel trim rings were wider, but a few early year 76H models were shipped with the 66H hubcaps and trim rings.

As late as 1947, Lincolns and Mercurys were still sold through Ford dealerships. Lincoln literature and advertising had never been exactly clear on this subject. Lincoln was referred to as Lincoln Motor Division of Ford Motor Company just prior to the war. Zephyr promotional material had varied from year to year in company titles. In 1940 they were by the Lincoln Motor Company Division and in 1941 Lincoln Motor Car Division. Ads during World War II were titled by Lincoln a Division of Ford Motor Company and Lincoln a Product of Ford Motor Company. In October, 1947, the Lincoln-Mercury Division was established, but T.W. Skinner remained the head of the new Lincoln-Mercury Division until January 30, 1948.

Skinner was replacement at Ford was Company vice president Benson Ford. Prior to this, Lincoln had operated under the auspices of a general manager. In the larger cities, dealerships began to be separated into Ford and Lincoln-Mercury, very much as they are today. However, there remain many combined dealerships in many small towns and there are still a few Ford-Mercury dealerships in existence at this writing.

The compression ratio on the 292 cubic inch HV-12 engine was raised to 7.2 to 1, from 7.0 to 1. This was primarily due to the availability of better grades of gasoline and a decreased demand for high-grade aviation fuel. The engine specifications rated the HV-12 engine as 125 horsepower at 4000 RPM. This translated into 33.1 brake horsepower. The drivetrain remained basically unchanged, with the specifications reading as follows: single, dual surface, ten-inch dry plate clutch; first gear ratio 2.12 to 1, second gear 1.43 to 1, third gear 1 to 1, with optional overdrive 0.70 to 1; Hypoid differential rearend ratio of 4.44 to 1; floating rear axles, 3/4-inch diameter shaft; tire size 7.00x15, 7.50x15 optional; steering ratio 18.4 to 1 with 4.75 turns lock to lock and a turning radius of 22.5 feet.

Body dimensions remained unchanged since the 26H models. The Continental convertible top bows caused the Cabriolet to be about an inch taller than the hardtop Coupe. Factory-new ground clearance was 7.66 inches. With age and the weight of the HV-12 engine, the sagging of the transverse leaf springs on the front axle would decrease this by an inch or two.

Shocks remained the old-style lever-arm type. The average weight of a 76H series Lincoln or Continental was approximately 4,100 pounds. Considering that these Lincolns were originally designed in the early 1930s, they ride quietly and comfortably even by today's standards

NINETEEN-FORTYEIGHT - In 1948, Lincoln produced 43,688 cars. Most were the new 9EL and 9EH models for 1949. These, however, are not generally thought of as 1948 model Lincolns. The new 876H series Lincolns were officially introduced on November 1, 1947. Production was mostly concluded by the following January. The last 876H was a Lincoln Continental Coupe type 57 and it rolled off the assembly line the end of March. These type 56 and 57 Lincoln Continentals were completed on the old Model-K assembly line as the regular Lincoln production line had already been shut down for retooling and major rework.

Exact 1948 production figures vary from publication to publication. One of the biggest variance is caused by the comparison of calendar year production to model year production figures. During research on this book, the actual handwritten Red Journals at the Henry Ford Museum archives were reviewed. Various departments like Production Programming and Control also made their own summary reports and this introduced a different viewpoint giving yet another set of numbers.

Considering all of these factors, the Appendix to this book gives a best-guess scenario to these figures. For example, there were 569 Lincolns produced in calendar year 1945. No Continental body styles were produced until February 1946. A large number of Continentals were produced in 1948 (1,299 to be exact) after Lincoln production supposedly had been stopped.

There was little change between the 76H and 876H Lincolns. An excellent indication of this is the series number itself. An eight for 1948 was simply prefixed to the 76H model designation. The Model-H had been in production for over a decade and 86H had been used as the 1938 series numbers.

Those who remember the cars new claimed the best clue to a new 876H model was the clear fog lamps. Amber lamps, however, could still be installed on cars shipped to states where clear lamps were illegal. In California, for example, it was illegal to move an automobile with only the parking lights on. The 6-volt parking lights on these Lincolns were dim, so driving lamps in this case would have been a desirable option.

The highest serial number recorded for a Model-H Lincoln was H182129. In all, there were 3,314 postwar Continentals and just over 40,000 standard Lincolns produced. With the conclusion of the Model-H, the name Continental was dropped from the Lincoln body-style lineup. Not until the mid-1950s when Ford brothers, Benson and William Clay collaborated on the Mark II, would the name Continental be used again.

The standard 876H series Lincoln was available in Sedan, Club Coupe and Convertible Coupe. These body styles continued to use pull-action outside door handles and the Continental retained the push-button door releases. The standard Lincoln used the script LINCOLN on the sides of the hood and retained the bright metal mold line strip. Whitewall tires were used in most display ads, but were usually footnoted, "When available, white sidewall tires at extra cost." The cross crest and knight's head logo continued as the main Lincoln symbol.

Advertising style and motif remained unchanged. The normal ad consisted of a two-color artist's rendering of a particular Lincoln body style. The "Nothing Could Be Finer" slogan and a paragraph of good words like, "The selection of a fine motor car is based on its beauty..." or "There are many measures of a Lincoln's worth..." were typical.

The Model H Lincolns remain popular with automobile hobbyists and car collectors to this day.

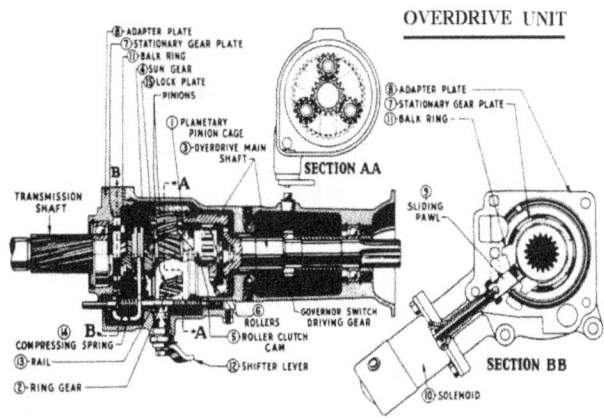

RESTORATION

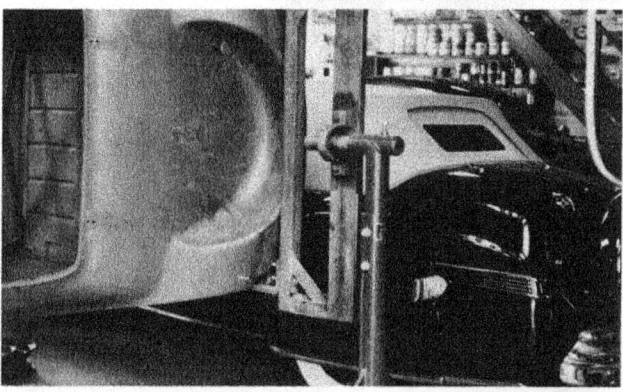

The Continental remains an apex of modern classic auto body design. These cars were so often photographed and shown today that it is hard to imagine so few were actually built.

Lee Iacocca always referred to the original Continental design as an example of the classic motorcar. He freely admitted that the Continental's lines had greatly influenced his thinking and the design of both the Ford Mustang and the Continental Mark III.

The Museum of Modern Art in New York selected the Zephyr-based Lincoln Continental as one of the eight most artistic automobile designs ever produced. Time magazine listed the Lincoln Continental, some ten years after its final production, as one of the top ten automobile designs in the world.

Above: Convertible in Ed Spagnolo's restoration shop; Continental body jig allows full rotation for repair and painting; 1939 Zephyr being restored in Chuck Knight's shop; Jake Fleming's 1941 Zephyr 3-window Coupe and Knight's 1941 restored Continental.

CHAPTER NINE
THOSE COSMOPOLITAN TIMES

Of Bulbous Beauties

Most major automobile manufacturers tend to have each succeeding model build on the prior year's design. Only once every couple of decades does this chronology break down. The Lincoln Zephyr in 1935 was an example of this. In 1948, the Lincoln Cosmopolitan was another such milestone. It was the production of a new and modern line of automobiles using outdated technology. It was the beginning of a new era for Lincoln, but not quite the end of the old. One must, however, return to the early days of World War II in order to fully understand the development of this rare and short-lived line of Lincoln automobiles.

A clay mock-up produced in November of 1941, which was essentially a Lincoln Zephyr Sedan with a one-piece, slightly curved windshield. The front fenders were faired into the body mid-door. The long, high hood line was retained. It had a rather unbecoming Oldsmobile style of grille, composed of arched bars.

By 1942, the clays mock-up had taken on the new bulbous shape and could be readily identified as related to the Lincoln Model-EH. By April, a torpedo backed or fastback Mercury body Club Coupe was sculpted. It featured a padded hardtop roof and convertible style side windows. In January of 1943, clay mock-ups were constructed of a fastback Club Coupe with the Model-EL fender line and a two-piece windshield. Except for the frowning 1946 Oldsmobile grille, it was clearly a small-bodied Lincoln. Front end and grilles seemed to be giving the designers more problems than the bodies themselves.

One of these voluminous body styles featured a tall narrow grille with flush door-covered headlights. By June of 1945, the Lincoln Cosmopolitan began to take shape as a new and radical looking style of automobile. The two single exceptions were the Mercury rolled wire grille and four large fender wings. The latter were obviously the forerunner to the smaller front fender chrome wings.

During 1944, several Model-EH Continentals had been on the drawing board, but that is about as far as any of these proposals ever got. Renderings of the Model-EH Continentals varied from a squared off Coupe that distinctly resembled a Mark II on a 121 inch wheelbase. The trunk design resembling a later year's Cadillac Seville and featured an outside rear-mounted spare tire. The Continental rear spare tire housing was faired into the lid of a hatchback trunk. The best-looking proposal was one that actually became the Model-EH Cosmopolitan. There was an earnest desire on the part of the design group to continue the name Continental in the Lincoln lineup. However, as the bulbous design was firmed up, it became more and more obvious that they were dealing with a uniquely different concept in automobile styling. Small items, like the side script logo LINCOLN COSMOPOLITAN, written in the same style as it was on the old LINCOLN CONTINENTAL, managed to survive. For a short period (July and August) during 1945, the Custom Sedan model was labeled as a Continental. Herman C. Brunn rendered several drawings of this proposal. They were of a Landaulet style Coupe and Sedan.

Marvin Arnold

Lincoln for 1951

LINCOLN AND CONTINENTAL

1945 outline drawings made by Herman C. Brunn applied coachbuilt and Continental concepts to EH Model. Additional drawings by Martin Regitko's design group applied sportsmen and convertible concepts during 1947 and 1948. Above right: Continental Sedan proposal for the EH Model.

The Brunn Sedan was an open-drive Brougham Limousine complete with padded roof and coach bars. The drawings were labeled the Brunn Brougham and included top and passenger compartment dimensions. One drawing was of a hardtop sedan and became the Custom Sedan proposal. These drawings are excellent examples of the coachbuilder's art applied to a modern body design.

Styling concepts for the next generation of Lincolns were well underway by 1943. In fact, what became the 1949 Mercury and small Lincoln would probably have been the 1945 model Fords and Mercurys had the war effort not intervened. Clay mock-ups of early forties Ford prototypes resemble a large fifties Volvo. Lincoln-Mercury seemed to be following the design trend of the period that resembled the postwar Nash, Hudson and Kaiser. This motif has often been referred to as the Upside-Down Bathtub look.

E.T. Gregorie, head of the design group at Ford until 1946, always prided himself on having never copied another car's styling. Thus, these bulbous designs were the natural evolution of the styling trends of this era. Gregorie's design group, from 1943 through 1945, was kept busy on defense projects such as camouflage patterns and glider airframe drafting. A few designers, however, continued to work on civilian automobile designs. During the short period that Gregorie was absent from Ford, September 1943 through March 1944, Tom Hibbard continued to develop new car designs.

A dozen or so full-size clay mock-ups were built and subsequently photographed. Most of the proposals for Lincoln and Mercury had retained some remnant of a front fender line.

The Early Years

The fender line feature would die as slow and as agonizing a death as did the running board. Drawings made by Robert Doehler in 1947 were of a Lincoln Sportsman Sedan. On a long 128 inch wheelbase, this Sedan was clearly a continuation of the Custom Continental concept. It featured a vertical rear-mounted spare tire housing that was partially imbedded in the trunk. It was called a Sportsman because of its Woody trim, Lincoln's answer to the Chrysler Town & Country models.

By June of the same year, the drawings John Cheek had made of the Sportsman Woody convertible on the small Lincoln chassis evolved into the Mercury station wagon. In May of 1948, J. Allward made drawings illustrating a Parade Sedan on the Lincoln body. Martin Regitko would head up a design team exploring these possibilities and later a Lincoln Parade Phaeton was produced.

As to the continuation of the Continental, the closest thing to it was the design sketches resembling a 1947 Kaiser-Fraiser with a forward-leaning, covered, rear-mounted spare tire. The hood lines on several of the wartime Lincoln clay mock-ups did retain, at least in impression, the high squared-off nose of the original Continental. This hood style was ultimately adapted for use on the Cosmopolitan, but flattened considerably. Without Edsel's guiding hand and with new Ford management, the design group was not sure that the Continental would be continued. Because of this, many Continental proposals were never fully developed. E.T. Gregorie indicated he felt that, "Had the Continental used different tooling than the standard Lincoln, it probably would not have been produced after the war at all."

Fastbacks were a popular body style on most of the Lincoln wartime mock-ups. Edsel, Gregorie and Harley Earl had all been partial to torpedo body styles. Ultimately, the 1949 Cosmopolitan Town Sedan type 73 did use just such a back end design. The two-piece flat windshield and front door wing windows were carried over on the mock-up, but the actual Cosmopolitan would be fitted with a single-piece curved windshield. One proposed logo design was round like the last Model-K logo with Lincoln in script letters.

Marvin Arnold

Wherever...whenever people of fine taste congregate...there is likely to be a new Lincoln Cosmopolitan. For ownership of this magnificently distinctive automobile is another means by which people of fine taste distinguish themselves today. Unquestionably, it is the First Car of the Land. Lincoln Division of Ford Motor Company.

All Lincoln cars equipped with improved HYDRA-MATIC transmission at extra cost

Lincoln...Nothing could be finer

This design drawing was made by Bill Schmidt in 1945 about the time Schmidt was made head of Lincoln-Mercury styling. It proposed a 1949 Lincoln Continental Cabriolet based on the currently popular bulbous design concept.

A major feature of the new Lincoln's front end design was hideaway or panel covered headlights. In photographs of these wartime Lincoln clay mock-ups shown on page 243, a Buick and a Chevrolet can be seen in the background. In an interview, Special Interest Autos asked E.T. Gregorie about the presence of these cars in the design area at Ford.

Gregorie explained, "We always had a representative group of these makes on hand. It was company policy to buy several of every make of car each year. We called them 'foreign cars' and we'd take them completely apart and inspect them piece by piece, lay them out on long tables. This way we could see all of the little tricks each manufacturer used in putting his cars together. We'd buy these foreign cars from local dealers. Whenever I had to go away on a trip, I would always drive one of them. Then we traded these cars back to the dealers. Each car had been completely disassembled and reassembled, but of course we had no specs to go by so it was put back together the best way we knew how. Anyway, the dealers would advertise these as low-mileage used cars, and they were, but the new owners might have been in real trouble due to our re-assembly. Nothing really fit the way it should."

The Ford styling cycle had caused a new body shell to be introduced every two years since 1933. The Mercury introduced in 1939 fell into step with this cycle, but Lincoln did not. Thus, it is difficult to guess what year that the Lincoln clay mock-ups in the design salon would have become had the war not came along. Clearly, however, they would have been produced several years earlier. Rather than improve or redesign the HV-12, Ford stayed with the V-8 engine. Any progress on a redesign had been slowed by the war time projects.

It does appear, at least by studying the photographs that the HV-12 engine was to have been phased out. The hood lines were shortened and the obviously heavier bodies would require more horsepower. In December of 1943, a prototype of a revolutionary concept engine was built. It was an aluminum block V-8 with dual single overhead worm gear driven cams. Al Esper, manager at the Dearborn Proving Grounds, reported that the engine was disappointing. The concept and the engine were scrapped after two months.

Early wartime Mercury designs resembled the Ford designs. Slowly, however, the thinking became that the Mercury should resemble the Lincoln more than the Ford. The Mercury was moved to the upper-middle market and the Ford was to reach a broader range of the lower-end market. There was one school of thinking in which the Ford name, and possibly the GM name, might be slowly elevated through the model lineup until they were the top of the line automobiles. This was already the case with Chrysler. The design trend of the early forties prototypes seemed in a small way to confirm this. Management decisions in 1946, however, cast the die in a more traditional direction.

In a 1949 paper to the SAE in Los Angeles, Harold Youngren described Passenger Car Design by saying that, "Foresight and guidance must come from information gained in various ways. Beginning with a rough sketch or a doodle, the idea is laid out on a one-tenth scale drawing. The design is then looked at from a market and manufacturing standpoint as well as cost and pricing class.

The two-model concept, Lincoln & Lincoln Cosmopolitan.

The next step in the design process would be a full-size blackboard layout followed by an engineering proposal to management. If approved, a full-size clay mock-up is built and trim is added using bright metal foil. If the design concept makes it through all of this, the body bridges and templates were made and engineering begins to produce the drawings and detailed specifications required to make the tooling and produce the automobile."

A special project, formed at Ford on April 12, 1946, was called the Light Car Division. The new model car lineup had originally begun by Edsel Ford and was further developed by Gregorie. It was a rather bulbous 118 inch wheelbase body for the new Ford. The Mercury was to be a Ford with some Lincoln and some pure Mercury features on a 120 or 123 inch wheelbase. The large Lincoln Zephyr was to be on a 125 inch wheelbase.

The latter actually became the Cosmopolitan. Two proposals that were ultimately dropped were the Custom and Continental Sedans that shared the Cosmopolitan body motif. The Continental with external rear-mounted spare tire was to have been on a 128 inch wheelbase and the Custom Sedan on a 135 inch wheelbase.

Ernest R. Breech, newly arrived at FMC, test-drove the new Ford prototype. He concluded that the car was too heavy and that the projected production costs were too high for the car to be successfully marketed as the Ford mainline. This seemed also to confirm the feelings of the Light Car Division people. Even if the Ford light car had been marketed in the United States instead of in Europe, there was too great a production gap between the proposed light Ford and the proposed Model-BA Ford. As it developed, by late 1947, the light Ford was not marketed in the U.S. It became the European Ford Vedette.

The result of several Ford Policy Committee meetings in August of 1946 was a crash program to develop a new Ford mainliner from scratch. In September of 1946, the Ford Motor Company showed its first monthly profit since midyear 1942. Things were definitely looking up. The Policy Committee met again on December 11, 1946. After a blind competition, they selected the Bob Koto and George Walker design for a new Ford. Gregorie's design was retained for the Mercury and Lincoln, but on December 15, E.T. "Bob" Gregorie resigned his position with the company. His first love had always been yachting and he would retire to Florida to follow a career as a custom marine designer.

The Koto-Walker design was to become both the Mainline and Deluxe Ford products, the HA and BA Fords for 1949 and 1950. Bob Koto had worked on the Tjaarda Zephyr front end redesign project under Gregorie. George W. Walker had worked under GM's Harley Earl before contracting with Ford as an outside stylist. Others involved in the project were Frank Hershey, who came from GM and Bill Schmidt.

Frank Hershey later became head of Ford styling and Schmidt became Lincoln-Mercury's chief of styling. The engineering and design staff for all of Ford-Mercury-Lincoln totaled only eight hundred people. By late 1947, Harold Youngren had increased the personnel level to 2,600. A new engineering center was under construction across from the Henry Ford Museum and Greenfield Village in Dearborn. Never again would a handful of men decide the production destiny of the Ford built automobile. By the 1948 new model introduction, Ford had spent $100 million on new tooling.

The original heavy Ford proposal became the 9CM Mercury and remained on the 118 inch wheelbase. The small 9EL Lincoln adopted the proposed Mercury wheelbase dimension of 121 inches. The 9EH Cosmopolitan remained on the originally proposed 125 inch wheelbase. The Cosmopolitan was almost scuttled at one point by Breech's group, but there continued to be some support on the Policy Committee for a large, top-of-the-line automobile.

Much of the 9EH tooling was already in place and the Cosmopolitan survived. Like many previous Lincoln models, it is not likely that the car was profitable. In this respect Breech was right, but it would have been sad had this bulbous beauty never appeared in the Lincoln genesis. With the new Ford design in place, the prototype models were all pushed up the product line one notch, except for the 9EH Continental and Custom Sedan and they were pushed off the planning table altogether.

Marvin Arnold

The Lincoln Cosmopolitan Convertible. White side-wall tires and road lamps optional at extra cost.

If you want a fine car that is one in a million, not like a million others... then you may drive the great new 1949 Lincoln Cosmopolitan anywhere, in any company, safe in the assurance you are driving the most distinctive fine car on the road. Lincoln Division of Ford Motor Company.

Lincoln makes America's Most Distinctive Cars

LINCOLN and CONTINENTAL CLASSIC MOTORCARS

NINETEEN-FORTYNINE - The 1949 9EL and 9EH series Lincolns were introduced to the automobile buying public on April 22, 1948. The new Lincoln's unveiling was followed on April 29 by the Mercury 9CM series that shared body components with the 9EL Lincoln. Production picked up rapidly. The small Lincolns were assembled at three sites in addition to the Michigan plant. The Los Angeles assembly plant began Lincoln production in May. A Metucheu, New Jersey, plant was opened in June and a St. Louis plant started production in September.

The new 9EL series "Light" Lincoln body styles were the six-passenger Coupe type 72 the lightest in weight (3,959 pounds), the Sport Sedan type 74 and the six-passenger Convertible Coupe type 76. All were on the 121 inch wheelbase. On the 125 inch wheelbase and built largely from separate tooling, were the four new 9EH heavy Lincoln body styles. They were the six-passenger Coupe type 72, the Town Sedan type 73 torpedo back, the Sport Sedan type 74 trunk back and the six-passenger Convertible Coupe type 76.

The 9EL Lincoln is often incorrectly referred to as the Sport Lincoln. Actually, the term applies to both the 9EL and the 9EH Sedans, which had the trunk back configurations. Yet another misunderstanding has the name Sport referring to the fastback Town Sedan type 73. The 9EL Convertible was only built this first year of production.

Additionally, the Cosmopolitan Town Sedan was dropped after this first year. The Cosmopolitan's headlights were to have been hidden or door-covered. Towards the end of development, however, engineering was still having problems with the door mechanism. Thus, a chromed metal trim tunnel was installed to mate the fender and headlamp assembly.

The result was a unique and stylish headlight motif, often referred to as Frenched or Frenched-in. The wide low profile grille had two horizontal grille bars with six teeth-like flutes located on either side of a small center egg crate pattern. At each end of the grille had large round parking light, reminiscent of the 876H series Lincoln's driving lamps.

The grille captured in appearance, if not in dimension, the older Lincoln's grille pattern. The Cosmopolitan had a curved single piece windshield while the standard Lincoln used a flat two-piece windshield with center bar. Both sedans and coupes had a rear door triangle wing-window. On the longer body Cosmo Sedans, the wing-window was aft of the door while on the smaller body sedans, it was part of the door window. The combination thumb push-button or hand-grip door handle was introduced this first year of the Cosmopolitan.

The Mercury and small Lincoln continued to use the old-style pull lever handles, but were changed to the new type the next year. The small Lincoln shared body dies with the Mercury was actually three inches longer than the Mercury. The extra inches were added to the forward section of the frame.

After the war, FMC had hired many of the GM design engineers. The body dimensions of the new Cadillacs were already known by these people. Thus, the new Lincoln body length was longer than the Cadillac even though its wheelbase was shorter.

The cabin or greenhouse area was 7.5 inches longer, affording more leg room front and rear. The Cosmo's bench seats were ten inches wider than that year's Cadillac. As it turned out, the standard Lincoln had more trunk room than either the Cadillac or the Cosmopolitan. The overall body length for the 9EL Lincoln was 213 inches while the 9EH Cosmopolitan measured 220.5 inches. The tread on both models was 58.5 inches front and 60 inches rear. Original equipment tire sizes were 8.20x15 and were the new super balloon type designed for lower profile and a more comfortable ride.

Rear fender skirts were standard equipment. The small Lincoln retained a body mold line resembling the outline of a front fender. It also had a large, full-body-length chrome strip on the sides. The Cosmopolitan was smooth sided except for a chrome wing or flange over the front fender wells. The cross crest and knight's head logo was on the center grille and on the full-moon hubcaps. Its silhouette was also molded into the door plate rubbers. The hood ornament was a missile suspended by a swept-back arch mount. The name LINCOLN was stamped into the center bumper chrome, front and rear. The bumper ends wrapped around the body to the wheel well in the front and most of the way in the back. Interiors for the period were plain, although they were luxurious compared with the average car interiors of the day. These were austere times. The opulence of the twenties and the Art Deco of the thirties had given way to the simplicity of modern. Salon Styling was the name given the new decorum. Soft foam rubber padding was extensively used in the seats. Fabric options were broadcloth and nylon. Cloth seat patterns were usually a wide pinstripe with contrasting solid seat back trim.

Fiberglass soundproofing insulation was used extensively and referred to as Quiet-Tone noise control. Power hydraulic on all four windows was an option. The vacuum operated power antenna was also still optional. Heater systems continued to be treated as optional equipment on cars of this period. The Lincoln heater used a positive fresh air system called Cross-Ventilation was controlled by three knobs on the lower part of the large instrument panel.

The instrument panel itself was massive in appearance and seemed to be a conglomerate of component parts. The round speedometer and engine cluster group were small, hard to read and separated by a center-mounted rectangular clock. A row of rectangular gold-colored pull knobs and switches were strung out along the lower panel. Chief Engineer H.H. Gilbert was quick to point out these controls were difficult to identify in daylight and impossible to read at night.

This panel arrangement wasn't dissimilar to one used on the early Beechcraft Bonanza airplanes. After several wheels-up landings in these aircraft, when the pilots extended the flaps instead of the wheels, Beechcraft redesigned the lower panel knob and switch arrangement. Fiascoes like these in the auto and aircraft industries probably caused the human factors engineering discipline to be taken seriously.

Page 240: Lincoln display ads and brochure illustrations from 1951. Page 242: Brochure for the 1951 model year. The Cosmopolitan was often illustrated with the dorsal chrome above the front fender-well, but many models were shipped without this accessory. Page 243: Clay mock-up built during 1942 and 1945. Page 244: Fox hunt scene depicts a 1950 Cosmopolitan standard Sedan with trunk. The torpedo back model was not offered in 1950. Page 246: Display ads from 1950 illustrated Lincoln Cosmopolitan Sedans and Lincoln Sedans in various scenic settings and provide colorful examples of that year's advertising art. Page 248: Advertising art work from 1949 display ads featured the roominess and ruggedness of the new models. 1949 Lincoln and Cosmopolitan introduced the two model concept for this series of Lincolns. Pages 249: Advertising art for 1949 model year which began in mid 1948, showing the two models of Lincolns in various scenic settings. Page 250: Full page color ad for the 1949 Lincoln Cosmopolitan Convertible. Above: Instrument panel used on 1949 Cosmopolitan was restyled after this model year. Note the round odometer and engine group with square clock between. Also, the lower panel bank of switches and pull levers.

The excitingly powerful new 1949 Lincoln—performance star of the fine-car field.

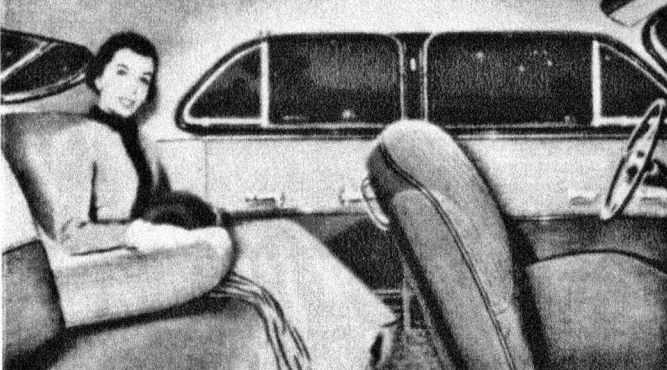

The excitingly powerful 1949 Lincoln

The Lincoln's upper panel, area directly in front of the passengers, was clear of knobs and obstacles in the interest of safety. This unique Cosmopolitan instrument panel was only offered the first model year. It would be extensively redesigned by Tom Hibbard at the request of marketing, who felt the panel was old-fashioned.

Henry Ford had always favored solid front axles. In the early forties, Lawrence "Larry" Sheldrick obtained permission to develop an independent front wheel suspension for the Ford. Engineer Joseph J. Felts, who was assigned to the project, was told to develop any type frontend so long as it did not look like a GM or Chrysler. A torsion bar design was ultimately chosen. In 1944, a hundred units were built and sent to dealers to be test driven.

When Harold T. Youngren, formerly Oldsmobile's chief engineer, came to Ford, he brought with him several young GM engineers. Among them was Earle S. MacPherson, who later developed the MacPherson Strut. A new independent coil spring frontend was developed for the EL and EH Lincolns. The old-style cross-member frame sometimes referred to as X-member or K-frame was retained.

During early production, the frame rails were increased by .015 inches in gauge. The new frontend used stamped steel suspension arms. The coil springs were mounted wishbone-fashion with the tubular shocks inside the coil springs. Heavier shocks and rubber frame bumpers were added during early production. The rear suspension retained the conventional dual semi-elliptic leaf springs.

A Hypoid or bottom offset differential rearend was used to allow the chassis to sit lower to the ground. This also lowered the center of gravity. With only 204 square inches of brake lining area, the Lincoln's brakes were inclined to grab with the slightest touch. Standard design Duo-Servo brake systems of this period all had this problem and the Lincoln brake system underwent several modifications during early production in an attempt to correct it.

Lincoln had used the three-quarter floating axle for many years. The new Lincoln used a semi-floating axle where the wheel bolts directly to the axle flange. This and the elimination of the drive shaft torque tube, decreased the sprung weight and improved the Lincoln ride. The rear axle ratio was 4.27 to 1, but a 3.07 to 1 engine to rearend final drive ratio was provided with the overdrive engaged. A Hotchkiss three-speed standard transmission was installed with the gear ratios of 2.526 to 1 in low, 1.518 to 1 in second and 1 to 1 in high. A Borg-Warner overdrive was optional on the small Lincoln and standard on the Cosmopolitan.

Lincoln returned to a V-8 engine for the first time since the early Model-K. The new flathead V-8 was rated as 152 horsepower at 3600 RPM.

The 152 V-8 develops 265 foot pounds of torque at 1800 RPM as compared to the older HV-12 that produced 225 at the same RPM. This C.C. Johnson designed engine was first installed on the F-8 Ford trucks in January, 1948. Frank Johnson, famed Ford and Lincoln engine designer of the twenties and thirties, had retired in 1947.) The new V-8 truck engine was adapted for both models of the new Lincoln. The engine had a 336.7 cubic inch displacement with a 3.50 inch bore and a 4.375 inch stroke. This relatively long stroke provided high torque. It differed from the popular engine design trend of squared engines in which the bore and stroke are the same dimension, i.e., 4x4. The compression ratio of 6.4 to 1 on the Ford truck engine was raised to 7.0 to 1 for the Lincoln version.

Standard engine accessories were a Holley two-barrel carburetor, mechanical fuel pump and six-volt electrical system. This three-main-bearing engine was 40 percent heavier than a Ford passenger car engine. The crankshaft alone weighed 104.5 pounds. Pistons were aluminum. The front of the large engine looked very much like other Ford V-8 engines with top-mounted generator and two water pumps driven by a single belt. The new rotary-type distributor was moved to the rear of the engine beside the fuel pump. This allowed the oil filler neck to be moved forward on the engine. A large oil bath air-cleaner was sidesaddle-mounted. Three exhaust ports were located either side of the V-block and the manifolds were connected with the traditional under-pan crossover pipe.

The most distinctive feature of this engine was its two broad, flat, cylinder heads. GM had already changed over to the OHV or overhead valve, but the new Lincoln engine was still of the valve-in-head design with the inverted L-combustion chamber. Lincoln would not change to the OHV until the 1952 models. Thus, these were the last of the big Ford flathead engines and were truly dinosaurs.

Ford engineering had not invested the time needed to develop an automatic transmission for the new V-8 engine. In fact, the engine itself was still suffering from a few developmental bugs. Additionally, there was some reluctance to proceed with a new automatic transmission design after
the Liquamatic fiasco. A deal was stuck with General Motors to use the GM Hydra-Matic transmission in Lincolns and Mercurys. Lincoln's manufacturing manager actually negotiated the deal with GM.

The new Hydra-Matic transmission for the Lincoln was introduced on June 26, 1949. Engineering manager Harold Youngren then turned to Borg-Warner to develop a Ford automatic transmission. Ford and Mercury went to the Borg-Warner designed Ford-o-matic and Merc-o-matic in 1951. Lincoln continued to use the Hydra-Matic until 1954.

The GM designed Hydra-Matic transmission coupled very well with the large Lincoln V-8 from a power train standpoint, especially at highway cruise speeds. The new Lincoln Hydra-Matic transmission gearshift lever arrangement placed "N" for neutral to the far left, "DR" for drive in the next position, "Lo" for low next and "R" for reverse in the far right position. There was no "Park" position and the car could be started in Drive.

These old-style selectors became the brunt of a popular joke about the hot rodder who figured out that "N" stood for nothing and so placed the selector into "L" for leap and then "D" for drag. Everything was going fine until he dropped the selector down into "R" for race.

Large two-page ads were taken out in popular magazines to hype the new Hydra-Matic transmission for the Lincoln. They read, "Simple as 1-2-3. Start the engine, set the lever in drive and step on the accelerator."

Lincoln ads for the period continued to feature realistic artist's drawings, usually in three colors. The "Nothing Could be Finer" Lincoln advertising slogan was dropped, one early ad read, "Nothing Could be finer or newer!" The most commonly used slogan was, "Lincoln has a new idea!" This was generally followed by phrases like, "What fine cars should be" or "Planned with you in mind."

There was a definite appeal to the female influence on the family's purchasing power with phrases like "Your wife has long been waiting for" and "For the lady behind the wheel." The early model introduction ads pitched, "Preview of Tomorrows Fine Cars" and "Two completely new 1949 Lincolns and the choice of magnificent body styles in two separate price ranges was now much broader.

Marvin Arnold

ROOM TO SPARE—For loads of luggage on the longest trip. Automatically illuminated compartment is safety-sealed against dust and water. The spare tire is at the right—convenient, yet out of the way.

THINKS WHILE YOU DRIVE—HYDRA-MATIC*, the road-proven, really dependable automatic transmission, is available on the Lincoln. No gears to shift, no clutch to press. Driving is as simple as 1-2-3.

Lincoln proudly presents...
the most beautiful "Salon Coupes" in the world

THE NEW *Lincoln Cosmopolitan Capri* bringing new meaning to luxury

THE NEW *Lincoln Lido* gay in spirit, young in heart

Lincoln... Nothing could be finer

CLASSIC MOTORCARS

The "Lincoln Makes America's Most Distinctive Cars" was also a popular slogan. The large-body style was called the Lincoln Cosmopolitan while the smaller was referred to only as the Lincoln. Often, the phrase "white sidewall tires and road lamps optional at extra cost" was footnoted. Not that this made much sense, as the price of these automobiles was never stated in the advertisements.

Even Borg-Warner got into the advertising act. They took out several full page ads showing a popular Lincoln ad with one corner folded down to reveal the "B-W" engineering logo. The Borg-Warner company boasted supplying nineteen out of twenty of the automobile makers with their parts. They manufactured everything from carburetors to gears, producing 185 different components for the auto builders.

During the 1949 National Association of Stock Car Auto Racing season, Lincolns won two of the nine Grand National NASCAR races. Additional publicity was obtained for the new Lincoln's mechanical prowess when Johnny Mantz of Englewood, California, drove the 9EL Coupe in the 1950 Pan-American Road Race across Mexico.

The car was sponsored by Bob Estes of Los Angeles. The Lincoln's side number was 38. It finished ninth in a field of sixteen Lincolns and twenty-two Cadillacs, but the race was won by an Oldsmobile 88. Known as the Carrera Pan-American, this race from Juarez to El Ocotal, Mexico was 2,178 miles long. Mantz's Lincoln ran well ahead on the straightaways.

At Mexico City, Johnny Mantz in the Lincoln had an eleven-minute lead on the entire pack. The heavy Lincoln started blowing tires on and at one point, the overheated brakes locked up and caused an hour delay. The Lincoln finished ahead of many respected rally cars and cars using the latest OHV and OHC engines. It was visions of things yet to come when, in the early fifties, the new lighter Lincolns would sweep these events for several years running.

The automotive press praised the new Lincolns highly. Publications like Newsweek and Iron Age wrote favorably about Lincoln's new styling. Popular Mechanics' Tom McCahill rated it as "conservative, fast and pleasing" after one of his famous Road Tests. McCahill further reported that both Lincolns were capable of 100 MPH speeds in overdrive.

In April of 1948, when the new models were introduced to the dealers, there was much enthusiasm about them. It soon became tough head-to-head competition. Chrysler introduced their new fender lines in the fall. They did not, however, come out with their new combustion dome Fire Power engine for two more years. Cadillac, on the other hand, used a mix of body styles for 1948.

Cadillac retained the old Fleetwood 75 series, but introduced an all-new straight-back front fender design on the 61 and 62 series. Hudson, Packard and Lincoln had all gone with the popular prewar thinking that the Slab-Side was the next design generation.

Harley Earl of GM made an end run around them all and it worked. Designer Julio Andrado retained the Cadillac's rear fender line, if not the front. Studebaker also retained the rear fender line, but GM expanded on the idea and introduced the Tail fin.

Designers Frank Hershey and Bill Mitchell claimed they had been inspired by a P-38 twin-tailed fighter airplane. The car-buying public loved it. Gregorie, too, had earlier sensed a need to retain some semblance of a fender line, as evidenced by the front fender silhouette on the Mercury and small Lincoln. Very little 1948 Lincoln 876H series dealer literature was published due primarily to the early Model E introductions. Large 32-page catalogues in 15x11 format were produced in great number for the new 9E series. Additionally, there were the standard-size color brochures.

Quick Facts, a small customer publication that began in 1936 and discontinued in 1942 was now offered again with the 9EL and 9EH series introduction.

The two Lincoln model concepts gave Lincoln a slight pricing edge. The small Lincoln was priced under the Packard and Chrysler by a couple of hundred dollars. The Cosmopolitan was priced about $500 under the top-of-the-line Cadillac. Lincoln dealers now had a model to compete with both the 60 and 70 series Cadillacs as well as Chrysler's six-cylinder Royal and Windsor and eight-cylinder Saratoga and New Yorker.

Chrysler's body styles shared components with the Dodge and DeSoto, similar to the Mercury-Lincoln scheme. The Packard's Twenty Century series was not dropped until 1950 and Packard continued to be a major competitor in the Lincoln market for several years. Almost more important than meeting the competition was the two Lincoln model concepts itself. It tied the Mercury to the Lincoln for the first time. Mercury could now be viewed as a baby Lincoln instead of a deluxe Ford.

The flathead V-8 had not hurt the sale of the Lincoln as much as the one-two punch delivered by the competition. The first punch, the lack of an automatic transmission had been circumvented, but the second punch was in the area of styling. Lincoln had unwittingly pioneered the hardtop coupe roof line with its Continental. Even today these type 57 Coupes are sometimes referred as Hardtop Coupes, but they clearly are not due to the rook posts between the two side windows. The competition introduced pillarless coupes and they became very popular. Marketing requested a study on the possibility of such a body style for the Lincoln.

Engineering said that the fundamental design of the bodies would not allow the removal of the center posts without extensive redesign. To answer this challenge, a series of sporty coupes was offered the following year. The EL and EH Lincolns had more nicknames hung on them than the Douglas DC-3. These bulbous Lincolns were referred to as bar-of-soap, upside-down bathtub, Moby Dick and beached whales to name a few.

Never before had Lincolns been turned out in such numbers The highest volume of Lincolns ever produced, heretofore, had been in 1937 when the combined Zephyr and Model-K production was just over thirty thousand units. One should, however, take into consideration that many of these new Lincolns were built early in 1948, making this an exceptionally long model year. These were, nevertheless, very impressive production figures for Lincoln. Had the standard Mercury body Lincoln never been produced, the Cosmopolitan alone would have turned in some respectable sales figures by Lincoln standards. The number of Cosmopolitans registered was 11,949 in 1948; 18,213 in 1949; 13,128 in 1950; and 11,642 in 1951. By the end of 1949, the Ford Motor Company had replaced Chrysler as the second largest auto producer.

NINETEEN-FIFTY - In 1950, a restyled Lincoln grille was introduced. While the 9E series Lincoln grille had held true to the massive postwar style, it did not look that good on the new bulbous Lincolns.

The cross crest and knight's head logo was now a standalone logo on the hood nose. It was winged with small square blocks. Between the 26H and 66H series, the crest logo had been moved from the nose to the grille. Now, the procedure had been reversed.

The grille itself was a single large horizontal bar, a style popular with custom shops of the period. A small vertical center bar was flanked on both sides by four flutes. The front parking lights were smaller with rectangular lenses. Plastic now replaced the traditional glass lenses on the front and rear parking lights.

The small Lincoln used the Mercury door handles last year, but both bodies received an improved push-button and grip door handle this year. Rocker panel chrome was added. Front and rear bumpers had dual top bumper guards. The front bumper was rotated slightly upward. "This so as to imply a faint smile and remove any impression of a frowning grille," this was according to Lincoln's chief engineer H.H. Gilbert.

On the Cosmo, the word LINCOLN was dropped and a larger script COSMOPOLITAN logo was located on the lower front quarter. The crest logo on the hub caps had been gold the first year, but was now chrome to match the wheel covers. Lincoln interiors for the last decade did not have much pizazz. Seats were living room couch comfortable and fabrics of excellent quality, but by today's tufted and rolled interior standards, they would be rather ho-hum. This year, new color and fabric choices were offered. Interior door handles were improved.

The new courtesy lights operated from front door switches. Only the Cosmo Sedan had rear door switches. The center post on hardtop models was upholstered to match the headliner.

The Convertible's rear window glass was now a single pane instead of two small panes. Actually, the Convertible had the sharpest looking of all the Lincoln interiors of this series. This year, however, the Convertible type 76 body style was only offered on the large Cosmopolitan. Of course, the smaller-bodied convertible was still available as Mercury. Additional fiberglass sound deadening was added in the roof of Sedans and Coupes.

Both the Cosmopolitan and standard Lincoln received an updated instrument panel. Tom Hibbard's design team went to work on a restyled dash soon after the first Model-E was introduced.

Hibbard had become chief designer after Bob Gregorie's departure. George Walker's consulting team also worked on the instrument panel redesign as well as many of the other restyled features from the 1950 models. The new instrument panel was Modern in the finest fifties tradition. The upsweep hooded two-tone panel covered two-thirds of the dash.

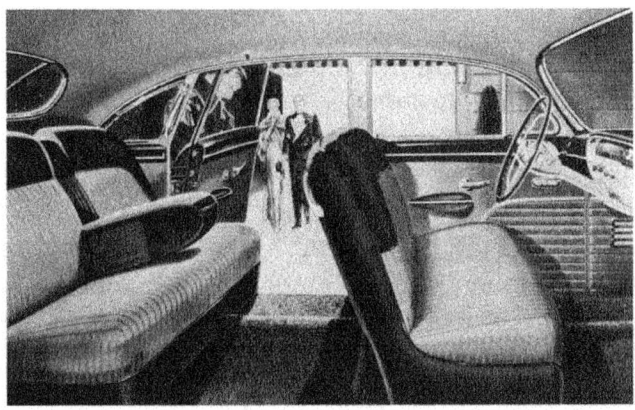
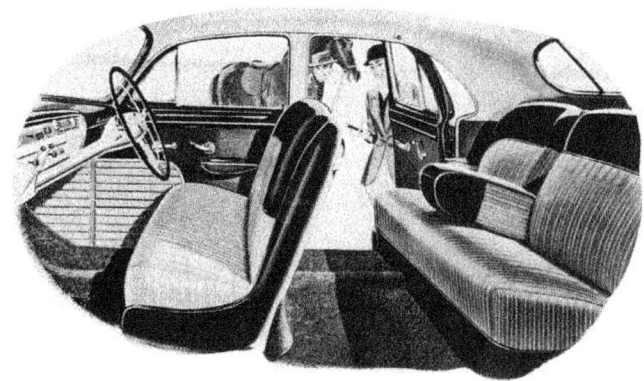

The instrument panel had a long, clear, plastic window enclosed a semicircular easy-to-read speedometer with engine gauges on either side. It extended to the right to encompass the push-button radio. The lower portion of the horizontally ribbed panel contained various easy-to-identify knobs and switches. The gear shift lever knob was also new. A pull-and-twist style hand brake replaced the less efficient lever handle and door locks were redesigned.

Optional equipment, in addition to radio and fresh air heater, included vacuum-power operated antenna, parking-brake-on warning light, hydraulically operated power windows and power front seat. In an effort to compete with the new hardtop coupes offered by other auto makers, Lincoln promoted the new Lido and Capri Coupes. The Lido was a dressed-up 0EL series type 72 with padded vinyl top and the Capri was a deluxe sport Cosmopolitan Coupe.

An optional padded roof for the Capri was offered in leather. The new Lido Coupe added a small logo forward of the new larger *LINCOLN* script logo on each side. On the Capri Coupe, a script *COSMOPOLITAN* was placed mid-door in line with the front fender chrome wing. Additionally, the Capri had rear fender well chrome wings, sometimes called gravel shields, to match the front.

Both Lido and Capri featured deluxe custom interiors with color-coordinated cloth and leather combinations. Engineering argued against the lack of structural integrity on the Lincoln's chassis for a hardtop seemed hollow, particularly in light of a convertible chassis already existed on which a top might have been permanently affixed. The Lido and Capri Coupes did not appear in the original new model brochures.

The dress-up job on the Lido was clearly an afterthought by marketing. The Cosmopolitan type 73 a torpedo back Town Sedan was discontinued at the end of the 1949 model year. The 0EH series Cosmopolitan was now offered as the type H-72 six-passenger Coupe, type H-72C custom Capri Coupe, type H-74 Sport Sedan and type H-76 Convertible Coupe.

The convertible was the heaviest of all these Lincoln bodies, weighing 4,419 pounds. The standard Lincoln 0EL series was available in the type L-72 six-passenger Coupe, type L-72C custom Lido Coupe and type L-74 Sport Sedan. The smaller Lincoln actually weighed only about 250 pounds less than the larger Cosmopolitan.

Lincoln's identification serial numbering method was changed this year and the preceding year's serial numbers began with 9EL or 9EH, which were followed by a production number, i.e., 1 thru 73563.

Series OE

Beginning with the 1950 model year, the prefix was 50 for the year, then LA or LP or SL for the assembly plant, followed by a serial number of 5001 thru 72521.

The standard Lincolns were assembled at Los Angeles (LA), Detroit Lincoln Plant (LP) and St. Louis (SL). The Cosmopolitans were only assembled at the Detroit plant. The ending letter was "L" for the Light 0EL Lincoln and "H" for the Heavy 0EH Cosmopolitan. Thus, the first Cosmo produced under the new numbering method was 50LP5001H.

Lincolns continued to be entered in stock car races and two of the nineteen NASCAR races were won by Lincolns. The new 1952 model Lincolns in design and the new found inclination towards racing would have a definite impact on their design concept, according to Bill Schmidt, chief stylist for Lincoln-Mercury.

A new factory was being built at Wayne, Michigan, to produce the Model 2H Lincolns that would be introduced in November of the following year. George Hackett, who was in charge of Ford auto shows, recalls that many types of experimental prototypes were also being developed during this period.

The 9E series bodies had undergone eleven design improvements to quiet road noise and chassis rattles. Additionally, eighteen other design change orders were issued to correct assorted mechanical problems. These early models suffered from water leaks, binding doors, hydraulic window switch failure and power units cracking the window glass. The rain shield was removed from the roof rail, over the forward wing-windows, to improve appearance.

The heater core was relocated outside of the firewall to reduce engine noise transmitted through the heater firewall. Overall, this second year's production was considered less prone to the worrisome minor problems. Hydra-Matic automatic and Touch-O-Matic overdrive transmissions were optional on all models. The overall engine design itself remained relatively unchanged, but numerous minor changes were incorporated.

During warm-up, the Hydra-Matic equipped cars would creep, so the automatic choke was redesigned. The oil filter was no longer mounted on the cylinder head. This location prevented proper torqueing down of the head bolts and had also been a long time problem with the old HV-12 engines. An improved steel alloy was now being used in the engine block castings.

These engines, as it turned out seemed to experience more than their normal share of cracked blocks. The oil dip stick was relocated to within easier reach under the hood. Pistons were changed from four-ring to three-ring with little effect on the engine's oil consumption rate.

The greatest improvement to engine performance came when the dynamic balance of each engine was checked and corrected. The front motor mounts were also improved as an indirect result of these tests. Hard steering remained a problem, so the steering gear box was reworked. Tire sizes on the standard Lincoln were 8.00x15 and on the Cosmopolitan 8.20x15.

The 0E series, a regular color brochure was offered, plus two smaller foldouts. A three-page, silver-gray pamphlet described the 0EL series and a four-page gold-tan pamphlet described the 0EH series. Separate color folders were issued midyear promoting the Lido and Capri Coupes.

Magazine advertising was art detail was progressively improving. A typical ad would picture a Cosmopolitan driving along an ocean shore or past a fox hunt scene. Photos were seldom, if ever, used in national advertising layouts during this period.

Officially Lincoln-Mercury Division brochures still read, "Lincoln Division of the Ford Motor Company." The Lincoln advertising motto of "Nothing Could Be Finer" was used.

Automotive writers of the period often compared Lincoln, Cadillac and Chrysler, but the comparison was more often of the companies. As the top line went, so did the rest of the fleet, particularly in closely associated body styles like Cadillac-Oldsmobile and the Chrysler-DeSoto. Styling exceptions were a trademark Cadillac's tail fin and the Continental's spare tire hump.

Various other body stylists attempted to copy them, none were very successful. Lincoln was not prepared for GM cutting its model run short this year. For 1950, General Motors hit its competition with both barrels, i.e., new body styles, which included a hardtop coupe and a 331 CID V-8 overhead valve engine.

Lincoln had chosen to drop the Custom Sedan, but Cadillac now offered an all-new Fleetwood series 75 limousine. Lincoln limousines had been produced by outside coachbuilders at great expense to the purchaser. Henney Motor Company of Freeport, Illinois, Hess and Eisenhardt of Cincinnati, Ohio and Dietrich Creative Industries of Grand Rapids, Michigan, were three of the coachbuilders who produced these custom Lincoln limousines.

The White House's Model-K Sunshine Special convertible limousine was still in service when Harry Truman came to the Presidency. At his January inauguration, however, Truman rode in a Cosmopolitan Convertible followed by two others. A custom Cosmopolitan convertible sedan, the famous Bubble Top Parade Car, was being built for White House service at the time.

Page 232 and 233: Lincoln advertising art from 1950. Page 233, top right: Interior views of Lincoln and Cosmopolitan. Opposite page, bottom: 1950 parade car in shop at Grand Rapids, Michigan; Next up, Harry Truman's personal limousine. This page: President Eisenhower in bubble top parade car, designed by Raymond Dietrich; "Sunshine Special" parked beside new 1950 Presidential Cosmopolitan convertible; Parade car with convertible top installed; and Secret Service convertible with retractable running boards.

President Eisenhower actually had the bubble top added four years later. Built on a 145 inch wheelbase, the Lincoln Cosmopolitan Parade Car weighed 6,450 pounds. It had rear fender well wings and a custom Continental spare tire kit. Footholds were affixed to the large rear bumpers for the Secret Service agents to stand on like carriage footmen. Unlike the Model-K Lincoln, the Cosmopolitan body style had no running boards on which they could ride.

Raymond H. Dietrich, famed designer of the coachbuilt era, had formed a new design company in Cedar Rapids. Dietrich was the design consultant on the Presidential Parade Limousine. His eye for what the large limo needed is evidenced in the open rear wheel well with added chrome wing and custom hub caps. Most of the body stretch was added to this limousine just forward of the rear wheel wells. There was only one Parade Car. However, nine other Lincoln Cosmopolitan custom Sedan limousines were built for the White House. Therefore, more than one collector may claim to own Harry Truman's Lincoln Cosmopolitan limousine and they probably do.

One limo was kept by Truman and followed him home to Missouri. It is retained by the Truman Museum in Independence. Another purchased by the Anchor Motel in Clearwater, Florida and was displayed there for years before it went to the Imperial Palace collection is Las Vegas. The Bubble Top Parade Car is presently owned by the Henry Ford Museum in Dearborn.

The standard White House limousines were stretched Sedan versions with raised roofs and padded tops. Their original cost was $30,000 each, but they were leased to the government for a few dollars a year. These limos did not have the external rear-mounted spare tire like the Parade Car.

The Number One car did have the retractable running boards, red lights and a slightly plusher interior with gold plated rear compartment trim, but not all were so equipped. All did, however, have rear heaters, rear radio and a compartment partition glass.

On the Number One car the rear passenger options included two built-in thermos bottles, fold-out writing desk, tobacco humidor and radio controls. These cars were rumored to have bulletproof glass and armor plating and this upped their weight 1,600 pounds over a standard Cosmo Sedan. Actually, the custom coach finish work itself accomplished this. The retractable running boards were later removed from White House Number One, due to clearance problems.

One other Secret Service car, a Cosmopolitan Convertible, was fitted with such running boards. The Parade Car remained in the White House service until 1961 and was driven over 100,000 miles. It was last used by President Kennedy in 1963, during a tour of Europe.

LINCOLN AND CONTINENTAL

NINETEEN-FIFTYONE - The 1951 Lincoln 1EL and 1EH series were officially introduced to the public on November 15th of the preceding year. It was the beginning of the end for these bulbous beauties. By Lincoln standards, their sales record had been phenomenal, the best in the company's history. By the new Ford Motor Company standards, it wasn't good enough. Now off the drawing boards and into engineering testing, the Race Era Lincolns were waiting.

Advertising and brochures underwent minor date and illustration changes, but only enough to classify them as 1951. On the cars themselves, the face lift job was mostly bright metalwork and chrome. The exception was the 1EL series, on which the entire back end was redesigned. This, of course, was also done to the Mercury that shared the same body. The back fenders were extended rearward past the trunk, an obvious design response to the Cadillac tail fin but far from a copy. The rear bumper actually followed the curvature of the fender extension. What a wonderful opportunity to have added a Continental spare tire kit, at least to the small Lincoln. By slightly insetting a spare into the trunk and bringing the rear bumper straight across the back, a Continental kit might easily have been installed. This could have become a unique distinguishing feature between the small Lincoln and the Mercury.

These Lincolns had suffered from lack of window area, which resulted in poor visibility, so this year the rear windows were enlarged slightly. The Cosmopolitan still retained the two chrome divider bars in the rear three-piece window. Both models, especially the small Lincoln, had always tended to look much like a California Barris custom and were not well endowed with greenhouse area, i.e. the glass-enclosed cabin area.

This increased open area required additional structure to be added to the steel roof frame and the addition of a box section to the rear window sill. There was a variety of side moldings offered this year. Wheel well wings were dropped from the Cosmopolitan. The body side molding was long, wide and straight. A forward leaning blade or dorsal was located at the leading edge of the chrome strip, but was not always installed. In Lincoln advertisements, the model name appeared below the chrome strip on the quarter panel, in the same location as in the previous year.

In actuality, it was located above the chrome strip directly over the front wheel well. The small Lincoln offered an additional chrome side panel molding and was a lightning-bolt strip that followed the fender mold line with a fluted filler plate at the center jog point on the strip. It was a less than attractive trim option.

The Cosmopolitan used a wide bright metal rocker panel kick plate. Both the Lincoln and Cosmopolitan got new trunk latch trim plates. Fender skirts were now optional on the small Lincoln, but remained standard equipment on the Lido Coupe

Most advertising pictured the Lincoln with rear fender skirts, but many units were shipped without them. The Cosmopolitan continued the use of fender skirts. Newly redesigned taillights were installed and replaced the round tri-star. These new tail lights were oval and looked much like a miniature version of what would appear on the 1952 Lincolns.

The grille was changed again this year, probably only because it was easy to do. The front parking light chrome trim now wrapped around to the front fender well and the center grille bar was an arch with five chrome flutes mounted on top. A new, more massive front bumper had two large bumper guards that formed the lower grille. This was a styling trend that Lincoln would incorporate into various models for the next eight years. The hood ornament and the hood nose logo remained unchanged. The headlights were moved outboard. Hub caps were restyled and looked ever so slightly like the Cadillac hub caps. They were plain and without a center logo.

The available body styles were unchanged from last year. The 1EL series Lincoln offered the type L-72B Club Coupe, the type L-72C Lido Coupe and the type L-74 Sport Sedan. The Lido Coupe featured a canvas or vinyl top and bright rocker panel molding. The 1EL series Cosmopolitan offered the type H-72B Club Coupe, the type H-72C Capri Coupe, the type H-74 Sport Sedan and the type H-76 Convertible Coupe. The Capri Coupe featured optional leather top and custom interiors. The Lincoln trademark of center opening doors would not be carried into the next model year.

These would be the last Lincolns to use the Suicide Door arrangement until it was used again on the Engle Continentals in 1961. They would be phased out for good at the end of the 1969 models. The Mercury sedans would never again use the forward-opening rear door, even on the models that shared body parts with one of the Lincoln models.

Sundry optional accessories were available on the Lincoln. They included items like a rear window wiper, engine compartment light, driving lamps, a tripod jack, curb buffers, rear door guards, seat covers, hand operated Seeing-Eye driver side hand operated spotlight, undercoating, a Porcelainizing finish coating, hydraulic power windows and white sidewall tires. An external sun visor was available for the standard Lincoln only. Heater and radio were optional. The radio had a four-position tone control, i.e., normal, bass, high fidelity and low noise. A vacuum operated power antenna and a rear-seat speaker were optional. High fidelity used a single speaker, as stereo had not yet been adapted to car radios.

The accessories received the full marketing treatment. They were grouped under headings like Utility and Safety options. Utility listed exhaust pipe extension, license plate frame and trunk lid lock. The Safety group listed a flashing parking-brake-on signal light, push-button operated windshield washer, backup lights and outside rearview mirror. Interior options included a wide new choice of colors and fabrics. The interior hardware like door handles and matched the instrument panel knobs.

The standard Lincoln had a robe rail or egress assist handles on the back of the front seats. A new non-glare rearview mirror was standard equipment. A lighted vanity mirror behind the sun visor was optional. New door switches operated the restyled interior dome light. The Lido and Capri Coupes offered an additional selection of custom deluxe interiors.

Mechanical changes included a redesigned baffle in the top of the radiator tank to prevent air pockets from forming. A higher pressure radiator cap was also used. Both of these modifications were affected to aid engine cooling. A stronger idler arm steering support was used for better steering stability. The engine itself was increased in horsepower slightly and now developed 154 horsepower at 3600 RPM (275 foot-pounds).

This engine would be the last of the Lincoln flatheads. It was a sturdy and powerful engine, but still suffered from minor oil consumption and vibration problems. In a further effort to lessen vibration, the shaft bearings and tappets were individually hand-fitted. The exhaust port cooling size was increased, which improved the directional flow through the exhaust tubes.

The new rear axle was high speed, a 3.31 to 1 ratio. An improved Holley 885-FFC two-barrel carburetor was designed to perform better at high altitudes. These two factors combined to improve the large Lincoln's performance both in the mountains and on the plains.

These were probably also good reasons for Les Viland's winning the March 8th Mobilgas Economy Run. He took the Grand Sweepstakes prize in a standard Lincoln with overdrive. His winning average was 25.448 MPG. Hydra-Matic was standard on this year's Lincolns, but a manual transmission with overdrive could still be ordered.

Overdrive combined with the new high-speed axle produced a final rearend gear ratio of 2.38 to 1. Fully aired 8.00X15 tires helped, but Ol' Feather Foot, Les' nickname, managed mainly to accomplish this high gas mileage through skillful use of the accelerator.

The run was carefully planned in advance, right down to the timing of the traffic lights at the starting point in downtown Los Angeles. Maintaining an exact cruising speed allowed the car to enter each intersection on a green light.

The Lincoln used in the Economy Run was impounded by the officials who looked for any non-stock modifications and there were none. In July, Motor Trend magazine used Viland's practice car to perform a similar economy test. They reported that even though the Lincoln's mileage was over 8 MPG better than the Chrysler and Cadillac entries, such mileage could be obtained at a steady 45 MPH in a stock Lincoln automobile.

Test reporter Griffin Borgeson put the large Lincoln through some additional tests. He reported that the Lincoln had a top speed of 100.67 MPH and obtained an average speed of 97.08 MPH over four runs. From a standing start, the Lincoln turned the quarter mile in 19.9 seconds. The Lincoln's clocked time from 0 to 30 MPH was 5.6 seconds and from 0 to 60 MPH was 15.8 seconds. Borgeson further commented that the 5.5 turns from lock to lock in the steering and the soft front suspension caused the Lincoln's tires to shriek with agony. His report went on to praise the hydraulic tappets and excellent crankcase ventilation on the large flathead engine.

The Korean War curtailed most automobile production to some extent, but Cadillac still out produced Lincoln three to one. The bulbous Lincoln's lack of popularity was borne out on the used car market and these large Lincolns lived up to their unbecoming nickname of beached whales. The Lincoln and Packard Blue Book prices for a four-year-old automobile were about one-third that of a Cadillac. All too often, these heavy motorcars were carted-off to scrap metal furnaces to rise like a phoenix as steel for yet another new model.

In terms of production numbers and management efficiency, these Lincoln models represent the threshold of the modern automobile. There are all too few of these fine examples of a milestone in the automobile engineering art form in existence today. These 1949 through 1951 models could easily be labeled as the beginning of the modern Lincoln automobiles, but they were not. Instead, they were the end of an era.

The new Lincolns being developed for the 1952 model year introduction would set the design standard into the early 1980s. Then once again, as before, technological developments would affect major changes in the industry and in the Lincoln motorcar. But, then that is another book, isn't it?

It is fitting indeed that the last designs of Edsel Ford and E.T. "Bob" Gregorie should survive in these, the last unique Lincolns. Henry Martyn Leland's dream of a permanent motorcar could not possibly have given him a vision of his total legacy. Nor could the vision of the artistically gifted Edsel Bryant Ford have conceived his hobby-like puttering with coachbuilt and custom automobiles would leave behind a worldwide respect for the motorcars known as the Lincoln and the Continental.

ABOUT THE BOOK

Of all the classic American motorcar marque stories, the story of the Lincoln personifies the American dream better than any other. The evolution of the Lincoln and Continental parallels the American automobile industry. Everyone who owns or appreciates fine motorcars like the Lincoln will enjoy reading this book. It is a book which combines the story of the marque with the technical and developmental aspects of the automobile itself. The book is richly illustrated with advertising art forms of the various eras. The text is both interesting and factually informative. The appendixes to this book provide production figures and detailed information on the various models. Beginning with the coming of the automobile to the Americas in the late 1800s and concluding with the beginning of the postwar modern automotive era, this book is an inside look at the forces which began and ended the classic American automobile era.

ABOUT THE AUTHOR

Marvin Earl Arnold grew up in Ohio and Oklahoma. In 1959, he and his wife moved to Dallas, Texas where they have made their home ever since. The author is a thirty year veteran of the aerospace industry. He is a senior systems design engineer and an experienced commercial pilot. Over the years, he has owned more than 100 makes and models of automobiles and has personally restored several dozen different models. Many of these cars were Lincolns and Continentals. He presently owns a 1941 and a 1942 Continental Coupe. The author is a member of the Society of Automotive Historians and the Antique Automobile Club of America. In 1952, the author purchased his first Lincoln, a used 1939 Zephyr Coupe, which began his long time interest in this Marque. This book reflects his many hours of research on the subject of Lincoln and Continental automobiles as well as the men and organizations which created them.

1984 Continental on Electra Glide Road, Monument Valley. But, then that's another story!

Marvin Arnold

APPENDIX I.

LINCOLN MODEL L 1920-1930

Abbreviations: AS 1 or 2-Passenger, Aux. Seats; AT Anderson Electric and Towson Body; AW All-Weather; BR Brougham; Conv Convertible; DC Dual-Cowl; HT Fixed-Top, Canopy; NC Non-Collapsible; OP Open; RS Rumble Seat, Dickey; S Stretch; SB Suburban; SC Semi-Collapsible; SP Sport; S3 3-Side Windows Sedan; TC Town Car; VR Various; WP w/Partition; WT w/Trunk; W2 2-Side Windows Sedan; W3 3-Window Coupe; W5 5-Window Club Coupe.

YEAR 1920—21, MODEL L, SERIES 101, Serial numbers 1 thru 834 thru 3001

TYPE	BODY	STYLE	Ab	SEAT	COACHBUILD	WB	WEIGHT	PRICE	BUILT
101	4dr	TOURING	OP	7	MURRAY/AT	130	4,185	$4,600	1,015
101A	4dr	TOURING	HT	7	MURRAY/AT	130	4,200	$4,700	18
102	2dr	ROADSTER	OP	3	MURRAY/AT	130	3,950	$4,600	78
103	4dr	PHAETON	OP	5	MURRAY/AT	130	3,135	$4,600	278
104	2dr	COUPE	W5	4	MURRAY/AT	130	4,140	$5,750	451
105	4dr	SEDAN	W2	5	MURRAY/AT	130	4,385	$6,000	352
106	4dr	LIMOUSINE	WP	7	MURRAY/AT	130	4,500	$6,600	101
107	4dr	BROUGHAM TC	TC	7	MURRAY/AT	136	4,300	$6,250	10
108	4dr	SEDAN	S3	7	MURRAY/AT	136	4,400	$6,200	26
109	4dr	SEDAN CABRIOLET	5/7	7	MURRAY/AT	136	4,425	$7,200	19
110	4dr	BERLINE	WP	7	MURRAY/AT	136	4,600	$6,600	6
111	2dr	ROADSTER	OP	2+1	MURRAY/AT	136	4,425	$4,500	45
111A	2dr	ROADSTER	OP	2+1	MURRAY/AT	136	4,050	$4,500	23
112	4dr	PHAETON DELUXE	OP	4	LANG	136	4,155	$5,200	196
113A	4dr	SEDAN	S3	4	AMERICAN	136	4,200	$5,200	25
113B	4dr	SEDAN	W2	4	JUDKINS	136	4,200	$5,200	25
114	4dr	SEDAN	OP	7	JUDKINS	136	4,419	$5,200	29
115	4dr	BERLINE	WP	5	JUDKINS	136	4,375	$4,900	25
122	—	CHASSIS	VR	—	LMC	136	3,205	$4,000	253
								Total	2,975

YEAR 1922 (LMC), MODEL L, SERIES 101, Serial numbers 3002 thru 3151 (150)

TYPE	BODY	STYLE	Ab	SEAT	COACHBUILD	WB	WEIGHT	PRICE	BUILT
101	4dr	TOURING	OP	7	MURRAY/AT	130	4,185	$4,600	3
104	2dr	COUPE	W5	4	MURRAY/AT	130	4,140	$5,750	3
105	4dr	SEDAN	W2	5	MURRAY/AT	130	4,385	$6,000	12
107	4dr	BROUGHAM TC	TC	7	MURRAY/AT	130	4,300	$6,250	1
109	4dr	SEDAN CABRIOLET	S3	5/7	MURRAY/AT	136	4,425	$7,200	1
111	2dr	ROADSTER	OP	2+1	MURRAY/AT	136	4,050	$4,500	2
112	4dr	PHAETON DELUXE	OP	4	LANG	136	4,155	$5,200	7
113A	4dr	SEDAN	S3	4	AMERICAN	136	4,200	$5,200	1
113B	4dr	SEDAN	W2	4	JUDKINS	136	4,200	$5,200	8
114	4dr	SEDAN	OP	7	JUDKINS	136	4,419	$5,200	14
115	4dr	BERLINE	WP	5	JUDKINS	136	4,375	$4,900	14
116	4dr	SEDAN	S3	7	JUDKINS	136	4,375	$5,200	19
117	4dr	SEDAN	SB	5/7	MURRAY	136	4,660	$5,800	23
118	4dr	LIMOUSINE	S3	5/7	MURRAY	136	4,590	$4,900	6
119	4dr	LIMOUSINE	TC	2	FLEETWOOD	136	4,785	$5,900	2
702	2dr	COUPE	W3	2	FLEETWOOD	136	4,270	$5,000	1
122	—	CHASSIS	VR	—	LMC	136	3,205	$4,000	20
									22
								Total	150

YEAR 1922 (FMC), MODEL L, SERIES 120, Serial numbers 3152 thru 8709 (5,558)

TYPE	BODY	STYLE	Ab	SEAT	COACHBUILD	WB	WEIGHT	PRICE	BUILT
101	4dr	TOURING	OP	7	MURRAY	130	4,185	$3,800	480
102	2dr	ROADSTER	OP	3	MURRAY	130	3,950	$4,600	6
103	4dr	PHAETON	OP	5	MURRAY	130	4,135	$4,600	37
104	2dr	COUPE	W5	4	MURRAY	130	4,140	$4,400	429
105	4dr	SEDAN	W2	5	MURRAY	130	4,385	$4,700	343
107	4dr	TOWN BROUGHAM	WP	7	MURRAY	130	4,300	$6,250	1
109	4dr	SEDAN CABRIOLET	S3	5/7	MURRAY	136	4,425	$7,200	10
111	2dr	ROADSTER	OP	2+1	MURRAY	136	4,050	$3,800	127
111A	2dr	ROADSTER	OP	4	LANG	136	4,155	$5,200	50
112	4dr	PHAETON DELUXE	OP	4	LANG	136	4,155	$5,200	763
113A	4dr	SEDAN	S3	4	AMERICAN	136	4,200	$5,200	200
113B	4dr	SEDAN	W2	4	JUDKINS	136	4,499	$5,200	125
114	4dr	BERLINE	WP	5	JUDKINS	136	4,785	$5,200	3
115	4dr	SEDAN	WP	4	JUDKINS	136	4,660	$4,900	6
117	4dr	SEDAN	SB	5/7	MURRAY	136	4,660	$4,900	615
118	4dr	SEDAN WT	S3	4	LANG	136	4,590	$5,100	102
118A	4dr	LIMOUSINE	S3	7	LANG	136	4,720	$5,100	433
120	4dr	TOWN CAR	W2	6	BRUNN	136	4,425	$5,100	120
121	4dr	LIMOUSINE	WP	7	BRUNN	136	4,425	$7,200	6
124A	4dr	TOURING	OP	7	AMERICAN	136	4,200	$6,200	2
125	4dr	SEDAN WT	W2	4	AMERICAN	136	4,590	$4,600	1136
126	2dr	COUPE	W5	4	BABCOCK/AT	136	4,290	$4,400	59
127	4dr	BERLINE	W2	5	BABCOCK/AT	136	4,510	$5,400	104
128	4dr	SEDAN	S3	7	JUDKINS	136	4,600	$4,600	74
129	4dr	SEDAN BERLINE	W2	6	MURRAY	136	4,600	$5,000	1
702	2dr	COUPE	W2	5	MURRAY	136	4,270	$5,000	14
122	—	CHASSIS	VR	—	LINCOLN	136	3,205	$3,400	265
								Total	5,512

YEAR 1923, MODEL L, SERIES 130, Serial numbers 8710 thru 16434 (7,724)

TYPE	BODY	STYLE	Ab	SEAT	COACHBUILD	WB	WEIGHT	PRICE	BUILT
111	2dr	ROADSTER	OP	2+1	MURRAY	136	4,050	$3,800	27
111A	2dr	ROADSTER	OP	2+1	LANG	136	4,050	$3,800	27
112	4dr	PHAETON DELUXE	OP	4	AMERICAN	136	4,155	$5,200	15
117	4dr	SEDAN	S3	5/7	LANG	136	4,660	$4,900	870
117A	4dr	SEDAN	SB	5/7	LANG	136	4,660	$5,100	101
118	4dr	LIMOUSINE	SB	5/7	MURRAY	136	4,720	$5,100	443
118A	4dr	LIMOUSINE	SB	5/7	MURRAY	136	4,720	$5,100	120
120	4dr	TOWN CAR	W2	7	BRUNN	136	4,425	$7,200	50
121	4dr	LIMOUSINE	WP	7	BRUNN	136	4,475	$6,200	18
123A	4dr	PHAETON WT	OP	4	LANG/AMERICAN	136	4,215	$3,800	1061
124	4dr	TOURING	OP	4	AMERICAN	136	4,290	$4,600	1182
125	4dr	SEDAN WT	W5	4	BABCOCK/AT	136	4,375	$4,400	365
126	2dr	COUPE	S3	4	AMERICAN	136	4,380	$4,400	816
127	4dr	SEDAN	W2	4	BABCOCK/AT	136	4,400	$5,400	532
128	4dr	BERLINE	S3	6	JUDKINS	136	4,510	$5,400	238
129	4dr	SEDAN BERLINE	S3	5	MURRAY	136	4,600	$4,800	1195
130	2dr	ROADSTER	OP	2	MURRAY	136	4,050	$3,800	48
131	4dr	CABRIOLET	HT	7	BRUNN	136	4,655	$6,200	14
132	4dr	SEDAN WT	W2	4	MURRAY	136	4,375	$4,600	93
133	4dr	SEDAN WT	SB	4	MURRAY	136	4,380	$4,600	269
702	2dr	COUPE	OP	2	JUDKINS	136	4,270	$5,000	208
2340	4dr	LIMOUSINE	S3	7	FLEETWOOD	136	4,690	$5,800	5
2421	4dr	TOWN CAR	W2	6	FLEETWOOD	136	4,630	$5,900	1
1225	2dr	EF COUPE	W3	2	CUSTOM	136	4,600	$3,400	1
122	2dr	CHUCK WAGON	—	2	CUSTOM	136	4,600	—	175
	—	CHASSIS	VR	—	LINCOLN	136	3,205	$3,400	
								Total	7,875

YEAR 1924, MODEL L, SERIES 134, Serial numbers 16435 thru 23614 (7,180)

TYPE	BODY	STYLE	Ab	SEAT	COACHBUILD	WB	WEIGHT	PRICE	BUILT
117	4dr	SEDAN	S3	5/7	MURRAY	136	4,660	$4,900	170
117A	4dr	SEDAN	SB	5/7	LANG	136	4,660	$4,900	101
118	4dr	LIMOUSINE	SB	5/7	MURRAY	136	4,720	$5,100	86
118A	4dr	LIMOUSINE	WP	6	BRUNN	136	4,425	$7,200	42
120	4dr	TOWN CAR	OP	4	LANG/AMERICAN	136	4,215	$3,800	12
121	4dr	PHAETON WT	OP	7	AMERICAN	136	4,290	$4,600	8
123	4dr	TOURING	W5	4	AMERICAN	136	4,380	$4,400	829
124	2dr	COUPE	S3	4	AMERICAN	136	4,380	$4,400	601
126	2dr	COUPE	S3	4	BABCOCK AT	136	4,400	$4,600	2
127	4dr	SEDAN WT	W2	4	JUDKINS	136	4,510	$5,400	424
128	4dr	SEDAN BERLINE	S3	4	MURRAY	136	4,600	$4,700	111
129	2dr	ROADSTER	OP	3	MURRAY	136	4,050	$3,800	351
130	4dr	CABRIOLET	HT	7	BABCOCK AT	136	4,655	$6,200	188
131	4dr	SEDAN WT	W2	4	MURRAY	136	4,375	$4,600	13
132	4dr	SEDAN WT	SC	7	MURRAY	136	4,890	$5,500	358
133	4dr	SEDAN WT	S3	7	MURRAY/BRUN	136	4,910	$5,600	899
134	4dr	LIMOUSINE	WP	7	MURRAY	136	4,865	$5,100	846
135	4dr	LIMOUSINE	S3	5	MURRAY	136	4,755	$6,600	482
136	4dr	SEDAN	NC	5	BRUNN	136	4,900	$6,600	928
137	4dr	CABRIOLET	HT	2	BRUNN	136	4,700	$4,700	6
138	4dr	LIMOUSINE TC	WP	7	MURRAY	136	4,945	$3,800	8
139	4dr	LIMOUSINE	S3	6	FLEETWOOD	136	4,800	$6,000	29
140	4dr	BERLINE WP WT	S3	2	JUDKINS	136	4,270	$5,400	20
702	2dr	COUPE	W3	2	JUDKINS	136	4,270	$5,000	393
2340S	4dr	LIMOUSINE	S3	6	FLEETWOOD	136	4,690	$5,800	77
2421S	4dr	TOWN CAR	W2	6	FLEETWOOD	136	4,630	$5,900	40
122	—	CHASSIS	VR	—	LINCOLN	136	3,205	$3,400	79
								Total	7,103

CLASSIC MOTORCARS

YEAR 1925, MODEL L, SERIES 141, Serial numbers 23615 thru 32029 (8,415)

TYPE	BODY	STYLE	Ab	SEAT	COACHBUILD	WB	WEIGHT	PRICE	BUILT
123A	4dr	PHAETON WT	OP	4	LANG/AMERICAN	136	4,215	$4,000	689
123B	4dr	SP PHAETON DC	OP	4	LANG/AMERICAN	136	4,565	$4,600	25
123C	4dr	SP PHAETON WT	OP	4	LANG/AMERICAN	136	4,565	$4,600	1
124A	4dr	TOURING	OP	7	AMERICAN	136	4,350	$4,400	106
124B	4dr	SP TOURING WT	OP	7	AMERICAN	136	4,290	$4,000	418
123D	4dr	SP TOURING DC	OP	7	AMERICAN	136	4,580	$4,200	324
124C	2dr	ROADSTER	OP	3	MURRAY/AT	136	4,740	$4,500	3
126	4dr	COUPE	W5	5	JUDKINS	136	4,750	$5,400	204
128	4dr	BERLINE WT WP	OP	4/6	BABCOCK/AT	136	4,885	$4,600	31
130	2dr	ROADSTER	OP	2	BABCOCK/AT	136	4,460	$5,400	126
132	2dr	SEDAN WT	W2	4	MURRAY/BRUN	136	4,575	$4,600	146
133	4dr	SEDAN	S3	4	MURRAY	136	4,585	$4,600	548
134	4dr	LIMOUSINE	TC	7	MURRAY	136	4,890	$5,500	829
135	4dr	BERLINE	WP	7	MURRAY	136	4,910	$5,600	443
136	4dr	SEDAN	S3	5	MURRAY	136	4,865	$5,100	541
137	4dr	CABRIOLET	NC	5	BRUNN	136	4,755	$6,600	58
138A	4dr	LIMOUSINE TC	SC	7	BRUNN	136	4,900	$6,400	9
138B	4dr	LIMOUSINE TC	HT	7	BRUNN	136	4,900	$6,000	9
139	4dr	LIMOUSINE	WP	7	FLEETWOOD	136	4,945	$6,000	197
140A	4dr	BERLINE WP WT	SC	6	FLEETWOOD	136	4,995	$6,000	100
140B	4dr	BERLINE WP WT	SC	6	JUDKINS	136	4,800	$5,400	148
141	2dr	ROADSTER	W2	2	JUDKINS	136	4,850	$5,600	100
142A	4dr	CABRIOLET	AS	5	MURRAY	136	4,500	$5,400	95
142B	4dr	CABRIOLET	NC	4	HOLBROOK	136	4,950	$7,200	6
143	4dr	SEDAN WT	W3	4	MURRAY	136	4,650	$4,775	470
144A	2dr	SEDAN WT	W3	4	MURRAY/LEBARON	136	4,700	$5,000	159
144B	2dr	SEDAN WT	S3	4	MURRAY/LEBARON	136	4,700	$5,025	433
145	4dr	BROUGHAM	WP	5	BRUNN	136	4,800	$6,400	15
146	4dr	SEDAN	S3	5	LINC/DIETRICH	136	4,850	$4,900	1095
147A	4dr	SEDAN	SC	5	MURRAY/DIETRICH	136	4,800	$5,000	398
147B	4dr	BERLINE	S3	6	MURRAY/DIET	136	4,850	$5,200	214
148	4dr	BROUGHAM	SC	5	DIETRICH	136	4,900	$6,800	80
149	3dr	CABRIOLET	—	—	DIETRICH	136	4,950	$7,200	12
150	—	HEARSE	—	—	JUDKINS	136	4,270	$5,000	345
—	2dr	COUPE	W3	2	LEBARON	136	4,750	$5,000	11
2686S	2dr	PATTY WAGON	—	—	DIETRICH	136	4,450	$4,600	2
122	—	AMBULANCE	W2	6/7	FLEETWOOD	150	4,450	$4,600	—
—	—	SPORT COUPE	—	—	—	—	3,300	$3,800	121
—	—	CHASSIS	VR	3	LINCOLN	—	—	—	—
								Total	8,452

YEAR 1926, MODEL L, SERIES 151, Serial numbers 32030 thru 39900 (7,871)

TYPE	BODY	STYLE	Ab	SEAT	COACHBUILD	WB	WEIGHT	PRICE	BUILT
123A	4dr	PHAETON WT	OP	4	LANG/AMERICAN	136	4,215	$4,000	147
123B	4dr	SP PHAETON DC	OP	4	LANG/AMERICAN	136	4,565	$4,500	283
123C	4dr	SP PHAETON WT	OP	4	LANG/AMERICAN	136	4,565	$4,600	41
124A	4dr	TOURING	OP	7	AMERICAN	136	4,290	$4,000	93
124B	4dr	SP TOURING WT	OP	7	AMERICAN	136	4,580	$4,200	324
123D	4dr	SP TOURING DC	OP	3	MURRAY/AT	136	4,740	$4,500	12
124C	2dr	ROADSTER	OP	3	MURRAY	136	4,460	$4,000	99
136	4dr	SEDAN	S3	5	BRUNN	136	4,865	$5,100	3
137	4dr	CABRIOLET	NC	5	FLEETWOOD	136	4,945	$6,600	52
139	4dr	LIMOUSINE	WP	7	FLEETWOOD	136	4,800	$6,000	40
140A	4dr	BERLINE WP WT	SC	6	JUDKINS	136	4,850	$6,000	20
140B	4dr	BERLINE WP WT	SC	6	JUDKINS	136	4,500	$5,500	173
141	2dr	ROADSTER	W2	2	MURRAY	136	4,950	$4,500	100
142A	4dr	CABRIOLET	AS	5	HOLBROOK	136	4,650	$7,200	150
142B	4dr	CABRIOLET	NC	4	JUDKINS	136	4,950	$7,200	6
143	2dr	COUPE	W3	2	MURRAY	136	4,700	$4,400	308
144A	2dr	SEDAN WT	W2	4	MURRAY/LEBARON	136	4,700	$4,800	513
144B	2dr	SEDAN WT	S3	4	MURRAY/LEBARON	136	4,700	$5,075	1350
145A	4dr	BROUGHAM	WP	5	BRUNN	136	4,850	$6,400	42
145B	4dr	BROUGHAM	WP	5	BRUNN	136	4,850	$6,500	3
146	4dr	SEDAN	S3	5	DIETRICH	136	4,800	$4,900	558
147A	4dr	SEDAN	SC	5	MURRAY/DIETRICH	136	4,800	$5,000	1590
147B	4dr	BERLINE	S3	6	MURRAY/DIETRICH	136	4,800	$5,200	1180
148	2dr	CABRIOLET	SC	4	DIETRICH	136	4,900	$6,800	2
149	4dr	CABRIOLET	AS	5	LOCKE	136	4,950	$7,200	101
151	4dr	SEDAN	S3	5	DIETRICH	136	4,850	$4,900	653
152	4dr	CABRIOLET	AS	4	DIETRICH	136	4,800	$7,200	10
153	2dr	SEDAN	W2	4	HOLBROOK	136	4,900	$4,800	263
154	4dr	ROADSTER	SC	2	LEBARON	136	4,830	$4,700	7
155	4dr	SPORT CABRIOLET	W3	5	DIETRICH	136	4,850	$6,500	10
157	2dr	COUPE	W3	3	JUDKINS	136	4,270	$6,700	371
702	—	CHASSIS	VR	—	JUDKINS	136	4,270	$5,000	8
122	—	CHASSIS	VR	—	LINCOLN	136	—	—	75
1225	—	CUSTOM	—	—	LMC/DIETRICH	150	3,300	$3,600	154
150A	—	HEARSE	—	—	DIETRICH	—	—	—	—
150B	—	CHASSIS	VR	—	LINCOLN	—	3,450	$3,900	37
								Total	8,787

YEAR 1927, MODEL L, SERIES 158, Serial numbers 901 thru 47500 (7,600)

TYPE	BODY	STYLE	Ab	SEAT	COACHBUILD	WB	WEIGHT	PRICE	BUILT
123A	4dr	SP PHAETON DC	OP	4	LANG/AMERICAN	136	4,565	$4,500	8
123B	4dr	SP PHAETON DC	OP	4	LANG/AMERICAN	136	4,565	$4,600	1
123C	4dr	TOURING	OP	7	AMERICAN	136	4,290	$4,000	2
124A	4dr	SP TOURING WT	OP	7	AMERICAN	136	4,580	$4,200	6
124B	2dr	COUPE	W3	2	MURRAY	136	4,650	$4,800	46
143	2dr	COUPE	W3	2	MURRAY	136	4,650	$4,400	400
144A	4dr	SEDAN WT	W2	4	MURRAY/LEBARON	136	4,700	$4,800	926
144B	2dr	SEDAN WT	S3	4	MURRAY/LEBARON	136	4,700	$5,075	63
145	4dr	BROUGHAM	WP	7	BRUNN	136	5,010	$6,600	3
146	4dr	SEDAN	S3	5	LMC/DIETRICH	136	4,850	$4,900	1193
147A	4dr	SEDAN	S3	5	MURRAY/DIETRICH	136	5,050	$5,300	1005
147B	4dr	BERLINE	TC	6	MURRAY/DIETRICH	136	5,100	$5,500	178
151	2dr	ROADSTER	AS	3	LOCKE	136	4,325	$4,000	917
152	4dr	SEDAN	S3	5	LMC/DIETRICH	136	4,850	$4,900	580
153	4dr	CABRIOLET	SC	5	HOLBROOK	136	4,500	$7,200	7
154	4dr	ROADSTER	AS	5	DIETRICH	136	4,830	$4,700	12
155	4dr	SPORT CABRIOLET	W3	5	LEBARON	136	4,900	$6,500	100
156	2dr	COUPE	W5	3	LINCOLN	136	4,815	$6,700	293
157	2dr	COUPE	W2	5	LMC/DIETRICH	136	4,850	$5,600	12
158	4dr	BERLINE SEDAN	AS	5	JUDKINS	136	5,090	$6,000	100
159	4dr	LIMOUSINE	SC	7	BRUNN	136	5,150	$6,800	54
160	4dr	BERLINE SEDAN	S3	7	WILLOUGHBY	136	5,000	$6,000	164
161	4dr	CABRIOLET AW	W3	7	JUDKINS	136	5,070	$5,500	352
162	4dr	SEDAN	W2	5	LEBARON	136	5,200	$7,000	20
163B	4dr	SPORT PHAETON	WT	4	LOCKE	136	4,840	$4,600	167
164	4dr	SPORT TOURING	DC	5	LOCKE	136	4,940	$5,000	90
702	2dr	COUPE	OP	2	JUDKINS	136	4,950	$4,500	173
122	2dr	CHASSIS	W3	2	JUDKINS	136	4,270	$5,000	205
1225	4dr	COACHING	VR	5	LOCKE/JUDKINS	136	5,100	$8,500	2
—	—	CUSTOM	BR	—	DIETRICH	136	3,000	$3,600	72
150B	—	CHASSIS	VR	—	LINCOLN	150	3,450	$3,900	22
								Total	7,148

YEAR 1928, MODEL L, SERIES 165, Serial numbers 47501 thru 54500 (7,000)

TYPE	BODY	STYLE	Ab	SEAT	COACHBUILD	WB	WEIGHT	PRICE	BUILT
144A	4dr	SEDAN WT	W2	4	MURRAY/LEBARON	136	4,700	$4,800	263
144B	4dr	SEDAN WT	S3	4	MURRAY/LEBARON	136	4,700	$4,800	529
145	4dr	BROUGHAM	WP	7	BRUNN	136	5,010	$6,400	3
147A	4dr	SEDAN	S3	5	MURRAY/DIETRICH	136	5,050	$5,000	1023
147B	4dr	BERLINE	S3	6	MURRAY/DIETRICH	136	5,100	$5,200	709
151	2dr	ROADSTER	AS	4	LOCKE	136	4,325	$4,600	65
152	4dr	SEDAN	S3	5	DIETRICH	136	4,850	$7,200	835
153	2dr	CABRIOLET	SC	5	HOLBROOK	136	4,500	$4,600	8
154	2dr	ROADSTER	AS	5	DIETRICH	136	4,830	$4,600	54
155	2dr	SPORT CABRIOLET	W3	3	LEBARON	136	4,900	$7,300	230
156	2dr	COUPE	W5	3	LINCOLN	136	4,815	$4,600	6
157	2dr	COUPE	W2	5	DIETRICH	136	4,850	$6,500	12
159	4dr	CABRIOLET	SC	7	BRUNN	136	5,150	$6,600	483
160	4dr	LIMOUSINE	S3	7	WILLOUGHBY	136	5,000	$6,000	348
161	4dr	BERLINE SEDAN	W2	5	JUDKINS	136	5,070	$5,500	66
162	4dr	BERLINE SEDAN AW	AS	5	LEBARON	136	5,200	$7,350	226
163A	4dr	SPORT PHAETON	WT	4	LOCKE	136	4,840	$4,600	150
163B	4dr	SPORT PHARTON	DC	4	LOCKE	136	4,940	$5,000	323
164	4dr	SPORT TOURING	OP	7	LOCKE	136	4,950	$4,600	347
165	2dr	ROADSTER	AS	4	BRUNN	136	4,740	$6,400	86
166	4dr	BROUGHAM	AW	5	BRUNN	136	4,925	$6,400	38
167	4dr	SEDAN CONV	W2	7	BRUNN	136	4,900	$6,600	2
168	4dr	SEDAN LIMO	S3	7	LINCOLN	136	4,850	$4,900	88
169A	2dr	TOWN SEDAN	W2	4	LINCOLN	136	5,165	$4,800	140
169B	4dr	TOWN SEDAN	S3	5	LINCOLN	136	5,010	$4,600	14
171	2dr	COUPE	W3	2	LINCOLN	136	4,720	$6,200	6
172	4dr	COUPE CONV	AS	5	DIETRICH	136	4,900	$5,600	1
550	4dr	BERLINE SEDAN	W2	5	JUDKINS	136	5,070	$7,200	40
2dr	4dr	CABRIOLET AW	SC	5	HOLBROOK	136	5,205	$5,000	110
702	—	CHASSIS	VR	—	LINCOLN	136	4,270	$3,600	105
122	—	CUSTOM	VR	—	LINCOLN	136	—	—	59
150B	—	AMBULANCE	—	—	BROWNELL	150	3,450	$3,800	24
150S									4
								Total	6,402

APPENDIX II.

LINCOLN MODEL K 1931-1940

Abbreviations: AN Non-Collapsible and All-Weather; AS 1 or 2-Passenger, Auxiliary Seats; AW All-Weather; Conv Convertible; DC Dual-Cowl; NC Non-Collapsible; PN Panel; RS Rumble Seat, Dickey; SC Semi-Collapsible; SP Special; S2 2-Side Windows Sedan; S3 3-Side Windows; WP w/Partition

YEAR 1929, MODEL L, SERIES 173, Serial numbers 54501 thru 61700 (7,200)

TYPE	BODY	STYLE	Ab	SEAT	COACHBUILD	WB	WEIGHT	PRICE	BUILT
151	2dr	ROADSTER	AS	4	LOCKE	136	4,325	$4,650	7
153	4dr	CABRIOLET	SC	7	HOLBROOK	136	4,500	$6,800	2
155	4dr	SPORT CABRIOLET	W3	7	LEBARON	136	4,900	$7,400	3
156	4dr	ROADSTER AS	W5	4	LINCOLN	136	4,815	$5,300	138
157	2dr	COUPE	W2	3	DIETRICH	136	4,850	$6,700	5
160	4dr	LIMOUSINE	S3	7	WILLOUGHBY	136	5,000	$6,200	155
162	4dr	CABRIOLET AW	W2	7	LEBARON	136	5,200	$7,400	88
163A	4dr	SPORT PHAETON	WT	4	LOCKE	136	4,840	$4,650	88
163B	4dr	SPORT PHAETON	DC	4	LOCKE	136	4,950	$4,500	58
164A	4dr	SPORT TOURING	OP	7	LOCKE	136	5,040	$4,900	18
164B	4dr	SPORT TOURING	DC	7	LOCKE	136	4,740	$4,900	225
165	4dr	ROADSTER AS	W5	4	LINCOLN	136	4,925	$7,400	78
166	4dr	BROUGHAM	AW	7	BRUNN	136	4,900	$6,900	60
167	4dr	SEDAN CONV	W2	5	BRUNN	136	5,165	$5,100	1380
168A	4dr	SEDAN	S3	5	LINCOLN	136	5,190	$5,100	837
168B	4dr	LIMOUSINE	S3	7	LINCOLN	136	4,945	$4,800	658
169A	4dr	TOWN SEDAN	W2	5	LINCOLN	136	5,010	$4,800	1513
169B	4dr	TOWN SEDAN	S3	5	LINCOLN	136	4,720	$5,200	270
170	2dr	COUPE	W3	2	JUDKINS	136	5,070	$5,800	69
171	4dr	COUPE CONV	AS	4	DIETRICH	136	4,900	$6,000	360
172	4dr	BERLINE SEDAN	W2	7	DIETRICH	136	4,840	$4,900	22
173A	4dr	SEDAN	S3	5	JUDKINS	136	4,840	$5,800	436
173B	4dr	SEDAN	W2	5	LINCOLN	136	5,370	$4,650	34
174	4dr	LIMOUSINE	S3	7	WILLOUGHBY	136	5,180	$6,200	228
175	4dr	BROUGHAM	W2	5	BRUNN	136	4,950	$7,200	50
176A	4dr	SPORT PHAETON	OP	4	LINCOLN	136	4,840	$4,650	92
176B	4dr	SPORT PHAETON	WT	4	LINCOLN	136	4,990	$5,050	42
177	4dr	SPORT TOURING	OP	7	LINCOLN	136	4,940	$4,650	174
178	2dr	SPORT SEDAN	W5	4	LINCOLN	136	5,150	$5,300	42
179	2dr	COUPE	W2	4	LEBARON	136	4,930	$4,800	209
180	4dr	BROUGHAM	AW	5	BRUNN	136	4,900	$7,200	15
181	4dr	COUPE CONV	OP	4	DIETRICH	136	5,000	$6,500	8
182	4dr	SEDAN CONV	W3	5	DIETRICH	136	4,920	$6,900	10
183	2dr	SEDAN	W2	5	LEBARON	136	4,920	$5,000	27
184	4dr	BROUGHAM	AW	7	LEBARON	150	5,140	$7,200	2
122	—	CHASSIS	VR	—	LINCOLN	136	3,300	$3,300	75
122S	—	CUSTOM	VR	—					70
122S	4dr	AERO PHAETON	OP	4			4,600	$9,800	1
150B	—	CHASSIS	VR	—		150	3,450	$3,500	43
								Total	7,632

YEAR 1930, MODEL L, SERIES 185, Serial numbers 61701 thru 66000 (4,300)

TYPE	BODY	STYLE	Ab	SEAT	COACHBUILD	WB	WEIGHT	PRICE	BUILT
165	2dr	ROADSTER AS	W5	4	LINCOLN	136	4,740	$4,600	12
168A	4dr	SEDAN	S3	7	LINCOLN	136	5,165	$4,900	458
168B	4dr	LIMOUSINE	S3	7	LINCOLN	136	5,190	$5,000	329
169A	4dr	TOWN SEDAN	W2	5	LINCOLN	136	4,945	$4,800	169
169B	4dr	TOWN SEDAN	W2	5	LINCOLN	136	5,010	$4,800	285
170	2dr	COUPE	W3	2	JUDKINS	136	4,720	$5,000	40
172	4dr	BERLINE SEDAN	W2	7	WILLOUGHBY	136	5,070	$5,600	72
174	4dr	LIMOUSINE	S3	7	WILLOUGHBY	136	5,180	$5,900	244
175A	4dr	BROUGHAM	W2	5	BRUNN	136	4,950	$7,200	36
175B	4dr	LANDAULET AW	OP	7	BRUNN	136	4,840	$7,200	53
176A	4dr	SPORT PHAETON	OP	4	LINCOLN	136	4,990	$4,200	90
176B	4dr	SPORT PHAETON	OP	4	LINCOLN	136	4,840	$4,800	79
177	4dr	SPORT TOURING	OP	7	LINCOLN	136	4,940	$4,200	8
178	2dr	SPORT SEDAN	W2	4	LINCOLN	136	5,150	$5,300	275
179	2dr	COUPE	W5	4	LEBARON	136	4,930	$4,800	18
180A	4dr	BROUGHAM	AW	5	BRUNN	136	4,920	$6,500	50
180B	4dr	BROUGHAM AW	W3	7	BRUNN	136	4,900	$6,600	42
181	4dr	SEDAN	W3	4	DIETRICH	136	5,000	$6,200	40
182	4dr	SEDAN CONV	W2	5	DIETRICH	136	4,920	$4,500	541
183	2dr	LANDAULET AW	BR	7	LEBARON	136	5,140	$7,100	49
184	4dr	CONV ROADSTER	W3	4	LEBARON	136	4,950	$6,900	100
185	4dr	SEDAN BERLINE	S3	4	JUDKINS	136	5,070	$5,600	100
186	4dr	BROUGHAM AW	W2	5	JUDKINS	136	4,950	$7,000	8
187	4dr	CONV PHAETON	W2	4	DERHAM	136	5,180	$5,900	1
188	4dr	CONV PHAETON	W2	4	DERHAM	136	4,950	$6,000	21
189	2dr	COUPE	W3	2+2	JUDKINS	136	4,720	$6,000	25
190	2dr	COUPE	W3	2	JUDKINS	136	4,850	$4,500	15
191	2dr	SPORT ROADSTER	W3	2+2	LOCKE	136	3,300	$3,600	47
122	—	CHASSIS	VR	—	LINCOLN	136	3,300	$3,600	47
								Total	3,212

YEAR 1931, MODEL K, SERIES 200, Serial numbers 65001 thru 70000 (5,000)

TYPE	BODY	STYLE	Ab	SEAT	COACHBUILD	WB	WEIGHT	PRICE	BUILT
202A	4dr	SPORT PHAETON	DC	5	MURRAY	145	4,940	$4,600	77
202B	4dr	SPORT PHAETON		5	LINCOLN	145	4,850	$4,400	60
203	4dr	SPORT TOURING		7	LINCOLN	145	5,030	$4,400	45
204A	4dr	TOWN SEDAN	S2	5	LINCOLN	145	5,200	$4,600	195
204B	4dr	TOWN SEDAN	S3	5	LINCOLN	145	5,205	$4,600	447
205	4dr	SEDAN		5	LINCOLN	145	5,300	$4,700	552
206	2dr	COUPE		5	LINCOLN	145	5,235	$4,600	225
207A	4dr	SEDAN		7	LINCOLN	145	5,420	$4,900	521
207B	4dr	LIMOUSINE		7	LINCOLN	145	5,370	$5,100	387
207C	4dr	LIMOUSINE		7	LINCOLN	145	5,370	$5,100	14
208A	4dr	CABRIOLET	AN	4	BRUNN	145	5,340	$7,400	15
208B	4dr	CABRIOLET	SC	4	BRUNN	145	5,440	$7,400	15
209	4dr	BROUGHAM	AW	4	BRUNN	145	5,370	$7,200	34
210	4dr	COUPE CONV		4	DIETRICH	145	5,220	$6,400	25
211	4dr	SEDAN		4	DIETRICH	145	5,250	$6,800	65
212	4dr	PHAETON	S2	4	DIETRICH	145	5,020	$6,200	11
213A	4dr	BERLINE	S3	5	DERHAM	145	5,460	$5,800	85
213B	4dr	BERLINE		4	JUDKINS	145	5,370	$5,800	86
214	2dr	ROADSTER	RS	2/4	LEBARON	145	4,800	$4,700	275
215	4dr	LIMOUSINE		6	WILLOUGHBY	145	5,370	$6,100	151
216	4dr	BROUGHAM	PN	7	WILLOUGHBY	145	5,400	$7,400	15
217A	4dr	CABRIOLET	AN	7	LEBARON	145	5,200	$7,100	10
217B	4dr	CABRIOLET	SC	7	LEBARON	145	5,420	$7,300	11
218	2dr	COUPE		2	JUDKINS	145	4,790	$5,800	86
219	2dr	COUPE		2	DIETRICH	145	5,800	$5,200	35
220	—	CHASSIS	SP	—	LINCOLN	150			3
221	—	CHASSIS	SP	—	LINCOLN	155			3
201	—	CHASSIS		—	LINCOLN	145			61
201S	—	CUSTOM	SP	—	LINCOLN	145			26
201R	—	RHD, EXPORT	SP	—	LINCOLN	145			21
								Total	3,556

YEAR 1932, MODEL KA, SERIES 500, Serial numbers 69001 thru 72041 (3,041)

TYPE	BODY	STYLE	Ab	SEAT	COACHBUILD	WB	WEIGHT	PRICE	BUILT
502A	2dr	COUPE		2	LINCOLN	136	5,090	$3,200	43
502B	2dr	COUPE	RS	4	LINCOLN	136	5,220	$3,245	43
503	2dr	ROADSTER CONV		2	DIETRICH	136	5,000	$3,400	40
504	4dr	TOWN SEDAN		5	MURRAY	136	5,330	$3,100	147
505	4dr	SEDAN		5	MURRAY	136	5,430	$3,200	921
506	4dr	VICTORIA		5	MURRAY	136	5,270	$3,200	265
507A	4dr	SEDAN		7	MURRAY	136	5,435	$3,200	508
507B	4dr	LIMOUSINE		7	MURRAY	136	5,520	$3,399	122
508	4dr	PHAETON		3	DIETRICH	136	5,135	$3,000	29
509	4dr	TOURING		7	DIETRICH	136	5,145	$3,200	82
510A	2dr	ROADSTER	RS	2	LINCOLN	136	4,925	$2,900	6
510B	2dr	COUPE		4	LINCOLN	136	5,055	$2,945	6
501	—	CHASSIS	SP	—	LINCOLN	136			5
501R	—	RHD, EXPORT	SP	—	LINCOLN	136			
								Total	2,224

LINCOLN AND CONTINENTAL

YEAR 1932, MODEL KB, SERIES 230, Serial numbers KB1 thru KB1666 (1,666)

TYPE	BODY	STYLE	Ab	SEAT	COACHBUILD	WB	WEIGHT	PRICE	BUILT
232A	4dr	SPORT PHAETON	DC	4	MURPHY	145	5,625	$4,600	30
232B	4dr	SPORT TOURING		4	MURPHY	145	5,600	$4,300	13
233	4dr	TOWN SEDAN		7	LINCOLN	145	5,720	$4,600	24
234A	2dr	TOWN SEDAN	S2	5	LINCOLN	145	5,870	$4,600	123
234B	2dr	SEDAN	S3	5	LINCOLN	145	5,880	$4,400	200
235	4dr	COUPE		5	LINCOLN	145	5,800	$4,400	216
236	2dr	SEDAN		5	LINCOLN	145	5,750	$4,700	83
237A	4dr	LIMOUSINE		7	LINCOLN	145	5,975	$4,700	266
237C	4dr	LIMOUSINE		7	LINCOLN	145	5,990	$4,900	41
238	4dr	CABRIOLET	AW	5	BRUNN	145	5,885	$4,900	135
239	2dr	SPORT BERLINE	AW	5	BRUNN	145	5,920	$7,200	14
240	4dr	SEDAN CONV		5	DIETRICH	145	5,605	$7,000	13
241	4dr	COUPE	RS	2	DIETRICH	145	5,560	$6,500	8
242A	2dr	COUPE	RS	2	DIETRICH	145	5,330	$6,400	20
242B	2dr	BERLINE	S2	5	DIETRICH	145	5,360	$5,000	9
243A	4dr	BERLINE	S3	5	JUDKINS	145	5,860	$5,150	8
243B	4dr	COUPE	RS	4	JUDKINS	145	5,860	$5,700	37
244A	2dr	LIMOUSINE		7	JUDKINS	145	5,610	$5,700	12
244B	4dr	BROUGHAM	PN	4	WILLOUGHBY	145	5,595	$5,350	11
245	4dr	LIMOUSINE		7	WILLOUGHBY	145	5,950	$5,100	64
246	4dr	BROUGHAM	PN	4	WILLOUGHBY	145	5,790	$7,100	4
247	4dr	VICTORIA CONV		4	WATERHOUSE	145	5,220	$5,900	10
248	2dr	ROADSTER CONV	RS	4	LEBARON	145	5,535	$4,600	112
249	2dr	SPORT ROADSTER	RS	2/4	MURPHY	145	5,605	$6,800	3
250	4dr	SEDAN		5	LINCOLN	150			18
231	4dr	SEDAN	SP	7	LINCOLN	145			100
231S	—	CHASSIS		—	LINCOLN	145			8
231R	—	RHD, EXPORT		—	LINCOLN	145			10
								Total	1,623

YEAR 1933, MODEL KA, SERIES 511, Serial numbers KA1 thru KA1140 (1,140)

TYPE	BODY	STYLE	Ab	SEAT	COACHBUILD	WB	WEIGHT	PRICE	BUILT
512A	2dr	COUPE		5	LINCOLN	136	5,200	$3,200	22
512B	2dr	ROADSTER CONV	RS	2	LINCOLN	136	5,250	$3,350	22
513A	2dr	ROADSTER CONV	RS	4	LINCOLN	136	5,050	$3,200	42
513B	4dr	TOWN SEDAN		5	LINCOLN	136	5,050	$3,245	43
514	4dr	SEDAN		5	LINCOLN	136	4,954	$3,200	201
515	2dr	VICTORIA		5	LINCOLN	136	5,270	$3,250	320
516	4dr	SEDAN		7	LINCOLN	136	5,159	$3,300	109
517A	4dr	LIMOUSINE		7	LINCOLN	136	5,184	$3,350	190
517B	4dr	PHAETON	DC	5	LINCOLN	136	5,040	$3,200	111
518A	4dr	PHAETON		5	LINCOLN	136	5,040		12
518B	4dr	PHAETON	RS	5	LINCOLN	136	4,750	$2,900	10
519	2dr	ROADSTER	RS	2	LINCOLN	136	4,780	$3,050	6
520A	2dr	ROADSTER		2	LINCOLN	136			7
520B	—	CHASSIS	SP	—	LINCOLN	136			23
511S	—	CUSTOM	SP	—	LINCOLN	136			4
511R	—	RHD, EXPORT		—	LINCOLN	136			
								Total	1,140

YEAR 1933, MODEL KB, SERIES 251, Serial numbers KB2001 thru KB2604 (604)

TYPE	BODY	STYLE	Ab	SEAT	COACHBUILD	WB	WEIGHT	PRICE	BUILT
252A	4dr	SPORT PHAETON	DC	4	LINCOLN	145	5,500	$4,500	9
252B	4dr	SPORT PHAETON		4	LINCOLN	145	5,500	$4,300	6
253	4dr	SPORT TOURING		7	LINCOLN	145	5,500	$4,500	6
254A	2dr	TOWN SEDAN	S2	5	LINCOLN	145	5,590	$4,500	39
254B	4dr	TOWN SEDAN	S3	5	LINCOLN	145	5,600	$4,400	41
255	4dr	SEDAN		5	LINCOLN	145	5,790	$4,700	52
256	2dr	COUPE VICTORIA		5	LINCOLN	145	5,710	$4,900	18
257A	4dr	SEDAN		7	LINCOLN	145	5,850	$6,900	100
257B	4dr	LIMOUSINE		7	BRUNN	145	5,685	$7,220	4
258C	4dr	CABRIOLET	NC	5	BRUNN	145	5,685	$6,850	13
258D	4dr	CABRIOLET	SC	5	BRUNN	145	5,730	$6,400	37
259B	4dr	BROUGHAM	AW	7	BRUNN	145	5,470	$6,600	15
260	4dr	VICTORIA CONV		4	WATERHOUSE	145	5,600	$5,000	25
261	2dr	SEDAN CONV		4	DIETRICH	145	5,200	$5,400	15
262	4dr	COUPE		5	DIETRICH	145	5,680	$5,500	12
263	2dr	SPORT BERLINE		4	DIETRICH	145	5,710	$5,500	12
263A	2dr	BERLINE	S2	5	JUDKINS	145	5,710	$5,500	12
263B	4dr	BERLINE	S3	5	JUDKINS	145	5,720	$5,000	30
264D	2dr	COUPE		2	JUDKINS	145	5,840	$5,900	2
265B	4dr	LIMOUSINE		7	WILLOUGHBY	145	5,850	$7,100	24
266B	4dr	BROUGHAM	PN	4	WILLOUGHBY	145	5,490	$4,600	22
267B	2dr	ROADSTER CONV		2/4	LEBARON	145	5,680	$4,900	1
242C	2dr	COUPE		2	DIETRICH	145	5,780	$5,800	4
308	—	CHASSIS	SP	—	JUDKINS				3
221	—	CUSTOM		—	LINCOLN	145		—155	
251	—	CHASSIS	SP	—	LINCOLN	145			
251R	—	RHD, EXPORT		—	LINCOLN				
								Total	604

(Total 1932 KA and ... KB 3,847)
(Total 1933 KA and KB ... 1,744)

YEAR 1934, MODEL KA, SERIES 521, Serial numbers KA1501 thru KA3176 (1,676)

TYPE	BODY	STYLE	Ab	SEAT	COACHBUILD	WB	WEIGHT	PRICE	BUILT
522a	2dr	COUPE		2	LINCOLN	136	4,989	$3,250	30
522b	2dr	COUPE		4	LINCOLN	136	4,959	$3,200	30
523A	2dr	ROADSTER CONV	RS	2	LINCOLN	136	4,924	$3,400	36
523B	2dr	ROADSTER CONV	RS	4	LINCOLN	136	4,934	$3,400	36
524	4dr	TOWN SEDAN		5	LINCOLN	136	5,140	$3,450	450
525	4dr	SEDAN		5	LINCOLN	136	5,044	$3,400	425
526	2dr	VICTORIA		5	LINCOLN	136	5,029	$3,400	115
527A	4dr	SEDAN		7	LINCOLN	136	5,203	$3,500	275
527B	4dr	LIMOUSINE		7	LINCOLN	136	5,228	$3,550	175
531A	4dr	PHAETON CONV		5	LINCOLN	136	5,024	$3,900	75
521	—	CHASSIS		—	LINCOLN	136			21
521R	—	RHD, EXPORT	SP	—	LINCOLN	136			8
								Total	1,676

YEAR 1934, MODEL KB, SERIES 270, Serial numbers KB3001 thru KB3744 (744)

TYPE	BODY	STYLE	Ab	SEAT	COACHBUILD	WB	WEIGHT	PRICE	BUILT
272	4dr	SPORT PHAETON	DC	7	LINCOLN	145	5,500	$4,400	2
273	4dr	SPORT TOURING		7	LINCOLN	145	5,220	$4,200	20
277A	4dr	SEDAN		7	LINCOLN	145	5,510	$4,500	210
277B	4dr	LIMOUSINE		7	LINCOLN	145	5,570	$4,700	215
278A	4dr	CABRIOLET	SC	5	BRUNN	145	5,316	$6,800	6
278B	4dr	CABRIOLET	NC	5	BRUNN	145	5,511	$6,600	7
279	4dr	BROUGHAM	AW	5	BRUNN	145	5,480	$6,800	15
280	2dr	COUPE CONV		5	BRUNN	145	5,045	$5,600	25
281	4dr	SEDAN CONV		5	DIETRICH	145	5,330	$5,600	25
282	4dr	LIMOUSINE		7	JUDKINS	145	5,570	$5,800	27
283A	4dr	BERLINE	S2	4	JUDKINS	145	5,710	$5,400	37
283B	4dr	BERLINE	S3	4	JUDKINS	145	5,740	$5,600	17
285	4dr	LIMOUSINE		7	WILLOUGHBY	145	5,605	$5,600	77
287	2dr	ROADSTER CONV		2/4	LEBARON	145	5,085	$4,400	27
271	—	CHASSIS		—	LINCOLN	145		$3,100	12
271C	—	CHASSIS		—	LINCOLN	157			10
271S	—	CUSTOM	SP	—	LINCOLN	145			7
271R	—	RHD, EXPORT	SP	—	LINCOLN	145			5
								Total	744

(Total 1934 KA and KB ... 2,420)

YEAR 1935, MODEL K, SERIES 540, Serial numbers K3501 thru K4919 (1,419)

TYPE	BODY	STYLE	Ab	SEAT	COACHBUILD	WB	WEIGHT	PRICE	BUILT
542	2dr	ROADSTER CONV	RS	2/4	LEBARON	136	5,030	$4,700	30
543	4dr	SEDAN	S2	5	LINCOLN	136	5,385	$4,300	170
544	4dr	SEDAN	S3	5	LINCOLN	136	5,680	$4,300	268
545	2dr	COUPE		2	LINCOLN	145	5,230	$4,400	44
546	4dr	PHAETON CONV		5	LINCOLN	146	5,665	$5,000	20
547	2dr	VICTORIA CONV		5	LEBARON	136	5,135	$5,500	15
548	2dr	COUPE		2	LEBARON	136	5,030	$4,600	23
541	—	CHASSIS		—	LINCOLN	136		$2,700	1
541R	—	RHD, EXPORT	SP	—	LINCOLN	136			5
								Total	576

YEAR 1935, MODEL K, SERIES 300, Serial numbers K3501 thru K4919 (1,419)

TYPE	BODY	STYLE	Ab	SEAT	COACHBUILD	WB	WEIGHT	PRICE	BUILT
302	4dr	SPORT TOURING		7	LINCOLN	145	5,225	$4,200	15
303A	4dr	SEDAN		5	LINCOLN	145	5,630	$4,600	351
303B	4dr	LIMOUSINE		7	LINCOLN	145	5,935	$4,600	282
304A	4dr	CABRIOLET	SC	5	BRUNN	145	5,415	$6,600	13
304B	4dr	CABRIOLET	NC	5	BRUNN	145	5,505	$6,700	13
305	4dr	BROUGHAM	AW	5	BRUNN	145	5,530	$6,700	10
307	2dr	SEDAN CONV		5	LEBARON	145	5,360	$6,500	20
308	4dr	BERLINE	S2	7	JUDKINS	145	5,645	$5,700	18
309A	4dr	BERLINE	S3	5	JUDKINS	145	5,545	$5,500	34
309B	4dr	COUPE		5	JUDKINS	145	5,555	$5,500	13
310	4dr	LIMOUSINE		7	WILLOUGHBY	145	5,695	$5,700	40
311	2dr	SPORT SEDAN		5	WILLOUGHBY	145	5,075	$6,800	8
301	—	CHASSIS		—	LINCOLN	145		$3,200	8
301S	—	CUSTOM	SP	—	LINCOLN			—145	
301R	—	RHD, EXPORT	SP	—	LINCOLN	145			13
								Total	843

(Total 1935 K/540 and K/300 ... 1,419)

275

The Early Years

YEAR 1936, MODEL K, SERIES 320, Serial numbers K5501 thru K7014 (1,514)

TYPE	BODY	STYLE	Ab	SEAT	COACHBUILD	WB	WEIGHT	PRICE	BUILT
323	4dr	SPORT TOURING		7	LINCOLN	145	5,276	$4,200	8
324A	4dr	SEDAN	S2	7	LINCOLN	136	5,426	$4,300	103
324B	4dr	SEDAN	S3	5	LINCOLN	136	5,476	$4,400	297
326	2dr	COUPE		5	LINCOLN	136	5,266	$4,200	30
327A	4dr	SEDAN		5	LINCOLN	145	5,591	$4,600	368
327B	4dr	SEDAN		7	LINCOLN	145	5,591	$4,600	370
328	4dr	LIMOUSINE		7	LINCOLN	145	5,591	$5,500	10
329A	4dr	VICTORIA CONV		5	BRUNN	136	5,176	$6,600	10
329B	4dr	CABRIOLET	NC	5	BRUNN	136	5,511	$6,600	10
330	2dr	ROADSTER CONV	RS	2/4	LEBARON	136	5,491	$4,700	20
331	4dr	BROUGHAM		5	BRUNN	145	5,571	$6,700	20
332	4dr	COUPE	RS	2/4	LEBARON	136	5,126	$6,700	20
333	4dr	PHAETON CONV		5	LEBARON	145	5,296	$5,500	30
334	2dr	SEDAN CONV		5	LEBARON	136	5,600	$5,500	15
335	4dr	LIMOUSINE		7	JUDKINS	145	5,605	$5,400	26
336	4dr	BERLINE		5	JUDKINS	145	5,495	$5,400	51
337A	4dr	BERLINE		7	JUDKINS	145	5,671	$5,400	13
337B	4dr	LIMOUSINE		7	WILLOUGHBY	145	6,661	$5,800	62
339	4dr	LIMOUSINE		5	WILLOUGHBY	145	5,561	$5,700	11
341	4dr	SPORT SEDAN			BRUNN	145		$6,800	9
321	—	CHASSIS			LINCOLN	145	—	—	6
322	—	CHASSIS	SP		LINCOLN	145	—	—	21
321S	—	CUSTOM	SP		LINCOLN	145	—	—	4
322R	—	RHD, EXPORT	SP		LINCOLN	136	—	—	15
321R	—	RHD, EXPORT			LINCOLN	145	—	—	
								Total	1,514

YEAR 1937, MODEL K, SERIES 350, Serial numbers K7501 thru K8490 (990)

TYPE	BODY	STYLE	Ab	SEAT	COACHBUILD	WB	WEIGHT	PRICE	BUILT
353	4dr	SPORT TOURING		7	LINCOLN	145	5,950	$5,550	7
354A	4dr	SEDAN	S2	5	LINCOLN	136	5,492	$4,450	48
354B	4dr	SEDAN	S3	5	LINCOLN	136	5,500	$4,450	136
356	2dr	COUPE		5	WILLOUGHBY	136	5,940	$4,750	6
357A	4dr	SEDAN		5	LINCOLN	145	5,697	$4,850	212
357B	4dr	SEDAN		7	LINCOLN	145	5,905	$4,850	248
358	4dr	LIMOUSINE		7	LINCOLN	145	5,660	$5,550	13
359A	4dr	VICTORIA CONV	NC	5	BRUNN	136	5,960	$6,650	10
359B	4dr	CABRIOLET	SC	5	BRUNN	136	6,020	$6,750	7
360	2dr	ROADSTER CONV	RS	2/4	LEBARON	136	5,490	$4,950	15
361	4dr	BROUGHAM		7	BRUNN	145	5,995	$6,750	29
362	2dr	COUPE	RS	2/4	LEBARON	136	5,172	$4,950	24
363A	4dr	SEDAN CONV	WP	5	LEBARON	145	5,880	$5,650	21
363B	4dr	SEDAN CONV		5	LEBARON	136	5,980	$5,950	37
365	4dr	LIMOUSINE		7	JUDKINS	145	5,732	$5,650	47
367A	4dr	BERLINE	S2	5	JUDKINS	145	5,880	$5,750	27
367B	4dr	BERLINE	S3	7	JUDKINS	145	5,682	$5,770	19
369	4dr	LIMOUSINE		5	WILLOUGHBY	145	6,115	$7,050	60
371	4dr	SPORT SEDAN		7	WILLOUGHBY	145	5,590	$6,850	6
373	4dr	BROUGHAM	PN	7	WILLOUGHBY	145	5,840	$7,050	4
375	4dr	CABRIOLET		7	BRUNN	145	5,640	$6,950	10
351	—	CHASSIS			LINCOLN	145	—	—	2
352	—	CHASSIS			LINCOLN	136	—	—	2
								Total	990

YEAR 1938, MODEL K, SERIES 400, Serial numbers K9001 thru 9450 (450)

TYPE	BODY	STYLE	Ab	SEAT	COACHBUILD	WB	WEIGHT	PRICE	BUILT
403	4dr	SPORT TOURING		7	WILLOUGHBY	145	5,557	$5,900	5
404A	4dr	SEDAN	S2	5	LINCOLN	136	5,527	$4,900	9
404B	4dr	SEDAN	S3	5	LINCOLN	136	5,537	$4,900	49
406	2dr	COUPE		5	WILLOUGHBY	136	5,407	$5,900	4
407A	4dr	SEDAN		5	LINCOLN	145	5,672	$5,100	78
407B	4dr	SEDAN		7	LINCOLN	145	5,600	$5,200	91
408	4dr	LIMOUSINE		7	LINCOLN	145	5,762	$5,900	8
409A	4dr	VICTORIA CONV	SC	5	BRUNN	136	5,322	$7,000	6
409B	4dr	CABRIOLET	NC	5	BRUNN	136	5,716	$7,000	5
410	2dr	ROADSTER CONV	RS	2/4	LEBARON	136	5,696	$6,300	8
411	4dr	BROUGHAM		7	BRUNN	145	5,136	$7,000	13
412	2dr	COUPE	RS	2/4	LEBARON	136	5,806	$5,300	12
413A	4dr	SEDAN CONV		5	LEBARON	136	5,227	$5,800	15
413B	4dr	SEDAN CONV	WP	5	LEBARON	145	5,126	$6,000	7
415	4dr	LIMOUSINE		7	JUDKINS	145	5,462	$6,000	11
417A	4dr	BERLINE	S2	5	JUDKINS	145	5,572	$6,100	11
417B	4dr	BERLINE	S3	7	JUDKINS	145	5,742	$6,000	19
419	4dr	LIMOUSINE		5	WILLOUGHBY	145	5,562	$6,100	11
421	4dr	SPORT SEDAN		7	WILLOUGHBY	145	5,632	$6,200	46
423	4dr	BROUGHAM	PN	7	WILLOUGHBY	145	5,826	$7,000	4
425A	4dr	CABRIOLET	NC	7	BRUNN	145	5,716	$7,400	6
425B	4dr	CABRIOLET	SC	7	BRUNN	145	5,840	$6,950	9
401	—	CHASSIS			LINCOLN	145	5,640	$6,950	9
402	—	CHASSIS			LINCOLN	136	—	—	0
401S	—	CUSTOM	SP		LINCOLN	145	—	—	25
								Total	450

YEAR 1939–40, MODEL K, SERIES 400, Serial numbers K9451 thru K9674 (224)

TYPE	BODY	STYLE	Ab	SEAT	COACHBUILD	WB	WEIGHT	PRICE	BUILT
403	4dr	SPORT TOURING		7	WILLOUGHBY	145	5,276	$4,800	1
404A	4dr	SEDAN	S2	5	LINCOLN	136	5,735	$4,800	12
404B	4dr	SEDAN	S3	5	LINCOLN	136	5,740	$5,800	22
406	2dr	COUPE		5	LINCOLN	136	5,615	$5,000	1
407A	4dr	SEDAN		5	LINCOLN	145	5,880	$5,100	50
407B	4dr	SEDAN		7	LINCOLN	145	5,970	$5,800	78
408	4dr	LIMOUSINE		7	LINCOLN	145	5,530	$5,800	2
409A	4dr	VICTORIA CONV	SC	5	BRUNN	136	6,030	$6,800	1
409B	4dr	CABRIOLET	NC	5	BRUNN	136	6,030	$6,900	1
410	2dr	ROADSTER CONV	RS	2/4	LEBARON	136	5,505	$5,200	2
411	4dr	BROUGHAM		7	BRUNN	145	6,120	$6,900	4
412	2dr	COUPE	RS	2/4	LEBARON	136	5,425	$5,200	3
413A	4dr	SEDAN CONV		5	LEBARON	145	5,670	$5,700	6
413B	4dr	SEDAN CONV	WP	5	LEBARON	145	5,780	$5,900	6
415	4dr	LIMOUSINE		7	JUDKINS	145	5,950	$6,200	2
417A	4dr	BERLINE	S2	5	JUDKINS	145	5,770	$5,900	2
417B	4dr	BERLINE	S3	7	JUDKINS	145	5,840	$6,000	1
419	4dr	LIMOUSINE		5	WILLOUGHBY	145	6,140	$6,100	4
421	4dr	SPORT SEDAN		7	WILLOUGHBY	145	6,030	$6,900	1
423	4dr	BROUGHAM	PN	7	WILLOUGHBY	145	5,840	$7,400	1
425A	4dr	CABRIOLET	NC	7	BRUNN	145	5,870	$7,100	2
425B	4dr	CABRIOLET	SC	7	BRUNN	145	5,890	$7,100	2
401	—	CHASSIS			LINCOLN	145	—	—	0
402	—	CHASSIS			LINCOLN	136	—	—	0
401S	—	CUSTOM	SP		LINCOLN	145	—	—	24
								Total	224

APPENDIX III. LINCOLN MODEL H 1936-1948

Abbreviations: AS 2-Passenger, Auxiliary Seats; BC Brunn, Custom; Conv Convertible; HT Sport, Hardtop; RH Right-Hand Drive; SP Special Order; WP w/Partition; W2 2-Window; W3 3-Window

YEAR 1936, MODEL H, SERIES 901, Serial Numbers H1 thru H15528

TYPE	MODEL	SN	BODY	STYLE	Ab	SEAT	WB	HT"	LGTH"	WEIGHT	PRICE	BUILT
902	ZEPHYR	H	4dr	SEDAN	W3	6	122	69	202.5	3,349	$1,320	13,983
902	ZEPHYR	H	4dr	TOWN-SEDAN	WP	6	122	69	202.5	3,379	$1,425	47
903	ZEPHYR	H	2dr	COUPE-SEDAN	W2	6	122	69	202.5	3,289	$1,275	1,498
											Total	15,528

YEAR 1937, MODEL H, SERIES HB, Serial numbers H15529 thru H45529

TYPE	MODEL	SN	BODY	STYLE	Ab	SEAT	WB	HT"	LGTH"	WEIGHT	PRICE	BUILT
700	ZEPHYR	HB	2dr	COUPE-SEDAN	W2	6	122	69	202.5	3,329	$1,240	1,500
720	ZEPHYR	HB	2dr	COUPE	W3	6	122	69	202.5	3,214	$1,165	5,199
730	ZEPHYR	HB	4dr	SEDAN	W3	6	122	69	202.5	3,369	$1,265	23,162
737	ZEPHYR	HB	4dr	TOWN-LIMO	WP	6	122	69	202.5	3,398	$1,425	139
											Total	30,000

YEAR 1938, MODEL H, SERIES 86, Serial numbers H45530 thru H64640

TYPE	MODEL	SN	BODY	STYLE	Ab	SEAT	WB	HT"	LGTH"	WEIGHT	PRICE	BUILT
700	ZEPHYR	86H	2dr	COUPE-SEDAN	W2	6	125	63.3	210	3,409	$1,355	800
720	ZEPHYR	86H	2dr	COUPE	W3	3	125	63.3	210	3,294	$1,295	2,600
730	ZEPHYR	86H	4dr	SEDAN	W3	6	125	63.3	210	3,444	$1,375	14,520
737	ZEPHYR	86H	4dr	TOWN-LIMO	W3	6	125	63.3	210	3,474	$1,550	130
740	ZEPHYR	86H	4dr	CONVERTIBLE	W2	6	125	63.3	210	3,724	$1,740	461
760	ZEPHYR	86H	2dr	CONVERTIBLE	W3	5	125	63.3	210	3,489	$1,650	600
											Total	19,111

YEAR 1939, MODEL H, SERIES 96, Serial numbers H64641 thru H85640

TYPE	MODEL	SN	BODY	STYLE	Ab	SEAT	WB	HT"	LGTH"	WEIGHT	PRICE	BUILT
H-70	ZEPHYR	96H	2dr	COUPE-SEDAN	W2	6	125	69.5	210	3,600	$1,330	800
H-72	ZEPHYR	96H	2dr	COUPE	W3	3	125	69.5	210	3,520	$1,320	2,500
H-73	ZEPHYR	96H	4dr	SEDAN	W3	6	125	69.5	210	3,620	$1,360	16,663
H-22	ZEPHYR	96H	4dr	TOWN-LIMO	W3	6	125	69.5	210	3,670	$1,700	95
H-74	ZEPHYR	96H	4dr	CONVERTIBLE	W2	6	125	69.5	210	3,900	$1,790	302
H-76	ZEPHYR	96H	2dr	CONVERTIBLE	W3	5	125	69.5	210	3,790	$1,700	638
H-56	ZEPHYR	96H	2dr	CABRIOLET	W3	5	125	62	214	4,500	$1,700	2
											Total	21,000

YEAR 1940, MODEL H, SERIES 06, Serial Numbers H85641 thru H107687

TYPE	MODEL	SN	BODY	STYLE	Ab	SEAT	WB	HT"	LGTH"	WEIGHT	PRICE	BUILT
72A	ZEPHYR	06H	2dr	COUPE	W3	3	125	69.5	209.5	3,375	$1,360	1,256
72B	ZEPHYR	06H	2dr	COUPE AS	W3	5	125	69.5	209.5	3,465	$1,400	316
73	ZEPHYR	06H	4dr	SEDAN	W3	6	125	69.5	209.5	3,535	$1,450	15,764
76	ZEPHYR	06H	2dr	CONVERTIBLE	W3	5	125	69.5	209.5	3,635	$1,770	700
77	ZEPHYR	06H	2dr	CLUB COUPE	W3	5	125	69.5	209.5	3,465	$1,400	3,500
22	ZEPHYR	06H	4dr	TOWN-LIMO	WP	6	125	69.5	209.5	3,575	$1,740	98
—	ZEPHYR	06H	4dr	SEDAN	SP	6	125	69.5	209.5	3,790	—	4
H-32	CUSTOM	06H	4dr	LIMOUSINE	WP	6	138	70.5	225.3	3,600	$2,751	4
H-36	ZEPHYR	06H	2dr	TOWN CAR	BC	6	138	70.5	225.3	3,790	$1,700	3
56	CONT'L	06H	2dr	CABRIOLET	*	5	125	62	209.8	3,615	$2,840	350
57	CONT'L	06H	2dr	COUPE	HT	5	125	62	209.8	3,700	$2,840	54
											Total	22,049

YEAR 1941, MODEL H, SERIES 16, Serial Numbers H107688 thru H129690

TYPE	MODEL	SN	BODY	STYLE	Ab	SEAT	WB	HT"	LGTH"	WEIGHT	PRICE	BUILT
72A	ZEPHYR	16H	2dr	COUPE	W3	3	125	69.5	210	3,560	$1,432	972
72B	ZEPHYR	16H	2dr	COUPE AS	W3	5	125	63.3	210	3,580	$1,464	178
73	ZEPHYR	16H	4dr	SEDAN	W3	6	125	63.3	210	3,710	$1,493	14,469
76	ZEPHYR	16H	2dr	CONVERTIBLE	W3	5	125	63.3	210	3,840	$1,801	725
77	ZEPHYR	16H	2dr	CLUB COUPE	W3	5	125	63.3	210	3,640	$1,493	3,750
—	ZEPHYR	16H	4dr	SEDAN	SP	6	125	63.3	210	3,790	—	4
31	CUSTOM	168H	4dr	SEDAN	W3	8	138	70.5	225.3	4,250	$2,622	355
32	CUSTOM	168H	4dr	LIMOUSINE	WP	8	138	70.5	225.3	4,270	$2,751	295
36	CUSTOM	168H	4dr	TOWN CAR	BC	8	138	70.5	225.3	—	—	5
56	CONT'L	16H	2dr	CABRIOLET	W3	5	125	62	209.8	3,860	$2,865	400
57	CONT'L	16H	2dr	COUPE	HT	5	125	62	209.8	3,890	$2,812	850
											Total	22,003

YEAR 1942, MODEL H, SERIES 26, Serial numbers H129691 thru H136254

TYPE	MODEL	SN	BODY	STYLE	Ab	SEAT	WB	HT"	LGTH"	WEIGHT	PRICE	BUILT
72A	ZEPHYR	26H	2dr	COUPE	W3	3	125	68.5	218.7	3,790	$1,748	273
72B	ZEPHYR	26H	2dr	COUPE AS	W3	5	125	68.5	218.7	3,800	$1,775	—
73	ZEPHYR	26H	4dr	SEDAN	W3	6	125	68.5	218.7	3,980	$1,801	4,412
76	ZEPHYR	26H	2dr	CONVERTIBLE	W3	5	125	68.5	218.7	4,190	$2,274	191
77	ZEPHYR	26H	2dr	CLUB COUPE	W3	5	125	68.5	218.7	3,810	$1,801	1,236
—	ZEPHYR	26H	4dr	SEDAN	SP	6	125	68.5	218.7	3,790	—	3
31	CUSTOM	268H	4dr	SEDAN	W3	8	138	70.5	234	4,380	$3,117	47
32	CUSTOM	268H	4dr	LIMOUSINE	WP	8	138	70.5	234	4,400	$3,248	66
56	CONT'L	26H	2dr	CABRIOLET	W3	5	125	63.1	217	4,020	$3,174	136
57	CONT'L	26H	2dr	COUPE	HT	5	125	63.1	217	4,060	$3,174	200
											Total	6,564

YEAR 1946, MODEL H, SERIES 66, Serial Numbers H136255 thru H152839

TYPE	MODEL	SN	BODY	STYLE	Ab	SEAT	WB	HT"	LGTH"	WEIGHT	PRICE	BUILT
73	LINCOLN	66H	4dr	SEDAN	W3	6	125	68.5	218.7	4,015	$2,337	16,179
76	LINCOLN	66H	2dr	CONVERTIBLE	W3	5	125	68.5	218.7	4,245	$2,883	—
77	LINCOLN	66H	2dr	CLUB COUPE	W3	5	125	68.5	218.7	3,915	$2,318	—
56	CONT'L	66H	2dr	CABRIOLET	W3	5	125	63.1	217	4,135	$4,474	201
57	CONT'L	66H	2dr	COUPE	HT	5	125	63.1	217	4,125	$4,392	265
											Total	16,645

YEAR 1947, MODEL H, SERIES 76, Serial numbers 7H152840 thru 7H174289

TYPE	MODEL	SN	BODY	STYLE	Ab	SEAT	WB	HT"	LGTH"	WEIGHT	PRICE	BUILT
73	LINCOLN	76H	4dr	SEDAN	W3	6	125	68.5	218.7	4,015	$2,554	19,891
76	LINCOLN	76H	2dr	CONVERTIBLE	W3	5	125	68.5	218.7	4,245	$3,143	—
77	LINCOLN	76H	2dr	CLUB COUPE	W3	5	125	68.5	218.7	3,915	$2,533	—
56	CONT'L	76H	2dr	CABRIOLET	W3	5	125	63.1	217	4,135	$4,746	738
57	CONT'L	76H	2dr	COUPE	HT	5	125	63.1	217	4,125	$4,662	831
											Total	21,460

YEAR 1948, MODEL H, SERIES 876, Serial numbers 8H174290 thru 8H182129

TYPE	MODEL	SN	BODY	STYLE	Ab	SEAT	WB	HT"	LGTH"	WEIGHT	PRICE	BUILT
73	LINCOLN	876H	4dr	SEDAN	W3	6	125	68.5	218.7	4,015	$2,554	4,820
76	LINCOLN	876H	2dr	CONVERTIBLE	W3	5	125	68.5	218.7	4,245	$3,143	—
77	LINCOLN	876H	2dr	CLUB COUPE	W3	5	125	68.5	218.7	3,915	$2,533	—
56	CONT'L	876H	2dr	CABRIOLET	W3	5	125	63.1	217	4,135	$4,746	452
57	CONT'L	876H	2dr	COUPE	HT	5	125	63.1	217	4,125	$4,662	847
											Total	6,119

REMARKS:
Right-Hand drive units shipped 1936 Sedans 908, Town-Sedans 7, 2dr-Sedans 25.
Disassembled overseas units 1936 were 302; 1937 were 477; 1938 were 720; 1939 were 282; 1940 were 259; 1941 were 176; 1942 were 48.
1937 HB730 Sedans, two were built into Convertible Sedan prototypes.
1938 730-B & 1939 H-73-B were Dluxe Sedans with custom interior appointments.
1939 H-74 Convertible Sedans, two were built into Continental Cabriolets.
1940 06H-56 Continental Cabriolets, 25 were built in calendar year 1938.
1941 16H Body width 73.38 inches. 1941 two 16H-56 and a 16H-57 were scraped.
1942 26H Body width was increased to 77.82 inches.
Continental 56 and 57 units 1940 were 404; 1941 were 1,250; 1942 were 336.
Continental 56 and 57 units 1946 were 466; 1947 were 1,569; 1948 were 1,299.
Total Continental 56 and 57 production 1939 thru 1948 was 5,326 units.

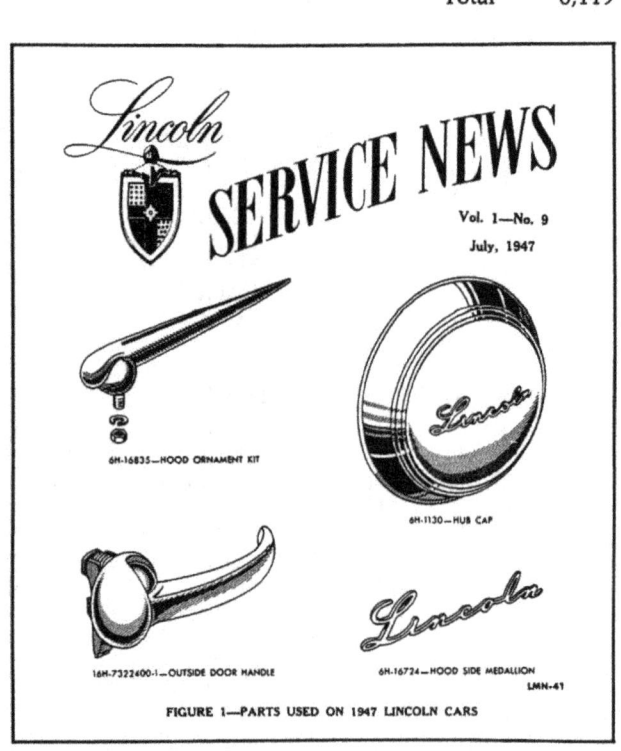

FIGURE 1—PARTS USED ON 1947 LINCOLN CARS

APPENDIX IV. LINCOLN MODELS EL & EH 1949-1951

Abbreviations: CONV Convertible; H Heavy; LA California; LP Lincoln Plant, Michigan; NB Notch Back; TB Torpedo Back; L Light, little; SL St. Louis

YEAR 1949, MODEL EL, SERIES 9EL Serial Numbers 9EL1 thru 9EL73559

TYPE	MODEL	BODY	STYLE	Ab	SEAT	WB	WEIGHT	PRICE	BUILT
72	LINCOLN	2dr	CLUB COUPE	NB	6	121	3,959	$2,527	38,384
74	LINCOLN	4dr	SPORT SEDAN	NB	6	121	4,009	$2,575	
76	LINCOLN	2dr	CONV COUPE		6	121	4,224	$3,116	————
								Total	38,384

YEAR 1949, MODEL EH, SERIES 9EH Serial Numbers 9EH1 thru 9EH73563

TYPE	MODEL	BODY	STYLE	Ab	SEAT	WB	WEIGHT	PRICE	BUILT
72	COSMOPOLITAN	2dr	CLUB COUPE	NB	6	125	4,194	$3,186	7,685
73	COSMOPOLITAN	4dr	TOWN SEDAN	TB	6	125	4,274	$3,238	7,302
74	COSMOPOLITAN	4dr	SPORT SEDAN	NB	6	125	4,259	$3,238	18,906
76	COSMOPOLITAN	2dr	CONV COUPE		6	125	4,459	$3,948	1,230
								Total	35,123
								Total Model Year	73,507

YEAR 1950, MODEL EL, SERIES 0EL Serial Numbers 50LP5001L thru 50LP20082L
and Serial Numbers 50LA5001L thru 50LA7252L

TYPE	MODEL	BODY	STYLE	Ab	SEAT	WB	WEIGHT	PRICE	BUILT
L-72	LINCOLN	2dr	CLUB COUPE	NB	6	121	4,090	$2,529	5,748
L-72C	LINCOLN	2dr	LIDO COUPE	NB	6	121	4,145	$2,721	
L-74	LINCOLN	4dr	SPORT SEDAN	NB	6	121	4,115	$2,576	11,741
								Total	17,489

YEAR 1950, MODEL EH, SERIES 0EH Serial Numbers 50LP5001H thru 50LP15701H

TYPE	MODEL	BODY	STYLE	Ab	SEAT	WB	WEIGHT	PRICE	BUILT
H-72	COSMOPOLITAN	2dr	CLUB COUPE	NB	6	125	4,375	$3,187	1,315
H-72C	COSMOPOLITAN	2dr	CAPRI COUPE	NB	6	125	4,385	$3,406	509
H-74	COSMOPOLITAN	4dr	SPORT SEDAN	NB	6	125	4,410	$3,240	8,332
H-76	COSMOPOLITAN	2dr	CONV COUPE		6	125	4,640	$3,950	536
								Total	10,692
								Total Model Year	28,181

YEAR 1951, MODEL EL, SERIES 1EL Serial Numbers 51LP5001L thru 51LP19317L
and Serial Numbers 51LA5001L thru 51LA7114L

TYPE	MODEL	BODY	STYLE	Ab	SEAT	WB	WEIGHT	PRICE	BUILT
L-72B	LINCOLN	2dr	CLUB COUPE	NB	6	121	4,065	$2,505	4,482
L-72C	LINCOLN	2dr	LIDO COUPE	NB	6	121	4,100	$2,720	
L-74	LINCOLN	4dr	SPORT SEDAN	NB	6	121	4,130	$2,553	12,279
								Total	16,761

YEAR 1951, MODEL EH, SERIES 1EH Serial Numbers 51LP5001H thru 51LP20813H

TYPE	MODEL	BODY	STYLE	Ab	SEAT	WB	WEIGHT	PRICE	BUILT
H-72B	COSMOPOLITAN	2dr	CLUB COUPE	NB	6	125	4,340	$3,129	1,476
H-72C	COSMOPOLITAN	2dr	CAPRI COUPE	NB	6	125	4,360	$3,350	1,251
H-74	COSMOPOLITAN	4dr	SPORT SEDAN	NB	6	125	4,415	$3,182	12,229
H-76	COSMOPOLITAN	2dr	CONV COUPE		6	125	4,615	$3,891	857
								Total	15,813
								Total Model Year	32,574

GENERAL INFORMATION
FOLLOWING IS A DIAGRAM OF THE BODY PARTS NUMBERING SYSTEM

```
              BODY TYPE        BODY GROUP
                    │           │
                    │           │   BODY GROUP DETAIL
                    │           │   │
                 8L 72 238 68-P Trim assembly
                 │                  (front door panel)—RH—Upper,
                 │                  Dark Gray Bedford Cord; Center,
                 │                  Blue Gray Broadcloth; Lower,
                 │                  Gray Bedford Artificial Leather
    PART NUMBER PREFIX            CHANGE IN FINISH, TRIM OR DESIGN

    SIX PASSENGER COUPE        FRONT DOOR TRIM ASSEMBLY R. H.
```

For Example—Should a Trim Assembly for a Right Hand Front Door Panel (Upper, Dark Gray Bedford Cord; Center, Blue Gray Broadcloth; Lower, Gray Bedford Artificial Leather) of a Lincoln Six Passenger Coupe be required the Alphabetical Index lists the group number as 23868-9. By referring to Group 23868-9 on page 61, BL-7223868-P is listed as Trim Assembly (front door panel)—R. H.—Upper, M-19141-P Dark Gray Bedford Cord; Center, M-19152-T Blue Gray Broadcloth; Lower, Gray Bedford Artificial Leather—Manual or Hydraulic Control

YEAR 19-	BODY TYPES	REMARKS	PART NUMBER	NO. REQ'D
		GROUP 23868-9 TRIM ASSEMBLY (FRONT DOOR PANEL)		
49	9L72	R. H.—Upper, M-19141-P Dark Gray Bedford Cord; Center, M-19152-T Blue Gray Broadcloth; Lower, Gray Bedford Artificial Leather—Manual or Hydraulic Control	BL 7223868-P	1
49	9L72	L. H.—Upper, M-19141-P Dark Gray Bedford Cord; Center, M-19152-T Blue Gray Broadcloth; Lower, Gray Bedford Artificial Leather—Manual or Hydraulic Control	BL 7223869-P	1
49	9L	Screw (oval head sheet metal)—No. 6 x ¾"	33000-S13	4

APPENDIX V. ENGINES & DRIVETRAIN: 1920-1951 LINCOLN, ALL MODELS

YEARS BUILT	ON MODEL	ENGINE TYPE	NUMBER CYLINDER	COMPRESS RATIO:1	BORE INCHES	STROKE INCHES	DISPLACE CUBIC IN.	CARB TYPE
1920-21	L	60d V L-HEAD	EIGHT	4.8	3.375	5.0	357.8	1-bbl
1922-27	L	60d V L-HEAD	EIGHT	4.81	3.375	5.0	357.8	1-bbl
1927-30	L	60d V L-HEAD	EIGHT	4.81	3.5	5.0	384.8	1-bbl
1931	K	60d V L-HEAD	EIGHT	4.95	3.5	5.0	384.8	2-bbl
1932	KA	60d V L-HEAD	EIGHT	5.32	3.5	5.0	384.8	2-bbl
1932-33	KB	65d V L-HEAD	TWELVE	5.25	3.25	5.0	447.9	2-bbl
1933	KA	67d V L-HEAD	TWELVE	5.61	3.0	4.5	381.7	2-bbl
1934	K	67d V L-HEAD	TWELVE	6.38	3.125	4.5	414.0	2-bbl
1935-40	K	67d V L-HEAD	TWELVE	6.38	3.125	4.5	414.0	2-bbl
1936-39	H	75d V L-HEAD	TWELVE	6.7	2.75	3.75	267.3	2-bbl
1940-41	H	75d V L-HEAD	TWELVE	7.2	2.875	3.75	292	2-bbl
1942	H	75d V L-HEAD	TWELVE	7.0	2.937	3.75	305**	2-bbl
1946	H	75d V L-HEAD	TWELVE	7.0	2.875	3.75	292	2-bbl
1947-48	H	75d V L-HEAD	TWELVE	7.2	2.875	3.75	292	2-bbl
1949	EL	90d V L-HEAD	EIGHT	7.0	3.5	4.375	336.7	2-bbl
1949	EH	90d V L-HEAD	EIGHT	7.0	3.5	4.375	336.7	2-bbl
1950	EL	90d V L-HEAD	EIGHT	7.0	3.5	4.375	336.7	2-bbl
1950	EH	90d V L-HEAD	EIGHT	7.0	3.5	4.375	336.7	2-bbl
1951	EL	90d V L-HEAD	EIGHT	7.05	3.5	4.375	336.7	2-bbl
1951	EH	90d V L-HEAD	EIGHT	7.05	3.5	4.375	336.7	2-bbl

APPENDIX VI.

FORD MOTOR COMPANY 1903-1951
Calendar Year Production
Figures from FMC News Release 75th Anniversary, Dearborn, Michigan.

YEAR	FORDS	TRUCKS	MERCURY	LINCOLN	Remarks
1903	1,708				FMC Ford car begins
1904	1,695				
1905	1,599				
1906	8,729				
1907	14,887				
1908	10,202				
1909	17,771				
1910	32,053				
1911	69,762				
1912	170,211				
1913	202,667				
1914	308,162				
1915	501,462				
1916	734,811	209			First Ford trucks
1917	622,351	41,725			
1918	435,898	62,444			
1919	820,445	120,597		0	First Leland Lincolns
1920	419,517	43,934		0	
1921	903,814	67,796		0	
1922	1,173,745	127,322		5,512	First Ford Model L Lincolns
1923	1,817,891	193,234		7,875	Model L Lincolns
1924	1,749,827	172,221		7,053	Model L Lincolns
1925	1,643,295	268,411		8,380	Model L Lincolns
1926	1,368,383	186,082		8,858	Model L Lincolns
1927	356,188	61,100		7,141	Model L Lincolns
1928	633,594	110,342		6,362	Model L Lincolns
1929	1,507,132	355,453		7,672	Model L Lincolns
1930	1,155,462	272,897		3,515	Model L; early K Lincolns
1931	541,615	186,207		3,592	Model K; early KA Lincolns
1932	287,285	105,283		3,388	Models KA:1,765; KB:1,623
1933	334,969	92,662		2,007	Model KA and KB Lincolns
1934	563,921	191,861		2,149	Model KA and KB Lincolns
1935	942,439	250,282		3,915	Model K; early H Lincolns
1936	791,812	223,779		22,001	Model H and K Lincolns
1937	848,608	268,621		29,293	Model H and K Lincolns
1938	410,048	151,079	17,282	19,751	First Mercury cars for 1939
1939	532,152	185,180	76,198	22,578	First Model H Continentals
1940	599,175	203,097	82,770	24,021	Last Model K Lincolns
1941	600,814	250,592	80,085	17,756	
1942	43,407	179,303	4,430	1,276	WW II halts car production
1943	0	142,357	0	0	
1944	0	154,761	0	0	
1945	34,439	124,300	2,848	569	Resume passenger cars
1946	372,917	201,280	70,955	13,496	Zephyr name dropped
1947	601,665	250,088	124,612	29,275	
1948	549,077	302,154	154,702	43,688	Model H end; EL/EH begins
1949	841,170	244,783	203,339	33,132	First million unit since '37
1950	1,187,122	345,851	334,081	35,485	
1951	900,770	317,252	238,854	25,386	Early 1952 models begin

APPENDIX VII.

LINCOLN COACHBUILT BODY NUMBERS

Unlike many coachbuilders, Lincoln assigned body number prefixes to all custom coach bodies for the Model L and Model K Lincolns. These numbers were usually found on the body sill just inside of the front right door or on the framework under the right front seat cushions. They were:

No. 1 Murray Corp. of America, Detroit, Mich. (Previously Murray Body Co., Towson Body and Anderson Electric Car Co.)

No. 2 American Body Co., Buffalo, N.Y.

No. 3 H.H. Babcock Co., Watertown, N.Y.

No. 4 Brunn & Co., Buffalo, N.Y.

No. 5 J.B. Judkins Co., Buffalo, N.Y.

No. 6 Lang Body Co., Cleveland, Ohio

No. 7 Fleetwood Metal Body Co., Fleetwood, Pa.

No. 8 Holbrook Co., Hudson, N.Y.

No. 9 LeBaron, Inc., Bridgeport, Conn.

No. 10 Lincoln Motor Co., Detroit, Mich.

No. 11 Dietrich, Inc., Detroit, Mich.

No. 12 Willoughby Co., Utica, N.Y.

No. 13 Locke & Co., Rochester, N.Y.

No. 14 Derham Body Co., Rosemont, Pa.

No. 15 LeBaron-Detroit Co., Detroit, Mich.

No. 16 Waterhouse & Co., Webster, Mass.

No. 17 Walter M. Murphy Co., Pasadena, Cal.

APPENDIX V cont'd. ENGINES & DRIVETRAIN: 1920-1951 LINCOLN, ALL MODELS

BRAKE HP	RATED RPM	TAXABLE HP	WHEELS TIRES	TREAD INCHES	AXEL RATIO:1	SERIAL NUMBERS	REMARKS:
81	2600	36.45	21x5.00	60 F & R	4.58	1 thru 3151	IRON PISTONS, FORK AND BLADE
90	2800	39.2	21x6.75	60 F & R	4.58	3152-47499	MINOR MODS, 4.90:1 OPT. AXEL
95	2900	39.2	20x7.00	60 F & R	4.58	47500-66000	IMPROVED ENGINE, MID-'27
120	2800	39.2	19x7.00	60 F & R	4.23	66001-70000	FOUR-RING ALUM. PISTONS
125	2900	43.0	18x7.00	60 F & R	4.23	70001-72041	OPT. AXELS 4.58 OR 4.90
150	3400	50.7	18x7.50	60 F & R	4.23	KB1-KB1666	KB2001-2604 IN '33
125	3400	43.2	18x7.00	60 F & R	4.23	KA1-KA1140	FOUR-MAINS, LIGHTER WT.
150	3800	46.8	18x7.50	60 F & R	4.23	KA1501-KA3176	KB3001-KB3744 FOR 145WB
150	3800	46.8	17x7.50	60 F & R	4.23	K3501-K9674	HYD. LIFTERS IN '37
110	3900	36.33	16x7.00	55.5/58.25	4.33*	H1-H85640	STL. 3-RING PIST, *4.44 '38
120	3500	39.75	16x7.00	55.5/58.25	4.44	H85641-H129690	COLUMBIA 3-SP., NEW OD IN '41
130	3800	39.9	15x7.00	59/60.75	4.44	H129691-136224	END PROD. FEB. '42, IRON HEAD
120	3500	39.75	15x7.00	59/60.75	4.44	H136255-H152839	**EARLY '46 MODELS, JUNE '45
125	4000	39.75	15x7.00	59/60.75	4.44	H152840-H182129	HYD. LIFTERS '38 AND BRAKES '39
152	3600	39.2	15x8.20	58.5/60	4.50	9EL1-9EL73559	MERCURY-BODY, HYDROMATIC OPT.
152	3600	39.2	15x8.20	58.5/60	4.50	9EH1-9EH73563	COSMOPOLITAN, FMC DEARBORN
152	3600	39.2	15x8.20	58.5/60	4.50	50LP5001L-20082	LA: 50LA5001L-50LA7252L
152	3600	39.2	15x8.20	58.5/60	4.50	50LP5001H-1570	MINOR ENGINE MODS
154	3600	39.2	15x8.00	58.5/60	4.50	51LP5001L-19317	LA: 51LA5001L-51LA7114L
154	3600	39.2	15x8.20	58.5/60	4.50	51LP5001H-20813	IMPROVED ENGINE

APPENDIX IIX. LINCOLN CONTINENTAL PRODUCTION

Figures by W.A. Currie, Production Programming & Control Dept. February 9, 1951, Lincoln-Mercury Division.

YEAR	MODEL	TYPE	JAN	FEB	MAR	APR	MAY	JUN	JUL	AUG	SEP	OCT	NOV	DEC	YR.TOT.
					v 1939 Models						v 1940 Models				
1939	96H	56		1		1					2	0	23		25
		57									0	0	0		0
				1		1					2	0	23		25
										v 1941 Models					
1940	06H	56	65	63	71	64	36	22	4	12	47	21	42	47	494
		57	0	0	0	1	7	32	14	20	69	80	107	111	441
			65	63	71	65	43	54	18	32	116	101	149	158	935
											v 1942 Models				
1941	16H	56	64	49	24	32	41	21	0	2	15	20	33	34	335
		57	99	98	62	42	72	88	0	2	27	36	53	49	628
			163	147	86	74	113	109	0	4	42	56	86	83	963
1942	26H	56	32												32
		57	33												33
			65												65
				v 1946 Model Year											
1946	66H	56		1	3	7	0	5	17	34	40	32	30	32	201
		57		0	1	3	0	9	16	35	35	47	63	56	265
				1	4	10	0	14	33	69	75	79	93	88	466
				v 1947 Model Year							v 1948 Models				
1947	76H	56	55	63	72	31	79	13	36	17	93	103	83	93	738
		57	85	66	74	105	65	18	32	22	84	105	83	92	831
			140	129	146	136	144	31	68	39	177	208	166	185	1,569
1948	876	56	90	357	5										452
		57	92	252	503										847
			182	609	508										1,299

Total Cabriolets . . . 2,277
Total Coupes . . . 3,045

Total Continental Production . . . 5,322

APPENDIX IX.

LINCOLN MODEL K

Spotter's Guide to 1931 through 1940 Model K.

1930 Model K, Series 200: Flat radiator, chrome shell, 34 cowl louvers each side, cowl lamps, oval bumper, chrome headlights and badge bar with oval Lincoln emblem. Dual trumpet horns, 145 inch wheelbase, 19 inch wheels, V-8 engine. Note: The body mold line which starts at the cowl and goes up over in front of the windshield, was styled by Raymond Dietrich and is called the LeBaron sweep. It is not indicative of any model year or manufacturer.

1932 Model KA, Series 500: Flat, slightly pointed at the top, radiator grille. Cowl lamps moved to top of front fenders. Straight, two-rib, one-piece bumpers. Five door panels in place of louvers on cowl. Trumpet horns, black fenders, 136 inch wheelbase, 18 inch wheels, V-8 engine. Lincoln medallion background is red.

1932 Model KB, Series 230: Same as KA except more massive round radiator grille shell, 145 inch wheelbase, V-12 engine. More luxurious appointments and wider choice of custom bodies. Lincoln medallion background is blue.

1933 Model KA, Series 511: Chrome rounded, snow plow, radiator shell, pointed mesh grille, downward curve in front bumper, and louvers on engine cowl. No external trumpet horns, valanced front fenders, 125 HP V-12 engine, and 136 inch wheelbase.

1933 Model KB, Series 251: Same as KA except 145 inch wheelbase, larger 150 HP V-12 engine, luxury appointments, and wider choice of custom body styles.

1934 Model K Series 521 and 270: Two wheelbases, 136 inch on the 521 and 145 inch on the 270. One engine both models. Painted radiator shell, not chrome. Return to cowl door panels, smaller headlight shell, more bug-eyed headlamps. Full skirted front fenders. Almost all body styles used dual side-mounted spare tires and the metal wheel covers for them had a new accent ring and side-case. KA and KB Serial numbers continued through this year.

1935 Model K Series 540 and 300: Same engine on both wheelbases, 136 inch on 540 and 145 inch on 300. All Serial numbers began with K. Bodies were further forward on the wheelbase. The cowl had horizontal trim above the cowl doors and below the mold line trim. New front bumper was convex and had two bumper guards. Painted headlight housings were longer and slightly smaller around. New instrument panel with two large round dials, the radio was placed in the center, and the glove box was larger.

1936 Model K Series 320: High round pontoon fenders were added this year. The windshield was sloped more. New fluted steel wheels were standard. Front fenders were shorter and running boards were longer. The grille was rounded, with more pronounced horizontal bars and a center vertical bar.

1937 Model K Series 350: The headlights were molded into the high, rounded front fenders. Roofs on hardtop bodies were more rounded as were the corners of all side-windows. Spare tire was inside trunk for first time.

1938 and 1940 Model K Series 400: Horizontal grille bars were reduced to 18 from 30. Cowl doors were replaced with five horizontal vent panels resembling louvers. Seven new sedan body styles were introduced in 1939.

1941 Model K Series 600: Never built. Drawings reveal that this Sedan Cabriolet resembled a Model H32 with Continental-style fenders and a long hood. The greyhound hood ornament was crouched low on the hood like a stalking panther. Wheelbase would have been 145 inches.

APPENDIX X.

LINCOLN MODEL L

Excerpts from MOTOR WORLD magazine —
1929 Characteristic Supplement.

1922 Model L, Series 120: Cowl lamps set out in cowl, not at base of windshield post. First year with cowl ventilators. Chassis body lower. Open models have a bead through the hood and cowl around top of body. More slant to windshield. Enclosed models have slanting windshield with triangle-shaped corner glass.

1923 Model L, Series 130: First year for Hoodye shock absorbers. Drum headlamps after April. Front spring leaves increased from ten to fourteen in number.

1924 Model L, Series 134: Motor cast in blocks of four arranged at 60 degree angle. Shutters controlled by thermostat located in upper radiator tank. Temperature of water from engine controls opening and closing. After July, radiator grille was changed from horizontal to vertical ventilating louvers.

1925 Model L, Series 141: Identical in many respects to 1924 models except fenders. Forced-feed engine lubrication with gear drive oil pump. Electro-Fog generator facilitates starting in cold weather. Centrifugal water pump. Delco electrical system. Worm and sector steering gear. Full floating rear axle. Torque tube encloses drive shaft and takes driving thrust. Fenders were longer with greater curvature.

1926 Model L, Series 151: No mechanical changes to chassis. Custom built bodies by different specialists added and bright color schemes adopted. Equipment includes Waltham speedometer and clock, Grolan gasoline cable-type gauge on dash, Yale ignition and transmission blocks, Cuno cigar lighter, smoking and vanity set, rearview mirror, stop light, visor, Folbert vacuum windshield cleaner, Biflex front and rear bumpers, Hoodye shock absorbers. Wood wheels on all models except Sport Phaeton and Sport Touring, which have wire wheels.

1927 Model L, Series 158: Adapted six brake system November, 1927. Bullet headlamps with two filament bulbs operated by lever in center of steering wheel. Most chassis features similar to 1926. Two open Touring models and closed custom bodies by Brunn, Holbrook, LeBaron, and Willoughby.

1928 Model L, Series 165: Improved V-type motor 3.5X5, 39.2 horsepower, 136 inch wheelbase, 32X6.75 tires. Bore of engine increased, optional tires 33 inch, coincidental ignition and steering lock. Hydraulic shock absorbers standard. Dash instruments grouped into oval panel. Rearview mirror, windshield wiper, Waltham eight-day clock, 80-mile air friction drive speedometer. Electric cigar lighter. One or two spare tires according to type.

1929 Model L, Series 173: Radiator increased in depth with larger cap and threads on outside of filler neck. Fenders shorter and follow less closely the contour of the wheel. New rubber engine mounts, transmission shift mounted on ball-and roller bearing. Automatic engine lubrication.

GLOSSARY

AERO — Having to do with aerodynamics. Aeroplane is an earlier spelling for airplane.

AIRFLOW — The aerodynamic flow around the body of a car. The term is also used as a noun to describe streamlined body designs of the 1930s.

AJUST-O-MATIC — Electrical servo switches in an early tube type radio for station signal seeking.

ALEMITE FITTING — Standard grease gun fittings used primarily on suspension, steering, and drive shafts.

ALL-WEATHER — Custom coach automobile with open front or rear passenger compartments, which could be enclosed during inclement weather.

ALAM — Association of Licensed Automobile Manufacturers.

ARMATURE — One meaning is the rotary part of a generator or motor, but as applied to auto body design, it is a mock-up fixture. See buck.

ARTILLERY WHEELS — Wheels with large wooden spokes like those used on early military horse-drawn caissons.

AUTO SALON — An auto show, usually by invitation only. They were popularized by the New York Auto Salons of the early twentieth century.

AUTOMOBILE — From "auto," meaning under its own power, and "mobile," meaning not stationary. Common name for popular motorized vehicle.

AUTOMOBILIA — Memorabilia relating to the automobile.

AUXILIARY SEATS — The fold-up opera seats located between the front and rear passenger seats. Also the small bench seat in a three-window coupe.

BANJO SPOKE — Spoke steering wheel design used in the early 1940s on Zephyrs and Mercurys.

BARRIS — Custom body design made popular by California body shops. It is a chopped, leaded-in, bulbous custom hot rod. Named for George Barris.

BATHTUB DESIGN — See bulbous.

BELTLINE — The mold line around the mid-body of an automobile usually starting just aft of the cowl and sometimes wrapping around the trunk.

BERLINE — Enclosed sedan, usually a seven-passenger model, with rear compartment divider (partition window behind driver's seat). Named for the German city. Normally a custom coach body.

BHP — Brake horsepower. Differs in method of calculation from standard horsepower.

BLACKWALL — Standard black tires, not white sidewalls.

BODY IN WHITE — Assembled body shell without engine, transmission, and drivetrain fitted.

BORE — The diameter of the cylinder and/or piston.

BOXY — General term applied to squared-off 1920s body styles which preceded the age of streamlining.

BRASS CARS — Early automobile designs, usually prior to 1920, so nicknamed because of their extensive use of brass fittings and accessories.

BRG — British Racing Green. Famous color of the British international race cars. A medium dark green.

BROADCLOTH — Densely textured woolen cloth with a plain or twill weave and lustrous finish. Sometimes has narrow rib pattern.

BROUGHAM — Large sedan with open driver section and with the rear passenger compartment enclosed. Normally chauffeur-driven. Also referred to as a Sedan de Ville. Sometimes confused with the custom coach builder, Brunn & Company. See limousine.

BUCK — The framework on which the clay mock-up of a body design is built.

BULBOUS — Bulb-like in appearance as a balloon or a bathtub. Inflated, large, and rounded.

BUSINESS COUPE — Fixed head coupe with no rear seat, also referred to as a Doctor's Coupe. Three-window coupes are of this body type.

CAR BUFF — An automobile enthusiast, not a rag used for polishing your car. Derived from the buff colored uniforms of volunteer firemen, said to be fire engine buffs.

CABRIOLET — Body style in which the roof above the driver can be converted from open to closed. Originally referred to sedan bodies similar to a Brougham, but later applied to convertible coupes in which the top could be partially or fully folded back.

CAISSON — Wagon wheel and axle used to transport cannon cases (case on wheels). See artillery wheels and spokes.

CALIFORNIA TOP — Early nickname for hardtop installed on Touring cars, and still used the side curtains.

CARBURETOR — Gasoline atomizer for injecting fuel into the intake manifold. Updraft type sits below a side-mounted manifold and draws air upward. Downdraft type sits on top of manifold and draws air downward.

CARRERA — Road race such as the Pan American Road Races held in Mexico during the 1950s and 1960s.

CARRIAGE — Device to carry. Word from which the shorter word "car" was derived.

CARROSSIER — French name for coachbuilder.

CARRY-OVER — Using a component from an existing model again on a newer model.

CATWALK — Area between the engine cowl and front fenders. Does not exist on modern automobiles.

CHROMED — Nickel plating of parts.

CID — Cubic Displacement in Inches.

CLASSIC CAR — Car of distinctive body styling and limited production. Normally characterized by long hood design and powerful appearance. The CCCA lists cars which they classify as classics. Term remains broad and is often misused.

CLOISONNE — Metal emblem with raised thin strips. A relief casting with enamel coloring within the recessed areas; cloisonnie (Fr.).

CLOSED — An enclosed body style such as a coupe or sedan.

CLUB COUPE — Two-door body style with trunk, and having a rear passenger seat. Often called five-window coupes. Not to be confused with a business coupe with an auxiliary seat installed or a two-door sedan which has a full-size rear seat area.

COACH BARS — Convertible tops with an outside brace bar which folds with the top. Also called Landau irons. Often installed as a dummy accessory, simulating a folding top.

COACHBUILT — The art of coachbuilding. Construction of a coach body on an existing manufactured chassis and power train. Such work is generally considered custom order or limited production.

COACHING BROUGHAM — Automobile body styling which imitated the famous stagecoach styling of the nineteenth century.

COACH SILL — That area along the top part of the body where the driver or passenger might rest an elbow. Where the convertible top or sidecurtain would be snapped on or where the top of the window would be when cranked down.

COINCIDENTAL LOCK — Steering column or gearshift pin locking mechanism operated by a key. Used to prevent auto theft.

COLUMBIA — Type of vacuum-shifted two speed rear axle.

CONCOURS D'ELEGANCE — French name for high-class automobile show or auto competition like a car meet.

CONTINENTAL — Body styling said to be influenced by mid-1930s European (the Continent) designs. Proper name for several Lincoln models.

CONVERTIBLE — Body style on which the top folds or retracts and having roll-up windows. May be a two-door or four-door body style.

COSMOPOLITAN — Citizen of the Cosmos. Having to do with modern city living. As applied to automobiles, the term would imply prestige or success.

COUPE — Two-door hardtop car, usually sloping to the rear, seating two or three persons in the front and may have a small rear seat. A coupe differs from a two-door sedan which has a full-size rear seat like a sedan.

COWL — Engine enclosure. Refers to the side panels below and on either side of the hood, and includes that area between the hood and the windshield.

COWL LAMPS — The small parking lights or running lights on the upper rear cowl.
CRUCIFORM — Dropping the floor board in between the frame. Also known as double dropped frame.
CUSTOM — To build or modify an automobile body in such a manner as to personalize it to the owner's specifications.
DASHBOARD — Area forward of the driver's compartment. Is sometimes confused with the instrument panel and firewall. Although technically incorrect, the instrument panel is often referred to as the dash or dashboard.
DICKY — Older term for rear outside auxiliary seat. Also called rumble seat. Derived from the old coach term for the seat where the footman rode. Also spelled dickey.
DISC WHEELS — Solid metal wheels with bolt-on outside rims, popular on automobiles during the period of wooden spoke and wire spoke wheels. They predate modern drop-center steel rim wheels.
DORSAL — Like the dorsal fin of a shark. A dorsal is a vertical blade shape molded into the auto body or the accessory.
DRIVE TRAIN — The mechanism which delivers engine power to the drive wheels. It includes transmission, driveshaft and differential.
DROPHEAD — British or sporting term for convertible top.
DRUM STYLE — Headlamp housing on an older body style car. Round and flat on the back. Predated cone or bowl-shaped types.
DUAL REARMOUNTS — The practice of mounting two spare tires on the back of an automobile. Popular in the period of time when flats were common due to poor rubber and bad roads.
DUAL-COWL — Touring body style where the front and rear doors are separated by a cowl section, usually containing a second windshield. Also closely resembles the tonneau cowl accessory.
DUESY — A popular slang term of the 1920s which made reference to something as being fancy and stylish like the Duesenberg.
DURO PUMP — Hydraulic power window pump.
DYMAXION — A term coined by designer, Buckminster Fuller. It refers to the construction of an object using maximum dynamic forces. It was also the name of a streamlined automobile designed by Fuller.
E MODEL — Lincolns built from mid-1948 through 1951. Known as the bulbous era Lincolns. Sub-Series EL & EH.
EDSEL — The first name of Henry Ford's son. Also used as the name for a model of car produced by Ford in the late 1950s.
EGG-CRATE PATTERN — Complex pattern grille work such as that used on 1946 through 1949 Lincolns.
ELECTRO-FOG — An electric-fog generator uses a coil to preheat the fuel during cold weather and help the engine to start more efficiently.
ELECTRICS — Term which applies to all early electrical powered automobiles.
ENGINE — See motor.
FACTORY-BUILTS — Term which differentiates the early custom body models built by the manufacturer versus the ones built by custom coachbuilders.
FAIRING — The body skin which bridges an opening, normally joining major components. The term faired-in refers to the installation of a fairing, generally sheet metal construction or body fill. Modern fairings are often rubber, plastic, or fiberglass.
FAIRLANE — Name of the Henry Ford estate in Dearborn, Michigan. Originally spelled Fair Lane. Became the model name of a popular Ford car and was the code name for a Ford research project.
FASCIA — The area in front of the driver below the windshield. It houses the instruments, switches and operator mechanisms.
FASTBACK — Body design on which the rear of the passenger compartment slopes into the trunk.
FIREWALL — The area between the driver's compartment and the engine, evolved from the early dashboard.
FLATHEAD — Where the cylinder head is cast solid (no rocker cover) and the valves are in the block.
FMC — Ford Motor Company.

FOB — Not including transportation, i.e., pick up at factory. From the shipping term Freight On Board.
FORK-AND-BLADE — A connecting rod and crankshaft design which has an extension to offset the throw, and thus provide a smoother running engine.
FORDOR — Ford spelling of a four-door sedan body style.
FREEWHEELING — A drive train mechanism which allows the engine to disengage and idle when the car is coasting.
FRENCHED — Also known as frenched-in. It means to smooth the gap between two body parts. Similar to faired-in, but more like lead-filled.
GEMMER GEAR — Steering gear on which the shaft screws a gear. Also referred to as worm gear.
GO-NOGO GAUGE — A tool used for checking parts of a specific dimension. It provides the minimum and maximum measurement that is acceptable for a cut or opening. Not normally used for critical tolerance measurements.
GORHAM — Designer of the greyhound symbol for the Lincoln Model L and Model K. Famous silversmith and jewelry house.
GREASE-CUP — A screw on cap in which grease can be placed. As the cap is tightened, the grease is forced into the shaft or bearing to be lubricated.
GREENHOUSE — The passengers' and driver's compartment of an automobile. So named because of the glass window area.
GREYHOUND — The decorative radiator cap ornament and symbol for the Lincoln Model L and Model K Lincolns. See Gorham and Lost Wax.
GRILLE — The decorative grate or bar work mounted in front of the radiator.
H MODEL — Several Series of Lincolns based on the original Zephyr design. Lincoln models built from 1935 through 1948.
H-PATTERN — Standard gearshift pattern with reverse gear in the upper left corner and neutral in the center. Originally used on floor shifts and later moved to the steering column.
HEADLAMP — Older name for headlight, from the time when coal oil lamps were used for headlights.
HEADLIGHTS — Forward facing lamps for night driving. Styling shapes are: drum, bell, bowl, cone, bullet, faired, enclosed, and hidden.
HO-DYE — Handaille shock absorbers. Early double action shock's nickname.
HOB-NOBBING — To travel in high society. Derived from Hobe Sound, Florida, where many luxurious winter estates were.
HOOD — Cover over the engine compartment. The British term hood means roof and bonnet means hood.
HYDRAMATIC — Automatic transmission developed by General Motors and used on vehicles from military to Lincolns.
HYPOID — Type of gear arrangement where the driveshaft sets off center of the gear to be driven. Normally used on differentials to allow the driveshaft to enter the rear axle at a lower point.
INDY — Indianapolis Speedway, also known as the Brickyard.
INTERNAL COMBUSTION — An engine in which power is generated internally by a mixture of fuel and air ignited by a spark.
JIG — Also referred to as a fixture, it is the framework which holds an assembly in position during construction.
JO-BLOCK — A standard dimension machined into metal blocks which are used as the master dimension for setting tools and gauges, designed by C.E. Johannsen.
K MODEL — Model of Lincolns following the Model L. Developed under Edsel Ford. Mostly coachbuilt bodies. Sub-Series KA & KB.
K-MEMBER — An angular brace on a chassis or framework forming a K.
KELLOGG — Type of tire pump which runs off of the transmission shaft.
KETTERING ELECTRIC — Electrical ignition system and self-starter designed by Charles F. Kettering, founder of Dayton Electric Company. Later known as Delco.
L MODEL — It stood for Liberty, Leland, and Lincoln. Lincoln automobiles built between 1919 and 1930.

L-FRAME — The angular steel used to construct the frame for an automobile chassis. Later chassis used U-shaped channels.

L-HEAD — Shape of the combustion chamber in a flathead engine. The valves are offset to the side of the cylinder and open upward into the combustion chamber.

L-SECTION — See L-frame.

LANDAU — Variation on the model terminology Landaulet.

LANDAU IRONS — See coach bars.

LANDAULET — Open driver compartment with all-weather top. The enclosed passenger compartment will also convert to an open body style by folding down a carriage-style top.

LEBARON SWEEP — Raised mold line beginning at the engine cowl and moving with a sweep down the midsection of the car body. Originated by Ray Dietrich to break up the boxy lines on 1920 body styles.

LELAND-BUILT — Motto of Henry Martyn Leland, founder of Cadillac and Lincoln. Meaning built by "The Master of Precision."

LENOIR — Earliest known design for a four-cycle gas internal combustion engine, dating around 1850. Held up as legal opposition to the Selden patent.

LEVASSOR ENGINE — Early European engine predating Benz. Better known as a System Panhard engine.

LIDO — Coastal resort in Italy. The word connotates holiday fun. The name used for a sport model Lincoln in the early 1950s. Also Lee Iacocca's first name.

LIMOUSINE — Similar to a Brougham with a large or extended passenger compartment. Driver's compartment may be open or enclosed, but if open includes a top and side curtains. Modern usage refers to stretched body custom sedan.

LINCOLN — Automobile and company founded by H.M. Leland. Named in honor of the 16th President of the United States, Abraham Lincoln.

LIQUAMATIC — First automatic transmission used on Lincolns. Introduced in 1942.

LMC — Lincoln Motor Company.

LOST WAX — A casting process in which wax is used to make the pattern and then melted out of the mold so that copies can be produced. This process was used in making the Gorham greyhounds.

LOUVER — A device used to allow or restrict the flow of air or light. A group of blades or veins arranged so as to form panels that open and close.

MAGNALIUM — An alloy containing aluminum.

MARQUE — Pronounced "Mark." It is a French word that means the first, but for automobiles it implies the beginning series in a group of designs.

MIDSIZE — A midsize car is neither large nor small in relation to other cars in current production. Definition has changed over the years, and a midsize modern car is approximately the size a small car was a few decades ago.

MOCK-UP — A model (usually full-scale) fabricated of nonstructural materials to look or function like the product to be built.

MODEL — Cars of the same make, design and period, i.e., Model L, Model K. An alternate meaning for the word model refers to the scaled down replica or toy of an airplane or car, and is generally not the meaning referred to when discussing automobiles.

MOHAIR — Early forerunner to velour upholstery, but is tighter in weave. Real mohair fabric is made from angora wool. Common mohair is obtained from the Nalga during the cleaning and preparation of Nalga hides.

MOLD LINE — Similar to beltline except with a decorative trim molding installed.

MONOCOQUE — A structure riveted or welded together to form a unit or subassembly construction.

MOTORCAR — Older term interchangeable with automobile, car, and motor vehicle. Generally, an American term. See Motor.

MOTOMETER — Temperature gauge with visual sight window built into a radiator cap. Indicates the coolant temperature.

MOTOR — Term commonly interchanged with engine, but such usage is not technically correct. An engine contains or transports its own propellant while a motor uses an external source of power.

NEOPHYTE — Early synthetic rubberized coating.

OHC — Overhead cam.

OHV — Overhead valves.

ONE-OFF — A single production or custom body style, usually referring to a prototype or one-of-a-kind development model.

OPEN — Top down or not installed, as in the case of a Roadster or Touring.

OPERA WINDOW — An oval window on the side of a coupe or sedan located where the rear seat passengers sit.

OVERDRIVE — A gear case located behind the transmission that provides for an additional drive gear. For example, if third gear allowed a 1 to 1 ratio, overdrive might provide a .7 to 1.

PADDED ROOF — Leather, canvas, or vinyl material placed over a hardtop roof and padded. Used as soundproofing and to enhance appearance.

PARTITION — The divider window between the passengers' compartment and the driver's compartment on a limousine or sedan. Usually glass, it often can be rolled down and up for privacy.

PHAETON — Deluxe version of a Touring, often built in dual-cowl versions.

PILLARLESS — On a sedan model where the posts between the front and rear doors are removable or nonexistent when the windows are rolled down. Early version of the hardtop sedan.

PILLARS — The uprights on an auto body which frame the doors and windows. The front pillar on either side of the windshield is the "A" pillar and the center one between the front and rear door is the "B" pillar.

PLACARD — A plate attached to the body of a machine which identifies or explains. Usually metal, embossed, and permanently affixed.

PLASTINE — An early type of plastic coating. Used to color-coat aluminum and prevent oxidation.

PLEXIGLAS — Early plastic glass, extensively used in aircraft during World War II. From plexius, meaning thin and pliable.

PNEUMATIC — Held up by air pressure. The term applies to tires filled with air. The term is not modern, and its usage predates the automobile.

POSH — The term means luxurious and is derived from the early English cruise ships which sailed south to Africa. Luxury accommodations were always on the shady side, Port side Out and Starboard side Home.

PRESS SHOP — The manufacturing area where the body panels are stamped out from sheet metal.

PRODUCTION — A car built in a series as opposed to a prototype, one-off, or custom.

PROTOTYPE — The original operational test model of a particular design.

PROW — The curved nose of a moving object such as the bow of a boat or the hood of a car.

PSI — Measurement of pressure, Pounds per Square Inch.

PURIST — Those who wish to restore vehicles to their authentic original conditions.

QUADRICYCLE — The name which Henry Ford gave his first hand-built vehicle. Named for its four bicycle wheels.

RADIATOR SHELL — The forward portion of the hood which enclosed the radiator and usually frames the grille.

READY-BUILTS — Meaning not custom built, and encompasses almost all mass produced body styles.

REARMOUNT — Spare tire mounted on the back of a car between the two rear fenders.

RESTYLE — As applied to auto body styling, the term means to rework an existing design.

RETROFIT — To update or replace an existing component with a later, improved version.

RHD — Right-Hand Drive, English style.

ROADABLE — Older terminology meaning to handle well on the open road or in the countryside. Implies a comfortable ride.

ROADSTER — Open body type with seating for two or three passengers. Has two doors, folding top, and side curtains. Some models have fold-down windshields. Convertible coupes are sometimes incorrectly called Roadsters. Rear luggage compartment sometimes has auxiliary seating. See Dicky.

ROBE RAIL — Bar or strap behind the front seat on which the back seat passengers may hang a blanket or lap robe. Sometimes considered as an egress assist for passengers.

ROCKER PANEL — Body panel below doors. Often adorned with a chrome strip called a rocker panel molding. Earlier model cars had running boards attached here.

RPM — Revolutions Per Minute. Over 100 RPM is always stated in hundreds, except even thousands.

SAE — Society of Automotive Engineers.

SAF — Ford France.

SALON — See Auto Salon.

SALOON — Conventional car body style, also known as a Sedan in which luggage is carried in a separate rear compartment.

SEATER — Names the number of seats in a sport automobile, i.e., two-seater.

SEDAN — Middle Eastern term meaning an enclosed transport normally having doors. In modern terminology, it refers to a four-door, standard family-style automobile.

SEDANCA DE VILLE. — Sedan, Brougham, or Town Car body style, "Sedan of Town."

SEMI-COLLAPSIBLE — Custom coach body having some convertible top capability, but leaves the pillars or other body structures in place.

SEMI-CUSTOM — Production model body style that is modified, i.e., modern limousine coachbuilding.

SEMI-MONOCOQUE — A structure consisting of prefabricated barrel or box units joined at assembly. See Monocoque.

SERIES — Group of body Types of same Make and Model. Model year or an unchanged style over several years.

SIDEMOUNT — Spare tire mounted at or in the rear part of the fender well, just behind the cowl. Can be a single sidemount or dual sidemounts.

SKIN — The external paneling of the automobile.

SPEEDSTER — Early sports car or racing version of a stripped-down standard body style. Predates the terms hot rod and street rod.

SPOKE — Refers to wheels which are constructed of spokes, normally early wooden automobile wheels. Also called artillery wheels. See caisson.

SPORT — Term used for early soft top coupe or sedan body styles. They were sporty because they appeared to have a convertible top.

STERKENBURG — Name given to the early streamline designs by John Tjaarda. Forerunner to the Zephyr.

STREAMLINE — (Streamlined) Popular design motif of the 1930s which moved away from boxy styling. See airflow.

STROKE — The distance which the piston moves from top to bottom. The movement of a connecting rod in relation to the crankshaft throw.

SUBASSEMBLY — The separate production of units such as doors and fenders feeding into the assembly line.

SUBURBAN — Dual-purpose estate body style, also called Shooting-brake, Utility Town Car, and Station Wagon. Rear seat usually folds down for loading luggage and equipment.

SUICIDE DOORS — Doors opening from the forward part of the body instead of from the rear. So named because if the door comes open while the car is in motion, the wind catches the door and flings it rearward. This design was popular on early autos that required engine cranking and later on many chauffeur-driven body styles.

SUSPENSION — That part of the automobile between the wheels and the frame.

SYNCHROMATIC — A method of synchronizing the transmission gears in order to prevent them from clashing during shifting. Also known as synchromesh.

TARP — Fitted canvas cover to enclose the passenger compartment on open body style models. Also a tonneau cover can be a fitted metal panel enclosing the same area.

TEARDROP — Body or component design which is streamlined into a teardrop or raindrop form. See airflow.

THERMOSTATICALLY — A method of controlling the movement of a device such as a louver or valve. Movement of a thermostatic control is obtained by the effect of ambient temperature on a bimetal.

THREE-BOX — The boxes of an automobile are the engine compartment, passenger compartment, and trunk area.

TONNEAU COWL — Similar to a dual-cowl, but it fastens over the rear doors instead of being in a fixed area between the doors. Usually with a second windshield attached. See Tarp.

TORPEDO BACK — See fastback.

TORSION BAR — The three major types of springs used on suspensions are leaf, coil, and torsion. The twisting of a torsion bar spring is said to be torsional.

TOUCH-O-MATIC — A Ford Motor Company commercial name for overdrive.

TOURING — Open body four-door sedan with folding top and side curtains. Front and rear seats carry four or five passengers. If installed, auxiliary seats will carry two more passengers. Also known as a Tourer.

TOWN CAR — A large formal sedan. See Brougham.

TRANSMISSION — Gear box which transmits the power to the driveshaft from the engine, allowing different ratios to be selected.

TRANSVERSE — Term generally applies to leaf springs which run sideways from wheel to wheel instead of fore and aft.

TRI-STAR — Circle divided into three equal pie-shaped parts. Popular design used on Lincoln Models L and E taillight lenses.

TRIFON — Arrow shaped, streamlined. See airflow.

TRIM — Soft finishings and interior items of an automobile such as carpet, upholstery, and interior panels.

TUDOR — Ford spelling of a two-door sedan body style. A two-door sedan differs from a coupe in that it has a full-size sedan rear seat.

TYPE — As applied to automobiles, the designation of a specific body style within the same Make, Model, and Series.

TYRE — British term for tire.

UAW — United Auto Workers.

UNIT BODY — See monocoque.

V-8 AND V-12 — Design of an engine in which the cylinders are opposed at an angle forming a V. Digits indicate total number of cylinders in the engine.

V-TYPE WINDSHIELD — Windshield which comes to a point. A two-piece flat windshield which replaced early flat one piece windshields, and predating modern curved windshields.

VELOUR — Soft, short pile upholstery. See mohair.

VENTURI — Physical narrowing of an opening such as a carburetor throat. Practical application of the theory that "as velocity increases, pressure decreases."

VICTORIA — Coachbuilt convertible or padded roof coupe body style with a large back seat. Popular name "Vickey."

VOLTA — Early experimenter with electrical spark. The electrical term volt was named after him.

WHEELBASE — The dimension from the center hub or axle of the front wheel to the center hub or axle of the rear wheel.

WHITEWALLS — Alternate name for white sidewall tires.

WINDSHIELD — Clear glass shield breaking the wind forward of the driver or passengers. British term is windscreen.

WIRES — Metal rimmed wheels supported by wire spokes.

WOODY — An estate or sport vehicle having external wood body trim.

ZEPHYR — Means a light wind or breeze. Zephyr was the name originally given to the Lincoln Model H series. Early GM diesel engines operating on the Burlington Line were also named Zephyr. Zephyr was a popular name for Art Deco objects of the 1930s. The first digital clock built in 1936 was named Zephyr.

LIST OF PUBLICATION REFERENCES (BOOKS): America Adopts the Automobile 1895-1910, James Flink, MIT Press, 1970; America on Wheels, Smith & Black, Morrison, 1986; American Automobile Advertising, Chronicle Books, 1988; American Automobile Album, W.H. McGaughey, Dutton, 1954; American Automobile Sales Literature Checklist, R.N. Tuthill, Bookman Dan, 1979; The American Automobile, Ralph Stein, Ridge Press, 1975; The American Automobile — A Brief History, John B. Rae, University of Chicago Press, 1965; American Automobiles, Georgano, Dutton, 1968; American Automobiles of the 50's & 60's, Martinez & Nory, Motorbook International, 1981; The American Car Since 1775, Automobile Quarterly, Dutton, 1971; American Car Spotter's Guide 1920-1980, Tad Burness, Motorbook International, 1986; American Cars from Harrah's Collection, L. Mandel, Stewart, 1982; American Cars of the 1930s, Fred Wayne, Olyslager, 1972; American Cars of the 1940s, Piet Olyslager, Warne & Co., Ltd., 1975; American Cars of the 1950s, Piet Olyslager, Warne & Co., Ltd., 1973; American Century — 100 Years of Style, Ralph Andrist, American Heritage, 1972; Antique Automobiles, Anthony Bird, Treasure Press, 1967; Antique Cars, Lord Montagu, Camden House; Art and the Automobile, D.B. Tubbs, Grosset & Dunlap, 1978; Auto Ads, Jane & Michael Stern, Random House, 1978; The Auto Album, Ted Burness, Houghton Mifflin, 1983; Auto Enthusiast's Dictionary, Carl Hungness, Indiana, 1976; Auto Parade International, Chilton; Automania — Man and the Motor Car, J. Pettifer, Little Brown, 1984; The Illustrated History of Automobiles, Burgess & Wise, Galahad Books, 1980; Saturday Evening Post Automobile Book, Curtis, 1977; 1927 Automobile History, Floyd Clymer, 1955; The Coming of Age of the Automobile Industry, E.D. Kennedy, Kelly Publications, 1972; Automobile Quarterly Vol. 1 No. 1, Vol. 12 No. 1, Vol. 12 No. 3, Vol. 14 No. 2, Vol. 14 No. 4, Vol. 15 No. 1, Vol. 17 No. 2, Vol. 2 No. 3, Vol. 2 No. 4, Vol. 23 No. 4, Vol. 6 No. 4, Vol. 17 No. 4, Automobile Quarterly, 1962-1985; Automobile and Culture, Silk & Fisher, Abrams, 1984; The Automobile in America, Sears & Stephen, Simon, 1977; 100 Years of the Automobile 1886-1986, Gallery Books, 1986; A Picture History of the Automobile, Peter Roberts, Triune Books, 1973; Automobiles of Yesteryear, Bergene, Dodds & Mead, 1962; Automobiles of the World, Lewis & Muscian, Simon, 1977; Automobiles and Automobiling, Viking Press, 1965; The Automotive Directory, Ralph Jennings, Dogan, 1969; Automotive Giants of America, Forbes & Foster, Forbes Publications, 1926; Automotive Mechanics, C.G. Barger, American Book, 1943; Automotive Yearbook, Wards, Detroit; Autos 1900-1905 America's Greatest Cars, Mayborn, Highland; Best of Old Cars Weekly Vol. 1 thru 6, John Gunnell, Krause, 1982; Big Book of Old Cars, Robert Jackson, McKay, 1978; The Book of the Motor Car, Bosch, St. Martin Press, 1975; Burlington in Transportation, Hardy & Corbin, Iowa, 1967; The Complete History of Cadillac, Maurice Hendry, Automobile Quarterly, 1973; The Car Culture, James J. Flink, MIT Press, 1975; Car Facts and Feats, Harding, Doubleday; Car Wars, Robert Sobel, Dutton, 1984; Car of the Year, Lent, Dutton; Cars 1886-1930, G.N. Georgano, Beekman House, 1985; The Cars That Henry Ford Built, Beverly Kimes, Dutton, 1978; The Cars of Lincoln-Mercury, Dammann & Wagner, Crestline, 1987; Cars of the 1930s, M. Sedgwick, Bentley, 1970; Cars of the 50s, Beekman House, 1978; Cars of the Early Twenties, Ted Burness, Chilton Books; Cars of the Stars, J. Davis, 1974; Cars — The Old Classics to 1945, Andrew Whyte; Chrome Dreams — Automobile Styling, Paul Wilson, Chilton Books, 1976; Classic American Automobiles, D.B. Wise, Galahad, 1980; Classic Cars, J.R. Buckley, Viking Press, 1964; Classic Tradition of the Lincoln Motorcar, Automobile Quarterly, 1968; Classic Cars Since 1945, Michael Twite, Blandford; Clymer's Motor Scrapbook No. 1 thru 8, Floyd Clymer, 1955; Collector's Guide to Car Values, Brian Jones, Bloomington, Indiana, 1983; Collector's Cars — Postwar Classics, Julian Brown, Chartwell Books, 1985; Complete Book of Collectible Cars 1940-80, Langworth, Beekman House; Complete Encyclopedia of Motor Cars, Georgano, Dutton; The Continental Story, Ford Motor Company, 1956; The Custom Body Era, Hugo Pfau, Baines & Co., 1977; Days to Remember America 1945-1955, Gunterh & Quint, Harper, 1956; The Designers, L.J.K. Setright, Follett Publishing, 1976; Dream Cars, R. Nichols, Gallery; Treasury of Early American Automobiles, Floyd Clymer, McGraw-Hill, 1950; Early Automobiles, Eugene Rachlis, Golden Books, 1961; Encyclopedia of American Cars 1930-1942, James Moloney, Crestline, 1980; Encyclopedia of American Cars 1930-1980, R.M. Langworth, Beekman House, 1984; Encyclopedia of American Cars 1946-1959, Moloney & Damman, Crestline, 1980; Encyclopedia of World's Classic Cars, Ray Bonds, Gallery Press, 1977; The Encyclopedia of the Motorcar, Phil Drackett, Crown, 1979; Esquire's American Autos & Their Makers, David Wilkie, Harper & Row, 1963; Essentials of Upholstery and Trim, Lee J. Locke, Post Motor Book, 1970; Famous Old Cars, Bowman, Arco; Fifty Years of Lincoln-Mercury, G.H. Dammann, Crestline, 1971; Ford 1903 to 1984, Lewis & Sorenson, Beekman House, 1983; The Ford Agency, H.L. Dominguez, Motorbook International, 1981; Ford Country, David L. Lewis, Amos Press, 1987; The Ford Dynasty, J. Brough, Doubleday, 1977; The Ford Industries, Ford Motor Company, 1924; Ford Motor Company — Complete History, R.M. Langworth, Beekman House, 1987; The 75th Anniversary Ford Road, Lorin Sorensen, Silverado, 1978; The Ford Shows, Loren Sorensen, Silverado, 1976; Ford — An Unconventional Biography, Boton Herndon, Weybright Publications, 1969; Ford — Decline and Rebirth 1933-1962, Allan Nevins, Scribner, 1962; Ford — Expansion and Challenge 1915-1932, Allan Nevins, Scribner's Sons, 1957; Ford — The Men and the Machine, Robert Lacey, Little Brown, 1986; Ford — The Times The Man The Company, Allan Nevins, Scribner's Sons, 1954; From Cycle to Space, Facts of File, 1987; General Motors — The First 75 Years, Automobile Quarterly, 1983; Giant Enterprise — Ford GM & the Auto, A.D. Chandler, Harcourt Brace, 1964; Golden Age of the American Racing Car, Grif Borgeson, Norton, 1966; The Golden Age of the Luxury Car, G. Hildebrand, Dover, 1980; Golden Anniversary of the Lincoln Motorcar, Automobile Quarterly, 1970; Great American Cars, Jonathan Wood, Gallery Books, 1985; Great American Convertibles, Wieder & Hall, Dolphin; Great Auto Races, Peter Heleck, Abrams, 1975; Great Cars of the Forties, Beekman House; The Great Cars, Ralph Stein, Grosset & Dunlap, 1967; Great Collector's Cars, G. Rogliatti, Madison Square, 1972; Great Lives Observed — Henry Ford, John B. Rae, Prentice-Hall, 1969; Great Marques of America, Jonathan Wood, Octopus Books, 1986; Guinness Book of World Records, Sterling, 1975; Harrah's Automobile Collection, Dean Batchelor, GF Publishing, 1984; Hemmings Vintage Auto Almanac, 5th Edition; Henry Ford, Regina Kelly, Follett, 1970; Henry Leland, Gloria May Stoddard, New England Press, 1986; History of World's Sports Cars, Richard Hough, Harper, 1961; A Pictorial History of the Automobile, Phillip Stern, Hearst-Viking, 1953; History of the Motor Car, Octopus Books; Horseless Vehicles — Automobiles, Gardner Hiscox, Henley, 1901; How Cars Are Made, John Taylor, Facts of File, 1987; Iacocca — An Autobiography, Iacocca & Novak, Bantam Books, 1984; Illustrated History of Ford 1930-1970, George Damman, Crestline, 1970; In the Age of Motoring, Pierre Dumont, Viking Press, 1965; The Kings of the Road, Ken W. Purdy, Little Brown, 1952; The Lincoln Continental, OCee Ritch, Clymer, 1963; The Lincoln Motorcar — Sixty Years of Excellence, Thomas E. Bonsall, Bookman, 1981; Lincoln — America's Car of State, Maurice Hendry, Ballantine, 1971; Lincoln — Classic Legend of Excellence, Mayborn, Highland, 1972; The Look of Cars, Henry B. Lent, Dutton, 1966; Man and the Motor Car, Prentice-Hall, 1949; Mark Lincolns — A Classic Source Book, T.E. Bonsall, Motorbook International, 1983; Master of Precision — Henry M. Leland, Mrs. W.C. Leland, Wayne Press, 1966; Men, Money and Motors — Drama of Auto, Macmanus & Beasle, Harper, 1929; Modern Classics — Great Cars Postwar Era, Rich Taylor, Scribner's Sons, 1978; Motor Auto Repair Manual, Hearst, 1951; The Motor Car — An Illustrated History, D.B. Wise, Putnam, 1977; Motor Service New Encyclopedia, A. Byke; Motoring, L.T. Rolt, Macmillan, 1956; My Forty Years With Ford, C.E. Sorensen, Collier Books, 1962; Never Complain Never Explain, Victor Lasky, Marek, 1981; The New Encyclopedia of Motor Cars, J.N. Georgano, Dutton, 1982; Official Price Guide to Collector Cars, Kruse International, 1983; The Old Car Books, John Bentley, Arco Publications, 1953; Old Car Value Guide 1985, Quentin Craft, 1984; The Olympian Cars, R.B. Carson, Knopf, 1976; On the Road Huck Scarry, H. Scarry, Putnam, 1981; Postwar Years Lincoln & Continental, P. Woudenberg, Motorbook International, 1980; Presidents on Wheels, H.R. Collins, Bonanza Books, 1975; Production Figures Book for U.S. Cars, Jerry Heasley, Motorbook International; Restoring Convertibles From Rags to Riches, Burt Mills, Dobbs-Mead, 1977; Road and Track — Illustrated Auto Dictionary, John Dinkel, Norton, 1981; The Roads We Traveled, D. Waitley, Messner, 1978; The Secret Life of Henry Ford, John Dahlinger, Bobbs-Merrill, 1978; The Serial Number Book 1900-1975, Grace Brigham, Motorbook International; Serials in Microform — 1987 Catalog, UMI, 1987; Service Manuals and Service Bulletins, Ford Motor Company; Special Interest American Cars 1930-1960, Peterson, 1975; Specification Book U.S. Cars 1920-1929, G.M. Naul, Motorbook International, 1978; Specification Book U.S. Cars 1930-1969, Motorbook International; Sports and Classic Cars, G. Borgeson, Prentice-Hall, 1955; Standard Catalog American Cars 1805-1942, Kimes & Clark, Krause, 1985; Standard Catalog American Cars 1946-1975, John Gunnell, Krause, 1982; Steam Power 1848-1956, Charles Knuden, Rand McNally, 1965; Summon the Stars, Joe Christy, Barnes & Co., 1970; The Survivors, H. Rosmussen, Picturama, 1977; The Sway of the Grand Salon, John Brinnin, Delacorte Press, 1971; Those Wonderful Old Automobiles, Floyd Clymer, Bonanza Books, 1953; Tin Goose — The Fabulous Ford Tri-Motor, D.J. Ingells, Aero, 1968; The V-8 Album, Early Ford Club, 1985; The Veteran Motor Car, David Scott, Scribner, 1956; We Americans — National Geographic, National Geographic, 1975; We Never Called Him Henry, Paul Marcus, Clifton, 1951; Wheels Within Wheels, Phillips Smith, Funk & Wagnalls, 1968; Wheels for a Nation, Frank Donovan, Crowell, 1965; Wheels on the Road, David Hebb, Macmillan, 1966; World Car Catalog, S. D'Angelo, Herald, 1967; The World of Automobiles, Columbia House, 1974; The World of Cars, Herald; World of Cars, Automobile Quarterly, 1971.

LIST OF PUBLICATION REFERENCES (PERIODICALS): Architectural Record; Antique Automobile; Autocar; Automobile Collector; Automotive Industries; Automobile Journal; Auto Sport Review; Business Week; Car Classics; Car Collector; Car Design; Car Exchange; Cars & Parts; Classic & Special Interest Cars; Classic & Sportscar; Collector Cars; Colliers; Congressional Digest; Continental Comments; Country Life; L'Illustration — Salon De L'Auto; Ford Times; Hemmings Motor News; Home and Garden; Horseless Age; Industrial Management; Life; The Lincoln; Lincoln-Mercury Times; Literary Digest; Motor; Motor Age; Motor Life; Motor Trend; Motor World; New Republican; New Yorker; Newsweek; Old Car Illustrated; Old Cars Price Guide; Old Cars Weekly; Popular Mechanics; Popular Science; Road & Track; Saturday Evening Post; Scientific American; Scientific Digest; The Way of the Zephyr; Special-Interest Autos; Thoroughbred Cars; Time Magazine; Town & Country; Vanity Fair.

ILLUSTRATION AND PHOTOGRAPHIC CREDITS: Applegate & applegate, Annville, Penn.; AACA Library & Research Center, Hershey, Penn.; Auto Expo, Salado, Tex.; Automobile Emporium, Dallas, Tex.; Gene Babow, Daly City, Calif.; John Bolen, San Antonio, Tex.; Henry Austin Clark, Jr., Glen Cove, N.Y.; Car Magazines, Arlington, Tex.; Col. Bill White, Louisville, Ky.; Color-ite Classic, Bethany, Conn.; Detroit Public Library, National Automotive History Collection; Ralph Dunwoodie, Sun Valley, Nev.; Dupont, Tampa, Fla.; Ford Motor Company, Dearborn, Mich.; Henry Ford Museum, Dearborn, Mich.; Imperial Palace Automobile Collection, Las Vegas, Nev.; Jay Ketelle, Amarillo, Tex.; Kruse Inc., Auburn, Ind.; Lincoln-Mercury Dealerships, Dallas, Tex.; Lincoln Stables, Tulsa, Okla.; Library of Congress, Washington, D.C.; Ted Leonard, Barrington, R.I.; McBride Publishing, Hartford, Conn.; Motorbooks International, Osceola, Wis.; Frank Masi, Denver, Colo.; Pate Museum of Transportation, Fort Worth, Tex.; Sandia Collection, Albuquerque, N.M.; Chris Stasko, New York, N.Y.

Genealogy of Lincoln

HENRY M. LELAND, founder

LINCOLN MOTOR COMPANY
Liberty aircraft engines, 1917-19

1921 "LELAND-BUILT" LINCOLN PHAETON

1929 "DIETRICH" MODEL L LINCOLN

EDSEL FORD, President, Ford Motor Company

FORD MOTOR COMPANY, purchaser of Lincoln Motor Company, February, 1922

1941 LINCOLN CUSTOM LIMOUSINE

1940 LINCOLN CONTINENTAL CABRIOLET

1948 LINCOLN CONTINENTAL COUPE

and Continental

Custom Coachcraft by
BRUNN
DIETRICH
FLEETWOOD
HOLBROOK
JUDKINS
LeBARON
LOCKE
WILLOUGHBY

1938 LINCOLN SEDAN TOWN CAR

1932 "JUDKINS" MODEL KB BERLINE

1938 LINCOLN ZEPHYR CONVERTIBLE

1949 LINCOLN COSMOPOLITAN SEDAN

1956 CONTINENTAL MARK II

Other books by the same author:

FLIGHT OF THE SETTING SUN
THE LIFE AND ADVENTURES OF
CAPTAIN JAKE MARTIN

by Marvin arnold

FLYING STORIES II
HOW I CAME TO BE A PILOT AND
ENGINEER AND WHAT HAPPENED AFTER THAT

by Marvin Arnold

Samco Publishing www.storydomain.com